CULTURE AND CONTEXT

A BASIC WRITING GUIDE WITH READINGS

W. DAVID HALL

PEARSON
Longman

New York San Francisco Boston
London Toronto Sydney Tokyo Singapore Madrid
Mexico City Munich Paris Cape Town Hong Kong Montreal

For Dottie,

who told me I should write many books.

Here is the first.

Vice President and Editor-in-Chief: Joseph Terry
Senior Acquisitions Editor: Steven Rigolosi
Development Editor: Ann Hofstra Grogg
Senior Marketing Manager: Melanie Craig
Senior Supplements Editor: Donna Campion
Production Manager: Ellen MacElree
Project Coordination, Text Design, and Electronic Page Makeup: Electronic Publishing Services Inc., N.Y.C.
Cover Design Manager: John Callahan
Cover Designer: Joan O'Connor
Cover Images: center photo: courtesy of CORBIS; bottom left photo: The Good E-Book, photographed by Anne Katrine Senstad; upper right photo: Jules Frazier, PictureQuest
Photo Researcher: Electronic Publishing Services Inc., N.Y.C.
Manufacturing Buyer: Al Dorsey
Printer and Binder: Courier
Cover Printer: Phoenix Color Corp.

Library of Congress Cataloging-in-Publication Data

Hall W. David (William David), 1965 Feb. 14–
    Culture and context: a basic writing guide with readings/W. David Hall.
        p. cm.
    Includes bibliographical references and index.
    ISBN 0-321-06755-X
        1. English language—Rhetoric—Handbooks, manuals, etc. 2. English language—Grammar—Handbooks, manuals, etc. 3. Report writing—Handbooks, manuals, etc
4. College readers. I Title

PE1408.H3135 2004
808'.0427—dc21

                                                                                              2002043428

Please visit our Web Site at **http://www.ablongman.com**

ISBN 0-321-06755-X

1 2 3 4 5 6 7 8 9 10—CRW—06 05 04 03

BRIEF CONTENTS

DETAILED CONTENTS

CHAPTER 2   Write: Selecting, Structuring, and Drafting   32

CHAPTER 25   Making the "Tools" Work: Sentences   453

CHAPTER 26   Punctuation and Capitalization   476

RHETORICAL CONTENTS

PERSUASION

WORKSHEETS AND CHECKLISTS

WORKSHEETS

CHECKLISTS

WORDS OF ADVICE

TIPS

WRITING WITH COMPUTERS

WRITING WITH OTHERS

PREFACE: TO THE INSTRUCTOR

Ever since I was ten years old, wandering around my small West Virginia neighborhood with a green notebook in one hand and a pencil in the other, I knew I was going to be a writer. I was one of those weird children who spent hours after school scribbling in notebooks. Words flowed, and I filled up notebook after notebook. I actually enjoyed writing assignments in English classes. Most of the notebooks are gone now, but the love of writing remains. I can think of no better pursuit than to produce that great sentence, paragraph, or essay.

Now I write and also teach writing. Teaching has opened up a new perspective on writing. On my first day of teaching, I hit the ice-cold water of this perspective face first. Students attend writing classes to learn to write more academically, and they expect true instruction—complete with guidance, tips, and actual help. What I knew about creating a good, solid, readable piece of writing—other than putting words on sheets of paper—was minimal. So I examined what I thought I knew about writing and set out to write—and teach writing—more effectively.

That is where *Culture and Context* comes from.

This book presents my most effective ways for teaching college students how to improve their writing skills beyond just putting sentences and paragraphs on paper and hoping for a good grade. For me, helping students find their writing voice is centered around these five elements: The Hook, The Readings, The Reality of Writing Situations, The Writing Strategies, and The Grammar Handbook.

THE HOOK

Some years ago, I took an informal survey of my students, and I was amazed to find that most saw writing as something only "smart" people could do. My students reasoned that, in terms of content alone, they were at a disadvantage. Smart people wrote about important issues of the day, not "silly" things from everyday life like why *The Matrix* is a good movie or what the Cincinnati Reds need to do to play in the next World Series. So my students chose artificial topics for their essays and forced an academic tone as they struggled to sound more interested in their subject than they really were. I told them to stop. I explained that when they write, they should focus on what matters to them. Students should write about what they know. After that, amazing things happened. They chose topics they had a passion for, and their writing improved.

When students write about what they know, they write about their culture. These cultures are the hook for *Culture and Context*. Students come from a variety of cultures—not only various backgrounds but various interests—and those different cultures are reflected in the readings found in this text. "The Good E-Book," by Jacob Weisberg, focuses on a old idea—books—and their place within our technological culture. "Learning What 'Team' Really Means," by Mariah Burton Nelson, discusses sports and female culture. Michael J. Bugeja's "Confrontations, Common Bonds" talks about conflict within a college culture. Popular culture is addressed through essays about television, movies, cartoons, and music.

Living with and drawing support from these cultures raises interesting ideas. These topics are what students know, and they are worthy of essays. Once a student knows how to write about something he or she is interested in, wrestling with more academic topics becomes much easier. But popular culture is also important to study, discuss, and write about for its own sake. Our world becomes smaller every day, and television, movies, music, and the Internet affect and connect people in ways we are just beginning to discover. Being able to write about popular culture is a great way to begin writing about all sorts of things.

THE READINGS

I love words. Most writing teachers I know do. We voluntarily sit, day after day, reading students' words, reading words in journals and magazines, in short stories and novels, and we create our own words. I want to instill this love for words in my students. After all, words are the tool of the writer; the greater the mastery over words, the greater the writing.

To this end, *Culture and Context* places reading in a prominent place. More than thirty readings are included and discussed in this book. Almost every chapter opens with a brief discussion of the topic, followed, immediately, by a reading. Background information about the author and the reading are presented, along with a lexicon or mini-glossary of the reading's challenging words. Questions for Thought accompany each reading to encourage students to think critically about what they have read. In Part 4: Reading and Writing about Popular Culture, Questions of Style prompt students to examine the author's use of words and phrases to get ideas across, and Questions of Strategy ask them to analyze approaches. Finally, in Questions for Writing, students use the readings as springboards for their own writing. Through these readings, students see how others talk about their culture and use these writings as models for their own writing.

THE REALITY OF WRITING SITUATIONS

Another, perhaps more damaging, misconception about writing my students bring into my classroom is that what is taught in class doesn't match the writing demands of the "real world." How could discussions of the use of detail or the strategy of comparison and contrast apply to writing a memo announcing a business meeting or a letter to the editor of the school's newspaper? The chapters on essay tests, business writing, and speaking out address these concerns. Advice on writing under pressure, filling out job applications, creating strong resumes, cover letters, and thank-you letters, along with writing effective letters to editors, can be found in this book. By structuring these chapters like the others, students can see that the techniques apply to the writing they'll do outside the classroom.

THE WRITING STRATEGIES

While a few of my students had no concerns about their topics, they approached every writing assignment the same way—as a narrative or as a persuasion essay. Students need more strategies than that, so in *Culture and Context*, each major writing strategy has its own chapter. These strategies include narrative, process, description, definition and classification, comparison and contrast, cause and effect, and persuasion. Like other chapters, these chapters open with a reading, followed by an explanation of that particular writing strategy. The writing process is integrated into these discussions as well. "Ready" features prewriting, describes the importance of knowing your topic, audience, and purpose, and suggests ways to gather information necessary for a particular piece of writing. "Write" deals with creating a rough draft and discusses introductions, thesis statements, conclusions, organization, and structure. "Revise" explains effective ways to polish drafts. In addition to the readings that serve as models, student samples of each strategy are also provided. Students see how other students have developed essays from brainstorming to the polished final draft. Ending each of these chapters are chapter reviews and a series of writing prompts, which include reading response exercises.

THE GRAMMAR HANDBOOK

One student was disappointed in a grade she received on an assignment. She thought it unfair that I took points off for fragments, awkward phrasing, and spelling mistakes. Her reasoning? "I thought that stuff wouldn't matter," she said.

"That stuff"—grammar, spelling, punctuation, and word choice—does indeed matter. Since that encounter with my student, I have given grammar greater emphasis in my classroom, and I include a grammar guide in this text. When a student is editing an essay and, as an example, a question of comma placement comes up, the student should be able to turn to the handbook and find a guiding rule. The handbook is located in the back of the book for a reason, however. In the writing process, editing and proofreading occur *after* the content of the essay is settled. So the placement of the handbook reinforces the idea that attending to grammar and mechanics comes last.

THE ANCILLARY PACKAGE

A complete **instructor's manual** is available to accompany *Culture and Context*. The instructor's manual includes: Suggested Discussion Topics addressing each reading; Writing Strategies; Discussion Tips for the readings' Questions for Thought; Chapter Concepts; Teaching Tips; Additional Grammar Exercised; and Worksheet Transparencies. Please ask your Longman sales representative for ISBN 0-321-06757-6.

In addition to the instructor's manual, a series of other skills-based supplements is available for both instructors and students. All of these supplements are available either free or at a greatly reduced price.

For Additional Reading and Reference

The Dictionary Deal.   Two dictionaries can be shrinkwrapped with any Longman English title at a nominal fee. *The New American Webster Handy College Dictionary* is a paperback reference text with more than 100,000 entries. *Merriam Webster's Collegiate Dictionary*, tenth edition, is a hardback reference with a citation file of more than 14.5 million examples of English words drawn from actual use. For more information on how to shrinkwrap a dictionary with your text, please contact your Longman sales representative.

Penguin Quality Paperback Titles.   A Series of Penguin paperbacks is available at a significant discount when shrinkwrapped with any Longman Basic Skills title. Some titles available are Toni Morrison's *Beloved*, Julia Alvarez's *How the Garcia Girls Lost Their Accents*; Mark Twain's *Huckleberry Finn*; *Narrative of the Life of Frederick Douglass*; Harriet Beecher Stowe's *Uncle Tom's Cabin*; Dr. Martin Luther King Jr.'s *Why We Can't Wait*; and plays by Shakespeare, Miller, and Albee. For a complete list of titles or more information, please contact your Longman sales consultant.

The Pocket Reader **and** *The Brief Pocket Reader,* **First Edition.**   These inexpensive volumes contain 80 brief readings and 50 readings, respectively. Each reading is brief (1–3 pages each). The readers are theme-based: writers on writing, nature, women and men, costumes and habits, politics, rights and obligations, and coming of age. Also included is an alternate rhetorical table of contents. *The Pocket Reader* ISBN 0-321-07688-0 *The Brief Pocket Reader* ISBN 0-321-07669-9

Penguin Academics: *Twenty-Five Great, Fifty Great Essays, and One Hundred Great Essays, edited by Robert DiYanni.* These alphabetically organized essay collections are published as part of the "Penguin Academics" series of low-cost, high-quality offerings intended for use in introductory college courses. All essay were selected for their teachability, both as models for writing and for their usefulness as springboards for student writing. For more information on how to shrinkwrap one of these anthologies with your text, please contact your Longman sales consultant.

100 Things to Write About.   This 100-page book contains 100 individual assignments for writing on a variety of topics and in a wide range of formats, from expressive to analytical. Ask your Longman sales representative for a sample copy. 0-673-98239-4

Newsweek **Alliance.**   Instructors may choose to shrinkwrap a 12-week subscription to *Newsweek* with any Longman text. The price of the subscription is 59 cents per issue (a total of $7.08 for the subscription). Available with the subscription is a free "Interactive Guide to *Newsweek*"—a workbook for students who are using the text.

In addition, *Newsweek* provides a wide variety of instructor supplements free to teachers, including maps, Skills Builders, and weekly quizzes. For more information on the *Newsweek* program, please contact your Longman sales representative.

Electronic and Online Offerings

The Writer's Warehouse. The innovative and exciting online supplement is the perfect accompaniment to any developmental writing course. Designed by developmental English instructors specially for student writers, The Writer's Warehouse covers every part of the writing process. Also included are journaling capabilities, multimedia activities, diagnostic tests, an interactive handbook, and a complete instructor's manual. The Writer's Warehouse requires no space on your school's server; rather, students complete and store their work on the Longman server, and are able to access it, revise it, and continue working at any time. For more details about how to shrinkwrap a free subscription to The Writer's Warehouse with this text, please consult your Longman sales representative. For a free guided tour of the site, visit <http://longmanwriterswarehouse.com>.

The Writer's ToolKit Plus. This CD-ROM offers a wealth of tutorial, exercise, and reference material for writers. It is compatible with either a PC or Macintosh platform, and is flexible enough to be used either occasionally for practice or regularly in class lab sessions. For information on how to bundle this CD-ROM FREE with your text, please contact your Longman sales representative.

The Longman Electronic Newsletter. Twice a month during the spring and fall, instructors who have subscribed receive a free copy of the *Longman Developmental English Newsletter* in their e-mailbox. Written by experienced classroom instructors, the newsletter offers teaching tips, classroom activities, book reviews, and more. To subscribe, visit the Longman Basic Skills web site at <http://www.ablongman.com/basicskills>, or send an e-mail to Basic Skills@ablongman.com.

For Instructors

[New!] *The Longman Guide to Community Service-Learning in the English Classroom and Beyond.* Written by Elizabeth Rodriguez Kessler of California State University-Northridge, this monograph provides a definition and history of service-learning, as well as an overview of how service-learning can be integrated effectively into the college classroom. Ask your Longman sales representative for a free copy. 0-321-12749-8

The Longman Instructor Planner. This all-in-one resource for instructors includes monthly and weekly planning sheets, to-do lists, student contact forms, attendance rosters, a gradebook, an address/phone book, and a mini almanac. Ask your Longman sales representative for a free copy. 0-321-09247-3

Electronic Test Bank for Writing. This electronic test bank features more than 5,000 questions in all areas of writing, from grammar to paragraphing, through essay writing, research, and documentation. With the easy-to-use CD-ROM, instructors simply choose questions from the electronic test bank, then print out the completed test for distribution. CD-ROM: 0-321-08117-X Print version: 0-321-08486-1

Competency Profile Test Bank, **Second Edition.** This series of 60 objective tests covers ten general areas of English competency, including fragments; comma splices and run-ons; pronouns; commas; and capitalization. Each test is available in remedial, standard, and advanced versions. Available as reproducible sheets or in computerized versions. Free to instructors. Paper version: 0-321-02224-6 Computerized IBM: 0-321-02633-0 Computerized Mac: 0-321-02632-2

Diagnostic and Editing Tests and Exercises, **Sixth Edition.** This collection of diagnostic tests helps instructors assess students' competence in Standard Written English for purpose of placement or to gauge progress. Available as reproducible sheets or in computerized versions, and free to instructors. Paper: 0-321-19641-3 CD-ROM: 0-321-19645-7

ESL Worksheets, **Third Edition.** These reproducible worksheets provide ESL students with extra practice in areas they find the most troublesome. A diagnostic test and posttest are provided, along with answer keys and suggested topics for writing. Free to adopters. 0-321-07765-2

Longman Editing Exercises. 54 pages of paragraph editing exercises give students extra practice using grammar skills in the context of longer passages. Free when packaged with any Longman title. 0-205-31792-8 Answer key: 0-205-31797-9

80 Practices. A collection of reproducible, ten-item exercises that provide additional practices for specific grammatical usage problems, such as comma splices, capitalization, and pronouns. Includes an answer key, and free to adopters. 0-673-53422-7

CLAST Test Package, **Fourth Edition.** These two 40-item objective tests evaluate students' readiness for the CLAST exams. Strategies for teaching CLAST preparedness are included. Free with any Longman English title. Reproducible sheets: 0-321-01950-4 Computerized IBM version: 0-321-01982-2 Computerized Mac version: 0-321-01983-0

TASP Test Package, **Third Edition.** These 12 practice pretests and posttests assess the same reading and writing skills covered in the TASP examination. Free with any Longman English title. Reproducible sheets: 0-321-01959-8 Computerized IBM version: 0-321-01985-7 Computerized Mac version: 0-321-01984-9

Teaching Online: Internet Research, Conversation, and Composition, **Second Edition.** Ideal for instructors who have never surfed the Net, this easy-to-follow guide offers basic definitions, numerous examples, and step-by-step information about finding and using Internet sources. Free to adopters. 0-321-01957-1

Teaching Writing to the Non-Native Speaker.   This booklet examines the issues that arise when non-native speakers enter the developmental classroom. Free to instructors, it includes profiles of international and permanent ESL students, factors influencing second language acquisition, and tips on managing a multicultural classroom. 0-673-97452-9

Using Portfolios.   This supplement offers teachers a brief introduction to teaching with portfolios in composition courses. This essential guide addresses the pedagogical and evaluative use of portfolios, and offers practical suggestions for implementing a portfolio evaluation system in a writing class. 0-321-08412-8

For Students

[NEW] *The Longman Writer's Portfolio.*   This unique supplement provides students with a space to plan, think about, and present their work. The portfolio includes an assessing/organizing area (including a grammar diagnostic test, a spelling quiz, and project planning worksheets), a before and during writing area (including peer review sheets, editing checklists, writing self-evaluations, and a personal editing profile), and an after-writing area (including a progress chart, a final table of contents, and a final assessment). Ask your Longman sales representative for ISBN 0-321-10765-9.

Researching Online, **Fifth Edition.**   A perfect companion for a new age, this indispensable new supplement helps students navigate the Internet. Adapted from *Teaching Online,* the instructor's Internet guide, *Researching Online* speaks directly to students, giving them detailed, step-by-step instructions for performing electronic searches. Available free when shrinkwrapped with this text. 0-321-09277-5

Learning Together: An Introduction to Collaborative Theory.   This brief guide to the fundamentals of collaborative learning teaches students how to work effectively in groups, how to revise with peer response, and how to coauthor a paper or report. Shrinkwrapped free with any Longman Basic Skills text. 0-673-46848-8

A Guide for Peer Response, **Second Edition.**   This guide offers students forms for peer critiques, including general guidelines and specific forms for different stages in the writing process. Also appropriate for a freshman-level course. Free to adopters. 0-321-01948-2

Ten Practices of Highly Successful Students.   This popular supplement helps students learn crucial study skills, offering concise tips for a successful career in college. Topics include time management, test-taking, reading critically, stress, and motivation. 0-205-30769-8

The Longman Writer's Journal.   This journal for writers, free with any Longman English text, offers students a place to think, write, and react. For an examination copy, contact your Longman sales consultant. 0-321-08639-2

The Longman Researcher's Journal.   This journal for writers and researchers, free with this text, helps students plan, schedule, write, and revise their research project. An all-in-one resource for first-time researchers, the journal guides students gently through the research process. 0-321-08530-8

State-Specific Supplements

[For Florida Adoptions] *Thinking Through the Test,* by D.J. Henry.   This special workbook, prepared specially for students in Florida, offers ample skill and practice exercises to help student prep for the Florida State Exit Exam. To shrinkwrap this workbook free with your textbook, please contact your Longman sales representative. Available in two versions: with answers and without answers. Also available: Two laminated grids (one for reading, one for writing) that can serve as handy references for students preparing for the Florida Exit Exam.

[For New York Adoptions] *Preparing for the CUNY-ACT Reading and Writing Test,* edited by Patricia Licklider.   This booklet, prepared by reading and writing faculty from across the CUNY system, is designed to help students prepare for the CUNY-ACT exit test. It includes test-taking tips, reading passages, typical exam questions, and sample writing prompts to help students become familiar with each portion of the test.

[For Texas Adoptions] *The Longman TASP Study Guide,* by Jeanette Harris. Created specifically for students in Texas, this study guide includes straightforward explanations and numerous practice exercises to help students prepare for the reading and writing sections of the Texas Academic Skills Program Test. To shrinkwrap this workbook free with your textbook, please contact your Longman sales representative. 0-321-20271-6

The Longman Series of Monographs for Developmental Educators

Ask your Longman sales consultant for a free copy of these monographs written by experts in their fields.

#1: The Longman Guide to Classroom Management.   Written by Joannis Flatley of St. Philip's College, the first in Longman's new series of monographs for developmental English instructors focuses on issues of classroom etiquette, providing guidance on dealing with unruly, unengaged, disruptive, or uncooperative students. Ask your Longman sales representative for a free copy.

#2: The Longman Guide to Community Service-Learning in the English Classroom and Beyond.   Written by Elizabeth Rodriguez Kessler of California State University–Northridge, this is the second monograph in Longman's series for developmental educators. It provides a definition and history of service-learning, as well as an overview of how service-learning can be integrated effectively into the college classroom. 0-321-12749-8

ACKNOWLEDGMENTS

I take this time to thank those people who helped during the writing of this book: Deanna, Gyasi, and Kai, for their love and patience; David Moore, for his support and proofreading talents; Holly Finnegan, Nancy Laughbaum, Celeste Bland, and other members of my department for their encouragement; Delores and Jack Davis, for understanding my absences; and William, Shirley, Chris, and Rob, for that Thanksgiving invitation when the last draft was due.

I would also like to thank the following reviewers for their insightful comments and suggestions on the manuscript: Jonathan Alexander, University of Cincinnati; John Lansingh Bennett, Lake Land College; Harold Brannam, Savannah State University; Edna Burrow, California State University, Northridge; Sandra Carey, Lexington Community College; Patricia Falk, Nassau Community College; Susanmarie Harrington, Texas Technical University; Charles Hood, Antelope Valley College; Margaret Karsten, Ridgewater College; Diana L. Kelting, Pikes Peak Community College; Mark Lewandowski, University of Louisiana, Lafayette; Patricia A. Malinowski, Finger Lakes Community College; Michelle Miller, Fullerton College; Jim Murphy, Southern Illinois University, Edwardsville; Karen Patty-Graham, Southern Illinois University, Edwardsville; Linda Perkins, Tarrant Community College; Carolee Ritter, Southeast Community College; Sandia Tuttle, Grossmont College.

I hope you find *Culture and Context* a book that will change your writing classrooms into writing generators and incubators. May your students find their voice as they talk and write about their shared cultures.

Thanks for giving the book a try! Enjoy!

W. David Hall
Columbus, Ohio

INTRODUCTION:
TO THE STUDENT

Welcome to *Culture and Context*. In these pages, you'll find guidance for communicating effectively in many writing situations, be it a 300-word paragraph assignment for an English class or a letter to your representative in Congress. This open letter from me to you previews what you can expect to encounter in this book and suggests ways you can use this book to its full potential. You can explore the meaning of culture and the importance of context as you reflect on the haunting question, "Can *anyone* be a writer?" Before we get there, however, let me explain why you need to learn to write more effectively.

WHY WRITE?

Writing is, and always will be, a fundamental skill. We live in an age of speedy technology and immediate information. As soon as a plane crashes in a country halfway around the world, we find out about it on a headline news cable channel. Information about stocks, sports scores, and even the weather is updated minute by minute. Via the World Wide Web, millions of pages of documents are at our fingertips where once a trip to the library would have been necessary. Getting information is the easy part; getting it in a well-written format is the challenge. Therein lies the need for good writing.

Strong writing skills are necessary for advancement in college and in the world of work. The academic push to increase the use of writing in all types of college classes reflects the increased expectations of leaders in business and in the professions. Where once we wrote memos and reports on occasion, we now send e-mail daily. Our writing skills are in every e-mail message. E-mail messages with words misspelled, plenty of typos, and a complete lack of format don't go over well with anyone—especially not your employer. Employers are most impressed by, and demand of their employees, strong writing skills.

WHY *CULTURE AND CONTEXT?*

All textbooks have a central concept. The central concept for this book is *culture*. The culture around you influences you and shapes your identity, your personal thoughts, and your worldviews. The culture includes the cultures of your campus and your classes as well as the cultures of your generation, your region, and the popular culture shared by millions through the media.

We are all, to some degree, connected to popular culture, and that connection can lead to great writing ideas. When I was an undergraduate student studying journalism, I signed up for a film class. Having spent many Saturday and Sunday afternoons in the Smoot Theater in Parkersburg, West Virginia, I thought I knew a lot about movies. I thought the class would be a breeze. I was wrong. We discussed plot, character development, setting, foreshadowing, and other aspects of storytelling. I knew the terms but had a difficult time applying them. The turning point came when the instructor showed *Chinatown*. I was hooked. On the surface, *Chinatown* is a good, old-fashioned detective story. However, the instructor showed me what was below the surface. Suddenly, I noticed snippets of dialogue that foreshadowed major events in the plot. Every scene, including shots of Jack Nicholson's bandaged nose, reflected some part of his character. All of the concepts taught in the class made sense after that, even in situations that had nothing to do with film. After that experience with *Chinatown*, I learned to use my love for movies as inspiration for writing about them in a more penetrating and academic way. I hope you will do the same.

Popular culture is not the only type of culture featured in this book. You will read about, discuss, and write about other cultures you know. Perhaps you are a man with children who works on rebuilding cars in your spare time. Perhaps you are a single woman in your late twenties with an extensive jazz and blues

The author from a different perspective. Artwork by his son, Kai Hall, age 8.

CD collection. Your context is your culture: male culture, female culture, parent culture, mechanic culture, young adult culture, jazz and blues culture. Being a student of a college or university makes you a member of your school's student culture. Even your English class has a unique culture.

Writing from a particular cultural point of view or writing about a particular aspect of a culture may feel a bit awkward at first. To some people, ideas generated from, say, a sports culture may not be seen as academic. However, as a developing writer, you should write about what you know. Using your own culture as a starting point for your writing is important for the following reasons:

- *Shared experiences make it easier for you to share ideas with others.* You have a context in which to discuss your insights and opinions. Popular culture is a good illustration of this point. Due to mass media, millions of people share the same experiences at the Cineplex watching the same movie, in their living rooms watching the same television show, or in the car listening to the same radio station. If you disliked a plot twist on *ER*, for example, you can share your opinion with a coworker who also watches the show. To explain your position, you can refer to scenes in previous episodes because you both know the context.

- *You already know how to investigate and support your ideas about your own culture.* Cable television, the Internet, movies, videos, newspapers, magazines, journals, and books can be great sources of ideas for writing topics and for information about them. Chances are, you already know how to locate and access these sources.

- *Your culture, and the way it changes, offers interesting perspectives for reflection.* As times change, so do cultures. I remember getting my first computer with Internet access. I thought I was truly part of the new computer culture when I logged onto America Online at 2400 bits per second and had to wait five minutes for a website to load. Ten years (and many upgrades) later, I have the option of connecting to the Internet through my cable company, and websites take only seconds to appear. Looking back at the way things used to be—when you were ten, or fifteen, or twenty—is not only a great topic for writing but an instant history lesson.

- *Your culture influences you and everyone else.* Many movies are truly forgettable; even if we enjoyed them, they make little impact on our lives. But every once in a while, a movie like *Star Wars* is released, and our popular culture is changed forever. Darth Vader, R2-D2, and lightsabers became a part of our language. Sixteen years passed between the release of *Star Wars: Return of the Jedi* and *Star Wars: Episode One: The Phantom Menace,* but the influence was still there. People camped out in front of movie theatres to get tickets. Newsmagazines ran cover stories of the *Star Wars* phenomenon. Many businesses even gave employees opening day off to see the new movie.

Writing about what you know is a great way to build and hone your writing skills. You are an expert in your culture; use your knowledge to your advantage.

HOW DO I USE THIS BOOK?

Culture and Context is designed to be your guide as you develop your skills as a writer.

Part 1 discusses the **writing process** by outlining a sure-fire system for writing and revising. First, you get <u>ready</u> (Chapter 1) to write by brainstorming ideas about your topic, audience, and purpose. Then, you <u>write</u> (Chapter 2) by selecting your best ideas, structuring them in paragraphs, and imposing an overall order that moves logically from introduction to conclusion. Finally, you <u>revise</u> (Chapter 3) by paying attention to content, structure, and mechanics.

Part 2 discusses **writing strategies** you can use to get your point across. Each strategy has its own set of rules, and you need to know them. Imagine Madonna is performing a concert in your town. Tickets go on sale in a few days, but you find yourself without any extra cash. You try a radio contest, but you aren't fast enough to be the winning caller. The choices are clear: ask for the money from your close friend (from whom you have already borrowed money), ask your parents (who may not appreciate Madonna's music in the same way you do), or borrow the money from your brother (who knows all about interest rates and won't hesitate to apply them to your "loan"). Your friend would probably give you the money and go to the concert with you. Your parents may be skeptical about the price of concert tickets and give you a lecture on spending money wisely before they give it to you. Your brother would want to know exactly how and when you were going to repay the money and may even charge you a late fee. You could get money from any of these sources; you would just have to approach each one differently.

Writing works the same way. The same words, ideas, and ways of discussing a subject cannot be applied to every situation. Different people are different audiences and have different expectations. This book is designed to prepare you for a variety of writing situations, especially the writing that takes place in academic and business settings, so mastery of many writing strategies is important to have.

Part 3 focuses on **writing situations** in the classroom and in the "real world." Here, you will get advice on responding to readings. You will learn about personal writing through self-reflection (looking in) and social awareness (speaking out). Because writing research papers will be a part of your college experience, a chapter on academic writing with research is included. A discussion of taking essay tests follows. A chapter on business writing concludes this section of the book.

The **readings** in Part 4 focus on various aspects of pop culture. For some people, readings in a textbook geared toward writing may seem strange, but there are good reasons for this inclusion, namely:

- *Reading expands vocabulary and inventory of ideas.* The basis of reading and writing is language. Language is represented by words. The more you read, the more words and ideas you encounter. Reading opens your mind to many uses of language which will improve your own writing.

- *Reading shows effective (and ineffective) use of language.* Reading bad writing clarifies what you should not do, while reading good writing directs you to what you should be doing. Because both can teach lessons in language, almost everything you read is an opportunity for learning.

- *Active reading requires writing.* Some people read books cover to cover but never have a true understanding of the content or a real appreciation for the style. Active reading fights against passive reading. Active reading demands that the reader scribble down thoughts and ideas as she analyzes what she reads. Reading helps create a dialogue with the text, which can also improve your writing.

Part 5 deals with **grammar, punctuation, and other mechanics.** Two schools of thought exist concerning the importance of learning the rules of grammar. One side insists developing writers need clear explanations and exercises for each part of speech in order to have a foundation to build on. The other side argues for a whole language approach—that the acts of reading and writing, by their nature, teach the parts of speech and other grammar rules. One idea, however, overshadows both sides of the argument: Poor grammar and punctuation produce poor communication. So, a grammar handbook is included in this textbook. Brief explanations of parts of speech and punctuation usage are also here, along with exercises for those who want to test their knowledge.

The book contains yet more features. The **exercises** found throughout the book are designed for practice and for product. In much the same way that Mia Hamm and Grant Hill warm up and practice before a big game, you should also warm up and practice your writing skills. The exercises in the book are designed for this. Take advantage of them. Write out your answers in order to truly stretch your writing muscles. Many exercises are open-ended, allowing many responses to the same exercise. This also means you can return and get a fresh workout each time. Starred exercises and writing assignments are appropriate for collaborative work. The worksheets are designed to help you organize your thoughts as you develop your ideas. By filling them out completely, you will capture your ideas and information on paper in an organized way. **Tips on writing with computers** and **tips for writing with others** will improve your techniques and communication skills. Because you will write research papers during your college career, **a section on MLA format and style** is included.

Become familiar with the parts and functions of the book that can offer you the most help. For example, if, for a music appreciation class, you have to write a report on three classical music performances, turn to the chapter on writing compare and contrast essays and read on. Remember: *Culture and Context* is a guide. Make it work for you.

CAN I WRITE?

Many people mistakenly think that only those individuals who write published work can write or have a talent for writing. True, their profession is writing. But writing is a part—some part—of every profession, every job, every relationship, every day-to-day activity. Writing is recorded communication. So instead of asking questions like "Can I write?" or "Do I have the talent for it?" ask yourself, "'How can I most effectively meet the challenge of the writing situation I am faced with?" When you change the question, you get a practical answer. This answer will help you communicate more effectively though writing.

Keep in mind that you must be willing to make a few mistakes in order to learn and to grow. Work hard to let go of any anxieties you may have about writing. Trust that you have something important to say and that you can say it on paper. Don't be deterred by bad writing experiences you have had. Focus on the task in front of you, seek the guidance you need, and make it a habit and a matter of pride to submit only your best work. The goal is clear: effective communication on paper. With a lot of effort and this book, you can reach that goal.

Thanks for using *Culture and Context* on your journey. May it serve you well.

PART I

The Writing Process

For some people, writing is a difficult task. These people see writing assignments as great mountains to climb and blank sheets of paper as vast, empty lands to cross. They immediately get tense and frustrated. Unfortunately, these people probably haven't learned that writing is a *process*, a series of steps designed to help anyone get from an idea to a polished draft. The writing process is the focus of this section of the book.

In Chapter 1, "Ready: The Writing Process Before You Really Write," we discuss prewriting. With prewriting, you develop a writing idea or topic by seeing how it relates to audience and purpose. In this chapter, you also see how you can generate ideas through brainstorming techniques.

Once you have a topic, an audience, and a purpose for your piece of writing, you can move to Chapter 2, "Write: Selecting, Structuring, and Drafting." Here, you explore the structure of paragraphs and essays, how to choose the appropriate information for your piece of writing, then how to organize that information effectively. Along the way, you see an example of how another student developed her ideas and wrote an essay.

Finally, in Chapter 3, "Revise: Improving Your Draft," you get advice on how to strengthen your essays. We discuss ways to revise the content of the essay, making sure what you want to say is on the page. After that, we talk about revising for structure, making sure your information flows smoothly throughout the essay. Later, we talk about revising for mechanics (grammar, spelling, punctuation, and the like), and we discuss proofreading strategies.

The writing process may seem time-consuming and difficult at first, but as you practice, the procedure will become second nature to you. Remember: Going through the steps of ready, write, and revise makes your writing task much more manageable and saves you a great deal of frustration.

READY:
The Writing Process Before You Really Write

Remember LEGO® toys? These multicolored, multishaped little plastic blocks are among the most imaginative toys ever invented, for they can be combined to create virtually any shape or design. Want a green house with white trim around the windows and a three-story doghouse in the backyard? Fine. Grab a bunch of LEGO bricks and start snapping them together. How about a car with wings and square wheels? You can build that contraption as well. Imagination is the only limit.

But something else is at work, too. If you attempt simply to snap pieces together without looking ahead, frustration will set in. You'll run out of green pieces. The windows will be uneven. The roof will look awkward. The person next to you, however, seems to have it all figured out. Her creation is balanced and orderly. The green blocks—just the right number of them—are in just the right place. Each window has shutters and the roof is perfect. Your first reaction may be that she is naturally talented and you simply can't create anything worthwhile, but that is not the case. She simply planned her house before she began. Maybe she first sketched out the design or looked at other designs. Probably she arranged the color, size, and shape of the pieces she would need and remembered to have a few extras on hand, just in case. Most certainly, she was aware that building requires a degree of trial and error and was determined not to give in to frustration. In essence, she planned ahead.

Building with LEGO pieces and writing a paragraph or essay are a lot alike. Both can cause frustration, for the process from start to finish is never smooth. Both can cause envy, for it seems—on the surface—that everyone else can do it better. And both also require a great deal of planning. The planning you will be doing for your writing is called **prewriting**, and that is the subject of this chapter. If you plan well, you'll spare yourself frustration and cause for envy.

Instead of rushing to complete the project, you should plan ahead. When it comes to writing, the success of a paragraph or essay is determined by how well you, as the author, have stayed focused in your subject or topic; how well you have kept in mind the audience or the people who will read your work, making sure they will understand what you are saying; and how well you fulfill your purpose or reason for writing in the first place. After you've planned for your topic, audience, and purpose, you're ready to begin writing.

This chapter examines the major elements of topic, audience, and purpose as well as the secondary concerns of time and resources. Together, we look at ways to select a topic, analyze the needs and expectations of the target audience, and sharpen your purpose for writing. Estimating how long you need to finish a writing assignment or compose an essay and determining what information you need and where you should get it fill out the rest of the chapter.

But first, read "Confrontations, Common Bonds" by Michael J. Bugeja.

Reading 1   Confrontations, Common Bonds
Michael J. Bugeja

BACKSTORY

Conflict and confrontation are a part of our lives. How do you react to confrontation? Do you immediately fight back? Do you compromise and try to make the situation better? Do you withdraw and hope it goes away? In the following essay, first published in *Writer's Digest*, Michael Bugeja, a creative writing instructor, finds himself in the middle of a confrontation during a writing class. Because he chooses to deal directly with the situation, Bugeja learns about the students, himself, and the nature of writing. After reading the essay, consider how you would have handled the situation.

LEXICON

Al Jolson: Actor most noted for his black-faced portrayal of an African-American singer in the silent movie *The Jazz Singer*

cliché: A word or phrase used so many times it becomes meaningless

enclave: A small area enclosed by a larger area

faux pas: A social mistake

isolation: The state of being alone or separated from a group

perpetuating: Continuing or causing to continue

plausible: Believable, understandable

salvo: Sudden attack

surname: Last or family name

1   I am trying to keep a black female writer from strangling a white male writer in my magazine workshop at Ohio University.

2   He has written a flawed piece of popular fiction from a black male viewpoint, and his apparent middle-class isolationism has resulted in a few misconceptions. First, the hero

resembles a white from an upscale enclave and sounds like Al Jolson in blackface. Second, there is no real story, only a bunch of white and black folks interacting clumsily with each other. Third, the writer fumbles technique, using dialogue to convey exposition; which means, in some passages, his black man doesn't even sound *human*. That stings.

3   The theme, however, is good, if a bit ordinary: "We should learn to get along."

4   The black woman writer misses the theme. What she sees is a white person perpetuating racial myths: His main character is phony, subhuman and stereotypical, she says. She is at wit's end.

5   For ten minutes she has seethed in her seat, listening to white students discuss dialogue and diction and now violates her vow of silence. She questions how this guy can get off writing about a black male and adds: "What does he know about my people?"

6   It escapes her momentarily that she has written a science-fiction piece from the viewpoint of a German sailor, and that she is neither male, white, German or a sailor. But she is a skilled writer, so the mistakes aren't as obvious, though a few stand out. For instance, some of her sailors behave like Nazis.

7   It occurs to me that the white student has a German surname.

8   Now nobody in the class is willing to critique his story. Why should anyone risk being called racist? After all, these are "someone's people."

9   I explain that the white student's story has a good message, noting that what appears stereotypical is actually poor execution. I make my points carefully without faux pas and impress the entire class, I think.

10   Then it is the white writer's turn to respond to my critique. He finds it amusing, he says, that I have gone to such lengths to pacify a complainer. Moreover, he believes his story is not nearly as flawed as I have indicated, and now the black student is about to strangle him.

11   I intervene. But first I allow myself a salvo about being diplomatic when I could have torn the story apart line by line, cliché by cliché. I'm not responding like a teacher now, but like an editor who has held back too much in the wake of bad work.

12   The black student wears an "I-told-you-so" smirk on her face. She says the white guy knows nothing about being black and rears up in her seat, ready to take on any comers. She says whites don't know how blacks feel inside.

13   This is a deadly argument in a writing workshop. If the students believe it, a chain reaction occurs: Men can only write about men; women about women; old people about the elderly; young about youth; plumbers about plumbing; convicts about crime; victims about other victims; blacks about blacks; whites about whites.

14   But luck is with me. I tell her that we all are of one race, the human one, and that while I may not experience humiliation on a regular basis, I have in my life, and so can bring forth that emotion in a piece about racism.

15   "No, you can't," she says. All whites think of blacks in stereotypical ways, she alleges. "So do *you*."

16   A silence sets in. She realizes she is in a white classroom and sits down, trying to fade away. Now the student with a German name is nodding with an "I-told-you-so" smirk on *his* face.

17   Someone is racist, and it isn't he.

18   I walk over to the black woman and tell her that I don't think about her as "black" or "African-American." Well, perhaps I did when I was taking attendance at the beginning of

the quarter. That much may be true. But now I see her as a writer and admire her because she loves words as much as I do.

19   We have that in common, I say.

20   She makes a face somewhere between anger and pain.

21   It is time to dismiss the class.

22   I am surprised when she comes to me afterward to apologize; she has learned something valuable, she says. How can she thank me? The white writer comes to me as well and demands an apology; he has not seen me react as an editor before, and my salvo about his story stings his ego. How can he rewrite?

23   There is only one way the black writer can thank me and the white one can rewrite his story. We will meet again in my office, heal and go to work.

24   In the next workshop, he has a more plausible version of his story and she, a better science fiction about the German sailor.

25   We are writers, after all.

QUESTIONS FOR THOUGHT

1. Two main forms of culture are the focus of this reading: popular culture and classroom culture. What other types of culture were evident? Explain.

2. Define *stereotype*.

3. Think about situations in which your writing has been critiqued. How did you view the criticism? How did you feel about making changes in your work based on someone else's thoughts about your writing?

4. Consider the author's solution to this tense situation. Do you agree or disagree with this method? What would you have done differently?

5. In the account, the black female writer questions the white male writer's ability to accurately portray African-American people. Bugeja responds in paragraph 14 by saying, "While I may not experience humiliation on a regular basis, I have in my life, and so can bring forth that emotion in a piece about racism." Is his response always true? Other than racism, what other situations exist in which one person cannot understand another person's culture or point of view, no matter how much one tries? Is one person's response more valid than another's? Explain.

6. Recall a popular movie or television show. Record the various cultures it features. What stereotypes do you notice?

TOPIC

Perhaps the single most important element to settle on during the prewriting planning stage is the topic. **Topic** is the idea or concept that functions as the basis for your writing. Think back to the LEGO project. Knowing what you want to build helps you generate images of what the final product should look like. With writing, knowing your topic helps you focus and decide on the information that goes into your piece. Topics can often be stated in a single word; however, for more complex writing, the topic may be as long as a sentence.

In "Confrontations, Common Bonds," the topic grows out of a classroom incident. The opening sentence provides clues: "I am trying to keep a black female writer from strangling a white male writer in my magazine workshop at Ohio University." The black female and the white male are at odds with each other throughout the piece, and the author—their instructor—describes how he tries to get them to see their "common bonds" as well as their differences. Ultimately, this short essay has a serious topic relating to stereotyping.

Where Do I Find Quality Topics for My Papers?

Perhaps you've struggled to find topics to write about. I hope you soon discover there are topics all around you. Your everyday life is full of them. Michael Bugeja, a teacher, found a topic in his classroom. You, as a student, can find a topic in every class you attend. Think about your life outside of class. What's on your mind right now—passing this writing course, your children, your weekend plans, caring for your cat? Any of these can serve as the basis of a piece of writing. Many times, though, you'll need or want to choose topics that reflect your thoughts and your intellect. To come up with these more serious kinds of topics, let's look at academic topics, self-reflection topics, and topics gleaned from outside sources.

Academic Topics.   Most college course assignments call for academic topics. Either the instructor will tell you point-blank what your topic will be, or you will be asked to choose from a limited selection. Sometimes you will have to find a narrow topic within a larger topic. For example, your instructor may ask you to write an essay about how technology has affected society. The aspect of technology you focus on—cell phone, the Internet, cable television—will be up to you.

Self-Reflective Topics.   Some college assignments call on you to write about yourself. These self-reflective topics often include ideas from diary or journal entries. To find topics for this type of writing, you look inside yourself for the ideas you want to get across in your writing. After reading "Confrontations, Common Bonds," for example, your instructor may have asked for a short essay on how you would have approached the situation. Self-reflection would lead to a true response to the assignment.

Outside Resources.   Information from resources other than yourself can be a great place to find topics. Songs, television programs, and articles can help generate ideas. Also consider investigating your campus clubs, activities, and your field of study for writing ideas.

How Can I Focus My Topic?

No matter where you find your topic, always keep in mind that you will be considered an expert on it—at least for the length of your paragraph or essay. The best way to show your expertise is to narrow your focus so you have something concrete to say. If you announce that you are making a "building" with those LEGO pieces, your range is very large; a building could be any structure from an outhouse to the Taj Mahal. If you say "house," you have narrowed the focus a bit, and if you say "a doghouse like the one Snoopy sleeps on," you've narrowed it even further. Now you have a better sense of the final product.

Say you've decided to write about a large topic such as "drug abuse," "crime," "movies," or "family vacations." Your range is huge. What can you say about crime in one essay? No matter how big the essay, crime is simply too large a subject. Narrow it. What do you really want to talk about? If you say, "I'm going to write a paragraph on the problem of people stealing book bags from students in the cafeteria," then you'll have a firmer idea of what the final product will be.

But limited topics don't have to be limiting. Often, by writing about something specific, you are able to make an important larger point. Michael Bugeja recounted a single incident and he used it to reflect on some pretty big ideas: stereotyping, the roles of students and instructors in the classroom, and even the qualifications of writers and the nature of writing.

Exercises

1. Jot down at least ten events that changed you in some way, such as giving birth to your first child or deciding to continue your education by attending college. Choose three that would make the best topics for writing. Explain why those would be good topics.

2. Glance through a textbook for another class. What concepts or ideas can you pick up from it that would make good topics for writing?

3. Read several articles from a newspaper or magazine. Write down the topic of each one, then jot down a short list of topics you could write about based on these articles. Trade articles with a few classmates, jot down a few ideas from their articles, then compare lists.

4. List ten groups or cultures with which you identify. What are the issues and ideas important to those cultures? Which would make good topics for writing assignments?

AUDIENCE

Audience describes the people you are writing to or for. Think back to the LEGO house you were making. If you are building the model for yourself and you want only one wall, no roof, and windows in the floor, then you should be happy with your creation. It is exactly what you wanted it to be. But you'll run into trouble if you offer that same structure to someone who has a more traditional idea of a house. Expecting four walls and a roof, he will be less than thrilled. Your creation won't meet his needs.

Most of the writing you will do in college is for an audience other than yourself, even if it's an audience of one—your instructor. Keeping your audience in mind as you write clarifies the idea of writing as *communication*. It is a two-way street. Getting your ideas across as you intend requires careful consideration of your readers and their expectations of the type of information as well as the style of language.

Audience and Topic

Look back at "Confrontations, Common Bonds." The essay was originally published in *Writer's Digest,* a magazine for aspiring and professional writers and writing teachers. This audience would naturally be interested in the topic: a writing teacher's dilemma in dealing with both hostile students and poor writing. This same article, as written, would have no place in *JAMA: The Journal of the American Medical Association* for the same reason that an article on cervical cancer and its treatment would not be published in *Money.*

Audiences are demanding. Readers expect your topic and presentation to be tailored to their interests. They don't appreciate their needs not being met. Recall the last bad meal you ate at a restaurant. Perhaps the lettuce in your salad was discolored or your vegetarian lasagne was overcooked. Regardless of what made it bad, chances are you didn't go back to that restaurant for a while and you cautioned others against eating there. Similarly, people stop reading when their expectations aren't being met, and they may be reluctant to read anything by the same author again.

The most effective way to make sure you meet the audience's expectations is to know those expectations before you begin writing. Here are some questions to guide you.

Audience Consideration Questions

- Who are the members of my audience?
- What style of language will my audience expect?
- What does my audience know about the topic?
- What has been their reaction to topics like this before?
- What has been their reaction to my other writing?

Imagine you are either the black female or the white male in "Confrontations, Common Bonds" and you have decided to write a letter of apology to the instructor. Now is the time to analyze the audience—the instructor you have offended. Your answers to the Audience Consideration Questions may look something like this:

- Who are the members of my audience?

  My instructor

- What style of language does my audience expect?
  Because the instructor has a graduate-level education and this was a serious conflict, I should use more formal language and a serious tone.

- What does my audience know about the topic?
  He witnessed the events, so I don't need to explain what happened in class. I should explain, though, why I reacted the way I did and why I am apologizing.

- What has been their reaction to topics like this before?
  He seems to be understanding when other people in class have had problems.

- What has been their reaction to my other writing?
  He has been fair in his evaluation of my work.

From this information, you could then begin to write a solid letter of apology that uses a style of language the instructor would appreciate, that explains things related to the classroom confrontation but not repeat everything he witnessed, and that is honest because he has been honest with you in the past. Because you have taken time to understand the instructor as your audience, the odds are good he will be receptive to what you have written.

Audience and Style

After you have determined your topic and audience, it's time to focus on language, which becomes a matter of style. **Style,** often referred to as **tone,** reflects the words and attitude used to express the ideas in the paragraph or essay.

Glance through a display of greeting cards at a drugstore or supermarket. You'll see a variety of topics; there seems to be a greeting card for almost every day of the year. Say you're looking for a birthday card for your brother. Do you want to tease him or to express your joy at having him in your life? Which card will he like best? In writing terms, the styles of the cards are different.

That difference in style also applies to writing. Traditionally, the style you will use in a college setting is straightforward and serious. Not many social work assignments call for gag lines or poetry! But consider these possible styles:

Humorous   Audiences who expect lightheartedness will appreciate this style. Exaggerations and jokes are often used to get the point across. In a serious piece, a humorous line or paragraph can add a little relief.

Sensitive   When you want to show the audience you empathize with their emotional state, use this style. Being sensitive to the feelings of others when discussing emotional topics such as death, aging, and unemployment shows the audience you care for them. Jokes, although they can add a little relief, may be out of place in this type of writing.

Frightening   Rather self-explanatory, this style or tone is used to scare the reader. A frightening tone can be used in fiction (as Stephen King does in many of his novels) or in nonfiction, when you want to warn the audience about certain aspects of the topic.

Poetic   The poetic style is designed to entertain and impress. While you may use standard English and traditional formats (paragraphs and essays), the audience for this style will appreciate the way you say something (repetition of words, use of rhyme, dialogue) at times even more than what you have to say.

Professional/Straightforward   You mean business when you write in a professional or straightforward manner. Your audience will want the information in an easy-to-grasp format and in language they can easily and quickly understand.

Informal   With the informal style, you are presenting information to your audience, but you are not concerned with standard format, grammar, spelling, or punctuation. This type of writing style is primarily used in e-mail to friends.

Finding the Right Style

Certain styles fit certain situations. If you are asked to write a memo or a report, you will naturally plan to be straightforward and professional. Your audience, primarily your employer or coworkers, may not have time for humor, and jokes may suggest you're not taking your work or your audience seriously. However, mixing styles can add strength to your writing. If the memo you are writing states the company is downsizing and workers need to prepare for layoffs, a sensitive touch to your straightforward approach will be effective. Here's a list of questions to guide you on the language and style to use.

Language Usage List

- What does the audience know about the topic?
- How will my audience receive (react to) this information?
- What tone would be best to deal with this situation?

The style of "Confrontations, Common Bonds" is primarily straightforward. Bugeja does add poetry, however. Consider these ending paragraphs.

> There is only one way the black writer can thank me and the white writer can rewrite his story. We will meet again in my office, heal and go to work.
> In the next workshop, he has a more plausible version of his story and she, a better science fiction about the German soldier.
> We are writers, after all.

He understands that if he tells the incident like a police report (with just the names of the people involved, the actions each person took, and the results of those actions), there would be no emotional impact and little reader interest. The audience reads *Writer's Digest* for insight on the writing life. By presenting the classroom confrontation almost as a short story, Bugeja involves the reader. The reader comes to care about the subject and thinks about how he or she would react in a similar situation.

Exercises

5. Select a topic from the lists generated in Exercises 1–4. With a partner, define several audiences that would be interested in that particular topic. Now choose an appropriate style to match. Explain your answer.

6. Read each of the following short paragraphs. Identify the writing style used. Discuss reasons the writers may have chosen those particular styles.

   a. I may circulate a petition to ban Mondays. I mean, seriously, who do you know that likes Mondays? Everyone is sleepy and slow to do anything on Monday mornings. Traffic is usually worse on a Monday morning than any other time of the week. I have even kept track of my worst days—the days where I am late for class, I spill coffee on my white skirt, or I lock myself out of my car—and they all happen to be Mondays. If we get rid of Mondays, we all get an extra day to settle into a new week. I think everybody should sign the petition. Let's get rid of Mondays!

   b. The school has no choice but to cut back on the number of hours the library will be open on weekends. Student use of the library on weekends, especially Sunday afternoons, has fallen over the past few terms. The students who do use the library on weekends usually get videos or short-loan materials like magazines and then leave. It is a rare occasion to see anyone in the library studying on weekends. While a few students will be inconvenienced by the closing, we hope that this cutback will lead to better use of the library during the week. For more information, please contact a member of the library staff.

7. Imagine you are writing three letters explaining the reasons why you don't like a certain course you are currently taking. One letter will be sent to an employer (who is paying your tuition), one to a good friend who isn't in the class, and the third one to the president of the college. Answer the Audience Consideration Questions for each audience. What writing style would you select for each letter? Share your lists with other members of the class or the instructor.

8. Select two websites that focus on the same topic and identify their target audience. Support your identification through detailed analysis of the sites. (Given that websites are visual as well, consider display and graphics, too.) Invite another member of the class to critique the websites, then compare notes.

PURPOSE

All writing has a purpose. Perhaps you want to share good news with a friend. Maybe you need to make other people in your school district aware of new proficiency testing. Maybe you just have to remind yourself to get bread and milk on the way home after class. In college writing, the reason you write a paragraph or essay is the **purpose.** Being clear about your reasons for writing before you begin helps keep your work on track.

Obviously, in a writing class, your primary purpose for writing is to complete an assignment and get a good grade. If you don't do the assignments, you won't pass the class. However, you should look beyond grades. Each piece of writing—even if it's a class assignment—has a purpose in and of itself. What is it you want to communicate? What emotion do you want to call forth in your reader? What action do you want your reader to take? From personal journal entries to letters to the editor to e-mail, the specific purpose of writing will determine the shape of that piece of writing.

As you ask yourself "Why am I writing this paragraph or essay?" keep in mind these possible answers:

- **To persuade:** to change the viewpoint of the audience on the topic
- **To inform:** to clarify the topic or enlighten the audience about certain aspects of it
- **To entertain:** to show the audience a humorous side to the topic
- **To question:** to raise issues related to the topic for the audience to ponder
- **To provoke thought:** to challenge the audience to think more critically about the topic
- **To satisfy a personal need:** to remind yourself, to explore your ideas, or for the sheer pleasure of writing

We can speculate that Michael Bugeja wrote "Confrontations, Common Bonds" to inform his audience (other writers and writing instructors) about what can go wrong in a writing classroom and how to fix that particular problem. Maybe he also had a personal need to share the experience with other writers, maybe he was hoping for feedback, or he may have needed to bolster his vita with a publication. Perhaps he was paid for his efforts. He may have been asked to write the article by the magazine's editors. We may never know Bugeja's personal motives, but we do know he wanted to describe, for fellow writing teachers, the bonds writers share.

Purpose and Audience

Your audience will have reasons for reading your work, just as you have reasons for writing it. As a reader, you expect to get information about stocks when you pick up the business section of *USA Today*; you expect to be entertained when you read one of Walter Mosley's Easy Rawlins mysteries. If those expectations aren't met, you will, most likely, stop reading. Your audience will do the same. So, in addition to asking "Why am I writing this paragraph or essay?" be sure to ask yourself, "What is my audience's reason for reading this? What do they expect from this piece of writing?" Your answers will help you make choices about the approach you should take to connect with your audience.

Purpose and Writing Strategy

To achieve a goal, you must have a plan. The coach of a baseball team will likely place players with strong batting averages lower on the batting roster to clean up or compensate for the weaker ones. A student may decide to study her most challenging subject in the school library, where she can get help from a tutor if necessary. She does the less challenging work at home and begins to see improvements in her grades. These examples illustrate planning or strategy at work.

In writing terms, plans are called writing strategies. **Writing strategies** are ways a topic can be presented in order to fulfill the writer's purpose. Imagine that the president of your college has announced a tuition increase. When you talk about this increase with your friends and classmates, you may express your outrage strongly. When talking about the increase to the president himself, you may find yourself toning down your anger a bit. In one case, the audience will be sympathetic and understanding; in the other case, your audience may become unsympathetic and be offended. Remember: Different writing strategies serve different purposes.

Unlike the limitless list of topics, writing strategies are generally broken down into the following categories, which will be explained in greater detail in Part II: Writing Strategies.

Narrative   **Narrative** is storytelling. Your purpose is to relay a series of events to the reader. Often, narratives are used to entertain an audience. The narrative strategy can be used, however, to show a more personal side of a topic as well as make a serious point. Instead of preaching about race and writing, Bugeja relates a narrative to illustrate his point. Narratives are made stronger with sensory detail and snippets of important conversation or dialogue.

Process   The **process** strategy is a step-by-step outline for successfully accomplishing a task. Your purpose here is to inform and educate your audience. This book is a good example of process. By reading this, you are learning a process for writing more effectively.

Description   **Description** calls on sensory details. To effectively describe something—an object, a person, a scene— in writing, you must appeal to the five senses (touch, taste, feel, smell, and hearing). The purpose behind description is to enhance your writing or to show your audience a certain person, place, or thing the way you see it. A brief paragraph about a suspicious-looking character hanging around your dorm is an example of descriptive writing.

Definition   **Definition** strategy centers on identifying the topic It includes categories, divisions, and other classifications. The purpose of definition is to go beyond information found in a standard dictionary and to add insight to meaning. An essay about what being a student is falls in this category.

Cause and Effect   **Cause and effect** strategy examines the relationship between events, either what created a certain event (cause) or the impact that event will have on subsequent events (effect). Wanting to have more knowledge in a certain field of study caused you to come to college. Obtaining that knowledge and getting a good job may be the effects of coming to college.

Persuasion   With **persuasion** essays, you give your point of view, then provide support for it in hopes that your audience will accept it as their own. Every four years, we are inundated with messages as to who would be the better candidate for the office of President of the United States. Each message has a single purpose: to grab your vote. These messages are examples of persuasion strategy.

Comparison/Contrast   **Comparison** shows how two things are similar, while **contrast** shows how two things are dissimilar. Although both writing instructors and math instructors often teach with textbooks, the similarities between those books are few. The differences, however, would be many and would make a good contrast essay.

Strategies in Combination   Each writing strategy can work well by itself. However, most strategies appear in combination. Think back to "Confrontations, Common Bonds" once again. The essay begins as a narrative. Bugeja tells what happened in his classroom. Within a few paragraphs, he helps his reader to fully understand his situation. He uses comparison/contrast strategy when talking about the differences between the two writers and their stories. The key for which strategy to use lies with the decisions you made earlier about topic, audience, and purpose. Your strategies must be aligned with your purpose.

Exercises

9. Take the topic and audience you selected in the previous exercises and add a short statement of purpose. What is your purpose in writing about that topic to that particular audience? What is the audience's purpose in reading about it?

10. For each of the situations below, select an audience and purpose, then choose the appropriate writing strategy or strategies. Explain each choice.

   a. Your parents are opposed to your desire to learn to snowboard. To them, it is just like skiing, which is dangerous.

   b. You see an article in the school paper stating that the library is reducing its hours because student traffic is lighter this semester. On the next page, you see an article describing brisk sales by local businesses in personal computers with Internet capability.

   c. Your friend, who is trying to improve her basketball skills, asks you for tips on shooting free throws.

   d. Your brother's band, the Pop Kulture Kids, wants to try out for a talent show. The problem is they play poorly even though they think they're great.

11. Read one article from each of three sections of a newspaper. Write down the purpose behind each article, then underline words and phrases that led you

to your conclusion. Trade articles with someone else, read his or her articles, and write down the purpose (and reasons to support your opinion). Trade back and compare notes.

12. Listen to your favorite radio station for ten minutes. Jot down what you hear—types of songs, types of commercials, and whatever else is on the air—then write down the purpose for everything you heard. Next, tune to another station that has a different format (music or talk) and follow the procedure you did for the first radio station. Compare the two. Are the purposes different? In what ways do they differ? What audience do you think each station targets?

13. Open a search engine on your Web browser and type in a topic you are somewhat familiar with—a hobby, a sport, a celebrity—and search three websites about that topic. Write down the purpose for each site and information that led you to your conclusion.

14. Look at the topic, audience, and purpose you selected in Exercise 9. Which writing strategy or strategies do you think will be the most useful in reaching your audience? Explain your answer.

SECONDARY PLANNING ELEMENTS

At this point, all the major elements in prewriting seem to be in place. You have a topic. You have determined the needs and expectations of your audience, you have refined the purpose for your writing, and you have chosen the appropriate writing strategy or strategies for this piece. You have even decided on the style you will use to get your message to the audience. Everything seems to be in order, but there are two more aspects to consider: time and resources.

Time

Time, obviously, is the number of minutes, hours, or days that can be devoted to a writing project, starting from the moment you finish your prewriting and ending with the moment you submit the final draft. The time you have available has a great impact on what you are going to write and how you are going to write it. Imagine, for example, you have been given the task of describing the id, ego, and superego for a psychology class. If you're asked to do this as part of a midterm or final written in class, your response will have to be completed in, say, one hour and will necessarily be brief. If, however, this task is assigned for a paper due in two weeks, your response will need to be much more thorough. You have time to include more detailed explanations and provide detailed examples as support. You even have time to research and gather more information. Your professor will expect more from you in a paper than in an exam.

The time you have available will shape your topic and your method. If you've chosen sexism in the original *Star Trek* series as a topic for a paper, you'd better have at least 79 hours to watch all of the episodes! Of course, you'll never have that much time, so choosing two or three representative episodes for your paper is a good alternative. You might choose the relationship between Captain Kirk and Lieutenant Uhura. Narrowing your focus is not taking the easy way out. It is doing what is possible in the time available. It also helps you be specific and concrete instead of broad and vague.

During prewriting, make a note of how much time you think the project will take. You won't be able to be specific about hours or minutes; having some idea of the amount of time it will take to complete the project will help you set a reasonable pace.

Tips

Make the Most of Time

As a student, your time is valuable. Here are tips for making the most of it.

▶▶▶ **Eliminate or contain distractions.** Watching television, surfing the Web, playing video games, and chatting online can be fun and relaxing, but don't let these activities run your life. My wife and I schedule one evening a week for television, and anything we want to watch at any other time throughout the week is taped. On our TV night, we relax; other evenings, we work.

▶▶▶ **Find your best writing time.** Creativity and energy levels hit people at different times. Some people are morning writers, and some people are evening or night writers. Try writing for five days in the early morning, then try writing for five days in the evening. Compare productivity rates for the ten-day period. Whenever you are most productive is when you should do most of your writing.

▶▶▶ **Adjust other time commitments.** If other class assignments, your job, family, or social life eat into your writing time, make rearrangements. Maybe, for a few weeks, you could change your work schedule. Maybe your son could stay at a friend's house one evening while you work on an important revision.

▶▶▶ **Schedule writing dates.** Feeling self-conscious about writing will slow you down. Find a buddy and get together for your writing sessions. Location and proximity aren't the issue; you can sit in one room at the library and she can sit in another. Just knowing someone else is going through the same experience you are, at the same time, can keep you on track.

▶▶▶ **Have all your materials ready.** Making numerous trips away from your desk or computer for paper, pens, a dictionary, and your class notes simply wastes time. Before starting, make sure you have everything you need.

Continued

▶▶▶ **Stop procrastinating.** Perhaps your biggest enemy is the temptation to do the work later. Waiting for inspiration or a better time or even a certain piece of information doesn't help you move forward. Actual writing, even as little as a paragraph or page each day, will stop the stalling.

▶▶▶ **Make time for breaks.** Writing for hours at a time can be just as detrimental as not writing at all. Writing is a brain activity and, just like any other muscle, the brain can get tired. When you feel you're having trouble staying focused, take a break. A walk around the dorm or around the block can do wonders for your head.

Resources

Expert testimony, dictionaries, thesauri, encyclopedias, websites, nonfiction books, newspapers, magazines, and academic journals are all examples of **resources,** or places where you can find information. Because you are writing about cultures you are familiar with, many times *you* will be your greatest resource. However, other writing projects may require outside information. The demands of your audience or the purpose for your writing may lead you to do research. Perhaps you are trying to persuade neighbors to start a neighborhood block watch. Your neighbors will want facts about the crime rate in the area and statistics on the success of other block watch programs. With this information, you'll be more likely to achieve your purpose. So, as part of your prewriting, jot down any resources (other than yourself) you may need to consult.

THE WORKSHEET FRAMEWORK

If you just want to see where your ideas lead, then begin writing. If you want to get to the point more quickly and, perhaps, more effectively, you should jot down your prewriting ideas. A way to do this is with a chart or a worksheet. Because writing is putting your thoughts, feelings, and ideas on paper, filling out a worksheet helps move those thoughts, feelings, and ideas to the forefront of your mind. Having your ideas on paper, even in a sketchy outline, can help you see what information will be useful, what will not be useful, and how you can arrange the information you will use.

The TAP Worksheet

To keep you on track as you settle on topic, audience, and purpose during the prewriting stage, use the **TAP (Topic, Audience, Purpose) Worksheet** on the following page. It outlines basic questions. Feel free to add notes to the sheet; any bit of information that can help focus your topic, your audience, and your purpose will move your writing forward.

TAP Worksheet

Topic: What is the topic of the writing project? _____

              What type of topic is it?   Academic   Self-reflection   Outside source

Audience: Who are the members of my audience?

_____

              What is the educational level or levels of my audience?

_____

              What does my audience know about my topic?

_____

              What has been their reaction to topics like this before?

_____

_____

              What has been their reaction to my previous writing?

_____

_____

Purpose: Why am I writing this particular piece?

_____

_____

              Why is the audience reading this particular piece?

_____

_____

Style: What style will work best with my topic and audience?

_____

_____

Strategy: What writing strategy or strategies may be used?

_____

_____

Time: How long will this writing project take? _____

Resources: What resources will I need?

_____

_____

I had to do a great deal of planning before I wrote this chapter. As I first began generating ideas and concepts to discuss, I filled in a prewriting worksheet similar to this one.

TAP Worksheet

Topic: What is the topic of the writing project? *Prewriting*

What type of topic is it?   (Academic)   Self-reflection   Outside source

Audience: Who are the members of my audience?
Students

What is the educational level or levels of my audience?
College

What does my audience know about my topic?
Can't answer that right now

What has been their reaction to topics like this before?
Can't answer that right now

What has been their reaction to my previous writing?
They haven't read anything else from me before.

Purpose: Why am I writing this particular piece?
To inform

Why is the audience reading this particular piece?
To learn ways to write more effectively

Style: What style will work best with my topic and audience?
Not clear on this yet

Strategy: What writing strategy or strategies may be used?
Not clear on this yet

Continued

Time:	How long will this writing project take? _A few weeks at the most_
Resources:	What resources will I need?
	Consult with editor and other writing textbooks

Overall, this prewriting worksheet gave me a framework for writing the chapter. Topic, audience, and purpose are covered, but look closely. A lot of my answers are still vague and unformed. "What does my audience know about my topic?" and "What has been their reaction to topics like this before?" are still unknown at this point. I originally thought these questions unanswerable, but the more I thought about them, the more I realized I might be able to find the answers through brainstorming.

BRAINSTORMING

Brainstorming allows your mind to run free and explore all the aspects of a particular topic. Some of these related aspects might be useful as you settle on a topic, an audience, or a purpose. Once you have chosen the topic, you simply begin listing aspects of the topic that fit your writing situation. You may even want to jot down a list of possible topics before choosing one. After you have chosen one, jot down ideas associated with that topic. The act of writing down your ideas may help trigger more and more ideas. To be honest, most likely you will not use all of the ideas you write down. The point is that each idea generates another.

Brainstorming can be done in a variety of ways, such as **freewriting, clustering,** and **jotting.**

Freewriting

Freewriting is writing without constraint in order to get to what you need or want to say. Often, an idea escapes us because a lot of other ideas (or distractions) demand our attention. Freewriting is designed to literally free your mind of those distractions so you can focus on the topic. Just write for a predetermined amount of time—say, ten to fifteen minutes or until you have filled a page. As you freewrite, don't worry about spelling, punctuation, sentence structure, or anything else. Stay focused on the act of writing and the topic, and don't stop writing until time is up. If you get stuck, just write, "I am stuck" or "I don't know what to say here" and keep writing. Once time is up, read through your freewriting result. Dig out the ideas that are appropriate for your writing situation and apply them to your prewriting.

Clustering

Clustering is a visual type of brainstorming where you group similar aspects of a topic together. However, you probably won't realize what aspects you are going to group until you actually begin this process.

In the middle of a blank page, write the topic and circle it. Draw a branch from that central circle to another circle. In this second circle, write down one aspect of the topic. Draw a different branch from the center circle and, within the circle at the end of that branch, write down a different aspect of the topic. Draw as many branches from the center as needed to divide the large topic into smaller, more manageable pieces. Branch out into even smaller circles, adding more and more detail about that aspect of the topic. See the sample of clustering in Chapter 2, page 48.

Jotting

Some artists' sketchbooks are filled with doodles, scribbles, and even parts of drawings never finished. Through these sketches, the artist is able to practice or warm up before working on the main project. At times, ideas for main points are captured through these random markings. **Jotting** is the writer's equivalent of doodling. Jotting is like freewriting, but instead of sentences, the writer uses words or phrases instead.

I chose two ways to brainstorm to answer the questions about audience for this book. First, I jotted down a few ideas about the students I knew who could benefit from this book. After that, I expanded that jotting into freewriting. "Beyond the list, who else could benefit?" was the prompt, and I began writing. Many more ideas appeared through freewriting.

I looked back at my prewriting worksheet for this chapter and found two areas that needed much more development: audience knowledge of the topic (prewriting) and previous audience reactions to the idea of prewriting. When I first filled out the sheet, these answers seemed accurate and, in fact, they were. However, I could be more specific. One of the brainstorming techniques (jotting, in this case) would help me develop these points a bit better. My new jot list looked liked this:

What Does My Audience Know?

They've written before

They struggle to generate ideas

May be unaware of audience and purpose

What Is Their Previous Reaction?

Class that hated the thought of prewriting

Students who turn papers in late

Most students like brainstorming

When I added this recently discovered information (and brainstormed some more answers for other sections), the prewriting sheet filled out quite nicely.

TAP Worksheet

Topic: What is the topic of the writing project? _Using prewriting techniques_
effectively

What type of topic is it? (Academic) Self-reflection   Outside source

Audience: Who are the members of my audience?
High school and college-level students, older students returning to school,
students repeating the course, students just needing a refresher on the
information

What is the educational level or levels of my audience?
Most will have a high school diploma or equivalent, some will still be in high
school

What does my audience know about my topic?
Has written before
May have struggled with generating ideas
Had many students unaware of the importance of audience and purpose

What has been their reaction to topics like this before?
Had half of one class last quarter who only did outlines and hated the
thought of prewriting
A few students disregarded time considerations and turned a few papers in
late
Most are open and willing to seriously explore prewriting and brainstorming

What has been their reaction to my previous writing?
They haven't read anything else from me before

Purpose: Why am I writing this particular piece?
To inform and to educate, to help beginning writing students develop their
ideas before they actually begin writing

Why is the audience reading this particular piece?
To learn ways to write more effectively
Reading Chapter 1 may also be an assignment

Continued

Style: What style will work best with my topic and audience?
Formal/Informal—while I want students to learn from this chapter, I also want them to feel relaxed, just like the students in my classroom

Strategy: What writing strategy or strategies may be used?
Definition—students may have heard of the terms I will be using in the chapter, but not completely sure about the meanings
Process—learning to write more effectively takes a how-to approach
Exemplification/Illustration—after I have defined something, I will need to explain it and give examples when necessary

Time: How long will this writing project take? A few weeks to write, a few days to revise

Resources: What resources will I need?
Consult with editor and other writing textbooks
Discuss brainstorming techniques with other instructors
Ask students how they go about preparing to write paragraphs and essays

Prewriting is a necessary stage in the writing process. The more attention you pay to prewriting, the easier it will be to write your rough draft. Fill out the TAP worksheet. Your answers will tell you what elements are developed and which ones need work. Brainstorm the ones that need work and fill in more complete answers. When you're satisfied with the worksheets, you're ready for the next step in the writing process—selecting and organizing. These are covered in Chapter 2.

CHAPTER REVIEW

Writing well often takes planning. First, you must choose a quality topic, or a solid idea that you are going to write about. At school, you will encounter academic topics, but often the topics will be self-reflective (coming from you)

or from outside resources. Once you have the topic, you then have to analyze your audience, or the people who will eventually read your work. You must also choose a style or tone that suits the needs of your audience. Styles include being humorous, sensitive, frightening, poetic, professional and straightforward, informal, and a combination of styles. After that, you must consider purpose, or the reason you are writing the paragraph or essay. Most often, the purpose will lead you to a specific writing strategy, or way a topic can be presented to the audience. Writing strategies include persuasion, process, description, definition, cause and effect, comparison/contrast, narrative, and a combination of strategies. Along with topic, audience, and purpose, you need to consider a few other planning elements, such as time and resources. Once all of these pieces have been developed, you can begin writing by brainstorming. Brainstorming is putting ideas down on paper. Three methods of brainstorming discussed here were freewriting, clustering, and jotting. Once all of this preparation has been taken care of, you can then move to the next chapter and the next step in the writing process.

Final Writing Assignments

1. List fifteen topics for writing (five academic, five self-reflective, and five from an outside resource). Choose one of the topics and fill out a TAP worksheet for it. (Keep the remaining topics handy for other writing assignments.) After that, choose the writing strategy you think will best work with the topic, audience, and purpose you have chosen. Finally, brainstorm aspects of the topic, using freewriting, clustering, and jotting.

2. Reread this chapter's opening essay, "Confrontations, Common Bonds." Put yourself in the place of the writing teacher. How would you have handled the confrontation? Brainstorm a list of possible ways to respond to the situation, then choose one and develop it by filling out a TAP Worksheet. Finally, write a short paragraph explaining how you would have handled the situation and why you would have taken that approach.

2

WRITE:
Selecting, Structuring, and Drafting

Although I am close to forty years old, Godzilla movies still thrill me. When I was younger, I would get so caught up in the adventure that I sometimes imagined *being* Godzilla! There I was, walking through Tokyo, smashing into buildings. Then I would see a huge, fire-breathing flying turtle that threatened the planet. I made my move. My fire breath would singe the monster's head while my tail slammed against his legs, causing him to tumble into the water. I roared my triumph, but then the monster reappeared, ready to do battle again.

Retelling these daydreams wouldn't take very much time. When I went to see an actual Godzilla movie and my friends asked about the story, I had to be more considerate. Recounting every scene would take at least two hours, and my audience would get bored quickly. "It was great," I would yell, and then describe the monsters, some general plot points, and, of course, a few of the fight scenes. The excitement would be infectious, and soon we would have an entire neighborhood of Godzillas.

Writing is about selecting. Like the kids in my neighborhood, your audience won't want to know—or have time for—everything you have to say about a topic. So you must select the highlights and arrange them in a way your reader will find interesting and easy to follow. As discussed in Chapter 1, selection and organization are influenced by topic, audience, and purpose. You also need to organize your material into paragraphs and essays. In this chapter, paragraph structure (topic sentence, body, and conclusion) and essay structure (introduction, thesis statement, body paragraphs, and conclusion) are also discussed.

First, let's read "The Good E-Book" by Jacob Weisberg.

Reading 2 | The Good E-Book
Jacob Weisberg

BACKSTORY

Many technological advances met resistance when they first arrived. Some skeptics criticized the automobile, never dreaming the machine would one day replace the horse and buggy. Even the personal computer was dismissed, for most people couldn't see the appeal of a computing machine at home. This trend continues with the electronic book, according to author Jacob Weisberg. Some writers and publishers think an electronic version of a book is just a fad. However, in the following essay, originally published in *The New York Times Magazine*, Weisberg argues the e-book represents the future of publishing.

LEXICON

cornucopia: an image of bounty, usually a goat's horn filled with fruits and vegetables

disseminate: to give away or to spread; to tell

edicts: official announcements

fancier: a person knowledgeable about a particular subject; an expert

issuance: distribution

lamentation: grief or regret

oeuvre: an entire collection of one's works

resolution: in computer terms, the final form of an image on a computer screen. The higher the resolution, the clearer the image.

technophobes: people afraid of technology

ventures: risks

1   In recent months, bulletins about e-books have been breaking almost daily. After Stephen King published his novella *Riding the Bullet* exclusively in digital form, others swiftly followed suit. Simon & Schuster announced it would bring out Mary Higgins Clark's complete *oeuvre* in digital form. Microsoft (which owns the magazine I work for, *Slate*) offered Michael Crichton's latest. *Timeline*, in its new Reader format, which triples the resolution of text on an L.C.D. screen.

2   Despite the fact that hardly anyone uses an e-book yet, the drumbeat of ventures and issuances is breeding alarm in some quarters that serious reading in the future may no longer require the accumulation of dust-catching objects made of cloth, glue, ink and wood pulp. Until recently, literary technophobes couched their dismay in skeptical pronouncements. "Nobody is going to sit down and read a novel on a twitchy little screen—ever," the novelist E. Annie Proulx said a few years ago when it was still possible to harbor such an illusion. The more up-to-date complaint is that e-books are unstoppable and will mean the death of literature. People will read novels on screens, but they will read only shallow entertainment from the likes of Stephen King, Mary Higgins Clark and Michael Crichton.

3   If this hostility feels vaguely familiar, it may be because every new form of literary discrimination has drawn the same sort of reaction. Medieval clerics greeted printed books as imposters of illuminated manuscripts—aesthetically inferior, textually unreliable and likely to breed a dangerous diversity of opinion. In the 1950's, the senior statesmen of publishing fretted that the paperback revolution would mean the further spread of low taste. The echo of such views is heard today in an equally misguided elite's hostility toward digital publishing; surely we will hear lamentations for the lost age of electronic literacy once scientists find a way to plant books directly into the brain.

4   Less jaded consideration suggests that serious and unserious readers alike have much to gain from the new technology. I came to this opinion a year ago, when I began using a Rocket eBook, the first well-designed electronic device built for reading. The Rocket, which has the heft of a folded-over paperback, is a portable screen that displays a single page of text at a time. You can think of it as a light plastic shell that allows you to take a night stand's worth of reading matter wherever you go. The availability of new works is spotty, but thousands of the classics of world literature—the texts that digital publishing is supposed to render obsolete—are all available for free download over the World Wide Web. If you haven't heard about this cornucopia, it may be because these classics' copyrights have expired, which means no one stands to make money from them.

5   A more advanced version of the Rocket is due out this fall, but the relatively primitive 1.0 version is already a thing of beauty. Putting aside the stares and questions, it is a no less comfortable way to read novels than the old hard-copy method. In fact, it is an improvement. Your book bag no longer causes backaches. You fall asleep reading and the book saves your place. And most of all, I find it more responsive to the way someone like me actually reads—not choosing one book at a time and reading it through from cover to cover but nibbling on several according to the mood that strikes, with interruptions for newspapers and magazines. There is no reason other than superstition to believe that using an e-book diminishes your personal relationship with what you read. And because an e-book doesn't require good lighting or two hands, it is bliss in situations in which a bound volume is an awkward appendage: while eating, in bed, on the StairMaster or in the car at night (with someone else driving, please). I've read more in the past year simply because my e-book has made doing so more convenient.

6   At another level, absorbing literature in a variety of ways—on screen, on paper, on tape—helps to dispel the false equation between text and book. Powerful associations from childhood—the smell of must, the flashlight under the covers—have bred generations that think of themselves as book lovers rather than story hounds or prose fanciers.

7   But to turn such preferences into edicts is simply prejudice. The book is the text's container, not its essence. Appropriate technology for the past 500 years, it now stands on the brink of improvement. What will replace the bound volume will be, in some ways, truer to the current process of literary creation. These days, novels are most often composed not on bound leaves but on computer screens. There is no reason to believe our culture will be poorer even in amorphous ways when people absorb them from screens as well. And in definite and obvious ways, readers and writers alike will be richer for the access they will gain to an electronic version of Borges's infinite *Library of Babel*. In the near future, books will cost little or nothing, never go out of print and remain eternally available throughout the wired world. Can anyone really be against that?

QUESTIONS FOR THOUGHT

1. In paragraph 5, Weisberg states "I've read more in the past year simply because my e-book has made doing so more convenient." Make a list of electronic items you use daily. What was your life like before you began using these items? In what ways have the items affected your life?

2. What are some pitfalls of electronic books?

3. What are some pitfalls of technological advances in general?

4. List some items that will never be replaced by technology. Explain.

SELECTING

Let's start where we left off in the previous chapter. You have chosen a topic. You have brainstormed a number of ideas related to your topic. Maybe you have done some research with outside sources. You now sit, facing notes and pages of information that may or may not make their way into your paragraph or essay. Obviously, you can't use everything—just as I couldn't tell the entire plot of the Godzilla movie to my friends and Jacob Weisberg can't tell you everything he knows about electronic books. You have to narrow what you know. This is a decision-making process known as **selecting**. Here, the ideas of **topic**, **audience**, and **purpose** come into play again.

Topic

When selecting information, you have to remember that every element needs to relate to the topic. Highlight or underline the sections of your brainstorming that relate closely to your topic. An anecdote about your uncle's experience with downloading online music files or a statistic on the number of video games sold to children ages ten and under may be interesting, but they don't belong in an essay on the changing technology of digital phones. Leave the other pieces of brainstorming untouched until you have written a rough draft of your document. You never know what you may need later on. Perhaps you'll discover that the ideas and information you generated aren't enough. In that case, brainstorm again, or collect more information from outside sources.

Audience

Consider again the people who are going to be reading your work. Refer to your TAP sheet and view every element from the point of view of the audience. Underline or highlight what will work and leave alone what is inappropriate. A paragraph explaining how a digital phone operates may not be necessary if your audience already knows this information. Again, at this point, simply move the unwanted information aside; do not throw it out completely.

Purpose

Your purpose will influence what information you select for your draft. Keep your TAP sheet handy to remind you of the purpose of your writing. Again, read through the brainstorming and highlight or underline the information that meets your purpose.

Jacob Weisberg is a contributing writer for *The New York Times Magazine* and chief political correspondent for the online magazine *Slate*. What do you think he could have told you about books and publishing? At least enough for a book! Instead, he focused on the e-book controversy, stating his opinion and supporting it with publishing history and personal experience. From his vast knowledge, he *selected* just what he needed to write an effective, convincing argument. His example is a good one.

Exercises

1. Complete a TAP worksheet as Weisberg might have completed it before he began to write "The Good E-Book."

2. Brainstorm a list of topics pertaining to students attending your college. Choose one and develop the idea through a TAP worksheet. Write a brief explanation of how you decided on topic, audience, and purpose.

3. With a partner, brainstorm a list of topics based on current events. Choose one and develop the idea through a TAP worksheet.

STRUCTURING: THE PARAGRAPH AND THE ESSAY

To be successful with your writing, you must present the information so it flows from one idea to the next and is easy to understand. You must shape your ideas by giving them structure—on a small scale in paragraphs and on a large scale with essays.

Examine the overall structure of the essay "The Good E-Book," which opens with a survey of the current state of electronic books. The next paragraph introduces

Paragraph and essay comparison.

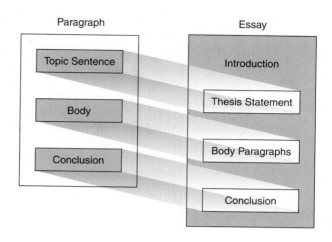

the controversy over their value and their consequences for literature. The third paragraph gives a brief history of technology and publishing conflicts. At paragraph 4, we begin to get Weisberg's point of view. Here he explains the pros of the e-books. Paragraph 5 goes into a discussion of a more specific aspect of the topic, namely the Rocket eBook (briefly mentioned in paragraph 4). In this paragraph, the pros for using this type of e-book are given in more detail. The two concluding paragraphs finish the discussion, where Weisberg praises e-book technology for moving publishing forward. This organizational structure isn't random; instead, the author understands both the structure of the essay and the structure of the paragraph and uses both to suit his topic, his audience, and his purpose.

To organize a piece of writing, you need to understand the structure of paragraphs and essays. In many ways, paragraphs and essays are patterned alike. A paragraph has a topic sentence or controlling idea, body sentences that develop the topic sentence, and a concluding sentence that wraps everything together. The essay has an introduction that presents the main idea, three body paragraphs that develop the idea, and a conclusion that reflects on the ideas. The following chart shows how the two structures are parallel.

Paragraph Structure

The **paragraph** is a collection of related sentences, a quick way to express information. At times, you will need only a few sentences to get your point across, and a paragraph is ideal for that task. As mentioned earlier, a traditional paragraph opens with a topic sentence. The idea stated in that sentence is developed through body sentences, and the paragraph ends with concluding sentences.

Topic Sentence   The **topic sentence** directs the focus of the other sentences in the paragraph. It introduces your topic and often reflects your opinion of the topic. A strong topic sentence immediately shows the reader your main idea. A weak topic sentence leaves your reader wondering about the overall point of the paragraph.

Consider paragraph 3 of "The Good E-Book," in which Weisberg describes resistance to change in texts:

> If this hostility feels vaguely familiar, it may be because every new form of literary dissemination has drawn the same sort of reaction. Medieval clerics greeted printed books as imposters of illuminated manuscripts—aesthetically inferior, textually unreliable and likely to breed a dangerous diversity of opinion. In the 1950's, the senior statesmen of publishing fretted that the paperback revolution would mean the further spread of poor taste. The echo of such views is heard today in an equally misguided elite's hostility toward digital publishing; surely we will hear lamentations for the lost age of electronic literacy once scientists find a way to plant books directly into the brain.

The first sentence makes a statement: Every new form of publishing is greeted with hostility. This sentence is the topic sentence. The audience now expects to see examples of this negative reaction to new forms of publishing, and Weisberg provides just that.

Tips

Make Your Topic Sentences Effective

Effective topic sentences have the following characteristics.

▸▸▸▸ **They state the topic.** Topic sentences give clear indications of the content of a paragraph. If your topic sentence is vague, the reader will have to guess at your meaning and may doubt your ability to discuss it effectively in a paragraph.

▸▸▸▸ **They often give a point of view.** Topic sentences that state opinions set the stage for sentences that support that opinion. Look at the first sentence of paragraph 5. It states that the Rocket eBook is "a thing of beauty." This is Weisberg's opinion, and the rest of the sentences in this paragraph explain why he feels so strongly about e-books.

▸▸▸▸ **They are supported by the rest of the information in the paragraph.** In this sense, the topic sentence is an anchor for the other sentences in the paragraph. Topic sentences control the movement and flow of the rest of the sentences. Without a topic sentence, the other sentences would read as though they were disjointed and loose.

▸▸▸▸ **They are often, but not always, the first sentence.** Topic sentences are organizers, so they usually appear first. But in one of Weisberg's paragraphs, the topic sentence is second. Can you find it? Look at paragraph 7. The controlling idea of this paragraph is "The book is the text's container, not its essence." Weisberg places this sentence at the end of the paragraph. Feel free to place your topic sentences in different places within a paragraph, but always strive for clarity and flow.

Continued

> ▸▸▸▸ **They are complete sentences.** Topic sentences are not headlines. Headlines in newspapers and magazines attract attention, but a topic sentence is different. The topic sentence is a complete thought and provides the audience with important information, so it should be as clear as possible.

Take a look at the following sentences. Which makes the best topic sentence?

1. Death of a Mall: How the Internet hurts local business
2. This paper is about shopping on the Internet.
3. Many local businesses are suffering due to online or Internet shopping.
4. It really is going to hurt a lot of people before it is over.

Number 1 is a headline. The phrase does mention a topic and hints at a point of view, but it is not a complete sentence. Number 2 is a complete sentence but lacks the author's opinion. Number 4 is not specific. What is going to hurt these people before it is over? Number 3 is a topic sentence. Both the topic and the writer's opinion are reflected in the statement.

Exercises

4. Read through each of the paragraphs, underlining the topic sentence. Make note of why you chose that particular sentence as the controlling idea, then discuss your answers with classmates.

   a. If the generous length of totality doesn't impress you, then the chance for clear weather should. At this time of year, southern Africa is well into its dry season and clear, sunny skies are the rule. The cool, dry weather also keeps mosquitoes at bay—a distinct bonus in a land where insects can carry unpleasant pathogens.

   (Talcott, "Hello, Darkness")

   b. He has written a flawed piece of popular fiction from a black male viewpoint, and his apparent middle-class isolationism has resulted in a few misconceptions. First, the hero resembles a white from an upscale enclave and sounds like Al Jolson in blackface. Second, there is no real story, only a bunch of white and black folks interacting clumsily with each other. Third, the writer fumbles technique, using dialogue to convey exposition; which means, in some passages, his black man doesn't even sound human. That stings.

   (Bugeja, "Confrontations, Common Bonds")

   c. Later, I discovered the truth. Deep Blue's computational powers were so great that it did in fact calculate every possible move all the way to the actual recovery of the pawn six moves later. The computer didn't view the pawn sacrifice as a sacrifice at all. So the question is, if the computer makes the same move that I would make for completely different reasons, has it made an "intelligent" move? Is the intelligence of an action dependent on who (or what) takes it?

   (Kasparov, "The Day I Sensed a New Kind of Intelligence")

▼   ▼   ▼

Body Sentences   Your topic sentence will be explained and developed through **body sentences**. Generally, paragraphs have at least two body sentences, but often many more. Refer again to paragraph 3 of "The Good E-Book."

> Medieval clerics greeted printed books as imposters of illuminated manuscripts—aesthetically inferior, textually unreliable and likely to breed a dangerous diversity of opinion. In the 1950's, the senior statesmen of publishing fretted that the paperback revolution would mean the further spread of poor taste. The echo of such views is heard today in an equally misguided elite's hostility toward digital publishing.

The body sentences explain the hostility people feel toward new forms of literary dissemination with examples from history. One example is from the Middle Ages, and one is from the 1950s. These examples are offered as an attempt to convince the audience that hostility to new forms of publishing is nothing new. Every thought expressed in the body sentences relates to the main idea or topic sentence.

Body sentences can support the topic sentence with statistics, details of a friend's personal experience, information gleaned from a website, an interview with an expert—whatever your brainstorming and research has uncovered. Any body sentence that doesn't develop your main idea in some way should be replaced.

Concluding Sentences   **Concluding sentences** are much more than just the endings of paragraphs. They connect the topic sentence and body sentences while reinforcing the controlling idea. Again, look at the third paragraph of the reading. This time through, focus on the last sentence:

> The echo of such views is heard today in an equally misguided elite's hostility toward digital publishing; surely we will hear lamentations for the lost age of electronic literacy once scientists find a way to plant books directly into the brain.

In the topic sentence, Weisberg said that resistance to changes in book forms is common throughout history. His final sentence mirrors this idea: "The echo of such views is heard today." Weisberg speculates—humorously—that the future practice of downloading books directly into the brain of the reader will make the current objections to electronic books obsolete. Through this speculation, he shows that hostility to electronic books will fade, just as earlier hostility to new forms has faded. The conclusion rounds off the essay's timeline; it has looked at the present, gone back to the past, and now forecasts the future. If your concluding sentences operate this way, your audience will grasp your message and remember it.

Exercises

5. Write a paragraph about a previous writing experience. Make sure your paragraph has a topic sentence, body sentences that state and develop details, and a concluding sentence.

*6. With a partner, write a paragraph encouraging students to get involved in extracurricular activities on your campus. Check your paragraph for a topic sentence, body sentences that highlight and detail the extracurricular activities, and a strong concluding sentence.

*Asterisks indicate exercises that can be done collaboratively.

Essay Structure

An **essay** is a carefully arranged set of paragraphs. Overall, most essays follow the three-part organizational structure: introduction, body, and conclusion. Paragraphs also share these features, but the difference lies in the amount of content and in the direction in which the piece of writing moves. Instead of a topic sentence as its lead, an essay has an **introductory paragraph.** The topic sentence becomes a **thesis statement**. Instead of being developed by a few sentences, as with paragraphs, points in an essay are developed through **body paragraphs**. Finally, instead of ending with a concluding sentence, as with paragraphs, essays end with a **concluding paragraph**.

Introduction   First impressions count. Imagine you're at your college's homecoming party and you see someone you find attractive. Immediately, you think to yourself, "How can I introduce myself without looking like a total loser?" You might adjust your hair, straighten your shirt, and think of a clever opening line, all in an effort to make a good first impression.

First impressions are just as important in writing. In the first paragraph, you must get the reader's attention and keep it. This paragraph—sometimes more than one—is the **introduction**. A strong introduction involves the reader and convinces her to read more.

In "The Good E-Book," Weisberg hooks you by name-dropping. He knows his audience in *The New York Times Magazine* will recognize the names of popular authors, and when these readers learn that familiar writers have published electronically, a connection is made. You see that your favorite author is publishing in this new form, and you will read on to find out more. As you continue reading, you learn that some publishers are up in arms over electronic books. Now you are hooked.

Introductions can bring out your creativity. If, perhaps, your opinion essay calls for lower ticket prices at professional baseball games played in your local stadium, you could begin with a short narrative about a family going to a game and the shocking amount of money they spend in one afternoon. Maybe in your research you discovered just how much ticket prices have gone up over the last few years and you want to make your audience immediately aware of the increase.

Tips

Make Your Introductions Matter

Whatever form your introduction takes, you still must keep these two rules in mind.

Be accurate. Don't make up statistics or exaggerate a point for the sole purpose of grabbing the reader's attention. Once she figures out you are not honest, she will be tempted to stop reading or, at the very least, begin to question the accuracy of other information you provide. The electronic book projects mentioned in the

Continued

opening of "The Good E-Book" are real; one simply has to log on to the authors' or publishers' official websites or call a nearby bookstore for verification.

Be efficient. More words don't always mean more power. An entire list of electronic book authors isn't necessary for Weisberg to get his point across. The short list works fine. Just hook the reader and let the rest of your essay provide the rest of the information to your audience.

Thesis Statement   The **thesis statement** controls the ideas in an essay. Like a topic sentence, it states the topic and the author's point of view. The major difference between a topic sentence and a thesis statement is size and scope.

In "The Good E-Book," each of the seven paragraphs has a topic sentence of its own. If stripped of all other sentences, the essay would look like this.

1. In recent months, bulletins about e-books have been breaking almost daily.

2. Despite the fact that hardly anyone uses an e-book yet, the drumbeat of ventures and issuances is breeding alarm in some quarters that serious reading in the future may no longer require the accumulation of dust-catching objects made of cloth, glue, ink and wood pulp.

3. If this hostility feels vaguely familiar, it may be because every new form of literary dissemination has drawn the same sort of reaction.

4. Less jaded consideration suggests that serious and unserious readers alike have much to gain from the new technology.

5. A more advanced version of the Rocket is due out this fall, but the relatively primitive 1.0 version is already a thing of beauty.

6. At another level, absorbing literature in a variety of ways—on screen, on paper, on tape—helps to dispel the false equation between text and book.

7. The book is the text's container, not its essence.

Each of these topic sentences controls the information within its respective paragraphs. The essay's thesis statement has to encompass them all. "…Serious and unserious readers alike have much to gain from the new technology" operates as the thesis statement for this particular essay. The other ideas expressed throughout the paragraph, those seven topic sentences above, are reflected in and are supported by the thesis statement.

Thesis statements are generally placed at the end of the introduction and before the body paragraphs start. However, just as with the topic sentence of a paragraph, you will occasionally find a thesis statement further along in the essay. Before you move your thesis statements around, however, get comfortable writing and placing them at the end of the introduction. This way, you will develop a sense of thesis statements and how the other paragraphs connect and relate to them.

Body Paragraphs   By definition, an essay allows more space for development than a paragraph. You have at least two or three **body paragraphs** in which to explain and explore these points. Reread this paragraph from "The Good E-Book":

> A more advanced version of the Rocket is due out this fall, but the relatively primitive 1.0 version is already a thing of beauty. Putting aside the stares and questions, it is a no less comfortable way to read novels than the old hard-copy method. In fact, it is an improvement. Your book bag no longer causes backaches. You fall asleep reading and the book saves your place. And most of all, I find it more responsive to the way someone like me actually reads—not choosing one book at a time and reading it through from cover to cover but nibbling on several according to the mood that strikes, with interruptions for newspapers and magazines. There is no reason other than superstition to believe that using an e-book diminishes your personal relationship with what you read. And because an e-book doesn't require good lighting or two hands, it is bliss in situations in which a bound volume is an awkward appendage: while eating, in bed, on the StairMaster or in the car at night (with someone else driving, please). I've read more in the past year simply because my e-book has made doing so more convenient.

If you break this paragraph into a thesis statement and supporting sentences, you can see how the author presents and supports his point.

Topic Sentence:
A more advanced version of the Rocket is due out this fall, but the relatively primitive 1.0 version is already a thing of beauty.

Supporting Points:

It is a no less comfortable way to read novels than the old hard-copy method.

Your book bag no longer causes backaches.

You fall asleep reading and the book saves your place.

I [can] nibble on several according to the mood that strikes, with interruptions for newspapers and magazines.

[It] doesn't require good lighting or two hands…bliss…while eating, in bed, on the StairMaster or in a car at night.

This well-unified paragraph convincingly explains the benefits of electronic books. Other paragraphs within the essay cite popular authors whose works have been published in e-books, give examples of hostility to new forms of publishing, and explain how e-books work and the relationship between reader and text. Placed together, these paragraphs create a strong essay.

Concluding Paragraphs   **Concluding paragraphs** finish your essays. They reiterate the essay's thesis statement and main points discussed in the essay. Concluding paragraphs also give the author a chance to reflect, offer advice or suggest a course of action relative to the topic. The exact content of the concluding paragraph may be determined by your audience and your purpose in writing the essay.

Reread the concluding paragraphs of "The Good E-Book":

> At another level, absorbing literature in a variety of ways—on screen, on paper, on tape—helps to dispel the false equations between text and book. Powerful

associations from childhood—the smell of must, the flashlight under the covers—have bred generations that think of themselves as book lovers rather than story hounds or prose fanciers.

But to turn such preferences into edicts is simply prejudice. The book is the text's container, not its essence. Appropriate technology for the past 500 years, it now stands on the brink of improvement. What will replace the bound volume will be, in some ways, truer to the current process of literary creation. These days, novels are most often composed not on bound leaves but on computer screens. There is no reason to believe our culture will be poorer even in amorphous ways when people absorb them from screens as well. And in definite and obvious ways, readers and writers alike will be richer for the access they will gain to an electronic version of Borges's infinite *Library of Babel.* In the near future, books will cost little or nothing, never go out of print and remain eternally available throughout the wired world. Can anyone really be against that?

The main idea of the essay is clearly expressed in this conclusion. His final sentence—a question—leaves the reader pondering. Weisberg gives us a lot to think about. He has accomplished his purpose.

Essay Unity   Having examined the components of an essay, now take a look at the structure as a whole. The first paragraph of "The Good E-Book" is the attention grabber and introduction to the topic. Weisberg describes the current state of e-books, explaining both what they are and what is being published in this electronic format. Paragraph 2 introduces the controversy behind the technology. In paragraph 3, Weisberg offers a quick history of publishers' attitudes toward new technology. Paragraph 4 introduces the thesis—that readers have much to gain from the new technology—and the following two paragraphs expand on positive aspects of e-books. Paragraph 7 concludes the essay by making this important point: "The book is the text's container, not its essence." Weisberg's purpose is to convince his audience that e-books are a good thing. He does that by examining—and refuting— the arguments against them.

Exercises

7. Write down the thesis statement for each of the following essays found elsewhere in this book. (Page numbers follow each title.) Explain your reasons.

   a. "One Poke Over The Line" (pages 407–409)

   b. "Is Rock Music Rotting Our Kids' Minds" (pages 379–382)

   c. "Ad to the Bone" (pages 422–424)

   d. "Learning What 'Team' Really Means?" (pages 370–372)

   e. "Underhanded Achievement" (pages 399–401)

*8. Brainstorm a list of topics that you could develop into an essay. Choose one and write a thesis statement for it. Share your thesis statement with other students for feedback.

WRITING WITH COMPUTERS

SELECTING

Computers can be a valuable aid when selecting information for a piece of writing. Open a new document and type the topic sentence at the top. Read through your TAP Worksheet and type out all the useful information below the topic sentence. Save this information as a separate document, then print out a hard copy for reference. As the information changes and the piece of writing begins to take shape, simply open the document and make necessary changes. Be sure not to delete or erase information that doesn't readily have a home in your document. Save it for future possibilities.

WRITING WITH OTHERS

SELECTING

Given that the final, polished draft of your piece of writing will be read by others, you should consider sharing your organizational structure and your selections for your paper with someone in your class whom you trust. An informal discussion works best. You simply talk out your plans for the paper (what the introduction and thesis statement will cover and how you plan to develop them, for example). The other person's job is to listen closely and offer suggestions. Because this is the planning stage, changes can be made easily.

9. Expand the topic sentences from Exercises 5 and 6 into thesis statements. Remember that these new thesis statements should include all the major points from the paragraph they came from.

OUTLINING: ORGANIZING YOUR PREWRITING IN ESSAY FORMAT

Outlines have gotten a bad rap over the years. Students (maybe even you) have myriad horror stories about creating lengthy outlines, complete with roman numerals, that seemed to take just as much work as writing the paper itself.

An **outline** is the skeleton or basic arrangement of information for a piece of writing. Think of an outline as simply a guide or a map for writing. Like directions, an outline helps you stay on track. As you write, you will probably discover a few ideas that were not part of the original outline. Be open to them. Feel free to reevaluate your outline and make changes at any point. Don't look at an outline as punishment or a way to stifle your creative energy. Outlines simply keep you centered on your writing task.

Organizational Patterns

Sentences and ideas are not just placed on the page at random, nor are all essays arranged in the same manner. If you were telling a story about applying to college, you would use a different structure than if you were attempting to convince a reader that everyone should go to college. Different writing strategies demand different organizational patterns, such as **chronological order**, **climax order**, and **spatial order**.

Chronological or sequential order. When you are writing a narrative, you need to explain the first event, then the second one, and so on. This pattern is called **chronological** or **sequential order**. If you fail to keep your ideas straight, the sequence of events will be disrupted and your essay won't flow well.

Climax order: From least to most important. When presenting information to your audience, you may want to save the most interesting or the strongest point until the end of the essay. This arrangement, called **climax order**, heightens suspense and keeps your audience's interest high throughout your essay. This type of organization works well with persuasive and response-to-reading essays.

Spatial order. Descriptive essays often focus on the arrangement of items in an area. This arrangement is called **spatial order**. Sensory details are important in this essay structure.

The Outline Worksheet

With your highlighted brainstorming ideas and essay structure in mind, try plotting your essay on a new worksheet.

Outline Worksheet

Topic: _____
_____

Audience: _____
_____

Purpose: _____
_____

**Thesis
Statement:** _____
_____
_____
_____

**Organizational
Pattern:** _____

**Reason or
Support #1:** _____
_____
_____
_____

**Reason or
Support #2:** _____
_____
_____
_____

**Reason or
Support #3:** _____
_____
_____
_____

Conclusion: _____
_____
_____

Time: _____

Resources: _____

STUDENT SAMPLE

Let's see how using the Outline Worksheet works. As an assignment in her writing class, Angie chose to write about athletes and academics. She had noticed that many student athletes were forced to sit out games because of their grades and that many students have demanded that more emphasis be placed on athletes' academics. Angie supports this idea, but she thinks these students need a balance.

Angie's clustering for her essay on children and sports.

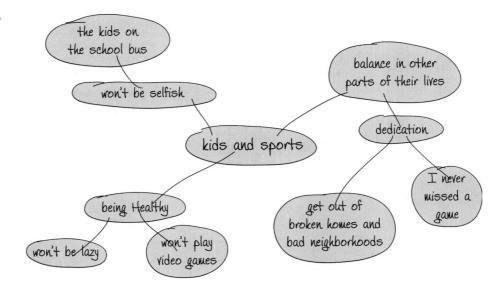

She tried out her ideas on kids and sports by clustering. Then she expanded her idea that young children should be encouraged to participate in sports as well as academics. Here is her TAP Worksheet.

Outline Worksheet

Topic: What is the topic of the writing project?

Children and sports

What type of topic is it?   (Academic)   Self-reflection   Outside source

Audience: Who are the members of my audience?

People who have children and want them to play sports.

Continued

What is the educational level or levels of my audience?
College level

What does my audience know about my topic?
Probably a great deal— but I have a unique
perspective—drove a bus all that time.

What has been their reaction to topics like this before?
Okay.

What has been their reaction to my previous writing?
I have done fine in class so far.

Purpose: Why am I writing this particular piece?
To educate people.

Why is the audience reading this particular piece?
To see my perspective.

Strategy: List the writing strategy or strategies that may be used in this writing project. Discuss reasons for using these selected strategies.
Persuasion—using some personal experience as support.

Style: What approach are you going to take with this topic? Discuss your choices
Straightforward.

Time: Estimate the amount of time needed for this writing project. (Consider the type of topic when estimating.)
1 week.

Resources: Jot down any outside resources that will be required for this writing project
None.

After she filled out a TAP Worksheet, Angie arranged the material to fit the structure of the essay: introduction, thesis statement, main points with details and examples, minor points with details and examples, and a conclusion. When sorted into categories, the information Angie wanted to include in her rough draft looked like this:

Outline Worksheet

Topic: _Children and sports._

Audience: _People with children interested in sports._

Purpose: _To educate them._

Organizational Pattern: _Persuasion_

Thesis Statement: _Children need to work hard in school, but they need balance, and playing sports will give them the balance and help with other stuff as well._

Reason or Support #1: _Children are overweight._

Reason or Support #2: _Children get selfish._

Continued

Reason or Support #3:	*Children need dedication.*
Conclusion:	*Athletics teaches our children a number of things.*
Time:	*1 week.*
Resources:	*None.*

WRITING WITH COMPUTERS

OUTLINING

Computers are wonderful tools, for they have made organizing your writing an easy task. Many word processor programs come equipped with ready-made outlines. Simply choose one and start filling in the blanks. If you don't have access to the outlining part of the program, create one of your own. Just set a tab every five or ten spaces on a blank document and save it. Next time you need to create an outline, open this file. When you start a new line, just hit the Enter key. When you need to indent, simply hit the Tab key. One note of caution: Outlines change as you organize the material. When that happens, make the necessary changes on the hard copy, type the changes on your outline, and print out a new working copy.

WRITING THE ROUGH DRAFT

A **rough draft** is exactly that: an unpolished version of a piece of writing. Gather all of your notes, outlines, and worksheets. Review your topic, your audience, and your purpose. Then start writing. Don't worry about development. Don't worry about sentence structure or spelling. You can take care of all those things later. The main idea of a rough draft is to get your ideas on paper.

A great place to begin writing is the middle of the piece, with either the body sentences or the body paragraphs. Starting in the middle allows you the opportunity to get to the sections of the writing you are most comfortable with and that will, most likely, be the strongest. As you write, embellish the information you have down in note form. Turn jottings into developed thoughts. After you have written the middle, work on the introduction and conclusion.

Keep your TAP worksheets handy. They may relieve some pressure when you can't think of what to write next. Be open to new ideas as well. Writing out the rough draft will generate more ideas.

Remember that you are writing a rough draft. Any part of it can be changed later on—so, for now, just let the words flow.

Tips

Make the Most of Rough Drafts

Your rough drafts are supposed to be rough. Keep these points in mind.

▸▸▸▸ **Remember, everything can be changed.** Writing goes through stages. You may have loved the idea of opening your essay with a series of questions, but after you wrote the body paragraphs, that idea no longer appeals to you. Change it. Just write what you want to write.

▸▸▸▸ **Expect the unexpected.** Have you ever gone shopping for one item and ended up buying something else? You took advantage of an unexpected opportunity. Do the same thing as you write. As new thoughts and ideas come into your head, jot them down as well. Some people keep a blank sheet of paper handy as they write a rough draft for the purpose of capturing the new ideas. Who knows? You may end up with the seeds of another piece of writing.

▸▸▸▸ **Don't throw anything out yet.** Some ideas from your outline may not make it to your draft. Don't force those ideas in. Just set them aside for the next writing assignment.

▸▸▸▸ **Don't sweat the grammar.** An entire section of this book is dedicated to grammar, spelling, and punctuation. These elements are important when it comes to polishing a piece of writing, but not when you are writing the rough draft. If you focus too much on correct grammar with your rough draft, you may block the flow of your thoughts. You can always fix the grammatical problems later.

▸▸▸▸ **Write now, research later.** When working on a writing project that requires gathering research or background information, you don't have to have all of the research completed before you begin writing. Being prepared is always a good goal, but if you find a statistic is missing or you don't know exactly how to spell an expert's last name, keep writing. Make a note in the draft of what you are missing, then go back and add it later.

Continued

> ▸▸▸▸ **Consider writing your essay as a paragraph you can expand.** Compare the paragraph structure with the structure of an essay. The paragraph's topic sentence equals the thesis statement of the essay, the body of the paragraph equals the body paragraphs of the essay, and the concluding sentence equals the concluding paragraphs of an essay. Given these comparisons, you might want to write a skeleton of the essay as a paragraph, making sure all the main points are expressed. From there, you can go through and add information.
>
> ▸▸▸▸ **If you find yourself getting off track, remember to TAP.** You did a great deal of preparation before you began writing the rough draft. Regardless of all your hard work, at times the words you are writing just won't be the ones you want. When this happens, take a few moments to review your topic, your audience, and the purpose behind your writing, then begin writing again. Refocusing your attention on these areas of your writing will provide you with more guidance.
>
> ▸▸▸▸ **Slow down.** Don't be in a rush to complete a draft. Take your time; complete one section, take a walk or watch television for a few minutes, then complete another section. Just be sure to remember your deadlines and keep your breaks short.

STUDENT SAMPLE

Let's go back to Angie. After completing the TAP Worksheet and Outline Worksheet, the next decision Angie had to make was where to begin writing. Her first impulse was to start with the introduction, but she chose the first body paragraph. She reviewed the information she had selected for that section and began writing. Here is what she started with:

Children can be lazy/overweight:

Kids can be fat if they sit around. They think that the only way to get anywhere is to drive, even for a short distance. But who is to blame for that? Parents can be because they don't motive their children well. Children need role models.

Here's what she ended up with:

Children's health can get bad because they sit around all day being lazy and overweight. You ask a kid today to check the mailbox, and they want the keys to drive to it. The problem is often that children are allowed to play video games, watch sports on television instead of playing them, and just sit around. Parents have to stop these destructive behaviors.

From this paragraph, the reader learns about the problem of overweight, lazy children. The reader also learns about Angie's solution: Parents need to regulate video games and other nonphysical activities. Angie rearranged her notes so the information would flow better in the paragraph. This paragraph is not perfect, Angie knows, but it is a good place to begin.

From here, Angie wrote the other body paragraphs, the introduction, and the conclusion. Her completed rough draft looked like this*:

> Children do need to work hard in school, but they need a balance and playing sports will give them that balance and help with other stuff in their lives as well. We have a problem with children being overweight in this country. We also have a problem with people suggesting that athletes should focus less on their academics and more on their talents in sports.
>
> Children's health can get bad because they sit around all day being lazy and overweight. You ask a kid today to check the mailbox, and they want the keys to drive to it. The problem is often that children are allowed to play video games, watch sports on television instead of playing them, and just sit around. Parents have to stop these destructive behaviors.
>
> If a child doesn't learn to share, then they will be selfish. They won't understand that the world doesn't revolve around then. I drove a school bus for years and I saw some of the worst kids imaginable. They would yell and cry and demand things from me because they were all about themselves. If they had played sports, they would have learned about respect and discipline and sharing.
>
> Dedication is the final thing that athletics can help a child with. I know that when I played sports in school, I loved being on the team and watching my team and playing the games. I was always there for practice and games, except for a few times. This is the type of thing that sports will give our children. A lot of athletes that were athletes as children through dedication and hard work have made life better for themselves and their families. Some come from bad neighborhoods and bad homes. Being dedicated to sports made them overcome their problems.
>
> Athletics teaches our children a number of things. We should focus on athletics and help children be successful.

---

*Many instructors require their students to use MLA formatting guidelines when submitting their final drafts. This textbook uses MLA formatting only for final drafts.

As a rough draft, this is a successful piece of writing. All of the parts necessary to explain and develop Angie's viewpoint are included. The first paragraph is an introduction. Angie opens with the thesis statement: "Children do need to work hard in school, but they need a balance and playing sports will give them that balance and help with other stuff in their lives as well." Then she goes on to discuss the important factors behind her thesis statement. Her approach presents her points clearly, making them very difficult to challenge.

In the next paragraph, Angie talks about children needing athletics to be healthy. She states her reason, plus she includes reasons children are not healthy: video games, watching sports on television instead of participating in them, and lounging around. She ends the paragraph by giving a directive, showing she does have solutions and is willing to share them.

Selfishness dominates the next paragraph. Here, Angie explains what she means by selfishness and gives a personal perspective on what she has witnessed. The years she drove the school bus add credibility to her argument. At the end of this paragraph, she explains how sports could have solved the problems she witnessed.

Angie devotes the last body paragraph to dedication and the idea that athletics can help children develop this virtue. Again, she includes a personal example, this time from her own experiences of being an athlete and having the dedication to attend all but a few of the games and practices. She develops this idea even further by talking about the situations in which some professional athletes grew up and how they were dedicated to that one thing that helped them achieve their dreams. As with her own experience, this insight helps with credibility.

Finally, in the conclusion, Angie restates her thesis statement, then offers a call to arms, encouraging the audience to support children in playing sports. Just two sentences long, this conclusion does what it is supposed to do; however, Angie knows it needs to be much more developed. She will take care of that during revision.

Now that you have a rough draft, congratulate yourself. Then take a deep breath. It is time to move on to Chapter 3: Revise, where you will learn how to improve your draft and make it stronger.

WRITING WITH COMPUTERS

CREATING THE ROUGH DRAFT

Word processing programs are ideal for rough drafts. When working with a computer, open a new file for each section you are working on. Once all the sections have been completed, create a new file incorporating all of the sections into one piece. Save all the documents. As you revise, you may have to change a certain section. Saving that section as a separate document will allow you to return to your original, untouched ideas. Also check your word processing program for special functions, such as Notes. Some programs allow the user to jot notes on a document that won't show up when the document is printed. As a last resort, your computer's operating system (Windows or Mac) should be equipped with a low-level note-taking program like Notepad (for Windows). Feel free to write short notes to yourself here.

CHAPTER REVIEW

After the prewriting is finished, it is time to write your rough draft. Writing the draft is a matter of selection and organization. Selection takes place on two levels. First, you must select information from your brainstorming worksheets for use in your essay. Next, select where each of the bits of information will go according to the structure of the essay introduction, thesis statement, major points, examples and details, minor points, examples and details, and concluding paragraphs. Organization is a matter of choosing the format and structure of your piece of writing, namely a paragraph or an essay. A paragraph is made up of a topic sentence (controlling idea), body sentences (main points you want to express within the paragraph), and a conclusion (a sentence or two tying all the ideas together). An essay is made up of an introduction (a paragraph or two that gets the reader's attention), a thesis statement (the controlling idea for the essay), body paragraphs (each structured like a regular paragraph and used to develop a particular point), and concluding paragraphs (a paragraph or two tying all of the elements of the essay together).

When you begin writing, start in the middle of the piece with the section you are most comfortable with. Once that section is written, move to the introduction and conclusion. Don't be afraid to add information in any given section. If the new ideas don't seem as though they will help you at that moment, jot them down in the margins or on another sheet of paper. Make sure everything is covered in the draft; be sure to keep the topic, audience, and purpose in mind, especially if you find yourself getting distracted or sidetracked. Disregard grammar, punctuation, and spelling concerns. Just write. Anything that needs to be cleaned up will be taken care of in Chapter 3: Revise.

Final Writing Assignments

1. Return to the final writing assignment you did for Chapter 1 and write a rough draft.

*2. With a partner, use one of the topics you developed in Exercise 2 or 3 and turn it into a rough draft. Write a short paragraph detailing your thoughts and feelings about working with someone else to create a rough draft.

3. Reread "The Good E-Book," then brainstorm a list of technological advances you think our society cannot function without. Choose one *you* couldn't live without and fill out a TAP Worksheet and an Outline Worksheet for it. What information did you decide to include in your piece of writing? Why? How will that selection affect the overall content of the piece of writing? Write a rough draft.

3

REVISE:
Improving
Your Draft

Almost everything you see in movies and on television or hear on the radio evolved from an original idea. Take the original *Star Trek*, for instance. The characters of Captain Kirk and Mr. Spock didn't start out as the characters that have become so popular. Spock, the stoic second-in-command of the starship Enterprise, was originally created as an overly emotional character. In the pilot episode, the captain was Christopher Pike. The second-in-command, known only as "Number One," was a woman. Test audiences didn't like Pike's somber approach to the unknown, so Captain James Kirk was created to be more action-oriented. The audiences didn't appreciate a woman in a leadership role, so Spock—now written as a logical, unemotional Vulcan—became first officer. That move wasn't popular, either, but the chemistry between the impulsive Kirk and the more cautious Spock impressed the skeptics. *Star Trek* as we know it today would not have been if it weren't for all of the early ideas. You could, in a way, consider these ideas the rough draft of the show.

Writing works the same way. The words and phrases you have in the rough draft have served you well up to this point. Now you have to change them to make them work better. Entire passages may need to be added, deleted, or reorganized. Such is the work of revision. **Revision** is the act of adding material, deleting material, reorganizing material, and otherwise changing a draft. The goal is to improve the draft so it meets the audience's standards as well as your own.

Understand that revision is not simply shuffling a few sentences here or taking out a word or two there. Strong revision demands taking a critical look at your writing, saving the parts that are working and changing the parts that aren't. Revision also involves **editing** or fixing problems with grammar, spelling, and punctuation you didn't stop to worry over as you wrote your first draft.

In this chapter, we focus on the most effective ways to revise. We talk about revising for **structure** and **content** as well as editing for **mechanics** (grammar), **spelling,** and **punctuation**. Checklists that can serve as guides through the revision process are included, as are tips on revising with computers and revising with others. To begin, let's take a look at "The Day That I Sensed a New Kind of Intelligence" by Garry Kasparov.

Reading 3   The Day That I Sensed a New Kind of Intelligence
Garry Kasparov

BACKSTORY

Intelligence is often thought of as the ability to reason through a problem. When confronted with a problem, humans are able to consider solutions and their consequences and choose the one that best solves the problem. Machines take a more methodical approach, trying solution after solution until they find one that works. This contrast between humans and machines can be seen in problem solving situations such as a game of chess. In an article originally published in *Newsweek*, Garry Kasparov, perhaps the best chess player who ever lived, writes about playing a match against Deep Blue, an IBM supercomputer. Through this match, he discovered a new insight to intelligence.

LEXICON

material: space on a chessboard

pawn formation: moves by pawns that aid other pieces

pawn sacrifice: allowing a pawn to be captured

1   I got my first glimpse of artificial intelligence on Feb. 10, 1996, at 4:45 p.m. EST, when in the first game of my match with Deep Blue, the computer nudged a pawn forward to a square where it could easily be captured. It was a wonderful and extremely human move. If I had been playing White, I might have offered this pawn sacrifice. It fractured Black's pawn structure and opened up the board. Although there did not appear to be a forced line of play that would allow recovery of the pawn, my instincts told me that with so many "loose" Black pawns and a somewhat exposed Black king, White could probably recover the material, with a better overall position to boot.

2   But a computer, I thought, would never make such a move. A computer can't "see" the long-term consequences of structural changes in the position or understand how changes in pawn formations may be good or bad.

3   Humans do this sort of thing all the time. But computers generally calculate each line of play so far as possible within the time allotted. Because chess is a game of virtually limitless possibilities, even a beast like Deep Blue, which can look at more than 100 million positions a second, can go only so deep. When computers reach that point, they evaluate the various resulting positions and select the move leading to the best one. And because computers' primary way of evaluating chess positions is by measuring material superiority, they are notoriously materialistic. If they "understood" the game, they might act differently, but they don't understand.

4   So I was stunned by this pawn sacrifice. What could it mean? I had played a lot of computers but had never experienced anything like this. I could feel—I could smell—a new kind of intelligence across the table. While I played through the rest of the game as best I could, I was lost; it played beautiful, flawless chess the rest of the way and won easily.

5   Later I discovered the truth. Deep Blue's computational powers were so great that it did in fact calculate every possible move all the way to the actual recovery of the pawn six moves later. The computer didn't view the pawn sacrifice as a sacrifice at all. So the question is, If the computer makes the same move that I would make for completely different reasons, has it made an "intelligent" move? Is the intelligence of an action dependent on who (or what) takes it?

6   This is a philosophical question I did not have time to answer. When I understood what had happened, however, I was reassured. In fact, I was able to exploit the traditional shortcomings of computers throughout the rest of the match. At one point, for example, I changed slightly the order of a well-known opening sequence. Because it was unable to compare this new position meaningfully with similar ones in its database, it had to start calculating away and was unable to find a good plan. A human would have simply wondered, "What's Garry up to?," judged the change to be meaningless and moved on.

7   Indeed, my overall thrust in the last five games was to avoid giving the computer any concrete goal to calculate toward; if it can't find a way to win material, attack the king or fulfill one of its other programmed priorities, the computer drifts planlessly and gets into trouble. In the end, that may have been my biggest advantage: I could figure out its priorities and adjust my play. It couldn't do the same to me. So although I think I did see some signs of intelligence, it's a weird kind, an inefficient, inflexible kind that makes me think I have a few years left.

QUESTIONS FOR THOUGHT

1. Think about the many ways computers can (and, in some instances, do) interact with people: teaching, entertainment, cooking, and banking, just to name a few. Can computers do a superior job in these areas, compared to human beings, or does the human element always rise above the computer's attempts?

2. In what ways is playing a game against a computer different than playing a game against a human opponent?

3. What are the advantages to playing against a computer opponent? What are the disadvantages?

4. Reread the essay, but consider the game from the computer's point of view. What are the advantages of a computer playing against a human opponent?

GETTING READY TO REVISE

Garry Kasparov was able to beat Deep Blue because his human mind had greater capacity to, as he put it, "figure out its priorities and adjust my play." That's exactly what you, as a writer, need to do when you revise. You have to figure out your reader's priorities and adjust your text. To do that, you have to step out of the role of writer and take on the role of reader. You need to imagine that someone else has written the paragraph or essay in front of you and has asked you to read it. As the reader, it is your job to be honest about the work. Ask yourself questions: Are the introduction and conclusion easy to follow? What about the second and third body paragraphs? Are the technical terms explained clearly? Does the story come across? Do the characters live? As you answer the questions, make changes that strengthen the overall essay. That is the nature of revision.

Some writers find revision overwhelming. Having a plan helps. Just as moves in chess should not be random, revision should not be random, either. Begin by focusing on two aspects of writing: **content** and **structure**.

REVISING FOR CONTENT

Initially, much of the revision you do will focus on content. **Content** is the information you convey to the reader. Begin revising by comparing your TAP worksheet to your draft. Does all of the information in your draft serve your audience and your purpose? Your ideas about your topic may have developed or shifted, but your audience and your purpose will have remained the same. Each section of a piece of writing must be scrutinized to see if it does follow audience and purpose considerations.

Topic

Topic is the subject of the paragraph or essay—who or what it is about. As you critique your work, make sure each part focuses on the topic. Do any sentences stray from the topic? Does each of the examples you provide connect to the topic? Is the topic clearly defined within your work? Be harsh as you answer these questions and consider other ones when revising. Because the topic is the focus of your piece, anything that moves away from that focus looks like fluff, and your work loses unity.

Audience

Keep in mind the audience's demands as you revise. Your readers should understand and receive your information with no problem. If a section isn't clear, however, the reader stumbles and may have to reread it a few times or abandon the piece of writing altogether. In order to be clear, explain unclear terms. Rewrite sentences that speak down to or that may be too sophisticated for your audience. Again, be sensitive to your audience and their demands.

In the reading, Kasparov is careful to explain how computers make their moves.

> But computers generally calculate each line of play so far as possible within the time allotted. Because chess is a game of virtually limitless possibilities, even a beast like Deep Blue, which can look at more than 100 million positions a second, can go only so deep. When computers reach that point, they evaluate the various resulting positions and select the move leading to the best one. And because computers' primary way of evaluating chess positions is by measuring material superiority, they are notoriously materialistic. If they "understood" the game, they might act differently, but they don't understand.

He does this in order for his audience (readers who may or may not play chess) to follow the intricacies of the game as well as the mechanics of Deep Blue's play.

Purpose

Focus on purpose as you revise. If you set out to entertain, for example, the words and phrases you use should do just that. Cut or rewrite any sentences that stray from your purpose. Kasparov's purpose for writing his essay was to discuss the concept of intelligence in a straightforward manner. He uses narrative to introduce his topic and weaves this narrative throughout the essay, but he does stick to the purpose.

Unity

All of the elements of an essay should work together. This connection among elements of a piece of writing is called **unity**. Revising for content means you have to examine how all of the words, sentences, and paragraphs fit together and work with one another. Areas that seem out of place or that slow you down as you read must be explained, condensed into other sections, or removed altogether. In the reading, Kasparov discusses Deep Blue's computational abilities. In order to put the whole piece together, however, he relies on the story of the chess match.

Coherence

An essay is a collection of paragraphs. At times, your writing may not be smooth as you move from paragraph to paragraph or from idea to idea. When this happens, you are lacking **coherence,** or clarity. Pay close attention to the sentences that connect ideas. Are these connecting sentences clear? Do they allow the essay to flow freely, or do they act as a barrier and slow the pace? Rewrite those sentences that do not help the reader get from one place to another easily. One suggestion is to use transitions. **Transitions** signal the end of one thought and the start of a new one. Some transitions are *first, second, also, finally, for example, however, nevertheless, on the other hand,* and *in conclusion.*

Length

One major consideration all writers face is length. Regardless of how well your essay is written, if the writing situation called for no more that 300 words and you have 523, you have a problem. Many writing instructors frown on such excess. Editors and publishers, always conscious of space, rarely consider pieces longer than their word requirements. Your memos and reports may be ignored or rejected if you use too many words to get your point across. Perhaps a bit of description can be taken out, or, if you have come up short and need more words, added. Be careful not to cut indiscriminately, however, or add filler material just to achieve a desired word length.

The Content Revision Checklist

At times, revision can be a complex job. You have a lot to remember. To make the job easier, use the following checklist:

Content Revision Checklist

Review the content of your rough draft carefully, then place checkmarks in the boxes that apply. Revise the paragraph in the areas with no checkmarks.

OVERALL ESSAY

Topic

☐ The topic sentence features the author's opinion about the topic.

☐ Each of the support sentences in the paragraph reflects the topic sentence.

☐ All of the information in the paragraph focuses on the topic sentence.

Audience

☐ The information provided in the paragraph is consistent with the demands of the audience.

☐ Word choice reflects the educational level and background of audience.

Purpose

☐ The paragraph expresses the author's reasons for writing it.

☐ Word choice reflects the author's overall purpose.

Clarity

☐ Each sentence is complete.

☐ Each sentence is easily read and followed.

☐ Unclear ideas have been reworked.

Coherence

☐ As a whole, the sentences in the paragraph support the topic sentence.

☐ The support is logical and consistent with the ideas expressed in the paragraph.

Length

☐ The paragraph meets the writing situation's required length.

☐ Long, unclear sentences have been rewritten into tighter sentences.

Other comments about the paragraph:

_____

_____

Exercises

1. Revise the following paragraphs for content, removing unnecessary passages and adding detail as needed.

   a. Video games are mind destroyers that cost too much money. Any good system with powerful graphics and many games costs a ton of money. An average board game is less than $15 at any toy store. A friend of mine bought a brand-new game system and then couldn't make his car payment because he had spent all his money on the stupid game. A baseball game that stars Mark McGuire costs about $75. You can't find any of them used, or I would be able to save money that way. Yes, video games cost a lot of money these days.

   b. Watching the Reds play against the Giants was great. The Reds were trailing 3–0 when one of the Reds hit a home run. The team then started to get excited and rallied. They made a really sweet play and tied the score 3-all. Finally, one of the players hit a triple, but the Giants players were so clumsy, they fell down, and the triple stretched into a home run. I can't believe I went to get popcorn and missed the first home run. Just my luck. Anyway, it was a great game. Hope the next one is even better, but it is supposed to rain.

   c. I read somewhere that movies are going to become completely computer-generated within the next ten years. Computers have already take over music. Some bands have better sounds with a computer accompanying them. Computers are in the classrooms, too. I had this one teacher who used computers to help us learn the subject matter. Computers are even in our cars. I rode with a friend who had a directional computer in his car. Computers are taking over the world.

2. Take a paragraph or essay you have written recently and trade it with a classmate. Within the margins, make note of areas that should be revised for content. Return the papers and discuss your comments.

3. Based on the comments from your classmate, revise the paragraph or essay from Exercise 2. Compare your original draft to the revision. How did the revision affect the overall content of the paper?

REVISING FOR STRUCTURE

Revising for structure in essays falls under the same guidelines as revising for content in paragraphs. However, there are some important differences. You must look at the arrangement of the content of the essay. For this new type of critique to take place, we have to consider new elements of the essay, including the beginning, middle, and ending.

Beginning

Often, when we write a rough draft, we simply start with the topic sentence or thesis statement (or, in some cases, without these sentences). Once we have everything written down in the rough draft, we can go back and add an appropriate opening for the piece of writing. To have an effective beginning to your work, you must pay attention to the introduction and the thesis statement.

Introduction   When critiquing rough drafts, make sure your introduction has punch, makes the reader want to read more, and reflects your interest in the topic. Kasparov's essay begins with the description of a particular moment in time, namely the moment when he "discovered" the computer intelligence. This places the reader right in the middle of the action. We are facing the computer in a game of chess, and that feeling draws us into the essay. All introductions should make us want to read on.

Thesis statement   A good thesis statement reflects the author's overall point of view toward the subject of the essay and is supported by every paragraph. Highlight your thesis statement, then see how it matches up with each of the paragraphs in the essay. If the body of the essay—the paragraphs discussing the various aspects of the thesis statement—seems to go in a different direction, or if it includes information not reflected in the thesis statement, you may want to adjust the thesis statement accordingly. If some of the ideas expressed in a few of the paragraphs stray while the rest fall right in line behind the thesis statement, the problem may reside within those paragraphs: that is where you should make changes.

Middle

The middle of the piece of writing is where the majority of the revising takes place. All of the major ideas are in the middle of the piece, so you need to focus closely on this section as you revise. Refer to your TAP Worksheet and make sure that you have a writing strategy in mind when you revise the middle section of your essay. Different strategies often suggest different paragraph arrangements, so it is important that the body paragraphs follow the demands of the chosen writing strategy.

Body paragraphs   Body paragraphs operate on two levels. First, they provide in-depth detail on one aspect of the topic. Next, they support the topic sentence or thesis statement. Consider the following body paragraph from Kasparov's essay:

Humans do this sort of thing all the time. But computers generally calculate each line of play so far as possible within the time allotted. Because chess is a game of virtually limitless possibilities, even a beast like Deep Blue, which can look at more than 100 million positions a second, can go only so deep. When computers reach that point, they evaluate the various resulting positions and select the move leading to the best one. And because computers' primary way of evaluating chess positions is by measuring material superiority, they are notoriously materialistic. If they understood the game, they might act differently, but they don't understand.

This paragraph explains the limitations of computers that play chess. Kasparov does a fine job telling the reader that computers try to take all they can get with every move. The paragraph also reflects the overall idea behind the essay—that Deep Blue displayed a certain type of intelligence.

Ending

Conclusions should reflect the introduction of an essay and remind readers of the essay's thesis statement and main points. When examining your conclusion, see if it reflects the same approach you started out with in the introduction and look for the main ideas. The conclusion to Kasparov's essay ties everything together quite well. He tells about the strategy he used to defeat the computer, thus ending the narrative. He also discusses the idea he mentioned at the beginning—he did see intelligence, but it was different than what he had expected. The reader carries away a good story and good insight on artificial intelligence for later discussions.

The Structure Revision Checklist

Structure revision can be done in your head, but a checklist is provided on the next page on the next page to save you that headache. Read through your draft, making comments on your checklist as you go. This way, you can pinpoint problems within the essay easily and revise it.

Structure Revision Checklist

Review the structure of your rough draft carefully, then place checkmarks in the boxes that apply. Revise the areas with no checkmarks.

BEGINNING

☐ The introduction provides a hook and draws the reader into the essay.

☐ The introduction is the appropriate length for the essay.

Topic Sentence/Thesis Statement

☐ This sentence has a topic and an opinion about that topic.

☐ This sentence reflects the main points of the essay.

Comments

_____

_____

MIDDLE
Body Sentences/Body Paragraphs

☐ At least three body paragraphs are present.

☐ Each paragraph has a controlling idea and appropriate support.

☐ Each paragraph is clear and concise.

☐ Each paragraph connects to the thesis statement.

Comments

_____

_____

ENDING
Concluding Sentences/Concluding Paragraphs

☐ Final paragraphs bring closure to the essay.

☐ Final paragraphs reflect the point of view expressed in the introduction and thesis statement.

Continued

Comments

_____

_____

WRITING STRATEGY

☐ I chose the following writing strategy:

_____

☐ Explanation for choice of this strategy:

_____

_____

_____

Additional Comments

_____

_____

GENERAL WRITING SITUATION CONSIDERATIONS

☐ Paragraph/Essay meets requirements for format, word length, etc.

Comments

_____

_____

General comments about the essay

_____

_____

_____

Exercises

4. Take a paragraph or essay you have written recently and trade with a class-mate. In the margins, note areas that need to be revised for structure. Return the papers and discuss your comments.

5. Based on the comments from your classmate, revise the paragraph or essay from Exercise 4. Compare your original draft to the revision. How did the revision affect the overall structure of the paper?

STUDENT SAMPLE

In Chapter 2, Angie began an essay about encouraging children to play sports. She did the prewriting and outlining and produced a rough draft. Next she needed to look at it with a more critical eye. Using the Content Revision Checklist and the Structure Revision Checklist as a guide, she went through her draft:

My topic sentence works here

Children do need to work hard in school, but they need a balance and playing sports will give them the balance and

Should I start a new paragraph

help with other stuff in their lives as well. We have a problem with children being overweight in this country. We also have a problem with people suggesting that athletes should focus less on their academics and more on their talents in sports.

Children's health can get bad because they sit around all day being lazy and overweight. You ask a kid today to check the mailbox, and they want the keys to drive to it. The problem is often that children are allowed to play video games, watch sports on television instead of playing them, and just sit around. Parents have to stop destructive behaviors.

I think this is funny—I like it

This I don't like—how can they stop the behaviors?

If a child doesn't learn to share, then they will be selfish. They won't understand that the world doesn't revolve around them. I drove a school bus for years and I saw some of the worst kids imaginable. They would yell and cry and demand things from me because they were all about themselves. If they had played sports, they would have learned about respect and discipline and sharing.

I could add so much more here

Dedication is the final thing that athletes can help a child with. I know that when I played sports in school, I loved being on the team and watching my team and playing the games. I

What am I saying here???

was always there for practice and games, except for a few times. This is the type of thing that sports will give our children. A lot of athletes that were athletes as children through dedication and hard work have made life better for themselves and their

I hate that phrase

families. Some come from bad neighborhoods and bad homes. Being dedicated to sports made them overcome their problems.

My teacher will wonder what I am talking about here

Athletics teaches our children a number of things. We should focus on athletics and help children be successful.

Content Revision Checklist

Place a checkmark in the boxes that apply. Revise the paragraph in the areas with no checkmarks.

Topic

☑ The topic sentence features the author's opinion about the topic.

☑ Each of the support sentences in the paragraph reflects the topic sentence.

☐ All of the information in the paragraph focuses on the topic sentence.

Audience

☑ The information provided in the paragraph is consistent with the demands of the audience.

☑ Word choice reflects the educational level and background of audience.

Purpose

☐ The paragraph expresses the author's reasons for writing it.

☑ Word choice reflects the author's overall purpose.

Continued

Clarity

☑ Each sentence is complete.

☑ Each sentence is easily read and followed.

☐ Unclear ideas have been reworked.

Coherence

☑ As a whole, the sentences in the paragraph support the topic sentence.

☑ The support is logical and consistent with the ideas expressed in the paragraph.

Length

☑ The paragraph meets the writing situation's required length.

☐ Long, unclear sentences have been rewritten into tighter sentences.

Other comments about the paragraph

Just work on clarity and clean up the rough spots.

Structure Revision Checklist

Place a checkmark in the boxes that apply. Revise the areas with no checkmarks.

BEGINNING

☑ The introduction provides a hook and draws the reader into the essay.

☑ The introduction is the appropriate length for the essay.

Comments

Continued

Topic Sentence/Thesis Statement

☑ This sentence has a topic and an opinion about that topic.

☑ This sentence reflects the main points of the essay.

Comments

_____

_____

_____

MIDDLE
Body Sentences/Body Paragraphs

☑ At least three body paragraphs are present.

☐ Each paragraph has a controlling idea and appropriate support.

☐ Each paragraph is clear and concise.

☑ Each paragraph connects to the thesis statement.

Comments

Some work on the body paragraphs is needed.

_____

_____

ENDING
Concluding Sentences/Concluding Paragraphs

☑ Final paragraphs bring closure to the essay.

☑ Final paragraphs reflect the point of view expressed in the introduction and thesis statement.

Comments

Conclusion needs more.

_____

_____

Continued

WRITING STRATEGY

☑ I chose the following writing strategy: persuasion.

☑ Explanation for choice of strategy: I am trying to convince readers about my point and I use reasons and examples to support my opinion.

_____

_____

GENERAL WRITING SITUATION CONSIDERATIONS

☑ Paragraph/Essay meets requirements for format, word length, etc.

Comments

_____

_____

General Comments About the Essay

_____

_____

Taking all of her new ideas into consideration, Angie set about revising her rough draft.

America is losing a generation of great athletes everyday; some of our kids have never tried sports. They think it's better to focus on academics. It is important for children to participate in athletics because we are raising lazy, overweight children who have no dedication to anything but themselves.

First, children do need to work hard in school, but they need a balance and playing sports will give them the balance and help with other stuff in their lives as well. We have a problem with children being overweight in this country. We also have a problem with people suggesting that athletes should focus less on their academics and more on their talents in sports.

Next, if parents would motivate their children to be a part of a sport that kids like, children would have more of a balance in their lives. Children's health can get bad because they sit around all day being lazy and overweight. You ask a kid today to check the mailbox, and they want the keys to drive to it. We have taught our kids to be lazy. The problem is often that children are allowed to play video games, watch sports on television instead of playing them, and just sit around. Parents have to stop destructive behaviors.

Finally, if a child doesn't learn to share, then they will be selfish. They won't understand that the world doesn't revolve around them. I drove a school bus for years and I saw some of the worst kids imaginable. They would yell and cry and demand things from me because they were all about themselves. If they had played sports, they would have learned about respect and discipline and sharing.

Dedication is the final thing that athletes can help a child with. I know that when I played sports in school, I loved being on the team and watching my team and playing the games. I was always there for practice and games, except for a few times. This is the type of thing that sports will give our children. A lot of athletes that were athletes as children through dedication and hard work have made life better for themselves and their families. Some come from bad neighborhoods and bad homes. Being dedicated to sports made them overcome their problems.

Athletes accomplish fame, go to the Olympics, earn millions of dollars, and are exceptionally talented. Athletics teaches our children more than the sport itself. It also teaches them values. I think if we focus on athletics as well as academics, we will find healthier, unselfish, and dedicated children.

The Peer Review Worksheet

Writing is a lonely task. While you may have bounced ideas off friends, you probably did most of your prewriting and wrote the first draft alone. But once you have a first draft, you have something solid for someone else to react to. In fact, this is a great time to test your writing with a practice audience, especially if the writing you are doing is for others or for your instructor. This test audience is also called **peer reviewers**. Peer review allows for feedback from fellow students that you can integrate with your paper before your audience reads it.

Another name for peer review is *constructive criticism*. The person reading and reviewing your manuscript pretends to be a friendly member of your audience. This person points out sentences that are awkward or confusing, questions the spelling of certain words, and makes suggestions for improving the essay's clarity. Peer review is not a license to insult people or trash their work. Peer review is not an opportunity to rewrite someone else's paper. Above all, peer review is not a way to sabotage someone else's work.

If you are the peer reviewer, reading and commenting on someone else's work may make you uncomfortable at first. After all, you too are a beginning writer. What position are you in to tell others how to improve their work? Truth be told, you are in a perfect position. You are a reader and what is not clear to you probably won't be clear to others. Also, keep in mind that, as a beginning writer, you understand how much harsh criticism can sting. You should be able to present your concerns in a manner the author will accept.

When you review someone else's work, that person will give background information about the piece of writing. Questions about topic, audience, and purpose should all be answered by the author. These questions will help guide you as you read. After those questions are answered, ask the author about any concerns he or she had about the paper. Again, this information can help guide you as you read. Then read the piece, making notes of first impressions. Read the piece a second time, focusing on the questions you asked earlier and noting any concerns you didn't see the first time through. Jot down your responses, then discuss your ideas with the author. Be sure to note the positive aspects of the piece and to comment on the strengths of the writing. By writing about all aspects of the piece, you show you are taking the writer seriously.

To guide you through the peer review process, a Peer Review Worksheet is provided on the next page. Feel free to make copies and use it when you edit. Also, feel free to make modifications if necessary.

Peer Review Worksheet

Author's Name: _____

Reviewer's Name: _____

Title of the work: _____

Background Information (provided by author)

Topic:_____

Audience: _____

Purpose: _____

Concerns the author has about the work: _____

_____

_____

_____

_____

The Review

What stuck out on the first reading? _____

_____

_____

_____

_____

What did you notice as you did a second reading? _____

_____

_____

_____

_____

In the margins, lightly mark problems with grammar, spelling, and punctuation.

Overall thoughts about the work: _____

_____

_____

_____

_____

Writing With Computers

REVISING

The greatest help any word processing program can give in terms of writing is with revision. It allows you a chance to see your many drafts change and take shape. Save a copy of your rough draft on a hard drive, floppy disk, or CD. Copy the entire file into a new document, then save and close down the original file. You may also access your program's revision function (called Track Changes in Microsoft Word). With this, you can make adjustments and still keep the original document. You now have a copy of the document that you can freely tweak and not lose any of the original work.

Also, in the case of peer review, you can send a copy of your rough draft to other students, instructors, or even online writing labs for advice (with your instructor's permission, of course). Again, make a copy of your draft, then go online and open an e-mail file. Write the person who will be receiving your draft a short note, then attach your file. Click on the Send button, and your draft will be on its way. If possible, set up a chat room (an online space where two or more people can type to each other) and a time where you two can discuss your work.

Always make changes on a hard copy of the document, then enter them in the computer file. Revision works best when you are able to actually mark on the document, as major adjustments are easier to write out on paper. Keep in mind, though, that with just a few inserts and deletes, you can actually save a great deal of rewriting time and effort.

REVISING FOR MECHANICS

Every piece of writing should be revised before it is submitted or printed. Revision is important because at this stage you ensure your work is presented in its best form. When you submit an essay to your instructor, in essence you are saying, "This piece of writing is the best I can do." The final draft represents all of your hard work, so it must look as good as possible. For this reason, the final step in the revision process is **editing**.

Grammar, word choice, spelling, punctuation, and capitalization—these are the elements of writing you were asked not to consider when writing the rough draft. You probably cleaned up some spelling errors here and there as you revised for content and structure. You may have made adjustments to phrases that were awkward or substituted interesting words for mundane ones. All stages of revision allow for changes in mechanics, but in this step, you are going to address mechanics in a more focused and formal way.

You may take a number of approaches to this type of revision. Whichever you choose, be sure to read each and every word carefully. You may even consider reading the paragraph or essay backward, sentence by sentence. Because the sentences are out of order, you can't concentrate on content, so your mind is free to focus on mechanics. This reading backward strategy works well with a piece of writing you have been working on for a long time because you may be so familiar with it you slide over problem spots.

Some beginning writers glance quickly through their work, convinced mechanics are not a problem. Often, this glancing reflects an uneasiness about revising with mechanics. Don't sweat it. Lots of resources can help you. Use Part V of this book, "Grammar and Mechanics Review," for reference. Grab your dictionary and look up any word you think may not be spelled correctly. Expect this stage to take a great deal of time. It is better for you to catch the problems than it is to have your audience catch them. You want your readers to pay attention to what you are saying with your writing, rather than be distracted by awkward sentence structure and misspelled words.

Whatever approach you take, the goal should be the same: the elimination of error. While searching for problems with sentence structure, word choice, verb tense, spelling, punctuation, and capitalization, here are specifics to look for.

Complete Sentences

As you jotted down ideas and wrote your first drafts, you were paying attention to ideas, not sentence structure. Now is the time to make sure all of your sentences are complete and grammatically correct. **Complete sentences** consist of a subject (what the sentence is about) and a verb (the action or the state of being of the subject), and they express a complete thought. Read each sentence carefully, checking for subject, verb, and complete thought. See Part V for more information.

Interesting Vocabulary

A strong vocabulary is necessary for writing and revising. When editing, pay attention to every word. If you repeat certain phrases when moving from one idea to another or you find bland wording in descriptions, make the necessary changes. For more on word choice, see Chapter 27.

Proper Punctuation

Punctuation marks—periods, quotation marks, commas, and the like—guide the reader through your sentences. Periods, for example, tell the reader that a sentence is over and a new sentence is about to begin. Poorly punctuated writing is confusing and can even be impossible to read, so make sure every mark is in the correct place. For more on punctuation, see Chapter 26.

Correct Capitalization

Even as you wrote your earliest drafts, you capitalized the first letter of the first word in every sentence. You may have also capitalized proper names out of habit. But what about other capitals that may or may not be needed in your final draft? You have to check your drafts carefully and apply any capitalization rules necessary. For a review of capitalization, see Chapter 26.

Writing With Others

REVISING FOR MECHANICS

Because you have lived with your piece of writing through at least two drafts, getting someone else to read it is a valuable aid to revision. An extra set of eyes may catch problems your eyes missed. Reading the draft aloud to someone else is also a good way to catch trouble areas, for two reasons. One, you may hear problems as you read the draft aloud. Two, your audience may notice awkward places that you didn't catch.

The Mechanics Checklist

To aid in revision, a checklist is provided on the next page. As you go through your draft, check the boxes in the areas where there are no problems. Make adjustments in the areas with no checkmarks. Be sure to check every sentence.

Mechanics Checklist

SENTENCE STRUCTURE

☐ Every sentence has a subject, a verb, and a complete thought.

☐ A variety of sentence structures (simple sentences, compound sentences, complex sentences, etc.) is used throughout the piece.

WORD CHOICE

☐ Every word is used appropriately.

☐ A variety of words is used.

SPELLING

☐ Every word is spelled correctly.

PUNCTUATION

☐ Every sentence ends with the appropriate punctuation (period, question mark, exclamation point).

☐ Commas are used correctly.

☐ Semicolons are used correctly.

☐ Colons are used correctly.

☐ Quotation marks are used correctly.

☐ Apostrophes are used correctly.

CAPITALIZATION

☐ Dates are capitalized.

☐ Proper names are capitalized.

☐ Words beginning sentences are capitalized.

☐ Brand names are capitalized.

☐ Religions and names of religious figures are capitalized.

☐ Specific courses are capitalized.

☐ Specific languages are capitalized.

TROUBLE AREAS I NEED TO CHECK:

_____

_____

_____

Exercises

6. Take a paragraph or essay you have written recently and trade with a classmate. In the margins, note areas that need to be revised for grammar and mechanics. Return the papers and discuss your comments.

7. Based on the comments from your classmate, revise the paragraph or essay from Exercise 6. Compare your original draft to the revision. How did the revision affect the overall grammar and mechanics of the paper?

STUDENT SAMPLE

To see revision in action, let's return to Angie and her essay. She already revised for content and structure; the essay says what it needs to say. She is now turning her attention to unity and coherence and making her entire essay stronger.

America is losing a generation of great athletes everyday; some of our kids have never tried sports. They think it's better to focus on academics. It is important for children to participate in athletics because we are raising lazy, overweight children who have no dedication to anything but themselves.

First, children do need to work hard in school, but they need a balance and playing sports will give them the balance and help with other stuff in their lives as well. We have a problem with children being overweight in this country. We also have a problem with people suggesting that athletes should focus less on their academics and more on their talents in sports.

Next, if parents would motivate their children to be a part of a sport that kids like, children would have more of a balance in their lives. Children's health can get bad because they sit around all day being lazy and overweight. You ask a kid today to check the mailbox, and they want the keys to drive to it. We have taught our kids to be lazy. The problem is often that children are allowed to play video games, watch sports on television instead of playing them, and just sit around. Parents have to stop destructive behaviors.

Finally, if a child doesn't learn to share, then they will be selfish. They won't understand that the world doesn't revolve around them. I drove a school bus for years and I saw some of the worst kids imaginable. They would yell and cry and demand things from me because they were all about themselves. If they had played sports, they would have learned about respect and discipline and sharing.

Dedication is the final thing that athletes can help a child with. I know that when I played sports in school, I loved being on the team and watching my team and playing the games. I was always there for practice and games, except for a few times. This is the type of thing that sports will give our children. A lot of athletes that were athletes as children through dedication and hard work have made life better for themselves and their families. Some come from bad neighborhoods and bad homes. Being dedicated to sports made them overcome their problems.

Athletes accomplish fame, go to the Olympics, earn millions of dollars, and are exceptionally talented. Athletics teaches our children more than the sport itself. It also teaches them values. I think if we focus on athletics as well as academics, we will find healthier, unselfish, and dedicated children.

Mechanics Checklist

SENTENCE STRUCTURE

☑ Every sentence has a subject, a verb, and a complete thought.

☑ A variety of sentence structures (simple sentences, compound sentences, complex sentences, etc.) is used throughout the piece.

PUNCTUATION

☑ Every sentence ends with the appropriate punctuation (period, question mark, exclamation point).

☑ Commas are used correctly.

☐ Semicolons are used correctly.

☐ Colons are used correctly.

☐ Quotation marks are used correctly.

☐ Apostrophes are used correctly.

Continued

CAPITALIZATION

- [ ] Dates are capitalized.
- [x] Proper names are capitalized.
- [x] Words beginning sentences are capitalized.
- [ ] Brand names are capitalized.
- [ ] Religions and names of religious figures are capitalized.
- [ ] Specific courses are capitalized.
- [ ] Specific languages are capitalized.

TROUBLE AREAS I NEED TO CHECK

_____

_____

_____

After Angie made her changes, her edited draft looked like this:

America is losing a generation of great athletes everyday; some of our kids have never given athletics a try. They have been programmed that it's better to focus on academics. It is important for children to participate in athletics because we are raising lazy, overweight children who have no dedication to anything but themselves.

First, children are lazy and overweight, causing their health to be at risk. Most kids today can't even run a block without getting tired or short of breath. You ask a kid today to check the mailbox, and they want the keys to drive to it. We have taught our kids to be lazy because they consume television commercials and video games. Parents stress education over exercise, but they go together. If parents would motivate their children to be a part of a sport that kids like, children would have more of a balance in their lives.

Next, if a child is not taught how to share early in life, most likely the child will be selfish. Being part of a team teaches kids that life is not all about them. I drove a school bus eight years and saw kids arguing daily about sharing with each other, but being athletic teaches a child about being a part of a team, teamwork, sharing, and getting along with others.

Last, being athletic teaches a child dedication. A lot of athletes that were athletic as kids through dedication and hard work have made life better for themselves and their families. Some have come from bad neighborhoods and broken homes. The obstacles that were in their way were pushed aside using the avenues of athletics that caused them to succeed far greater than academics.

Athletes accomplish fame, go to the Olympics, earn millions of dollars, and are exceptionally talented. Athletics teaches our children more than the sport itself; it also teaches them values. I think if we focus on athletics as well as academics, we will find healthier, unselfish, and dedicated children.

PREPARING THE FINAL COPY

Once the last word has been written and the last period has been placed at the end of the last sentence, you will have an incredible feeling of a job well done. In your jubilation, you may want to simply hand it in and wait for your grade. However, you need to take a few minutes to proofread and check format to make sure the final copy is ready for submission.

Proofreading

Proofreading is the act of checking the final product for errors of any type. Give yourself time to do this carefully. You may already have, for example, corrected the misspelled words you found in the introduction when you expanded it during revision, or changed the comma to a semicolon in the next-to-last sentence in paragraph 2 during the editing stage. Proofreading is a separate stage in which you check the corrections, but it is much more than this. Good, effective proofreading requires that you scrutinize every paragraph, sentence, word, and letter contained in your writing so your final draft looks its best.

When proofreading, some writers choose to read their work aloud to themselves, making corrections as they go. Some read backward, from the last word to the first. Some read through their final draft five, six, or even more times, each time searching for something different—one pass for periods, one for capitalization, one for spelling. Whichever method you decide to use, be sure to give yourself adequate time. Take some time away from your revised essay before you proofread it. Even a few minutes will clear your head. Also, be sure to pace yourself as you proofread a draft. Quickly glancing through a draft may reveal some problems, but a slower reading will reveal many more. Also, be sure to mark changes to your draft clearly. Fewer things are more frustrating than looking back at a draft that has been proofed and not being able to read the marks for correction. Make your symbols and marks large and heavy enough so when you actually make the changes, you will have no questions and will not overlook anything. Solid marks also enable you to find the problem areas more quickly.

One valuable tool for proofreading is the abbreviated Proofreading Symbols and Marks List on page 85. These symbols and marks, universally used by teachers, writers, and editors, tell you what changes to make to the draft. Because these marks are used by almost everyone who works with the written word, they can be a great help when editing collaboratively. No guesswork about proposed changes will occur because everyone involved with the proofreading uses the same set of marks and symbols.

Exercises

8. Read the following sentences. Make changes using the proofreading symbols. Not all sentences need changes.

   a. Fining problems in a paragraph sentence or a word can be difficult.

   b. My instructor said You'd better Be prepared for a quiz on thursday.

   c. I said, "Thursday isn't good for me." He said, "Why not?" I said, "Because I have two other other quizzes that day."

   d. He looked at me like I had two heads.

   e. I couldtell that he would Not chaneg his quiz day for mee

9. Read the following essay, correcting errors by using proofreading symbols and marks along the way. Remember that not every sentence will need changes.

Movies derived from old Television shows are a watse of a good two hours. First, it just shows a great lack of imagination. At one time, screenwriters had to actually think up plots and dialogue for *Casablanca, 2001: A space Odyssey*, and *Some Like it Hot*. These original stories excited movie audiences. When Luke Skywalker blew up the Death Star, we were on the edge of our seats seats. Those movies showed how powerful an imagination can be. Next, many of the Television shows that become movies today weren't great to begin with. *Star Trek*'s series of movies came from a short-lived television show that had pathetic special effects and bad acting. *The Brady Bunch*, which spawned not only one but two movies, was just a silly show. These

Proofreading Symbols and Marks

Symbol	Meaning	Example
⌒	Close space	Ther e should be no extra space.
ℰ	Delete	There is an an extra letter at the ende.
/	Insert space	Too many times/we run ideas together.
/	Lower case	David said his House was for sale.
¶	New paragraph	"Should we wait?" he asked. "Well, of course," I replied.
/	Corrections	"If yoo say so," she replyed.
↗	Insert comma	1175 E. 26th Ave, Boston, MA 99909
⌣ ⌣	Insert quotation marks	Frankie said, Everyone should dance every day.
≡	Capitals	Lynese saw that movie at the omniplex west.
' ''	Don't make change	Friday will be a big day for me.
∽	Transpose characters or words	I have a bda feeling about this test.
		I have a feeling bad about this test.

shows were fun to watch, but not worthy of multi-million dollar productions. Finally, the screenwriters change so much of the ideas from the television shows that they should have started with a clean slate. *Lost In Space* was a goofy science fiction show in the '60's complete with bad acting, crazy costumes, and incredibly low budget special effects very little was explained about how the Robinson's got lost in space. When the movie remake came out a few years ago, all of that changed. Major actors were hired, making the dilemmas and situations much more real than before. Fashion designers had bigger budgetsand created costumes that looked good and was very practical, like retractable armor. Along with the money came state-of-the-art computer generated special effects. Adding a sense of wonder the television show never could. Outiside the Robinsons' name and the fact that they were eventually lost in space, the movie baredlittle resemblance to the show. Why not just call it something else? It is a shame people don't demand original movies at the movie theater and get their nostalgia from TV Land.

Writing with Computers
PROOFREADING
Computers have enhanced many areas of the writing process. Unfortunately, proofreading isn't one of them. Spelling and grammar checking programs are limited. Words they don't recognize, spelled correctly or not, are flagged as incorrect. Often, homonyms (words that sound alike but are spelled differently and have different meanings) are bypassed by these programs. For example, your computer reads *to, two,* and *too* as spelled correctly without regard for their context. The most effective way to proofread with a computer is to read the draft on the screen and make any changes. Print out a hard copy of the work and proofread it again. Make changes, then print out another hard copy, proof it, and make changes. Finally, print out another hard copy as the final draft to be submitted. By following this procedure, you will be able to ignore what your computer may say and actually do real proofreading.

Formatting

Final formatting is as important as proofreading. **Format** is the layout or physical arrangement of the written material on the page. Format includes such concerns as where your name goes on the page, how big the side and bottom margins are and how each page is numbered. At this stage, you should also have finalized a title for your piece. While you are working on creating that piece of writing, you may have written some sections in pencil and some in ink, or you may have scribbled changes in the margins and on the back of each page. The act of creation is never neat. But when you are submitting the final draft for a grade, neatness counts!

Your instructor may give you specific instructions for formatting submissions in your writing class. Follow these exactly. Here are additional tips.

Tips

Make the Format Right

The way you present your writing is important to the impression it makes. Here are points to keep in mind.

▸▸▸▸ **Identify yourself.** All final drafts need identification, namely your name, the date the assignment is turned in, the hour you attend class, and the course number for the class. While students are often tempted to attach a clean, crisp cover sheet to their work, identification information can be placed in the upper right hand corner of the first page. By placing the identification material here, you conserve paper and make it easier for your instructor to keep track of all the pages to your draft.

▸▸▸▸ **Give your work a title.** Center the title at the top of the first page, about three or four lines under the identification material. The title should be bold-faced. Unless you are told to do so by your instructor, do not underline or in any other way enhance the title. Anything other than boldfacing will distract the reader, thereby drawing attention away from your work. Remember to keep the title short and to the point.

▸▸▸▸ **Make margins and spacing adequate.** An inch of blank space should frame every page of your final draft. On the first page, skip three or four lines before you write the title, then skip another three or four lines before you begin the introduction. The body of the paper should be double-spaced, with the beginnings of new paragraphs indented five spaces.

▸▸▸▸ **Avoid fussy formats.** Some beginning writers are seduced by the fancy layouts or fonts (type of printing style) their computers can provide. These students usually attempt to imitate those fancy layouts in their final draft, adding pictures or placing the text in an awkward position on the page. Be warned: Playing around with layout or adding these extras only distracts the

Continued

reader. When formatting a final draft, let the strength of your writing attract attention to itself. Your instructor expects a clean, clear, well-written final draft unadorned with extras. Remember that the articles you read in magazines were submitted in much the same way you are submitting your work. Leave all that other design jazz to the art department.

▸▸▸▸ **Make handwritten submissions presentable.** At times, submitting a handwritten final draft may be acceptable. Always use black or blue nonerasable ink for the last draft of your work to elimimate possibility of smudging. Every letter should be as neat as you possibly can make it so your reader will not have to guess. If you see a mistake, carefully cross it out and write the correct word beside or above it. If you find three or more mistakes on a page, recopy that page.

Writing with Computers
FORMATTING

Often, computers can be a valuable help when formatting. Word processing programs often have 1-inch margins as a standard feature, and you can double-space text simply by highlighting it, pulling down a menu bar, and selecting Double under Spacing. However, be sure to preview the document before printing out the copy you are going to submit. What you see on the screen is not always what comes out of your printer. The title, for example, might appear double-spaced on the screen but single-spaced on the printed page. Carefully examine the final copy you will submit.

One way to preview the draft in printed format before you actually print is to change the screen to Print Layout. Click on View, then click on Print Layout. You should see the document as it will be printed. You can make changes in Print Layout just as you would in any other form of View.

STUDENT SAMPLE

Let's return to the essay Angie has finished editing. The grammar seems to be in order; now all she has to do is proofread the piece. She is aware that she has been working fast and may have introduced some errors. Using the proofreading symbols, Angie marked the draft in the following manner. She also put the essay in the right final format.

America is loosing a generation of great athletes every day, some of our kids have never given athletics a try. They have been programmed its better too focus on academics. It is important for children, To participate in athletics because we are raising lazy, overweight children who have no dedication two anything but themselves.

First, children are lazy overweight, causing their health to be at risk. Most kids today can't even run a block without getting tired or short of Breath. You ask a kid today to check the mailbox, and they want the keys to drive to it. We have taught are kids to be lazy because they consume television commercials and video games. Parents stress education over exercise, but they go together. If parents would motivate their children to be a part of a sport that like kids, children would have more of a balance in their lifes.

Next, if a child is not taught how to share early in life most likely the child will be selfish. Being part of a team teaches kids that life is not all about them. I drove a school bus eight years and saw kids arguing daily about sharing sharing with each other, but being athletic teaches a child about being a part of a team. Teamwork, sharing, and getting along with others

Last, being athletic teaches a child dedication. A lot of athletes that were athletics as kid through dedication and hard work have made life better for themselves and their families. Some have come from bad neighborhoods and broken homes. The obstacels that were in there way were pushed aside using the avenues of athletics that caused them to succeed far greater than academics.

Athletes accomplish fame, going to the Olympics, earn millions of dollars, and are exceptionally talented. Athletics teaches our children more than the sport itself; it also teaches them values. I think if we focus on athletics as well as academics, we will find healthier, unselfish, and dedicated children.

Once Angie cleaned up the problems, her final draft looked like this*:

Angie S____

01/20/2000

ENGL 100

Children and Sports

America is losing a generation of great athletes every day; some of our kids have never given athletics a try. They have been programmed to think it's better to focus on academics. It is important for children to participate in athletics because we are raising lazy, overweight children who have no dedication to anything but themselves.

First, children are lazy and overweight, causing their health to be at risk. Most kids today can't even run a block without getting tired or short of breath. You ask a kid today to check the mailbox, and they want the keys to drive to it. We have taught our kids to be lazy because they consume television commercials and video games. Parents stress education over exercise, but they go together. If parents would motivate their children to be a part of a sport that kids like, children would have more of a balance in their lives.

Next, if a child is not taught how to share early in life, most likely the child will be selfish. Being part of a team teaches kids that life is not all about them. I drove a school bus for eight years and saw kids arguing daily about sharing with each other, but being athletic teaches a child about being a part of a team, teamwork, sharing, and getting along with others.

* Note that this final draft uses MLA formatting guidelines. Throughout this textbook, all final drafts will be shown in MLA format..

Last, being athletic teaches a child dedication. A lot of athletes that were athletic as kids through dedication and hard work have made life better for themselves and their families. Some have come from bad neighborhoods and broken homes. The obstacles that were in their way were pushed aside using the avenues of athletics that caused them to succeed far greater than academics.

Athletes accomplish fame, go to the Olympics, earn millions of dollars, and are exceptionally talented. Athletics teaches our children more than the sport itself; it also teaches them values. I think if we focus on athletics as well as academics, we will find healthier, unselfish, and dedicated children.

CHAPTER REVIEW

The final stage of the writing process comprises editing and proofreading. When editing, an author takes a close and careful look at grammar, complete sentence structure, appropriate punctuation, and vocabulary. If changes in these areas are needed, the author makes them, then gives the draft to another person to review. This peer review allows others to comment on the content of the material as well as to point out awkward places the author may have overlooked. After editing, proofreading takes place. During this part of the final stage, the author examines the draft, making sure all the elements are in their correct places. After all the typos are cleared, then formatting becomes an issue. Here, the author concentrates on the layout or the arrangement of the information on the page. Once all this has been accomplished, the draft, in its final, finished form, is ready to be presented to the audience.

Final Writing Assignments

1. Revise the rough draft you wrote at the end of Chapter 2, following all the steps described in this chapter. Be sure to use the Content Revision Checklist, the Structure Revision Checklist, and the Mechanics Checklist as guides. Proofread and correct your essay and put it in the format your instructor requires. Then submit it to your instructor for a grade.

2. Trade drafts from Writing Assignment 2, Chapter 2, with a classmate. Work as peer review partners as you revise your draft for content, structure, and mechanics. When you finish your work together, write a paragraph or brief essay on what you learned from your partner.

PART II

Writing Strategies

In Part 1, we discussed the writing process and the procedure for turning an idea into a final draft. If all writing assignments and situations were the same, Part 1 would be all you need. However, all writing assignments are not the same. You may be asked to write an essay about an event that changed your life. Later, you may be asked to give your opinion on a critical issue on your college campus. Using the writing process will help you in both cases, but you can't use the same approach to each topic. Different writing situations require different approaches or strategies. Those writing strategies are the focus of this unit.

The seven basic writing strategies are narration, process, description, definition and classification, comparison and contrast, cause and effect, and persuasion. Each strategy has its own chapter. Within each chapter, the elements of that particular writing strategy are explained in terms of the writing process (ready, write, and revise) as well as essay structure (introduction, body paragraphs, and conclusion). Because each strategy is unique, discussions of additional considerations (dialogue with narrative or evidence with persuasion, for example) are also included. Student samples for each strategy are also included to help illustrate why a particular strategy was chosen and how the essay for that strategy developed.

The writing process introduced you to a good way to create a piece of writing. Writing strategies will now introduce you to effective and appropriate ways to reach your audience.

4

NARRATION

I sat in a booth at the Burger King, a cup of orange juice nearby, staring at the papers before me. Excitement and joy swelled inside me. I was looking at my first writing contract, the one for this textbook. I had been a writing teacher for almost ten years and spent the better part of my free time writing. I had short stories, poems, and the opening chapters to a few novels, but nothing had really sold. I know that writers are first and foremost focused on the quality of their words and language, but don't be fooled. Getting published is a rush like no other.

As I read through the contract, I reflected on the events that had led to this moment. A textbook publisher representative had come to my office a few months prior to see if I was interested in adopting another textbook for my writing course. I told her I liked what I saw, but none of the books really jumped out at me. Then she asked an important question.

"Do you have any ideas for a book?"

I had a hundred ideas floating around in my head. "Well, yes," I said, without hesitation.

She gave me a business card and a few papers that explained how to submit ideas for books. "Follow these directions and we'll see what happens."

Later that day and for many days afterward, I wrote down ideas, changed them, tossed them away, and wrote down some more. Finally, I stumbled upon the idea of using popular culture as a way to teach writing skills. I have been doing that in my classroom; why wouldn't it work in as a book?

After six months of writing and rewriting and discussions with editors, I had my contract. I knew the hard work had just begun, but I also knew I had achieved something important in my teaching and writing career.

Narration, or storytelling, is a natural form of human expression. Most everyone has a favorite book, movie, or television show episode. Our ancestors told stories about their ways of life, and we pass those stories to our children. Many psychologists believe adults should tell the stories of painful childhood in order to heal. Stories are the primary way we convey news and other important information. Storytelling is an essential part of being human. In this chapter, we discuss the ways to write narration and to use a variety of storytelling elements, such as dialogue and strong action verbs, to enhance the stories you tell.

First, read a good story from writer Anne Lamott's *Bird by Bird*.

Reading 4   Polaroids
Anne Lamott

BACKSTORY

Many people think writers have an unlimited amount of ideas and energy from which they draw their inspiration and their story lines. Nothing could be farther from the truth. Writers often work hard to find a focus for their writing. This selection by writer Anne Lamott, who also teaches writing, illustrates the difficulty writers can have and also the thrill they experience when their writing takes shape. Lamott talks about herself writing about the Special Olympics, a series of sporting events where athletes who have physical and mental challenges compete.

LEXICON

excruciating: unbearable

Preakness: championship horse race

1   Six or seven years ago I was asked to write an article on the Special Olympics. I had been going to the local event for years, partly because a couple of friends of mine compete. Also, I love sports, and I love to watch athletes, special or otherwise. So I showed up this time with a great deal of interest but no real sense of what the finished article might look like.

2   Things tend to go very, very slowly at the Special Olympics. It is not like trying to cover the Preakness. Still, it has its own exhilaration, and I cheered and took notes all morning.

3   The last track-and-field event before lunch was a twenty-five-yard race run by some unusually handicapped runners and walkers, many of whom seemed completely confused. They lumped and careened along, one man making a snail-slow break for the stands, one heading out toward the steps where the winners receive their medals; both of them were shepherded back. The race took just about forever. And here it was nearly noon and we were all so hungry. Finally, though, everyone crossed over the line, and those of us in the stands got up to go—when we noticed that way down the track, four or five yards from the starting line, was another runner.

4   She was a girl of about sixteen with a normal-looking face above a wracked and emaciated body. She was on metal crutches, and she was just plugging along, one tiny step after another, moving one crutch forward two or three inches, then moving a leg, then moving the other crutch two or three inches, then moving the other leg. It was just excruciating. Plus, I was starving to death. Inside I was going, Come on, come on, come on, swabbing at my forehead with anxiety, while she kept taking these two- or three-inch steps forward. What felt like four hours later, she crossed the finish line, and you could see that she was absolutely stoked, in a shy, girlish way.

5   A tall African American man with no front teeth fell into step with me as I left the bleachers to go look for some lunch. He tugged on the sleeve of my sweater, and I looked

up at him, and he handed me a Polaroid someone had taken of him and his friends that day. "Look at us," he said. His speech was difficult to understand, thick and slow as a warped record. His two friends in the picture had Down's syndrome. All three of them looked extremely pleased with themselves. I admired the picture and then handed it back to him. He stopped, so I stopped, too. He pointed to his own image, "That," he said, "is one cool man."

6   And this was the image from which an article began forming, although I could not have told you exactly what the piece would end up being about. I just knew that something had started to emerge.

7   After lunch I wandered over to the auditorium, where it turned out a men's basketball game was in progress. The African American man with no front teeth was the star of the game. You could tell that he was because even though no one had made a basket yet, his teammates almost always passed him the ball. Even the people on the other team passed him the ball a lot. In lieu of any scoring, the men stampeded in slow motion up and down the court, dribbling the ball thunderously. I had never heard such a loud game. It was all sort of crazily beautiful. I imagined describing the game for my article and then for my students: the loudness, the joy. I kept replaying the scene of the girl on crutches making her way up the track to the finish line—and all of a sudden my article began to appear out of the grayish green murk. And I could see that it was about tragedy transformed over the years into joy. It was about the beauty of sheer effort. I could see it almost as clearly as I could the photograph of that one cool man and his two friends.

8   The auditorium bleachers were packed. Then a few minutes later, still with no score on the board, the tall black man dribbled slowly from one end of the court to the other, and heaved the ball up into the air, and it dropped into the basket. The crowd roared, and all the men on both teams looked up wide-eyed at the hoop, as if it had just burst into flames.

9   You would have loved it, I tell my students. You would have felt like you could write all day.

QUESTIONS FOR THOUGHT

1. In what ways are the Special Olympics the same as other sporting events? In what ways are these games different? How are the audiences different?

2. Lamott goes to the Special Olympics to write an article. What did she expect the article to be about? What was the actual article about?

3. Lamott reveals a lesson she learned while attending the Special Olympics. What was that lesson? What other lessons did she learn?

4. How honest is Lamott—with herself and with you, the reader? What would have been your reaction to seeing the last runner when you thought the race was over? How hard do you think it is to write with honesty? What difference would it make in your writing?

5. The title of the reading is "Polaroids." What are Polaroids? Where in the story do Polaroids, or the development of Polaroids, figure? How is writing a story like watching a Polaroid develop?

READY

Everyone has a story to tell, or so it has been said. In this chapter, I'm going to try to convince you this is true. Your stories are inside your experiences, waiting to emerge.

All stories begin with ideas and thoughts that are worked out before any part of the story hits the page. When you prepare to tell a story, you don't just blurt out everything that happened. You must recount the events in such a manner that the reader will share in the adventure as well. To do this, you must focus on the way your topic relates to your audience and purpose.

Topic, Audience, and Purpose

When choosing a topic for a narrative essay, step inside yourself. Examine your experiences. What situations and events have you witnessed or been a part of that you could write about? What are some of your earliest memories? Think about habits you have. When did that certain habit begin, and why did it start? Think of the emotional times in your life as well. Think about when a close friend or relative died or when your daughter was born. What were your reactions? How did you deal with the situation? Your life is filled with events that have affected you, and these events would make fine narrative topics.

Audience has a big impact on a narrative simply because you are sharing a personal event with people who—most likely—are strangers to you. Yes, you may have a writing class together or live in the same dorm, but these are probably not people you grew up with. How much background information will they need in order to fully appreciate your story? How much of yourself do you want to reveal to people who barely know you? How honest can, or should, you be? What parts of the story will appeal to a wide audience, and what parts will appeal only to the people who were present at the events you recount? These questions should not scare you away from telling the story you want to tell; on the contrary, they will help you write the strongest stories you can.

Stories serve many purposes in our lives. Perhaps the most popular reason to tell stories is entertainment. You laugh when your sister tells you about a recent date that turned into a disaster. Another reason is to educate. People hear and understand information better if it is presented in story form. We also tell stories to persuade. A friend will advise you not to eat in a certain restaurant and gives you the gruesome story about her only time having lunch there. You may also tell a story to speak out. Imagine trying to register for a writing class and having to go to five different offices, spending six hours, and still failing to get registered properly. When you write a letter of complaint to the head registrar, telling your story will have an impact. Carefully consider what your reason is for telling the story, and stay with it as you write.

Consider Anne Lamott's essay about the Special Olympics. Her topic is not so much about the Olympic event but about what she learned from that experience. She went looking for a piece to write, and, in the end, the piece she was supposed to write found her. She opens herself up on the page, explaining that she was impatient with the last runner who was simply trying to finish the race. The essay was originally published in a larger work by Lamott about the writing life, so her audience would be wide but primarily focused on those interested in writing. She was also writing a piece for her students, as she mentions in the concluding paragraphs of the essay. She also understands that some of her readers may never have had the opportunity to write about a Special Olympics or even attend the games themselves, so Lamott fills in those details for them. Finally, Lamott's purpose is to educate the readers. Instead of giving page after page on how writing ideas develop, Lamott illustrates the point with her own experiences and the images of a Polaroid photograph emerging before her eyes. She had topic, audience, and purpose all working together to help the story shine.

The Six Journalists' Questions

As you begin to focus your ideas for the story you will tell, think about it again from the point of view of your audience. They are going to need some secure information to picture your story as you unroll it for them. It might help to ask, and answer, the same questions journalists keep in mind as they write news articles: **who, what, when, where, why,** and **how**. Well call these the **Six Journalists' Questions**. A short explanation of each follows:

1. **Who** are the main players in the story? Who is the narrator? What relationship do they have with each other? Is important information about the main players included in the story?

2. **What** happened? Give the details of the plot of the story, or make a quick list of events.

3. **When** did the story take place? Be as specific as possible by citing day, month, calendar year, or even season of the year, as well as the passage of time.

4. **Where** does the action in the story take place? What is the setting for the story? Are important elements about the setting in the story?

5. **Why** did this event happen? Why did you react the way you did?

6. **How** do the events in the story affect the main players? How could the events affect the audience?

Apply these six questions to the reading that opened this chapter, "Polaroids."

1. **Who?** Main characters include Lamott herself, the runner at the end of the race, and the man playing basketball.

2. **What?** Lamott sets out to write a story about the Special Olympics. During a race, she deals with her impatience waiting for a very slow runner to finish. Later on, she watches a man play basketball in a game where the athletes seem more interested in playing than in winning. Lamott finds that effort is more important than the outcome.

3. **When?** Lamott wrote the story six or seven years ago, but it takes place in a single day.

4. **Where?** The story takes place during the Special Olympics. The first scene is the runner's track, and the second scene is the basketball court.

5. **Why?** Lamott agreed to write an article on the Special Olympics. What she didn't know was that the assignment would give her insight into the writing process.

6. **How?** When the sixteen-year-old girl and the African-American man display the beauty of sheer effort, Lamott realizes that the success of human experience is in *being there*, in participating, and that's the real story. The runner is stoked after she finishes the race. The basketball player makes a shot, and the crowd goes wild. Both athletes are excited and elated by their achievements.

The Narrative Brainstorming Worksheet

To be sure all these questions are answered somewhere in your narrative, use the following brainstorming sheet. Be sure to be as complete as possible with the details of your stories as you fill out this sheet.

Narrative Brainstorming Worksheet

Topic: _____

Audience: _____

Purpose: _____

The Six Journalists' Questions

1. **Who** are the main characters in the story? What relationship do they have to each other?

   _____

   _____

2. **What** takes place in the story? Outline the events.

   _____

   _____

3. **When** did the story take place?

   _____

   _____

4. **Where** did the events in the story take place?

   _____

   _____

5. **Why** did the event take place? Why did you react as you did?

   _____

   _____

6. **How** did the events affect the lives of the main characters?

   _____

   _____

Feel free to use the back of this sheet or other pages to write down additional information.

Exercises

1. Brainstorm a list of occasions when you struggled to do something well and succeeded. Choose one from the list and develop the idea through the Narrative Brainstorming Worksheet.

2. Brainstorm occasions when you learned something, but it wasn't what you set out to learn. Choose one from the list and develop the idea through the Narrative Brainstorming Worksheet.

3. Write about your first writing experience or a memorable writing experience. Brainstorm the highlights of the event, then fill out the Narrative Brainstorming Worksheet to develop the idea.

WRITE

The Narrative Brainstorming Worksheet includes the information you want to include in your story, but it is the bare minimum. In drafting, you'll probably experiment with how the events fit together and how many details to include. Here are points to keep in mind.

Select

Look at Anne Lamott's story again. It is just 789 words long, yet it has quite an impact. When she talks about some of the runners being confused, she writes "They lumped and careened along, one man making a snail-slow break for the stands, one heading out toward the steps where the winners receive their medals; both men were shepherded back." Every detail counts; every detail adds to the story.

Details **Details** are the bits of information that will help your audience understand the point of the story. For example, Lamott explains that she has been assigned to write an article about the Special Olympics. We don't have any other information about how she got to the games and, frankly, we don't need it. However, she is good about giving us her background with Special Olympics: She goes to the local games, and she loves all types of sports. These details help us understand her mindset as she continues with the story. Without these details, we question her connection to the events.

Dialogue For narration, you have the option of selecting actual speech, or **dialogue**, to help you tell the story. Compare these two passages. Which one is stronger?

1. The rude waiter greeted us as we entered the restaurant.

2. The waiter thrust two menus in our faces and growled, "You just gonna stand there or are you going to sit down already? What do you want, an engraved invitation?"

While the first sentence tells what happened, the second sentence actually shows it through the dialogue. We know the waiter is rude because of what he says. Dialogue adds strength and vividness to the story. Notice the impact of the only two lines of dialogue in "Polaroids": An African American man tugs at Lamott's sleeve and shows her a Polaroid of himself and two friends. "'Look at us,' he said," and "'That,' he said, 'is one cool man.'" With just two lines of actual dialogue, we get a picture of the man and the scene. He is proud of his friends and himself. Lamott is careful not to manipulate the dialogue in any way. What the man says reflects his character, and that is all that is important. Later in the story, this bit of dialogue becomes almost emblematic of the lesson Lamott learns that day: "It was about the beauty of sheer effort. I could see it almost as clearly as I could the photograph of that one cool man and his two friends."

Lamott also uses internal dialogue to let us know what she is thinking; "Come on, come on, come on." The slowness of the race is excruciating, and she is starving. Through this internal dialogue, she is being honest, which adds dimension to her as a character in the story.

Make Dialogue Real

When selecting dialogue, be true to the story you are writing and to the characters you are describing.

▶▶▶▶ **Avoid dialect. Dialect** is the way someone enunciates words. People from the South are said to speak with a slight drawl in their words, while people in the North tend to speak faster and through their noses. Dialect can also represent the speech of people from other countries. The British, for example, are said to drop the harsh *h* sounds from the front of certain words. Although you want your narrative to be true to the events, be careful not to overdo the dialect. Unintentionally, your use of dialect may project a negative aspect of a character you didn't intend. "Garsh, duh, I ain't gots no ideer where he be" may be a bit more colorful than "I don't know," but it makes the speaker appear uneducated and may offend your audience.

▶▶▶▶ **Avoid Hollywood style.** Television dialogue works differently than real life dialogue. In situation comedies, the dialogue is centered on the joke, either as a setup or a punch line. In dramas, dialogue is centered on suspense, making a trip to the mall seem as life-threatening as open-heart surgery. More often, dialogue serves to advance the plot, not to reveal character. These exchanges may be entertaining, but they are not real. If you want to hear what real dialogue sounds like, stop watching television and start listening to people.

Continued

▶▶▶▶ **Be true to your characters.** Although you are writing about real events, take some advice from fiction writers. Dialogue is used to make people real. We don't always say what is on our minds, and we don't always say the right things. However, what we do say reflects who we are. When you are sorting out the dialogue, make sure that what your characters say shows them for who they are.

Exercises

4. Write a short dialogue for the following events.

   a. The registrar tells a tired, frustrated student that the class she needs for that semester is closed.

   b. A man who is down on his luck is approached by a representative of Sweepstakes International and told, in front of a camera crew, that he has just won $25 million dollars.

   c. A young woman tries to break a date.

   d. A young man tries to break a date.

   e. An instructor tells a sensitive student he is in danger of failing a course.

5. Read "The Day That I Sensed a New Kind of Intelligence" (page 58). Consider Garry Kasparov's thoughts about the rematch with Deep Blue, then write a short dialogue he might have with the computer. Have the computer respond, but be sure to stay true to the computer's character.

6. Take the stories you brainstormed in the previous exercise set and write a bit of dialogue for each one. Be sure to be true to the characters involved and to pay strict attention to topic, audience, and purpose.

Structure

Even with the most exciting details, you just can't write everything down and hope it all turns out. Narratives require paying close attention to structure, for you want your story to move slowly from beginning to end, and you may want to convey some sense of suspense as you tell it. Knowing your high school football team won the inner-league championship by one field goal is nice, but if that information is in your first sentence, then the reader's reason for reading the story is gone. You must focus on a structure that allows you to tell the event the way it happened, adding in background information and other details along the way. This is called *chronological order.*

Chronological Order   Many narratives follow chronological order. With **chronological order**, events happen in a linear, often logical sequence. Think of the event you are going to write about and work your way backward to a good starting point. Usually, the hours before the big event, when everything is normal, are a good place to begin. Then move forward, telling what happened first, and next, and so on, as you move toward the end of the story. You could also employ a flashback and start in the middle or even at the end of the story, then move back to the beginning of the event.

Regardless of where you begin, your story must have a plot, a climax, and a resolution. The plot is the basic series of events. The climax is the turning point of a story, where the main characters change in some way. The resolution is the end of the story, usually followed by a reflection on the changes that occurred during the climax.

Examine Lamott's "Polaroids." It begins with information about how Lamott arrived at the Special Olympics and the event she is watching. It then moves to the race in which the sixteen-year-old girl participates, continues with Lamott's encounter with the African-American man, and ends with the basketball game. This is the basic plot of the story. Along the way, Lamott makes a discovery about herself, which the audience gets to share with her as it evolves. She realizes her article is about "tragedy transformed over the years into joy" and "the beauty of sheer effort." This is the climax of the story. Had Lamott revealed this change earlier, the story would have lost much of its power. The chronological structure would have been damaged, and the audience may not have read much farther.

The revelation about writing doesn't happen the moment Lamott begins her story. It happens gradually, throughout the day, and Lamott shows the passage of time effectively. She talks about cheering and taking notes all morning long, watching the race before lunch, then watching the basketball game after lunch. These subtle references to time illustrate the length of the day and show her progression of thought.

Introductions and Conclusions   Remember reading fairy tales or Aesop's fables when you were younger? Although many of the stories were steeped in fantasy and magic, they all had morals or lessons we as children were supposed to learn. The idea of a moral, or, at the least, the reason we are telling our stories should be previewed in the introduction and revealed in the conclusion of the narrative.

Use the introduction as a springboard into the story itself. Reflect on the purpose of the essay, then on the audience. What could you write that would reflect the purpose of the narration and include the reader? To answer that question, focus on the main idea behind the story itself and write it as a problem statement to be placed at the end of the introduction. The **problem statement** acts as a thesis statement for the narrative. To flesh out your introduction, include background information necessary for your audience to fully appreciate your story.

For an example, look at the opening paragraph for "Polaroids."

> Six or seven years ago I was asked to write an article on the Special Olympics. I had been going to the local event for years, partly because a couple of friends of mine compete. Also, I love sports, and I love to watch athletes, special or otherwise. So I showed up this time with a great deal of interest but no real sense of what the finished article might look like.

This first paragraph introduces us to the writer, Anne Lamott—who, as narrator, is a character in her story. We learn about her background in relation to Special Olympics (she is on assignment and has friends who compete), then get a hint at what is to come within the essay (she doesn't know what form the article will take). We become interested in finding out more now that she has set up the story for us.

Conclusions are not just the end of the story. Conclusions for narratives are paragraphs that involve reflections on the situation and the lessons learned— the moral, if you will. Don't simply start a conclusion with "In conclusion, I learned…" or "The moral of the story is…." Work your reflections into the context of the narrative.

Lamott's conclusion for "Polaroids" begins in the last few sentences of a body paragraph and continues into the final paragraphs of the work.

> I had never heard such a loud game. It was all sort of crazily beautiful. I imagined describing the game for my article and then my students: the loudness, the joy. I kept replaying the scene of the girl on crutches making her way up the track to the finish line—and all of the sudden my article began to appear out of the grayish green murk. And I could see that it was about tragedy transformed over the years into joy. It was about the beauty of sheer effort. I could see it almost as clearly as I could see the photograph of that one cool man and his two friends.
>
> The auditorium bleachers were packed. Then a few minutes later, still with no score on the board, the tall black man dribbled slowly from one end of the court to the other, and heaved the ball up into the air, and it dropped into the basket. The crowd roared, and all the men on both teams looked up wide-eyed at the hoop, as if it just burst into flames.
>
> You would have loved it, I tell my students. You would have felt like you could write all day.

Exercises

7. Outline a plot for a story about an occasion when you participated in a sporting event. What would make a good introduction, conclusion, and lesson?

8. Outline each of these plot ideas. Be sure to create an introduction, conclusion, and lesson learned.

   a. My beloved dog, Watson, died on the day my baby brother was born.

   b. My first day on my new job, February 26, 1997, showed me I could handle anything.

   c. Rain ruined our picnic at Linden Park, but that was the best thing that could have happened.

9. Expand one of the stories you worked with in Exercise 6 into a rough draft. Add detail, dialogue, and any necessary information to the draft.

REVISE

Revising a narrative may be the easiest part of writing one. All the larger elements of the story should be on paper. It's now a matter of strengthening each element and enhancing the story. As you work through your draft, check chronological order to be sure all of the scenes are in the right sequence. Once that is done, look closely at the way the story is written. Are some of the verbs lacking excitement? Are more details and description needed? Is the dialogue effective? All of these are important considerations when revising a narrative. However, keep one thing in mind: Revising doesn't mean changing the truth of the event. In the beginning paragraphs of "Polaroids," Lamott focuses on the girl struggling to finish the race. Lamott doesn't say the girl dashed by everyone else and came in first place. That may also be a good story, but it didn't happen. Lamott could have said she was riveted to her seat during the entire race, but that wasn't true. She was honest in saying she wished the race had ended sooner so she could eat lunch. The writer stuck to the truth, and so should you.

Flow

Read the story for flow the first time through. Do the events occur in a logical manner? Can you as reader (rather than writer) mentally move from one scene to another with ease? These questions deal with flow, or movement, in a piece of writing. If you've been struggling to get all the elements from the Narrative Brainstorming Worksheets into your writing, your sentences may come across as choppy. Now is the time to make them flow smoothly. Pay close attention to transitions at this stage, too. Some transitions are needed when you move from scene to scene, but beginning each paragraph with "Next, I…" or "After that, I…" will sound too artificial.

Word Choice

People are movement and action. Your five-year-old doesn't move around; he jumps, skips, runs, races, slides, leaps, dodges, climbs, glides, and meanders through life. Your chemistry professor doesn't simply talk; he lectures, cajoles, teases, whines, screams, rants, laughs, sighs, and projects during each lesson. The heart of good storytelling is using strong verbs that convey action, and in revising, you have a chance to replace weak words with vivid ones. Have fun with the action words, but be careful not to overdo it. Look for a balance between the sections that demand strong words and sections where simpler words will do.

In "Polaroids," Lamott uses powerful action words to describe the runners at the last track and field event: "lumped and careened along, making a snail-slow break for the stands, both were shepherded back." These actions are juxtaposed with the detail of the young woman at the end of the race, moving one crutch forward two or three inches, then moving a leg, then moving the other crutch two or three inches. Because the pace of the narrative has slowed and because "move" works well in the description, the verbs change.

Now, go back and edit your narrative. Fight the urge to keep in every word and every detail and focus on the topic, audience, and purpose of the essay. Everything extra must be eliminated.

Exercises

10. Revise the rough draft you wrote in Exercise 9. Let topic, audience, and purpose be your guide, and pay attention to flow and word choice.

11. Write a short essay about a pet from the pet's point of view. Fill out a Narrative Brainstorming Worksheet and write a rough draft, then revise it for an animal audience. Carefully consider what the animal audience may or may not know about the topic and this audience's attitude toward the topic.

STUDENT SAMPLE

Chris brainstormed a list of childhood events for his first writing assignment in English class—a narrative. At the top of the list was the one event he wanted to share with everyone: the time he was in a bread commercial. He had always remembered this episode as fun, and he hoped he could reflect that fun in his writing.

He started by filling out the Narrative Brainstorming Worksheet.

Narrative Brainstorming Worksheet

Topic: _Being in a commercial_

Audience: _class members_

Purpose: _Explain my adventures in front of the camera_

The Six Journalists' Questions

1. **Who** are the main characters in the story? What relationship do they have to each other?

   Me – brother – other kids – tiger

   Continued

---

2. **What** takes place in the story? Outline the events.

   me and my brother asked to be in a bread commercial
   I got very excited, but found that filming the commercial
   was different than I expected.

3. **When** did the story take place?

   Quite a few years ago— when I was in grade school.

4. **Where** did the events in the story take place?

   Parkersburg, WV—my home town

5. **Why** did the event take place? Why did you react as you did?

   I was invited to be on the commercial. I had never done anything
   like that before.

6. **How** did the events affect the lives of the main characters?

   I was a star for a day and learned to take things as they come.

Feel free to use the back of this sheet or other pages to write down additional information.

From there, Chris wrote his rough draft.

A long time ago, I was in a bread commercial. See, Brawny Bread was a very popular type of bread when I was a kid. So I thought it would be cool to be in the commercial. We were all there at the playground, and the tiger ran by. The tiger I refer to here is the tiger on the side of the bag of bread. He was just a guy in a big suit. Anyway, to make a long story short, my brother and I and the other kids in the commercial—there were about seven of us, if I remember right—chased after the tiger. He waved his arms and acted as though we were all playing together. When it was all over, I got paid $100, which was big money back then. I only saw the commercial one time, but that was good enough for me. I knew I was a star.

Chris knew he had some work to do expanding this draft when he read that the assignment was to be 2–3 pages long. To get some more ideas on where to go with the draft, Chris referred to his brainstorming sheet. He also asked Lydia, a classmate, to read his work to see what questions she had about the story itself. Here are the notes Chris ended up with.

A long time ago, I was in a bread commercial. See,
Not much of an intro — Brawny Bread was a very popular type of bread when I was
a kid. So I thought it would be cool to be in the commercial. — *Who? Where?*
We were all there at the playground, and the tiger ran by. The
tiger I refer to here is the tiger on the side of the bag of bread.
Doesn't fit—I am — He was just a guy in a big suit. Anyway, to make a long
telling the long story story short, my brother and I and the other kids in the
commercial—there was about seven of us, if I remember
right—chased after the tiger. He waved his arms and acted as — *More detail*
though we were all playing together. When it was all over, I
got paid $100, which was big money back then. I only saw
Needs something more — the commercial one time, but that was good enough for me.
I knew I was a star.

The verdict was in: The story would be a good one if Chris just slowed down in telling it. Discouraged, he wanted to abandon the project, but he let the draft sit a day. When he came back to it, he saw the feedback was right. There was a good story here; it just needed some work. He added more detail-specific events and vivid action words. He added a problem statement to the first paragraph. And he added dialogue—lots of dialogue.

After a few more tries, the final draft looked like this:

Chris J_____

ENGL 100

11/14/00

Star for a Day

One of the most wondrous and surreal experiences I have ever had was when I became a television star. Okay, so it was only a minute-long, locally produced Brawny Bread commercial that most people never saw, but to my 8-year-old self, I was Hollywood with a capital *H*.

My mother explained the entire setup to me and my brother one day after dinner. A former Miss America had been asked to find a group of five or six children to be in a bread commercial and she called my mother, who immediately volunteered us.

"So, we gotta eat sandwiches or something?" my brother asked.

"No," my mother said. "You just play in the playground at school with the tiger."

I was lost in time and space. The Brawny Bread tiger. Cool. Each loaf of Brawny Bread came packaged in a standard, thin plastic bread bag. The part that made it different—and therefore, way cool—was the open end of the bag. It was decorated with orange and black stripes so that it resembled a tiger's tail. "Grab a tiger today" was emblazoned on each bag. The tiger mascot, large and strapping because it ate so much of the bread, roared, MGM lion style, at the end of each commercial. Whether we ate the bread or played or simply stood in place for a minute, we were going to be a part of this fantastic thing.

I didn't have any lines, but I practiced anyway: eating a sandwich with a smile, grabbing the tiger's tail, even playing on the swing sets at school. Every day for a week, I counted out the steps to the right side of the swing set. If I grabbed a swing first, I could steady it, swing around, plant myself in the seat, and begin swinging, all in one fluid motion. It would look great on film.

The Sunday of the filming came. A van was parked across from the jungle gym and two camera operators were in place. We were directed to stand with the other children at the edge of the playground.

"Remember to smile."

"Don't run too fast. Just stay with the other children."

"Don't look into the camera. Just make it look real."

Their parents were coaching the other children; we just stood there and watched. At least my brother just stood there. I listened, trying to absorb any and all of the rules that I could. Right after I found out about only showing your good side to the camera, a woman with jet black hair motioned us to follow her.

Standing at the edge of the playground, she said, "Okay, kids, when the tiger comes running by, chase him."

A six-foot man in a tiger suit emerged from the van. He adjusted his headset, exaggerated a nod, and then ran straight for the swing set. When he ran past us, we followed. I took off in a full sprint, then relaxed when I realized I was ahead of everyone else. Just short of the jungle gym, the tiger began jumping up and down, patting each of us on the head.

Then he stopped and the commercial was over. The kids wandered back to their parents, the equipment was packed away in the vans, and everyone left.

I have only seen the commercial once, by accident at that. We were running with the tiger as the narrator said something about Brawny Bread giving kids healthy bones and lots of energy. Then the animated tiger crept across the screen and roared. Fade to black.

So it wasn't *Dawson's Creek* or *Buffy the Vampire Slayer*. But it was good television for me. Not many kids, after all, can say they were television stars for a day.

CHAPTER REVIEW

When you write a narrative essay, you are relating a story. Strong stories answer the Six Journalists' Questions: Who are the main characters? What happened? When did the events take place? Where did the events take place? Why did they happen? How did it affect the main characters? As you write the story, make sure you have a good introduction, a solid conclusion, and a lesson learned. The introduction should include a problem statement, a thesis statement that hints at the lessons to be learned in the story. The conclusion includes the climax of the story, or the turning point where the main characters change. The conclusion should also include a reflection of the lessons learned by the main characters. When you revise a narrative, focus on the verbs. Strong verbs make for exciting stories.

Final Writing Assignments

1. Polish the revised draft you worked on in Exercise 10. Submit your finished essay to your instructor.

2. Reread "Polaroids" and write a reading response, following the format described in Chapter 11.

3. Write a narrative essay about something miraculous or inexplicable that happened to you. Start with what you were doing before the event, then explain the event in detail and discuss how it affected your life. Add background information to help the reader share your experience. Focus on strong action verbs.

4. Retell your favorite fairy tale from a different point of view, perhaps that of the villain. Include as many relevant details as necessary. Don't forget to use strong verbs.

PROCESS

The process of eating out requires much more planning and energy than most people think. What starts as a good idea becomes a matter of logistics. First, you have to decide what kind of food you want: hamburgers, chicken, tacos, or a vegetarian dish. After you wade through that list of possibilities, you need to choose a restaurant. Say you have a craving for Italian food. Do you want to eat the pasta dishes in the school cafeteria, or would you rather go to a fancier place? Money will influence that decision. You may not have received that emergency loan from your parents yet, so the cafeteria is your only choice. However, you may have been paid this week and find yourself with an extra $30.00 to spend. So off you go to that fancy place across town. Regardless of where you eat, a few more steps in the process of eating out follow. You need to choose your dining partners, if you want any. Then you have to decide what to wear. Seems like a lot of work just to grab a bite to eat, doesn't it?

Process writing strategy is the main focus of this chapter. **Process** is the step-by-step explanation of how to complete just about any task, from brushing your teeth to eating out to running for president of the United States. As we discuss process, we look at the choices writers make when creating process essays (what steps to include, what steps to leave out), the arrangement of the steps, and other elements that must be considered when telling someone how to do something.

But first, read "Hello, Darkness, My Old Friend," by Richard Talcott, an article about solar eclipses and the most effective way to watch one.

Reading 5 Hello, Darkness, My Old Friend
Richard Talcott

BACKSTORY

We often go about our daily routines and never stop to consider the world around us. When was the last time you smelled a rose and listened to the birdsong that greets you every sunny morning? Have you ever noticed even more spectacular phenomenon such as an eclipse? In this essay, which first appeared in *Astronomy* in 2001, author Richard Talcott explains the grandeur of a solar eclipse and explains how to properly view one.

LEXICON:

pathogen: a disease-causing agent

totality: the moment during an eclipse when the moon completely covers the sun

1   Racing across Earth's surface at more than 1,000 miles-per-hour, the moon's shadow seems eager to cast its magical spell. An almost palpable sense of wonder grips the waiting throngs as totality approaches. Then, as the last glimmer of sunlight disappears behind the moon's limb, day turns to night and the eerie sounds of silence descend upon the land.

2   Thanks to a remarkable coincidence that renders the moon almost exactly the same size as the sun in our sky, this majestic display lasts just a few fleeting moments. But it impresses so much that nearly everyone who has witnessed a total solar eclipse vows to see another.

3   Well, the opportunity has arrived: On the afternoon of June 21, the longest total eclipse in nine years traverses southern Africa. The path of totality cuts a narrow swath across Angola, Zambia, Zimbabwe, Mozambique, and the island nation of Madagascar. As many as 4 ½ minutes of totality await those on the center line along the Angolan coast, a number that dwindles to 3 minutes in coastal Mozambique and about 2 ½ minutes in Madagascar.

4   If the generous length of totality doesn't impress you, then the chance for clear weather should. At this time of year, southern Africa is well into its dry season and clear, sunny skies are the rule. The cool, dry weather also keeps mosquitoes at bay—a distinct bonus in a land where insects can carry unpleasant pathogens.

5   Such unpleasantries shouldn't frighten you, however. Check with your doctor to line up any needed shots—some immunizations take weeks before they become effective. Then, as you're getting ready to pack, be sure to throw in a good insect repellent.

6   Once you're in Africa and the big day is at hand, reach your viewing site a couple hours before the eclipse begins. That leaves plenty of time to set up before the show starts. Dur-

Totality: the brief midpoint of the eclipse.

ing the partial phases, eye safety is paramount: Sunlight can quickly and painlessly damage the eye's retina. For a direct view of the sun, use only Mylar filters, metal-on-glass filters, or #14 arc-welder's glass.

7   You can also view the partial phases indirectly by projecting the sun's image. Take two pieces of cardboard and punch a tiny hole in one of them. Then let the sun's light pass through the pinhole onto the second piece of cardboard. Local citizens may want to watch the eclipse too; a projection device or extra filter material will go a long way toward making their day a memorable one as well.

8   Once the moon covers more than half the sun, watch for subtle changes. Look for solar crescents under trees and bushes, images projected by the tiny gaps between leaves. Shadows in general will appear sharper as the eclipse progresses. And wildlife will sense something's going on, preparing for nightfall even though it's the middle of the day.

9   In the last minute before totality, the solar crescent breaks up as lunar mountains poke through it. Known as Baily's beads, this string of pearls shrinks as the moon continues its relentless march. Finally, just a single bead remains—the glorious diamond ring.

10   When the advancing moon extinguishes the diamond ring, totality has arrived. Remove the solar filters and examine the eclipsed sun with your eye, binoculars, or a telescope. After your eyes adjust to the sudden darkness, the corona blazes into full view. The gauzy, pearly-white corona, the sun's outer atmosphere, typically stretches a few times the sun's diameter. Watch for delicate loops, swirls, and streamers in the corona. Also look for fiery red prominences, features that lie close to the sun's surface and will appear just above the moon's outline.

11   Also take the time to observe your surroundings. Notice the color of the sky and the twilight hues that ring the horizon. You should see the brightest planets and stars during totality. Most prominent will be Jupiter, located 5° west of the sun. Saturn, Sirius, and Canopus should also be conspicuous. Although Venus shines brightest of all, it

A map of the path of the eclipse.

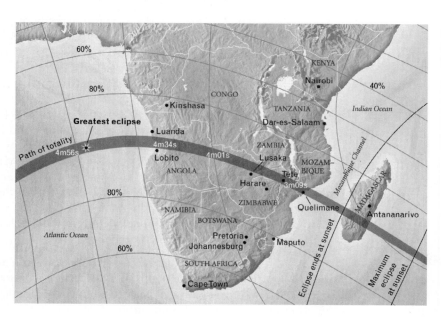

lies near the horizon as seen from western Africa and sets before totality begins in spots east of central Zambia.

12   Totality ends when a second diamond ring appears on the moon's opposite side. That's the signal to replace all solar filters. Although the sequence of partial phases now plays out in reverse, most people pay scant attention—they've seen the show they came for. It's time to relax and contemplate the next total eclipse, 18 months from now in southern Africa and Australia.

QUESTIONS FOR THOUGHT

1. What is the most impressive natural phenomenon you have ever witnessed?
2. Why does Talcott choose supernatural overtones to begin an article on the practical way of viewing an eclipse?

READY

When written well, a process essay can be engaging, a true learning experience for the reader. You shouldn't just begin by scribbling a list of instructions. These essays aren't created on a whim or pulled out of thin air; they are planned. The basis of the plan includes thoughts on topic, audience, and purpose, as well as a list of materials and an explanation of jargon.

Topic

Topics for process papers abound. Think about everyday tasks, such as washing your hair or getting ready for class. Some people may think these activities are trivial, but keep in mind that almost everyone has a different way of performing a routine task. Sharing your unique way may give others insight on the way they perform a certain task. Because this is a writing textbook, let's use my writing experience as an example. When I began writing, I would sit down at the computer and start writing at nine or ten P.M. After a long day of teaching, attending meetings, and tutoring students, I was sluggish, exhausted, and unproductive when it came to my evening writing time. My wife made a simple suggestion: Write in the morning. See, when she wants to complete a task (her creative talent is making things), she examines her day and jots down times when she will be most caught up in her routine. She jot down hours to be spent with family and friends. She looks at her schedule and blocks out a few hours during the week to devote to her projects. This approach worked for her, and she suggested I try reevaluating my schedule to see what time would be best for me to write. I looked at my schedule and found that the only time I could truly devote myself to my writing was at 5 A.M. I set the alarm for 5 A.M. the next morning and wrote for an hour. I was a bit groggy at first, but eventually the words began to flow. I was much more productive. Now I try to write every day, first thing in the morning.

Step-by-Step Approach   Topics for process essays usually fall within one of two categories: step-by-step and formula. When writing with the **step-by-step** approach, you must explain how a procedure is done, starting at the first step and moving through the explanation until you reach the last step. Each step-by-step approach is organized according to chronological (or time) order.

"Hello, Darkness, My Old Friend" is a good example of the step-by-step approach. According to Richard Talcott, the author of the essay, if you wish to see the eclipse, then you should get immunized, fly to Africa, grab a pair of specialized sunglasses, and wait. Once the eclipse begins, you should look at the moon crossing the sun, keeping the protective eyewear on until totality arrives. Only then can you take off the eyewear and view the eclipse with your naked eyes. If you do this procedure out of time order, either by taking off your sunglasses before totality or not wearing sunglasses at all, you run the risk of damaging your eyes permanently. Likewise, you would be crazy to wait until being bitten by an infected mosquito before you get a preventative shot. Processes arranged in the step-by-step approach must be followed in the order the steps are presented or you won't be successful.

Formula Approach   The step-by-step approach focuses on the order of the steps in the process. The **formula** approach, however, focuses more on the steps themselves. In other words, as long as you follow the steps regardless of the order, you will perform the task successfully.

For example, you may read in a psychology journal that, in order to raise healthy children, you must have a loving family atmosphere, a healthy diet of fruits and vegetables, and plenty of opportunities for artistic expression. Do you give the children a banana before saying "I love you" or after? With a formula approach to this process, when you give the banana relative to when you say "I love you" doesn't matter. What does matter is that all of the desired elements are present and you do them all.

Audience

Once you have chosen your topic, find out what your audience already knows about this topic, then write to their level of understanding. In "Hello, Darkness," Talcott explains what type of sunglasses to use and why using sunglasses is important during a solar eclipse: "Sunlight can quickly and painlessly damage the eye's retina. For a direct view of the sun, use only Mylar filters, metal-on-glass filters, or #14 arc-welder's glass." The article was first published in *Astronomy*, a space science magazine targeted at a general audience with an interest in science. Talcott knows the audience probably has some knowledge about using eyewear to watch a solar eclipse. However, because he is writing for a general audience, he also understands they may not know the extent of the damage that can occur or what types of glasses can be worn safely. So Talcott includes this information in the essay. The important information is included and presented to the audience in a way that they will understand.

Purpose

Finally, you write process essays to either instruct (by the step-by-step approach) or to explain (by the formula approach). Avoid giving advice or opinions that lead the writing away from instruction or explanation. Talcott's purpose was to enlighten readers about the proper way to view a solar eclipse. Readers aren't distracted by the history of solar eclipses or a prolonged discussion of the author's experiences watching them. I am sure Talcott has had many interesting experiences, but he sticks to his purpose. Every word and paragraph aids in the education of the reader, as should all the information in your process essays.

Materials

Imagine baking a cake and finding out you don't have enough sugar or are short one egg simply because the recipe didn't list all of the necessary ingredients. Few things are more frustrating than beginning a project, then finding out that you don't have everything you need at hand. To keep your reader from this frustration, list all necessary items. Be as specific as possible with your list. Tell what materials are needed as well as the specific amounts for each one. Explain the necessity of any unusual items. For example, to properly view the solar eclipse, Talcott suggests eye protection. However, he doesn't say, "Grab a pair of sunglasses." He suggests certain types—"mylar filters, metal-on-metal filters, or #14 arc-welder's glasses" and explains that these are best for maximum safety and pleasure.

Visuals

Pictures and other types of graphics can also help us understand and follow a procedure. Visuals work well as a supplement to written instructions that may be a bit dense. You may not need a picture to show how to crack an egg, but you might need one to illustrate assembling a bicycle or connecting a monitor, printer, and scanner to a new computer. Visuals can also provide your audience with instructions without the aid of text. Say, for example, a friend from out of town is coming to visit you and she needs directions. You could write out two paragraphs, detailing each major highway, all the exits, and every turn she has to make, or you could draw her a map. Whether or not to use a visual is your choice; just make sure it is clear and provides information that reflects your topic, audience, and purpose.

The visuals that accompanied "Hello, Darkness, My Old Friend" in *Astronomy* served as supplement and provided information not found in the article itself. One example is the picture of the eclipse at totality, where the sun's rays provide a halo or "diamond ring" around the moon. This picture clarifies the discussion of totality in paragraph 10 and gives the reader an image by which to compare their own experiences. Another example is the map illustrating the path of the eclipse over southern Africa. This map provides new information about the eclipse, showing the paths the sun and moon travel and the point at which the eclipse will be greatest. The map gives the reader a clear view of where the phenomenon will take place.

The Process Brainstorming Worksheet

As you develop ideas for a process essay, fill out the Process Brainstorming Worksheet on the following page. Be sure to fill it out in its entirety; materials you do not think are important to the process may turn out to be invaluable later on. Also, as you fill out the worksheet, choose a category or approach for your process: the step-by-step approach or the formula approach. If you plan to include a visual, sketch it on another sheet of paper.

Process Brainstorming Worksheet

Topic: _____

Audience: _____

Purpose: _____

Approach: _____

Materials Needed

Steps Involved

1. _____
2. _____
3. _____
4. _____
5. _____
6. _____

Explanation of Material and Steps

1. _____
2. _____
3. _____
4. _____
5. _____

Conclusion

_____

_____

_____

_____

Visual: On your paper, draw a visual aid that could supplement your process essay or that could add more information overall.

Feel free to expand any section of this Process Brainstorming Worksheet by writing on additional paper.

Exercises

1. Review the writing process discussed in the previous sections of this book. Now write your own writing process, describing the procedure you use to write essays. What extra steps or additions have you made to the writing process?

2. Read through the list of ideas for process essays. Choose one and develop it by filling out a Process Brainstorming Worksheet. Share your worksheet with others.

   a. The most effective way to reduce governmental red tape

   b. How to increase the student body population at your school

   c. How to bake a "Death by Chocolate" dessert

   d. How meteorites ended the reign of the dinosaurs

   e. How to get out of debt

WRITE

Process essays are tricky; you must present information in an orderly fashion but not sound as though you are barking out orders like a general. Of course, you must present a complete set of steps in your process as well as a complete list of all the materials needed. As your write, you should be aware of the tone of your writing. A measure of creativity is needed to make the process interesting to your audience as well as to you. A place to begin is selecting the most appropriate steps for your procedure.

Select

Being thorough in a process essay doesn't mean you have to include hundreds of steps in your explanation. Review the brainstorming worksheet and select only the materials and steps that will serve your purpose (informing or explaining) and that will allow your audience to understand the overall procedure easily.

"Hello, Darkness, My Old Friend" focuses only on the safest way to view a solar eclipse. Although international travel is briefly mentioned, Talcott doesn't include steps on how to choose a travel agent, how to get a good deal on travel rates, or how to choose the best and cheapest hotels in the area. Getting to Africa is definitely part of the process; however, additional information about travel agents, airplane ticket fares, or hotels would pull the reader away.

Structure

For an idea of how process essays are to be structured, watch the cooking shows on The Food Network. First, the chef parades a delicious-looking dish, in its best presentation, in front of the screen. She tells us, the viewers, how easy it is to make the dish, then turns to the well-stocked kitchen and begins cooking. She explains the procedure and, when the hard part is over, she produces a previously prepared dish, takes a bite, and tells us how good it is. The structure of a process essay parallels the structure of cooking shows. First, you entice the audience to try the procedure through the introduction. Next, you list the materials, much like the chef in the well-stocked kitchen. From there, you write the essay, putting the steps in order and offering information or explanations as you go. Finally, you conclude the essay by reflecting on the procedure itself.

Bon appétit!

Introduction   Cooking shows are successful, in part, because the chef entices the viewers right up front with magnificent and exotic foods and drinks. The food doesn't look like I prepared it, with dry chicken just lying on the plate surrounded by bleached white rice. On television, the chicken has been browned just right and the rice seems to sparkle on the decorative serving platter. The presentation makes me want to learn how to prepare that dish. Introductions are the presentation of the idea to the audience. If you are going to explain how to repair a flat on a bicycle, don't start out by saying, "I will tell you how to fix a flat bicycle tire." Instead, enliven the presentation by saying, "Your trusty old bicycle, your traveling companion for all these years, has a flat tire. You want to ride in the weekend race or escape to your favorite spot in the forest to catch up on some reading, but now it looks like you are stranded in your apartment with your noisy roommates. Well, maybe not. With a few tools and a little bit of time, you can fix that flat and be on your way to freedom."

See the difference? You have enticed the audience to learn.

To help your audience become intrigued enough to try a procedure, appeal to one or more of the basic emotions most human beings respond to: love, frustration, fear, empowerment, wonder, and so on. Reflect on the type of audience your procedure would appeal to, then reflect on the emotion connected to that audience.

Take a closer look at the introduction to "Hello, Darkness, My Old Friend."

> Racing across Earth's surface at more than 1,000 miles-per-hour, the moon's shadow seems eager to cast its magical spell. An almost palpable sense of wonder grips the waiting throngs as totality approaches. Then, as the last glimmer of sunlight disappears behind the moon's limb, day turns to night and the eerie sounds of silence descend upon the land.

> Thanks to a remarkable coincidence that renders the moon almost exactly the same size as the sun in our sky, this majestic display lasts just a few fleeting moments. But it impresses so much that nearly everyone who has witnessed a total solar eclipse vows to see another.

> Well, the opportunity has arrived: On the afternoon of June 21, the longest total eclipse in nine years traverses southern Africa. The path of totality cuts a narrow swath across Angola, Zambia, Zimbabwe, Mozambique, and the island nation of Madagascar. As many as 4 ½ minutes of totality await those on the center line along the Angolan coast, a number that dwindles to 3 minutes in coastal Mozambique and about 2 ½ minutes in Madagascar.

The author understands that, given the distance to the region in which the eclipse will take place, namely southern Africa, many readers naturally can't run out and catch the next plane. However, he makes viewing the eclipse seem an ancient adventure, complete with magic that turns day into complete darkness. He also explains that this phenomenon happens only occasionally, again adding to the adventure of the experience. Finally, he tells his audience when and where it will take place, which means more and more adventure. Now, even the most stalwart homebody will read to see what this totality stuff is all about and maybe even book a flight to Africa.

Materials   On television cooking shows, the kitchens are always properly stocked. You never see Emeril Lagasse, for example, scramble for his chili powder to kick a dish up a notch. Follow this example when you are writing a process essay. On the Process Brainstorming Worksheet, list all of the materials needed, then work them into the draft. If a particular device or a piece of equipment is needed, explain why when you mention it in your paper. This will prevent people from substituting materials that may not work or that could possibly cause them harm.

Let's go back to the reading that opened this chapter. To get the total eclipse experience, Richard Talcott suggests the following materials: plane tickets to southern Africa, immunizations, eye protection, and two pieces of cardboard. The tickets will take you to the place where you can see the eclipse, and immunizations will prevent you from getting sick. Notice that Talcott indicates certain types of eyewear for proper protection: Mylar filters, metal-on-glass filters, or #14 arc-welder's glass. You can use the cardboard to see it as well. Talcott makes it clear that anything else will not be adequate protection against the sun's rays. With these materials, anyone can watch the eclipse without any problem.

Sequential Order   Steps in a process must be presented in **sequential** or **chronological order**. The first step of the process must be stated at the beginning, followed by the second step, then the third step, and so on. When I watch a cooking show, I am amazed that the chef can make a complicated process seem easy. As a writer, though, I understand that it looks so easy because the chef is showing me, step by step, how to prepare a dish. When writing your process essay, you must make sure all the necessary steps are listed in the correct order and that each one is clear. While watching one of those cooking shows, I learned that adding oil before you heat a pan makes the food taste different than if you add it after you heat the pan. The same can be said for the sequencing of the steps. If Step A has to be done before Step B or the outcome will be disastrous, by all means make sure that Step A comes before Step B.

Also make each step clear. Two teaspoons of sugar are drastically different than 2 tablespoons of sugar. Just as a chef is clear when discussing measurements of ingredients, you must be clear in your process writing. Include explanations as you write your steps so your audience will understand what you are doing and why you are doing it a particular way.

In "Hello, Darkness, My Old Friend," Richard Talcott is careful to tell us we must have strong eye protection, such as #14 arc-welder's glass, because "During the partial phases, eye safety is paramount: Sunlight can quickly and painlessly damage the eye's retina." He goes on to talk about the other steps in the process, but this step is necessary at the beginning of the procedure and is well explained.

Conclusion   At the end of the cooking shows, the chefs eat their creations. They don't just eat; they seem to savor each and every morsel. We see how successful the process was, and we may even want to try the process ourselves. The conclusion to your process essays works the same way. You shouldn't just stop the essay at the last step. You should explain to the audience the outcome of the process and suggest that they now go out and follow the same procedure.

Look at the end of Talcott's essay.

> Totality ends when a second diamond ring appears on the moon's opposite side. That's the signal to replace all solar filters. Although the sequence of partial phases now plays out in reverse, most people pay scant attention—they've seen the show they came for. It's time to relax and contemplate the next total eclipse, 18 months from now in southern Africa and Australia.

Talcott explains that the eclipse is over (and cautions us to wear eye protection as the eclipse fades). He also explains that we may see the formation of the eclipse in reverse. With his last sentence, however, he teases us to try out what we have learned. Eighteen months is not that far away, mind you. Now that we know what to do, we would be more than prepared to experience the next eclipse. You want your audience to have that same enthusiasm for the process you describe.

Exercises

3. Write a process paragraph for a routine you do often, such as getting ready for the day or going to class. Brainstorm all of the materials needed and be sure to list the steps in sequential order. Finally, add a strong topic sentence and a conclusion.

4. Review the brainstorming worksheet you filled out for Exercise 2. Which approach do you think will be the most beneficial to you, your topic, your audience, and your purpose for writing the paper? What adjustments, if any, are you going to have to make in your essay to fit this approach?

5. With a partner, look over the series of steps in your brainstorming worksheet. Place these steps in chronological order. Discuss the process of arranging the steps. What did you have to leave in? What did you have to leave out?

REVISE

What you don't see on the cooking shows are all the changes that go into creating a dish. A chef starts out by putting all the ingredients together, adding a bit of heat, and hoping for the best. As the dish progresses, the chef samples it. If the food is not to his liking, he throws it out and starts again. This time, he makes subtle changes in a few ingredients or adjusts the cooking temperature. Again, he samples his creation, throws out the concoction, and starts again. He repeats this process until the dish is just right. Revising process essays works the same way. You may have some idea of what the procedure was when you wrote it down, but now you must make sure the procedure works perfectly. If you identify problems with content, you must adjust the sequence of steps or add materials to your list. If you find problems with grammar and mechanics, you must make sure all the sentences are clear and that you are using appropriate word choice. You may not have to throw out your drafts and start over each time, but you should make changes if and when necessary.

Sequence Check

To effectively revise your process essay, train yourself to unlearn the procedure and then relearn by reading and following the steps in your own essay. Gather the materials, then move through each step. Pay close attention to what you are doing and make note of any materials you need to add, modify, or delete. Also, make sure all the materials are listed together near the beginning of the essay. After that, pay attention to sequential order, making sure the steps are arranged logically. Again, pay strict attention to each step as you perform it. Perhaps you do something subconsciously that must be part of the procedure; perhaps an extra step can be removed. Note it and make adjustments in the appropriate places.

Jargon Check

One enemy of clarity in a process essay is jargon. **Jargon** consists of technical or specific language that only a certain group or audience understands. For example, if you have never used a computer before, terms such as *download, SGRAM,* and *operating system* will confuse you. Using jargon with a general audience only complicates the process. The reader now has to master the new vocabulary as well as follow the procedure. To help control your use of jargon, analyze your audience. How involved is your audience with the topic? How have they read about the topic? If you are writing to people who are knowledgeable about the topic, the technical terms won't be a problem. However, if you are writing to a broad audience, the technical terms should be replaced with words more accessible to a general audience. The purpose of the essay is to instruct, which means keeping the steps simple, clear, and free of jargon.

Just like any other science, astronomy is filled with technical terms. If "Hello, Darkness, My Old Friend" had been published in an astronomy journal, then the jargon would have been expected. However, Richard Talcott understands that the audience for *Astronomy* magazine is general. He may need to remove or explain technical terms. Talcott chooses to explain terms, such as *totality.* " The author explains that "totality" refers to the time of total eclipse. The term appears throughout the essay, but we understand it because of the explanation.

Transitions

With a process essay, you may be tempted to move from one step in the procedure to another by relying on numbers (1, 2, 3, and so on). Don't. You should

Writing with Others

PROCESS

You have completed your process essay. You have all the materials listed, you have every step needed, and you have followed all of the rules for writing a process essay. But how can you tell if your directions are successful? This is where a peer reviewer can help.

Once you have completed your process essay, give it to another student and have her try it out. Sit back and observe. Look for confusion or for steps done in the wrong order. Make note of any materials the peer reviewer may request to complete the task at hand. Finally, when the peer reviewer is finished, ask about any steps or materials that could have been added to make the process go more smoothly.

A peer reviewer can act as your test audience. If the test subject can perform the procedure well, then others can do it well, too. Chefs test their recipes on friends and family before their recipes are published. The reviewer is doing you the same favor.

choose transitions that reflect chronological order and will retain your audience's interest. Good transitions are often found in verbs. Move the verbs to the front of the sentences and, instantly, you have transitions to your next steps.

Talcott's essay flows because he moves logically from point to point. An excellent example of this good use of transitions is paragraph 10:

> When the advancing moon extinguishes the diamond ring, totality has arrived. *Remove* the solar filters and *examine* the eclipsed sun with your eye, binoculars, or a telescope. *After* your eyes adjust to the sudden darkness, the corona blazes into full view. The gauzy pearly-white corona, the sun's outer atmosphere, typically stretches a few times the sun's diameter. *Watch* for delicate loops, swirls, and streamers in the corona. *Also look* for fiery red prominences, features that lie close to the sun's surface and will appear just above the moon's outline.

The reader is not simply told to do one thing and then another. Talcott placed the transitions in such a way that the order of the sentences seems natural. These transitions make the presentation of the procedure seem more like an essay than a set of instructions.

STUDENT SAMPLE

When Janice moved into her dorm, she was surprised that it was wired. That is to say, she was surprised that her dorm was networked or connected to other computer stations on campus. "Cool," she thought. "I can write my papers here, save on the network server, and then print my work out on the nice laser printers in the library." Janice was excited, but her roommate Diane was not. Diane's computer had Internet access, but that was the extent of her computer knowledge. Words like wired, networked, and server confused her and the literature provided by the college didn't help matters at all. All the helpful hints and inch-thick documents were full of jargon. Janice spent an entire evening explaining things to Diane. The next day, Diane told a few other students in the dorm and soon Janice was teaching almost everyone. "This would be a lot easier," Janice thought, "if I wrote it all down."

And so she did.

To begin, Janice examined her audience. While these were women in college who had some idea about computers, her audience had no idea how some of the technical aspects worked. They would be sending email home or to friends, so information about that wasn't necessary. The purpose was to instruct these women on how to use the network at school. By looking at the audience and purpose, Janice determined her topic: the basics of using the school's computer network.

Janice then filled out a Process Brainstorming Worksheet.

Process Brainstorming Worksheet

Topic: _Computer network_

Audience: _Women in my dorm_

Purpose: _To teach them about using the server_

Materials Needed

computer	
password	

Steps Involved

1. _Log-on_
2. _Save file to server_
3. _Log off_
4. _____
5. _____
6. _____

Explanation of Material and Steps

1. _Log-on to get computer access_

Continued

2. _Must save files to server—otherwise this won't work_ _____

3. _____

4. _____

5. _____

Conclusion

This is very easy and will save you tons of time and trouble.

_____

_____

_____

Visual: In the space provided, draw a visual aid that could supplement your process essay or that could add more information overall.

Feel free to expand any section of this Process Brainstorming Worksheet by writing on additional paper.

Sitting at the dorm computer, with notes and worksheet by her side, Janice wrote the following rough draft:

> We have access to the network here at school. First, you have to log-on. Your password is on a sheet of paper attached to your admission stuff. After you log-on, go to File an click on Save as. From there, you can save your work on the server X12. That server is connected to all the computers on campus and you can then pull up your documents whenever you want to. That's all there is to it.

Janice read through her draft, following her own advice through the procedure. As she tried to use email following her own directions, she made notes for improvements.

> We have access to the network here at school. First, you
>
> *Too much jargon* have to log-on. Your password is on a sheet of paper attached
>
> to your admission stuff. After you log-on, go to File an click
>
> on Save as. From there, you can save your work on the server
>
> *I need to make* X12. That server is connected to all the computers on campus   *Nothing is really*
> *it more* *explained*
> *interesting like* and you can then pull up your documents whenever you want
> *Diane said.* to. That's all there is to it.

Janice revised her draft, making the directions themselves more clear.

We have access to the network here at school. First, you have to log-on. When you log on, you type in your password. Your password by the way is on a sheet of paper attached to your admission stuff. After you log-on, you will have access to all of the programs in the network. The computers connected by cables and wires to each other. When you are a part of the network, you too are connected to other computers. Do whatever you want to do and then click on file click on save as and then click on server X12 Students. This server, as it says, is for students to download their work. When you save to this server, you can then go anywhere and open the file. No need to cart around all of those diskettes. That's all there is to it.

Finally, Janice revised the draft for sharper writing, grammar, and mechanics and came up with this final draft.

We have access to the network here at school. Now, to some of you, this might not seem like a big deal, but it is. We have a wired dorm, which means that all of our computers here are connected to all of the computers on campus. You can write something here and print it up on the nice laser printers anywhere on campus. And believe me, the procedure is simple. First, you have to log-on to your computer. To log-on, just type in your password. (Your password, by the way, is on a sheet of paper attached to your admission forms.) Once you log-on, you are free to work with whatever program you want. Most of you will probably write papers using the word processor program. Whatever program you use, you will most likely want to save your work. Save like you always would (click on File, then on Save As). When you get to Save As, be sure to click on X12 Students Server. Instead of saving your work to a diskette or a hard drive, your work will be saved on a server. A server is like a giant hard drive where millions of bits of information are stored. The great thing about saving your work to the student server is that you can access your work from anywhere on campus. When you save to this server, you can then go to any other computer on campus, open your file, and work on it. You can even print your work on the laser printers. Your work, but the way, is password protected, which means no one can get to your documents but you. See how easy it is? Now there is no need to cart around all of those diskettes. That's all there is to it.

She gave copies of her directions to the other women in the dorm and they loved it.

CHAPTER REVIEW

When you write a process essay, you are either instructing or explaining how to perform a certain task. To do this effectively, you must take into account what the audience knows about the topic and what needs to be added to that knowledge. Once you begin writing the process essay, make sure you have a complete list of materials or items the reader will need in order to perform the task successfully. After that, make sure the steps for the procedure are in chronological order, with each step leading naturally into the next. To help with this flow, pay attention to transitions. Strong verbs make for good transitions. Finally, as you revise, watch out for jargon, technical words, or phrases that need explaining to those unfamiliar with the topic. Explain the jargon as you use it, or avoid it altogether. Before you present your final draft to your audience, have someone try the procedure as you have explained it.

Final Writing Assignments

1. Write a process essay explaining some aspect of a hobby you enjoy, such as finding stamps for your collection or growing prize-winning tomatoes in your patio garden. Brainstorm all of the materials needed, list the steps in sequential order, and then add a strong introduction, thesis statement, and conclusion. As you revise this essay, make sure all jargon is explained in the context of the paragraph.

2. With a partner, write a self-help process essay about breaking a bad habit. First, choose a bad habit many people share, then brainstorm ways people could break that habit. Focus on just one of those solutions and brainstorm the materials and steps needed to break the bad habit.

3. Revise the rough draft of the process essay you began in Exercises 4 and 5. Be sure to examine each step carefully and make adjustments as necessary. Also, find any jargon and evaluate its reason for being in the essay. After you have revised for content, be sure you have revised for grammar and mechanics as well. Submit your essay to your instructor.

4. Reread "Hello, Darkness, My Old Friend," and then write an essay on the best way to experience an outdoor activity such as taking a hike, building a snowman, birdwatching, or in-line skating. As Talcott did in his essay, begin with an enticing introduction. From there, discuss the best place to experience the activity, and don't forget to list all the materials needed for the activity. After that, list the steps involved, adding any necessary information. Finally, write a conclusion that invites the reader to try the procedure.

5. Choose a simple procedure, such as greeting someone. Interview people from different cultures to see the various ways they greet one another. Write a process essay explaining different greeting processes to the audience.

DESCRIPTION

When a batter steps up to the plate, the audience, no matter how big, goes silent. The pitcher, his hardened face tightly squeezed as he concentrates on the catcher's fingers, shakes off signal after signal from the catcher, beads of sweat dripping off his face. Finally satisfied that a curveball has been signaled, the pitcher nods. He stands, still and straight, a hand holding the baseball against his weatherbeaten glove. As he pulls his arm back to hurl the ball, his leg rises and rises. Once his arm is cocked, he lets go with a massive throw that seems to wind his entire body around the mound. At nearly 100 miles an hour, the little ball speeds toward the batter. Quickly and carefully, the batter pulls his arms back, stick at the ready. At the exact moment, wood smashes against white leather as the bat strikes the ball, sending it over the heads of the infield players. Not waiting for an invitation, the batter drops the bat and begins a mad dash toward the first base. With legs pumping and chest pounding, he runs with full speed. His right foot brushes against the base, and he continues to run. The strain of the momentum can be seen on his face as he rounds second base and sprints toward third. Still moving on the energy of the moment, the runner tags third and heads toward home plate. The crowd is on its feet, cheering him with a deafening roar. Home plate seems farther away now than it did when he left just seconds ago, so he turns his run into a slide. Dirt, dust, and desperation billow up in a cloud that covers the batter and the base. He stops, suddenly, and then feels the soft pat of a catcher's glove against his leg. He cracks his eyes enough to see the umpire standing, knees slightly bent, hands and arms extended out. He has beaten the ball and hit a home run.

Whether you are writing about home runs, watching television, or taking a trip to Europe or just down to the library, you need to enhance your writing through description. **Description** is a writing strategy in which you provide information about a person, place, thing, event, idea, or emotion by appealing to one of the five senses: sight, taste, touch, hearing, and smell. Our senses are our windows to the world and, when we use description, we are allowing the audience the opportunity to experience the world as we experience it.

This chapter helps you develop your skills for writing descriptive essays. Here, we talk about the five senses and how to write in a way that makes these senses react. We also discuss a few organizational patterns for descriptive essays, such as spatial order, time order, and order of importance. Tips on strengthening your eye for detail are also provided.

For another example of descriptive writing, let's read a piece describing the early days of baseball, called "Preliminaries."

Reading 6   Preliminaries
Leonard Koppett

BACKSTORY

Often, when we think of professional sports, we focus on current information, such as scores, players, championships, and the like. But what about the history of these games? How did baseball, basketball, or soccer begin? In this piece from the opening chapter of *Koppett's Concise History of Major League Baseball*, historian Leonard Koppett describes the early days of the sport.

LEXICON

promenading: strolling

provincial: unsophisticated

venerable: respectable, honorable

villas: small houses

virulent: harmful, hostile

sacking: attacking

smiting: striking hard

wicket: a set of three poles; in cricket, the object is to deflect a ball away from the wicket with a paddle

1   Imagine that you are a young man—say, 25—of comfortable means living in New York City in the 1840's.

2   It is already one of the most important cities in the world, but far more provincial than the large cities of Europe. All of it is contained within the southern third of Manhattan Island. From the Battery north to almost 30th Street, it is built-up solid. Beyond that, along Broadway and Fifth Avenue, stretch the villas of the very rich. The waterfront, along the East River (which is mostly south) and the Hudson River to the west, is a forest of masts, a maze of ferry boats, a collage of sails, ropes, barrels, wooden piers, and wooden warehouses.

3   A house taller than four stories is a rarity, since the only way to reach upper stories is to walk (and carry things) upstairs. The skyline's peaks, therefore, are church steeples. To get around the narrow streets, paved with cobblestones if at all, you have three alternatives: ride a horse, be pulled by a horse, or go on foot.

4   Your grandfather most likely fought or was otherwise involved in the Revolutionary War (which he probably calls the War of Independence), and he remembers clearly George Washington's inauguration downtown as the first president of the new country. Your father remembers vividly the anxiety and disruption of the War of 1812, when he was courting your

mother. You yourself recall the financial panic of 1837 and the riots it generated, when the city's unemployed protested high rents and high food prices by sacking the city's warehouses.

5   But now (let's pretend the year is 1842) times are relatively peaceful and prosperous. The president is John Tyler because William Henry Harrison, who was selected on the slogan of "Tippecanoe and Tyler too," had died 31 days after making his inaugural address in March 1841, during which he caught pneumonia. Tyler is a Virginian, generally at odds with his own party, the Whigs (dominant among antislavery Northerners). Abolitionists are still considered wide-eyed radicals although your own sympathies are basically in that direction, and the real struggle is still about the spread of slavery to the new territories and about the slave trade, rather than about slavery's established existence. Arkansas is the most recent, and westernmost, of the 23 United States of America.

6   For heat you depend on coal or wood in a fireplace or stove. Illumination comes from candles or torches. Among the things you have never imagined are elevators, typewriters, cameras, sewing machines, safety razors, or safety pins.

7   This year, two exciting new features have been added to the bustling social life and recreational opportunities of Little Old New York: Phineas T. Barnum has opened his fascinating museum at Broadway and Ann Street, and the huge new reservoir, which runs along the west side of Fifth Avenue from 40th to 42d Street, has massive stone walls suitable for fashionable promenading along the water's edge.

8   But you already have a favorite entertainment, a hobby you share with your social equals. Whenever the weather is nice enough, a bunch of you get together and play a game you have learned to call Base Ball.

9   It is not really new, but it has a fascination all its own. You hit a ball with a stick and run around "bases." In some versions, it is as old as humankind. Specifically, it is an adaptation of two venerable English games, rounders and cricket. And that's natural enough, because your family's roots are English or Dutch, wars notwithstanding. Almost every "good" family in town is from this background. The waves of Irish Catholics starting to flow into the city generate an anti-Catholicism so virulent that by 1844 New York will elect a mayor (James Harper) from a party (the American Republican Party) that makes anti-Catholicism one of its basic principles. You derive all your ideas—and limitations—of "gentlemanly" behavior, your definition of social class, and your models of fashion from contemporary England, where a young queen named Victoria has reigned for five years and where industrialism has started upheavals that will soon cross the ocean.

10   For any activity, then, an exclusive "club" is as natural in this New York as in that London, and you and your fellow Base Ball players long to form one. Among other things, open fields on which to play are rapidly disappearing in this growing city whose population has reached 250,000; and ferryrides to the abundant open spaces of Brooklyn (a village of some 30,000) or New Jersey are time-consuming and hopelessly complicated if not properly organized. So when you gather at Madison Square, where Fifth Avenue and Broadway meet at 23d Street, and play ball and argue about what rules to use, you talk more and more of formalizing your group and its activity into a respectable club.

11   Meanwhile, you become more and more captivated by the special features of the game itself: catching the ball on the run, throwing it hard and straight, the greater primitive satisfaction of smiting the ball as hard as possible with a level swing (instead of guarding a

wicket against a bouncing delivery, as in cricket), the variety of having more than one station to run to after hitting the ball.

In some such fashion, it all began—baseball as we know it in New York and, therefore, baseball in America.

QUESTIONS FOR THOUGHT

1. This essay is written from a second-person point of view, characterized by the use of the pronoun *you*. Why does Koppett use this point of view? In what ways does it affect the reader?

2. In paragraph 6, Koppett writes, "Among the things you have never imagined are elevators, typewriters, cameras, sewing machines, safety razors, or safety pins." Why does the author mention devices and items that don't exist in the 1840s?

3. How would you describe baseball as it is played today?

READY

Imagine an outdoor scene where everything is in two tones: light gray and dark gray. The grass is gray, growing from a dark gray ground where the gray-faced children are playing baseball on a dreary day. Then imagine the same scene, but this time add all the colors of a rainbow. The deep green grass springs to life from the dark brown and black earth while the children, dressed in blue jeans and white t-shirts, pink dresses, and red baseball caps, play baseball under a brilliant blue sky.

What a difference!

When we talk about description as a writing strategy, we are talking about creating a scene in words that closely reflect the mood of a scene in real life. We are also talking about adding detail to other writing strategies, such as narrative, to give them more spice. Description is more than simply sticking colorful adjectives into an essay. You must begin with considerations of topic, audience, and purpose that will help establish the tone of your descriptive writing. In other words, they will show you where to add detail and to find the type of detail that should be added.

Topic, Audience, and Purpose

Anything and everything that can be described can be a topic. To narrow this field, work with items with which you have strong connections or feelings. Having easy access to the item you wish to describe is also important. *Ideas* can come from memory, but actual *description* is best when it comes from recent contact.

Audiences strongly guide the content of a descriptive essay. For an audience that has little knowledge of the topic, you need to choose details that will educate. For an audience that is somewhat familiar with your topic, your focus should be on the tone you are trying to convey. Your readers will be able to see what you are describing through a new perspective.

The purpose of a description essay can vary. Primarily, you write descriptive essays to educate or inform your audience. You may also choose to use description to entertain an audience. Another reason to write a descriptive essay is to persuade. Description can be a strong tool for getting people to change their minds. For example, say you wish for better-quality food to be served in the school cafeteria. A paragraph describing soggy French fries, rubbery chicken salad, and week-old boiled eggs would go far in getting people to join your cause.

The Five Senses

Descriptive writing relies heavily on an appeal to the five senses: sight, touch, taste, hearing, and smell. These senses govern the way we experience life, so it is natural that they should help guide the contents of your descriptive writing. At first, as you brainstorm details about your topic, you may find yourself focusing on obvious traits. You must retrain yourself to actually observe your topic, to go beyond the obvious and bring out the less obvious details. To do this, use the Description Brainstorming Worksheet on page 138.

The Description Brainstorming Worksheet

After you have chosen a topic, fill in as many details as you can. Consider the senses and the questions related to them as you brainstorm. This information may be sketchy—some questions may not apply to the topic at all—but the idea is to get you observing and reporting on those observations.

Description Brainstorming Worksheet

Topic:_____

Audience: _____

Purpose: _____

Senses Chart

Senses	Questions	Details
Sight	What objects are here? What people do I see? What are they wearing? What shape is the room? What colors are here? What does what I see remind me of?	
Hearing	What immediate sounds do I notice? What background sounds are there? What do these sounds remind me of?	
Smell	What odors can I identify? What odors can I not identify? What do the unknown odors remind me of?	
Touch	What textures do I feel? What do these textures remind me of?	
Taste	What can I taste here? What does the taste remind me of?	

Dialogue

What we say reflects who we are. This makes dialogue an interesting and important part of describing people. Listen for snippets of dialogue when people talk. Listen to the way Jill says "I'm sorry" over and over when something goes wrong, even if she is not at fault. Listen to Bill blame the president of your school when he can't schedule a class. Listen for the tremble in Lisa's voice when she is lying. Listen to your own use of language. What do you say that reveals your character? As you listen and jot down ideas, include those bits of dialogue in the description.

Carefully choose the bits of language you are going to use to reflect character. For example, Bill may have been making excuses out of fear in a particular situation, but normally he would own up to his mistakes. If you only write down the excuses and not the explanation, he may be portrayed as having a completely different personality. For more discussion on dialogue, see Chapter 4: Narration.

Exercises

1. List ten people, places, or things with which you are familiar. Choose three and write a sentence or two about why each would make a good subject for a descriptive essay.
2. Select five newspaper and magazine paragraphs. Read through them, underlining all descriptive words. Fill out a Description Brainstorming Worksheet for each paragraph and make note of where even more description could be added.

WRITE

So where do you go once you have completed the Description Brainstorming Worksheet? How do you actually write a descriptive essay? To begin, establish the tone or feeling you want to convey about your topic. Next, choose details from your brainstorming worksheet that reflect the overall tone. Finally, choose an organizational pattern for your description, such as spatial order, time order, and order of importance. All of these elements are necessary for a good, solid piece of descriptive writing.

Select

Description is much more than just a laundry list of information. The detail you include should reflect a specific tone or feeling you want your audience to have about the topic. A Halloween night should be especially creepy, while your high school graduation party should be full of life and laughter. For Halloween, put in those dark shadows, distant screams, and cold breezes. For the graduation party, include your best friend's throaty laugh and the blues music heard in the parking lot. The details you choose will influence your audience's perception of your topic, so choose well.

Dominant Impression   **Dominant impression** is the overall feeling or attitude reflected in the detail. Dominant impression guides the use of detail in descriptive writing. Without a good dominant impression, your writing will be flat and uninspired. The dominant impression can be stated outright within a paragraph, as it is in paragraph 2 of "Preliminaries."

> It is already one of the most important cities in the world, but far more provincial than the large cities of Europe. All of it is contained within the southern third of Manhattan Island. From the Battery north to almost 30th Street, it is built-up solid. Beyond that, along Broadway and Fifth Avenue, stretch the villas of the very rich. The waterfront, along the East River (which is mostly south) and the Hudson River to the west, is a forest of masts, a maze of ferry boats, a collage of sails, ropes, barrels, wooden piers, and wooden warehouses.

The first sentence—"It is already one of the most important cities in world, but far more provincial than the large cities of Europe"—establishes the tone of the paragraph and is therefore the dominant impression. Some dominant impressions are implied—that is, the details in the paragraph lead toward an overall tone, but that tone isn't stated. Check paragraph 9:

> It is not really new, but it has a fascination all its own. You hit a ball with a stick and run around "bases." In some versions, it is as old as humankind. Specifically, it is an adaptation of two venerable English games, rounders and cricket. And that's natural enough, because your family's roots are English or Dutch, wars notwithstanding. Almost every "good" family in town is from this background. The waves of Irish Catholics starting to flow into the city generate an anti-Catholicism so virulent that by 1844 New York will elect a mayor (James Harper) from a party (the American Republican party) that makes anti-Catholicism one of its basic principles. You derive all your ideas—and limitations—of "gentlemanly" behavior, your definition of social class, and your models of fashion from contemporary England, where a young queen named Victoria has reigned for five years and where industrialism has started upheavals that will soon cross the ocean.

The details—the English games rounders and cricket, English or Dutch background, waves of Irish Catholics, Queen Victoria—all show that baseball had been influenced by cultures other than American. But you won't find a sentence that directly tells you this. The dominant impression here, then, is implied.

Whether stated or implied, all the details in your descriptive writing must center on the dominant impression. Otherwise, they float on the page without any direction.

Details and Dialogue   When talking about detail and description, another consideration should be dialogue. Dialogue is words and phrases that people say within a written work. With good dialogue, what people say or how they say it can reveal detail about that person. For example, imagine having a conference with your history professor about a possible topic for a research paper. When you first mentioned the idea, she seemed excited. But during the conference, she says, "I have had other students write about this topic and their papers weren't very good. Are you sure you can find enough information for your paper? Scholars have tried for decades and still haven't cracked that mystery." Through this dialogue, you can get the idea that the instructor doesn't want you to work on that topic. She never comes right out and says, "Change your topic." But through the dialogue, we get the impression she is discouraging you.

For more on dialogue, see page 139.

Structure

Details must be arranged in an order that serves both the reader and the author. You must organize the detail to reflect the dominant impression and the purpose of the essay while enticing the audience. To do this effectively, you should rely on one of three types of organizational patterns: spatial order, time or chronological order, and order of importance.

Spatial Order   Spatial order revolves around the arrangement of objects in any area or space. Many descriptive essays begin by placing the audience in the middle of the area or space and then describing the area and its contents. Imagine walking into your classroom. As you enter the room, what do you see on the opposite wall? To the right? To the left? On the floor? What about the ceiling? Describing your classroom would be a matter of spatial order.

Time Order (Chronological Order)   With chronological order, you describe a series of events in the order in which the events happened. Paragraph 4 of "Preliminaries" is a great example of description through chronological order. The author talks briefly about the Revolutionary War, the War of 1812, and the financial panic and riots of 1837. By using chronological order, the author is able to show the arrangement of events that helped shape the New York of the 1840s.

Order of Importance   Reflect on your topic before you begin describing it. What is the most important aspect of the topic? What is next on the list? Third? Rearrange these aspects so the important one comes first and the rest follow in descending order. In the conclusion to "Preliminaries," Koppett writes a paragraph that describes special features of baseball—catching, throwing, batting, and running. Although he could place these features in any particular order, he chose to place catching over everything else. To Koppett, catching is the most important aspect of the game, and so he places it first.

Introductions and Conclusions

Like any other type of essay, a descriptive essay must have an introduction and a conclusion. The introduction should get the audience interested in reading more and should contain a fair amount of detail itself. The focus of the introduction should be the dominant impression, which leads into the essay itself.

Take a close look at the opening paragraphs for "Preliminaries." Notice the detail and the dominant impression.

> Imagine that you are a young man—say, 25—of comfortable means living in New York City in the 1840's.
>
> It is already one of the most important cities in the world, but far more provincial than the large cities of Europe. All of it is contained within the southern third of Manhattan Island. From the battery north to almost 30th Street, it is built-up solid. Beyond that, along Broadway and Fifth Avenue, stretch the villas of the very rich. The waterfront, along the East River (which is mostly south) and the Hudson River to the west, is a forest of masts, a maze of ferry boats, a college of sails, ropes, barrels, wooden piers, and wooden warehouses.

The descriptive essay should end with a strong conclusion. Like the introduction, the conclusion should reflect the dominant impression, as it will be the last thing that the audience reads. Check out the conclusion for "Preliminaries" and note how it reflects the wispy wonder of the early days of baseball.

> For any activity, then, an exclusive "club" is as natural in this New York as in that London, and you and your fellow Base Ball players long to form one. Among other things, open fields on which to play are rapidly disappearing in this growing city whose population has reached 250,000; and ferryrides to the abundant open spaces of Brooklyn (a village of some 30,000) or New Jersey are time-consuming and hopelessly complicated if not properly organized. So when you gather at Madison Square, where Fifth Avenue and Broadway meet at 23rd Street, and play ball and argue about what rules to use, you talk more and more of formalizing your group and its activity into a respectable club.
>
> Meanwhile, you become more and more captivated by the special features of the game itself: catching the ball on the run, throwing it hard and straight, the greater primitive satisfaction of smiting the ball as hard as possible with a level swing (instead of guarding a wicket against a bouncing delivery, as in cricket), the variety of having more than one station to run to after hitting the ball.
>
> In some such fashion, it all began—baseball as we know it in New York and, therefore, baseball in America.

Exercises

3. Fill out a Description Brainstorming Worksheet for one of your topics from Exercise 1. Next, determine the dominant impression and a topic sentence or thesis statement. Is the dominant impression one that you expected? Could you give a different impression with the details from this chart?

4. Study an everyday item, such as a pencil, a toaster, your notebook, or this textbook carefully. Fill out a Description Brainstorming Worksheet, and then write a paragraph (at least 100–150 words long) describing the item. Remember to appeal to the five senses.

5. Using spatial order, write an essay describing a place you frequent. Make that place sound appealing to someone who has never been there before.

6. Using chronological arrangement, write a descriptive essay about a job you have had. Provide details that put the reader inside the experience. Be careful not to write a process essay in which you tell the reader how to do the job.

REVISE

Revising a descriptive essay can be a simple matter of focusing on the dominant impression. In other words, if a word, phrase, or certain bits of description don't support the dominant impression, they should be replaced. If these useless words stay, they may end up damming the flow of your details. The flow of the details, by the way, could also be called the *organizational path* or *structure* of the descriptive essay. Each type of organizational path, whether order of importance, chronological, or spatial, has a certain flow or rhythm. Make sure your words follow that flow.

STUDENT SAMPLE

Sheila was surprised to have this writing assignment in her college success course: "Throughout our lives, we all have to pick and choose what to keep and what to throw away. Write a short essay about something you have kept with you most of your life. Why is it important to you? How will it help you in college?" Sheila didn't have to think hard; Buttons the Bear had been with her since she was three years old and, seventeen years later, it traveled with her to college. She couldn't imagine having gone to a school halfway across the country without it.

In her dorm room, Sheila propped Buttons on her pillow and looked at him closely. As she examined him, she filled out the Description Brainstorming Worksheet and made a few notes.

Description Brainstorming Worksheet

Topic: Buttons the bear.

Audience: Instructor, other students

Purpose: To introduce them to Buttons

Continued

Senses Chart

Senses	Questions	Details
Sight	What objects are here? What people do I see? What are they wearing? What shape is the room? What colors are here? What does what I see remind me of?	teddy bear—light brown, missing an eye
Hearing	What immediate sounds do I notice? What background sounds are there? What do these sounds remind me of?	
Smell	What odors can I identify? What odors can I not identify? What do the unknown odors remind me of?	My perfume on his body & a slight musty smell—cried into him a lot
Touch	What textures do I feel? What do these textures remind me of?	soft—cottony very flexible—reminds me of being a kid
Taste	What can I taste here? What does the taste remind me of?	

After that, she wrote a rough draft.

Buttons the bear has been with me since I can remember. I got him for my third birthday. Mom says that I liked everything I had gotten that year and that Buttons wasn't my favorite toy. But she wanted me to have a teddy bear. Over time, I learned how important Buttons was going to be to me.

He is eighteen inches long, with a light brown cotton soft body and a dingy brown-green bear head. His left ear and eye are missing, but Mom sewed them up. Buttons got in a fight with Tommy, our golden retriever, who torn him to shreds one day. Mom was able to patch him up, but the dog ate the ear and eye and we never saw those again. Buttons is overstuffed and a small tear in the seam in the back has little bits of orange fluff seeping out of it. That happened a few months ago when I got excited about coming back to school and tossed the bear in the air. I didn't get a chance to get it fixed yet. But I will. Buttons has light brown legs that are stubby and cute little tiny feet. One foot is torn and mom said there wasn't enough stuffing to fix it so she let it just hang open. I cried and cried when she told me she wasn't going to fix it.

The bear has been a friend. That's is why it is important to me. It will help me get through college because it has helped me get through everything else.

Sheila noticed a few things as she reread the draft. Her topic sentence and dominant impression were at the end, just tacked on to the draft. Moving those two elements to the beginning would make the entire essay stronger. She also remembered why the bear's foot had gotten torn open: She pulled on the seam as she was going to the hospital to have her tonsils taken out. She knew she had to add that to the draft and make additional changes as well.

Need to talk about Buttons more

Buttons the bear has been with me since I can remember. I got him for my third birthday. Mom says that I liked everything I had gotten that year and that Buttons wasn't my favorite toy. But she wanted me to have a teddy bear. Over time, I learned how important Buttons was going to be to me.

He is eighteen inches long, with a light brown cotton soft body and a dingy brown-green bear head. His left ear and eye are missing, but Mom sewed them up. Buttons got in a

I like this part

Do I get off the subject a bit? Who cares how he got ripped up?

fight with Tommy, our golden retriever, who torn him to shreds one day. Mom was able to patch him up, but the dog ate the ear and eye and we never saw those again. Buttons is overstuffed and a small tear in the seam in the back has little bits of orange fluff seeping out of it. That happened a few months ago when I got excited about coming back to school and tossed the bear in the air. I didn't get a chance to get it fixed yet. But I will. Buttons has light brown legs that are stubby and cute little tiny feet. One foot is torn and mom *How old was I then?* said there wasn't enough stuffing to fix it so she let it just hang open. I cried and cried when she told me she wasn't going to fix it.

I will add more to the conclusion

The bear has been a friend. That's is why it is important to me. It will help me get through college because it has helped me get through everything else.

After making these changes and doing some more editing, Sheila wrote the following final draft.

Sheila L _____

ENGL 101

March 1, 2000

Buttons the Bear

Buttons the Bear has been with me since I can remember. I got him for my third birthday from my mother. She told me she wanted me to have a teddy bear for a friend. Now that I am older, I understand what she meant. Buttons has been a good friend to me. He will help me get through college because he has helped me get through everything else in my life.

When you look at Buttons, you may see a ratty old teddy bear, but I see our lives together. Buttons is eighteen inches long, with a light brown cotton soft body and a dingy brown-green bear head. The first casualty was Button's left eye and ear. Tommy, our golden retriever, was being very playful one day but I wanted to be left alone. I used Buttons to hit Tommy and Tommy tore my bear to pieces. Mom was able to patch him up, but the dog swallowed the ear and eye.

Buttons is quite round; he is overstuffed. In fact, he is so overstuffed, little bits of orange fluff are seeping out a seam in his back. That happened a few months ago when I first found out I was going to college. I tossed the bear up in the air a few times and pulled the seam apart. Buttons has light brown stubby legs and a cute little left foot. The right foot is nothing more than a few pieces of loose fabric. He had a foot there once, but when I went to the hospital to have my tonsils removed, I was scared. I took Buttons along to help me and, during the trip to the hospital, I pulled the seam apart. Mom told me later that all of the fluff had fallen out and that there was nothing she could do to fix it.

As you can see, Buttons has been a friend to me. It might seem odd that a grown woman brings a teddy bear to college with her, but I couldn't leave him behind. We have been through a lot together, and he will help me get through college just by being himself.

CHAPTER REVIEW

Descriptive writing is writing that appeals to the five senses: taste, hearing, smell, sight, and touch. A well-written description is controlled by a dominant impression, or the overall idea or feeling that you want your reader to experience.

Of all the details that may be generated on the brainstorming worksheet, only the details that support the dominant impression should be used. Dialogue can also be used as a way to add detail to a piece of writing. Your descriptive essay should be organized around one of three patterns: spatial order (the arrangement of objects in a particular space or area), time order or chronological order (what event took place first, next, and so on), and order of importance (the most important aspect of the topic first, next, and so on). After you have your details and organizational pattern, write the essay and then refer back to the dominant impression as you revise. Remember: If a word, sentence, or phrase doesn't support the dominant impression, replace it with one that does.

Final Writing Assignments

1. Expand one of the exercises you wrote earlier in this chapter to a complete, polished essay. Be sure to refer to your Description Brainstorming Worksheet and the dominant impression as you revise. Also remember to appeal to the five senses as you write.

2. Describe an event or ritual that you and your family partake of every year, such as a holiday gathering or a family reunion. Use the Description Brainstorming Worksheet to help get started. Make sure you add dialogue and appealing details.

3. Read a recent article on a neighborhood or place around your town that has a certain reputation. Perhaps it may be the "poor" part of town or the "rich, snobby" area. Visit the area, taking note of the people, places, and things you see there. Write a descriptive essay that supports or challenges the general reputation of the area.

4. Read through a brochure about student life at your school. With a partner, create a mock brochure describing student life as you and your partner have experienced it. (For added authenticity, illustrate your brochure with pictures of students.)

5. Write a reading response to "Preliminaries." Highlight sections of the essay that appealed to you and explain why. To get you started, it may help to complete a Description Brainstorming Worksheet. Be sure your response follows basic essay structure.

6. Take a look at the picture my son, at age 8, drew of me (page 2). Then ask a child (8–10 years old) to draw a picture of you. Write a descriptive essay about the picture. Go beyond what you see on the page. What emotions are expressed in the picture? What clues helped you identify those emotions?

DEFINITION AND CLASSIFICATION

Before I got to college, I thought professors came in two basic forms. The men were all in their fifties, with gray hair and tweed jackets, smoking pipes and waxing philosophical. The women all wore glasses, had their hair pulled back tightly in buns, and always wore skirts or power suits. After I got to college and, years later, became a teacher myself, my image of teachers changed drastically. *Teacher* is a loose term for anyone who trains or educates others. There are many types of teacher, including the Outgoing Spirit, the Showoff, and the Guide.

The most unusual teacher is the Outgoing Spirit. This type of teacher wants to be your friend and buddies up to you a lot, all while still being in charge. Mrs. Morgan, a science teacher I had my freshman year, was like that. She wore loud clothes that didn't match and treated students as though she had known them for years.

Another type of teacher is the Showoff. A showoff is more interested in impressing students than in teaching. My political science teacher, Dr. Granger, was a showoff. Every day, he read a passage from our textbook, shook his head, apologized for making us read such drivel, and then told us the "truth" about the topic. He recalled dates and people as though he lived during the times.

My favorite teacher is the Guide, the person who shows you the way to understanding. I had become increasingly frustrated with my literature class when Mrs. Stevens, my English teacher, suggested I learn how to read for meaning by watching the movie *Chinatown*. I thought she was a nut, but she had my full attention during class. As we watched the movie, she pointed out all the elements of literature and then showed us how to transfer that analysis to written work. My grade improved drastically after that.

Regardless of style, each teacher was able to do the job of instructing students well. As I teach, I draw from each of their styles and, probably, create a style of my own. Consider the types of teachers you have had throughout the years. What sort has influenced you the most? What kind of teacher would you make?

Definition and classification essays examine topics in terms of what they are or are not (definition) and how a certain topic can be sorted into types (classification). In the opening essay, I defined the word *teacher* as "anyone who trains or educates others." In the body paragraphs, I classified *teacher* into three smaller

149

groups: the Outgoing Spirit, the Showoff, and the Guide. In this chapter, we discuss effective ways to define and classify topics with respect to topic, audience, and purpose. We also look at the basic structure of definition and classification essays and watch while one is created.

We started this chapter talking about teachers. Now, let's talk about the students. Different styles of teaching exist, but what about different styles of learning? This idea is the focus of "The Seven Learning Styles," by Stacy Mantle.

Reading 7   The Seven Learning Styles
Stacy Mantle

BACKSTORY

What is the best way for you to learn something, such as facts from the Civil War or all of the bones in the human body? Do you prefer lectures and notes, or are you more comfortable with interactive or hands-on lessons? In an essay from an Internet site about teaching, educator Stacy Mantle suggests that seven learning styles exist and that learning about these seven styles can help teachers be more effective in the classroom. As you read, study each style to see which one fits you.

LEXICON

adept: skilled

empathetic: sharing the feelings someone else feels

linguistic: related to language

1   How many ways are there to learn about a subject? According to the latest findings by several leading psychologists, there are seven specific types of learning styles. This means that in order to maximize learning advantages, you must define the type of learner that you have, and cater the lesson to that particular learning style. For example, if your child is primarily a linguistic learner, you could incorporate several novels into your curriculum. You could encourage short stories to explain scientific developments, or allow the student to rewrite a difficult math problem into a story problem. If he/she is primarily logical, you will want to emphasize charts, tables, and diagrams. Venn diagrams work well with a logical learner.

2   Read each description below to determine which style best describes your student. Remember that it is possible to have more than one style of learning, particularly in the intrapersonal and interpersonal categories (numbers six and seven), which have traditionally been interpreted as personality types.

3   **1. Linguistic:** This type of learner loves to read, write, and tell stories. They tend to memorize places, dates, names, and trivia very easily, and are always mesmerizing you with their incredible tales. They have a remarkable ability to repeat back everything you have ever told them, word for word. Encourage their creativity, and do your best to distin-

guish between the truth and exaggeration (it is all well intended). These students learn best by saying, hearing, and seeing words. Ask them to write down a word or a phrase, and it is forever locked into their memory. Encourage them to participate in spelling bees and creative writing courses. You could have another Shakespeare on your hands!

4   2. **Logical:** This child is very mathematically inclined. They enjoy solving problems, particularly if they are math related. They are similar to Dr. Spock, on *Star Trek*, in that they are very logical, straightforward types of learners. They will plague you with questions on how things work, how things relate to one another, and why things are here. Their favorite toys as young children were likely building blocks and pattern puzzles. Answer their ongoing questions with as much patience as you can muster, and know that one day they may likely become an engineer. This type of student learns best by categorizing, classifying, and working with abstract patterns or relationships. Ask them to make a chart or to show relationships between different items. For example, "What kind of effect does the El Nino have on the stock market?". They will not only come up with an answer, but they will be able to explain the process and developmental stages of the relationship.

5   3. **Spatial:** These are the visualizers. They spend most of the day dreaming, watching movies, and staying as far away from reality as possible. If they seem particularly "down," asking them to draw a picture will get you much further into the nature of the problem, than asking them to tell you about it. Allow them to develop their senses and their natural artistic abilities. They are very good at working with colors and pictures, and using the "mind's eye." Allow them to play a couple of educational computer games, such as *Civilization* or the *Oregon Trail*, or to daydream under a tree. They could be hard at work thinking about a particular problem, but have yet to put it on paper. These types of learners are very artistic, although they often have problems expressing it. Encourage any type of creative endeavor. They may become the next developer of an international theme park.

6   4. **Musical:** If your child is always walking around the house humming a tune, or always needs music to study by, then he/she is likely a musical learner. This type of learner is best at noticing details, pitches, and rhythms that escape the normal listener. They are excellent at keeping tune, and are adept at turning the abstract into concrete objects. They learn best through rhythm, melody, and music. For memorization techniques, ask them to write a song about the lesson (rap works well as a narrative), or teach them a song. Encourage their natural love of music, and try to incorporate music into as many lessons as possible.

7   5. **Bodily:** This type of learner is always on the move. They constantly walk around, they have to touch everything, and they use body language to convey their feelings. They would rather play sports or do a craft than sit down and read a book. They need active education! Keep them moving. Play word games in the pool, have spelling lessons during tennis. Take them camping to learn about geography and nature. These are the learners who can do more than one thing at a time. Generally recognized as ADHD (Attention Deficit Hyperactivity Disorder), many are misdiagnosed. Allow them to use all of that extra energy to learn. Remember to incorporate sense development and interaction with space during their lessons. Attempt to keep the duration of each lesson down to a minimum (10–20 minutes depending on age), and change subjects frequently. Interdisciplinary lessons are very successful with these types of learners.

8   6. **Interpersonal:** These are the "social butterflies." They adapt easily to any type of social situation, have many friends, and are excellent leaders. They are patient, understanding, and very empathetic, which makes them a favorite among their playmates. They generally make good leaders because of their ability to mediate conflict, and are often referred to as "the Peacemaker" of the family. Encourage their love of people, and allow them to be with many different types of people. They will likely bring home a number of different types of friends. Although this can be difficult at times, it is important to support and accept all of them. This type of learner will do best in a group situation as they compare, share, relate, and interview other people. If no group is available, don't be surprised to see them create one in their animals or toys!

9   7. **Intrapersonal:** These strong-willed people work best alone. They pursue their own interests and have a deep understanding of themselves. They pride themselves on being independent and original, and they tend to stand out from the crowd without even trying. They are the "strong, silent type." They do best in self-paced instruction, individualized projects, and working alone. Allow them to be by themselves, but continue to encourage their socialization skills. Create a number of situations for them to socialize, yet allow them to maintain their own space. These children work best alone, and often need to be encouraged to socialize.

10   In conclusion, we all have elements of each learning style. But the truth is that one or two types stand out in each of us. Determine which style of learner your child is, and figure out ways to incorporate that learning style into your teaching. Continue to encourage the student to figure out alternative styles, and teach them how to bring each type into their life.

QUESTIONS FOR THOUGHT

1. Mantle suggests allowing spatial learners (type 3) to daydream. How would daydreaming during class time benefit a student?

2. Reread the seven learning types and then reflect on the education you have received. Which type of learner are you? Explain.

3. How would you recommend a teacher incorporate music into a math or a writing class?

READY

Take a close look at this textbook. Feel its heft. Flip the pages and notice the smell and sound. Look at the print on the spine and the back cover. Once you have studied the book, write a short paragraph explaining what a textbook is. Begin with these words: "A textbook is…".

Whatever you write about the textbook will become your definition of a writing textbook. When we talk about **definition**, we are talking about explaining a concept to an audience. In defining the concept *textbook*, you may have written something like this:

> A textbook is a printed collection of information for both student and teacher. Students use textbooks for information, and teachers use textbooks to guide lectures and lessons for students' understanding of the information within the book. The textbook we use in this writing class, *Culture in Context*, explains how to write for a college audience. It also has a set of readings and a grammar handbook.

This paragraph describes or defines what a textbook is and includes a strong example as well. But does one single definition truly define all textbooks? Think of all the types of textbooks you have seen. Some textbooks are online, accessible only through the Internet. Some textbooks are on CD-ROM, which means the student must have access to a computer. Some textbooks are workbooks, while others are reference sources. Remember the Showoff from this chapter's opening essay? He spoke all the information his students needed. Would his lectures count as a textbook?

We find that our definition is adequate in some ways, but not in every way. To make some definitions more complete, we need to break the larger idea into separate compartments. This breaking down is known as **classification**. Under the umbrella topic of textbooks, we have several classifications or types of textbooks, such as online textbooks, CD-ROM textbooks, and oral notes.

Classifications are not random or arbitrary. Classifications are chosen based on thoughtful analysis of the concept being defined. When you choose your categories for classification, be sure to use appropriate criteria, or elements on which differences can be based. The best place to start is your topic, audience, and purpose.

Return to the textbook example. *Culture in Context* has a certain shape and size, with a cover pattern unlike that of your math textbook or your biology textbook. An audience interested in art and design would be interested in the visual differences between the books, so the classifications would focus on visuals. An audience interested in writing styles, however, would be more attracted to classifications that focused on those styles, which may include point of view, paragraph structure, and sentence length. Either set of classifications is fine, as long as your audience is in agreement.

Definition and classification can work separately or hand in hand. For concepts unfamiliar to your audience, the definition writing style would serve you well. The information you provide would help educate your audience about the topic. Classification would be better used with an audience more familiar with the general topic. Through that strategy, the audience would see this topic in new ways. Notice the approach taken with "The Seven Learning Styles." The article was originally published on a website for teachers, so the concept of learning wasn't foreign to the audience. However, Stacy Mantle, the author, wants to educate these teachers about the types of learners in a classroom. To do this, she breaks the idea of *learner* into seven basic categories: linguistic, logical, spatial, musical, bodily, interpersonal, and intrapersonal, and then explains each style in more detail.

Topic, Audience, and Purpose

Most everything in the world can be explained, categorized, catalogued, indexed, arranged, or sorted in one way or another. So choosing a topic for a definition or classification essay doesn't have to be a daunting task. What you write in your definition or classification essay will depend on your audience. If your audience has a limited knowledge of your topic, then go with a definition essay. If your audience has greater knowledge of the topic, then develop categories of that topic through a classification essay. Determine your purpose for writing this type of essay by studying your audience and your topic. Primarily, your purpose is to educate, to define an unknown concept to your audience. Beyond that, your purpose could be to enlighten your audience and call them to action. For example, Mantle's essay educates teachers about learning styles in order for the teachers to enhance their teaching methods. Students need the information to become more effective students.

The Definition/Classification Brainstorming Worksheet

Using TAP as a guide, you can fill out a Definition/Classification Worksheet to help generate and develop your ideas. Be as detailed and as clear as you possibly can on the worksheet; sketchy explanations or categories may confuse you when you develop the idea into a full-blown essay.

Definition/Classification Brainstorming Worksheet

Topic: _____

Audience: _____

Purpose: _____

Definition of Topic: _____

_____

_____

_____

_____

Example for Topic:

_____

_____

_____

_____

Classifications for Topic:

Criteria	Characteristics	Examples

Additional Information for the Essay:

_____

_____

_____

_____

_____

_____

_____

Exercises

1. Prepare a list of topics that can be defined beyond dictionary definitions. Good pets, pleasant people, bad food, and nice restaurants are just a few examples. Choose one and fill out the Definition/Classification Brainstorming Worksheet. Why did you choose this particular topic? What categories are you using for classification? What elements are you highlighting in your definition?

2. Consider your chosen program of study. What topics or ideas in that area could be used for a definition/classification essay? Brainstorm a list and then choose one topic. Fill out a Definition/Classification Brainstorming Worksheet for that topic.

3. Think of one type of entertainment you enjoy, such as television, music, or movies. What categories could you generate for that type of entertainment? Choose a type and fill out a Definition/Classification Brainstorming Worksheet.

WRITE

As you write your definition/classification essay, remember that you are explaining a concept to your audience. You may be tempted to write little more than a dictionary definition of your topic, but your audience will demand more. As with other types of essays, be sure to provide thorough development and include specific examples. If you are writing a classification essay, you should first provide your audience with a general definition of the topic. That way, everyone has a basis for understanding the classifications. From there, you should provide insight on the classifications and the criteria you used to determine the categories. After that, you should simply choose the appropriate categories and write about each one in a separate paragraph. As with the definition essay, you should include explanations and specific examples for each of the categories you choose.

Select

In theory, you could write a novella defining a topic like *hard work* or *tasty food.* You could also write a book explaining the classifications and types of *work* or *food.* In reality, however, you need to be discriminating with your definitions and classifications. You should select only the information that will appeal to your audience and serve your purpose.

With definition essays, select information about the topic that will educate and enlighten your audience. Select the strongest elements of the topic and use them as a starting point for your writing. Strong elements are ones that are obvious to your reader and to you, such as size, shape, and color. Once those are in place, select less obvious elements for discussion in your essay. Less obvious elements may include background information.

Classification essays provide the same challenge. The categories you choose should reflect the demands of your audience. If your topic is somewhat unfamiliar to your audience, use classifications that are easy to follow. You can use categories that go beyond the basics when you are talking to an audience that is knowledgeable about the topic.

Refer to the reading for this chapter. Teachers should be familiar with the concept of learning. However, those same teachers may not be as familiar with the seven learning styles, so the author expands on each style she discusses. Within each discussion, she is careful to select only information that explains that learning style through examples and then provides teaching assistance. Look closely at the paragraph about interpersonal learners.

> These are the "social butterflies." They adapt easily to any type of social situation, have many friends and are excellent leaders. They are patient, understanding, and very empathetic, which makes them a favorite among their playmates. They generally make good leaders because of their ability to mediate conflict, and are often referred to as "the Peacemaker" of the family. Encourage their love of people, and allow them to be with many different types of people. They will likely bring home a number of different types of friends. Although this can be difficult at times, it is important to support and accept all of them. This type of learner will do best in a group situation as they compare, share, relate, and interview other people. If no group is available, don't be surprised to see them create one in their animals or toys!

Be sure to narrow your categories to about three or four. A small group of well-supported, well-explained categories will be better appreciated than a laundry list of poorly supported, weakly explained categories.

Structure

The structure of a definition/classification essay should be straightforward. Your thesis statement should explain the concept you are going to define or the categories you are going to use to classify the topic. If you are writing a definition essay, use the body paragraphs to explore and give more detail about various aspects of the topic. If you are writing a classification essay, devote each of the body paragraphs to a single classification, offering in each an explanation and specific examples. Finally, conclude both types of essays with a reworking of the thesis statement and a brief summary of the points discussed in the essay.

Mantle opens "The Seven Learning Styles" by explaining why teachers should be aware of the different learning styles in their classrooms. From there, she moves into seven paragraphs, each addressing one learning style. Within each of the paragraphs, Mantle develops her discussion. Finally, she draws all the styles back together, echoing the point she made in the introduction: Knowing about learning styles can enhance the classroom and the lives of the students.

Introductions   Read the two opening paragraphs of "The Seven Learning Styles."

> How many ways are there to learn about a subject? According to the latest findings by several leading psychologists, there are seven specific types of learning styles. This means that in order to maximize learning advantages, you must define the type of learner that you have, and cater the lesson to that particular learning style. For example, if your child is primarily a linguistic learner, you could incorporate several novels into your curriculum. You could encourage short stories to explain scientific developments, or allow the student to rewrite a difficult math problem into a story problem. If he/she is primarily logical, you will want to emphasize charts, tables, and diagrams. Venn diagrams work well with a logical learner.
>
> Read each description below to determine which style best describes your student. Remember that it is possible to have more than one style of learning, particularly in the intrapersonal and interpersonal categories (numbers six and seven), which have traditionally been interpreted as personality types.

In this introduction, the author challenges the audience with what would normally be a typical question: "How many ways are there to learn a subject?" A traditional answer may be one or two, but Mantle explains that there are actually seven. This information immediately piques the interest of the audience . Following up on the announcement of seven learning styles, Mantle explains why studying these styles is important to teachers: This knowledge helps maximize learning, thus making teachers more effective in the classroom.

The introduction of your definition/classification essay should follow the same path. Brainstorm approaches to your topic and the ideas you want to present to your audience. Will readers be more interested in a discussion of the topic itself? Should you open with a dictionary definition and then challenge it with your new insights and information? Just about any approach will work as long as you focus on the topic, the demands of your audience, and your purpose in writing the paper.

Body Paragraphs   The structure of the body paragraphs within definition/classification essays is fairly standard. Each paragraph consists of the point or idea you are trying to get across to the reader, a brief explanation of that point, and an example or other type of development. Of course, the major difference is that body paragraphs in a definition essay focus on various aspects of the topic being defined, while the body paragraphs in a classification essay are devoted to each of the categories relating to the topic.

Read paragraph 6 of "The Seven Learning Styles," which focuses on music as a learning style.

> **Musical**: if your child is always walking around the house humming a tune, or always needs music to study by, then he/she is likely a musical learner. This type of learner is best at noticing details, pitches, and rhythms that escape the normal listener. They are excellent at keeping tune, and are adept at turning the abstract into concrete objects. They learn best through rhythm, melody, and

music. For memorization techniques, ask them to write a song about the lesson (rap works well as a narrative), or teach them a song. Encourage their natural love of music, and try to incorporate music into as many lessons as possible.

The author is thorough in her discussion of the musical learning style. Mantle explains the characteristics of a musical learner and goes on to explain, in general terms, the learning style. Toward the end of the paragraph, she offers specific examples of activities that work well for musical learners.

Make sure each body paragraph deals with a single idea and that all of the elements of the paragraph focus on that idea. It may be tempting to compare characteristics of your topic within the body paragraphs, but this may confuse readers. Simply present the information and move on to the next point.

Order of Body Paragraphs   If you have ever consulted a dictionary for a definition, then you have the idea of standard definition organization: A term is introduced, followed by its meaning. This is one way to organize a definition, but it is not always the most effective or interesting. Your definition and classification essays should include more insight and explanation than a definition found in a dictionary in order to serve both your audience and your purpose. When organizing a definition essay, start with a frame of reference common to you and your audience (which may be the dictionary definition) and then expand into your insight. With a classification essay, start with a definition of the topic so you and your audience share a frame of reference, as mentioned earlier.

Details within each type of essay can be presented in either chronological order or climax order. With chronological order, the information is sort of a historical account. This approach works well when explaining how a topic has changed over the years, such as how computers have evolved from warehouse-sized mainframes to hand-held personal data assistants. With climax order, information is arranged so the least impressive information is presented first and the most impressive information is presented last.

The distinctiveness and development of the categories is as important as their order. For example, in "The Seven Learning Styles," the bodily learning style could have been placed first or last on the list. However, it is important that the paragraph starts with a sentence helping the reader identify that particular type of learner: "they constantly walk around, they have to touch everything, and they use body language to convey their feelings."

Regardless of the type of essay you choose to write, you and your audience must start at the same point. Misunderstandings at the beginning of the essay lead to a confused and unsatisfied audience by the end. When you start at the same point, however, your audience will stay with you.

Conclusions   Conclusions for definition and classification essays can either restate your thesis statement or call your audience to action. A typical conclusion consists of restating the thesis statement and the main points you discussed. With this traditional conclusion, the audience is likely to remember what you said in the essay. With a call to action, you encourage your audience to act upon the information provided. While either type of conclusion is fine, make sure you stay true to your purpose for writing the essay.

Stacy Mantle chose a call to action for her conclusion. In paragraph 10, she writes:

> In conclusion, we all have elements of each learning style. But the truth is that one or two types stand out in each of us. Determine which style of learner your child is, and figure out ways to incorporate that learning style into your teaching. Continue to encourage the student to figure out alternative styles, and teach them how to bring each type into their life.

She is asking teachers to apply this newly acquired knowledge in the classroom in order for both teacher and student to be more successful. Success for teacher and student was her purpose for writing the essay, and the end of the essay fulfills that purpose.

Exercises

4. Choose one of the topics you developed in Exercises 1–3 and expand it into a rough draft. Remember that each category or criterion must be explained and then followed by specific examples.

5. Trade lists of topics for definition/classification essays with another student. Choose one topic from the list, fill out a Definition/Classification Brainstorming Worksheet, and then write a rough draft. Exchange your draft for another student's draft and critique the draft.

REVISE

Revising definition and classification essays means returning to the reasons you decided to write the essay in the first place. As you revise, keep in mind that you are educating people. If you are revising a definition essay, make sure that the definition of the topic is clear from the beginning. As you move through the essay, look for weak explanations or examples and strengthen them. If you are revising a classification essay, focus on a clear general definition at the beginning of your essay and then move to the categories. Make sure each is distinct, developed, and is appropriately illustrated by examples. In either case, make sure your points are clear and concise. Getting someone else to look over your essay would be helpful as well.

STUDENT SAMPLE

All of his life, Jorge has liked toys, and he has an extensive collection of action figures, model cars, plastic spaceships, and other items. Many of his friends are puzzled, however, with Jorge's idea of collectibles. Some toys he displays openly, while others he keeps in the original packaging. When he was assigned a definition/classification essay for his English class, he thought this would be a good way to educate noncollectors on types of toys and to educate his friends on his seemingly bizarre collecting habits.

To begin, Jorge went home and surveyed all his things. He thought about jotting down a list of the types of toys he has—types of cars, action figures, and so on—but the list would be extensive and the essay would be much longer than the 300–400 word limit. So he adjusted his strategy a bit. Why not look at the characteristics of the toys that were the prizes of his collection? They were all different, but they still shared some of the same elements. Those elements would be the basis of his discussion. He filled out the Definition/Classification Brainstorming Worksheet this way:

Definition/Classification Brainstorming Worksheet

Topic: _Collectible toys_

Audience: _People who don't collect toys_

Purpose: _To enlighten them_

Definition of Topic: _Toys that are special to me for more than one reason._

Example for Topic:

Classifications for Topic

Criteria	Characteristics	Examples
Age	Toys that have been around awhile	G.I. Joe
Price	Some toys are expensive	Barbie Doll: $50.00
Availability	Can't find them everywhere	'ER' Ambulance
Sentimentality	Toys that just mean something to me	my viewmaster

Continued

Additional Information for the Essay

Show that toys can be grouped in different ways

From here, Jorge wrote a short paragraph for each of the characteristics, making sure he included both a definition and the necessary detail.

Characteristics of Collectible Toys

1. Age: Some toys are just old and will be worth a lot of money some day. I have a number of old toys, including an original 13-inch G.I. Joe doll with a footlocker. He has his original uniform as well.

2. Price: I paid $50.00 for a Barbie doll dressed like the superhero Wonder Woman. It is the only Barbie I have, but I thought it was worth the money.

3. Availability: Some people think that any toy can be found any place and that isn't necessarily true. A toy can become a collectible if there is a limited quantity or if that toy can be found only in a certain location. For example, I have a model ambulance from the show *ER*. There were less than 15,000 of these models made, which means instant collectible.

4. Sentimentality: Some of the toys I have in my collection are there because I just like them. Someone special gave them to me or I got them during a memorable time in my life. My Viewmaster is one of those toys. It was given to me when I was a kid and I never really liked it much, but I keep it because it helps me remember being a kid. I don't even know if I have any of the slides any more.

Taking these notes, Jorge created this rough draft and made notes for revision:

What kinds of toys am I talking about?

I love toys of all types. Of course, what kid doesn't like to play with dolls or cars or model airplanes? But how many adults do you know that like to play with toys? Well, I am one of those people. Although I have a lot of toys, not all

I like this

are collectibles. To me, for a toy to be collectible, it must fall under one of these guidelines: age, price, availability, and sentimentality.

Fragment

First, age. Some toys are just old and will be worth a lot of money some day. I have a number of old toys, including an original 13" G.I. Joe doll with a footlocker. He has his original uniform as well.

More about age

Next is price. I paid $50.00 for a Barbie doll dressed like the superhero Wonder Woman. It is the only Barbie I have, but I thought it was worth the money.

Not long enough

Another category is availability. Some people think that any toy can be found any place and that isn't necessarily true. A toy can become a collectible if there is a limited quantity or if that toy can be found only in a certain location. For example, I have a model ambulance from the show <u>ER</u>. There were less than 15,000 of these models made, which means instant collectible.

Another fragment

Finally, sentimentality. Some of the toys I have in my collection are there because I just like them. Someone special gave them to me or I got them during a memorable time in my life. My Viewmaster is one of those toys. It was given to me when I was a kid and I never really liked it much, but I keep it because it helps me remember being a kid. I don't even know if I have any of the slides anymore.

I wonder if everyone knows what a viewmaster is

Toys are fun to play with, no matter what age you are.

More—not long enough Some toys, however, have more meaning than others. These are my criteria for collectible toys.

After making a few major and minor changes, Jorge produced this final draft:

Jorge _____

ENGL 099

4/28/00

Characteristics of Collectible Toys

How many adults do you know who like to play with toys? Running a few Hot Wheels cars through a track or painting a model World War II bomber I just built is relaxing. I have a lot of toys, but only certain ones are what I would consider collectible. A collectible is something that holds special meaning for the owner. My collectible toys hold special meaning for me because of their age, the price I paid, their availability, and sentimental reasons.

The first criterion is age. Some toys are collectible simply because they have been around a long time. In this case, I look for an original edition of the toy. For example, I have an original 13-inch G.I. Joe action figure that was first produced about twenty-five years ago. G.I. Joe has gone through some changes, so this particular edition is valuable.

Another criterion is price. If I pay more than $20 for a toy, I think it is a collectible. Recently, for example, I paid $50 for a Barbie doll. Now, this Barbie doll was not a usual Barbie. This one was dressed like the superhero Wonder Woman. Its uniqueness made it worth the money to me.

A third criterion is availability of the toy. Some people think any toy can be found any place, but that isn't necessarily true. A toy becomes a collectible if there is a limited quantity or if that toy can be found only in a certain location. For example, I have a model ambulance from the show ER. Fewer than 15,000 of these models were made, which means instant collectible.

Finally, the last criterion is sentimentality. Some of the toys I will never part with because they hold special meaning for me. One such toy is the Viewmaster. A Viewmaster is shaped like a pair of binoculars. You can insert slides into the viewer and see three-dimensional images with them. I got this Viewmaster when I was ten years old and played with it a lot. It is beat up and I don't have any of the slides anymore, but I still call it a collectible.

Everyone should play with toys. If you are inclined to collect them, feel free to use my criteria or create some of your own. Remember, a collectible is only a collectible because it means something to you.

CHAPTER REVIEW

Definition and classification writing strategies allow writers to describe and categorize things beyond traditional dictionary definitions. Because the primary purpose of this type of writing strategy is to educate, the definitions and classifications should include insights not found anywhere else. Once you choose a topic, gauge the audience's knowledge of that topic. If your audience is only slightly familiar with the concepts, write a definition essay. If the audience is very familiar with the topic, write a classification essay in which you break the topic into categories. For a classification essay, the selection of categories is based on criteria, or specific elements appropriate to the topic. A definition/classification essay consists of an introduction, body paragraphs (in which the author explains aspects of the topic or explains subgroups or categories of that topic in detail), and a conclusion. Information within body paragraphs should be arranged in chronological order or climax order. With chronological order, information is arranged in time sequence. With climax order, information is arranged from the least impressive to the most impressive. At any rate, make sure your body paragraphs are clear and concise. With a definition/classification essay, the conclusion may either restate the main ideas behind the essay or call the audience to action.

Final Writing Assignments

1. Expand the topic you developed in Exercise 4 into a full essay. Revise your rough draft by making your language more concise and including the appropriate examples.

2. Read "The Day That I Sensed a New Kind of Intelligence" by Garry Kasparov (page 58). Generate a list of types of intelligence, then fill out a Definition/Classification Brainstorming Worksheet using intelligence as a topic. From here, write a definition/classification essay.

3. Reread "The Seven Learning Styles." List three or four friends or classmates that exhibit different styles. Using each student as an example for a learning style, complete a Definition/Classification Brainstorming Worksheet and then write a draft. Polish this draft and submit it to your instructor.

4. With a partner, read through several newspapers and magazines and create a list of topics that have become popular recently. Choose one, define it, and write a definition essay. You and your partner can complete separate brainstorming worksheets and then combine the two as you write the draft of the essay.

5. Brainstorm a list of non-English words that are a part of the English language. Choose one and define it. Consult the Internet, your school librarians, or someone who speaks another language and find out other ways the term can be defined or classified. With this information, write a definition or classification essay.

8

COMPARISON
AND CONTRAST

Before you arrived on campus, you may have thought that college was little more than high school. In some ways, you were right. In high school, you were required to attend classes and should have been prepared for every session. In college, if you don't attend class or are not prepared, you may end up failing. In high school, you had certain events and activities, such as homecoming dances or football games, which helped you relax and cultivate school spirit. The same can be said for college, with all of its athletic competitions and parties. High school and college also share the same basic structure. In both, you attend lectures, do assigned work, and then have some sort of assessment of your work. What you may not realize, however, is that high school and college do have key differences. In college, you have more freedom. You wake up and go to bed if and when you want to, not because your mom comes knocking on your bedroom door. In college, you are expected to be more self-directed with respect to attending classes and studying. If you don't understand a concept, you must take the responsibility to ask the instructor after class or find a tutor. Finally, someone is paying your college tuition, whether it is you, your parents, or the government. You must make sure you are able to pay for classes the following term or you won't be able to attend.

High school does share a number of important traits with college, but it may not have completely prepared you for college. Yet, your experiences in high school will help you adjust to college.

Just as college is unlike high school, comparison and contrast essays are unlike other types of essays. Usually, you focus on one topic in an essay, but with a comparison and contrast essay, you write about two. In the opening sequence, I talked about aspects of two types of educational experience—high school and college—and showed how they were alike in some ways and different in others. In this chapter, you will find out how to select appropriate topics for a comparison and contrast essay, how to select traits to use as the basis for discussions, how to organize a comparison and contrast essay, and, finally, tips on how to make your comparison and contrast essays stronger.

This chapter's reading is "Family Ties Put a Face on the Faceless Issue of Free Speech," written by reporter Eric Slater for the *Los Angeles Times*. In this article, Slater discusses freedom of speech through a comparison and contrast of two very different people: Shawn Thomas, a rapper who recorded "Deadly Game," (a song that "advocates the killing of cops") and Blake, the author's brother, who is a police officer.

Reading 8 Family Ties Put a Face on the Faceless Issue of Free Speech
Eric Slater

BACKSTORY

The First Amendment of the Constitution of the United States declares that "Congress shall make no law respecting an establishment of religion, or prohibiting the free exercise thereof; or abridging the freedom of speech, or of the press; or the right of the people peaceably to assemble, and to petition the government for a redress of grievances." Because of this amendment, people in this country are able to write and distribute their ideas freely. But what happens when these ideas call for violence against others? In 1992, rapper Ice-T released a song called "Cop Killer," which included lyrics such as "I'm 'bout to bust some shots off / I'm 'bout to dust some cops off." In the following article from the *Los Angeles Times*, reporter Eric Slater writes about the song, freedom of speech, and his brother, who is a police officer.

LEXICON

beget: create or produce

demigod: a being that is more than human but less than a god

derided: insulted

fervor: earnest enthusiasm

flailing: moving wildly

gangsta rap: a type of hip-hop music spotlighting crime and violence

mantra: holy word or phrase, often repeated for power

mottling: staining with a different color

1   Newspaper writers and rap stars, it is not widely known, have much in common.

2   Stereotypically speaking, both groups are almost impossibly bad dressers—rappers opting for gold, gold, Armani and gold; journalists for lightly stained Dockers. Both work with language and, on the rare fine day, spin mere words into music. And most notably, both are frequently saved from a societal whipping behind the woodshed by the protections of the First Amendment.

3   Brothers of a sort, we are.

4   What, then, to make of my dilemma with rapper Shawn Thomas? In a song called "Deadly Game," Thomas, my free speech brother, advocates the killing of cops.

5   But I hear his words with new ears because now my real brother *is* a cop.

> It's a deadly game of baseball
> So when they try to pull you over
> Shoot 'em in the face, ya'll.

6   Thomas' song is of course not the first by an angry young rock 'n' roller to lash out at police officers, the symbol and sometime instrument of real oppression, racism and brutality. Bob Marley shot the sheriff, but spared the deputy, in his spare, deceptively mellow classic.

7   Ice-T rose to the status of gangsta rap demigod when, in 1992's "Cop Killer," he declared:

> I'm 'bout to bust some shots off.
> I'm 'bout to dust some cops off.

8   But my younger brother Blake wasn't a cop then, he was a high school kid. And when a group of Texas lawmen threatened to disrupt a Time Warner shareholders meeting if the label didn't drop the Ice-T album, I derided them as simple, predictable reactionaries. I defended the rapper with a simple predictable free speech mantra: art does not beget violence. Today, I defend Shawn Thomas, who records under the name C-BO, with equal fervor but more thought, and—whether art begets violence or not—with the image of my little brother lying by the side of a road, shot in the face.

9   It was a year ago that the shades of gray began mottling my black and white mental canvas of artistic expression.

10   Two other reporters and I had stopped at the Tower Records in Northridge on our way back to the office from lunch. I don't recall which albums I picked up, or which the other passenger picked up. I only recall that the reporter who was driving that day grabbed Ice-T's 5-year-old album, "Body Count." Back in the car, he slid it into the CD player and punched up the song that made Ice-T a star, "Cop Killer."

11   We all cackled—not at the notion of killing cops, certainly, but because this rant of true and deep urban anger seemed a little silly now, having become a hit in Toledo and Yakima as well as South-Central L.A., and because Ice-T had become a well-paid movie actor with a television sitcom in pre-production.

12   My laugh, though, was not as hearty as it might have been. My little brother had become a cop by then, a deputy sheriff in Boise, Idaho. I figured I could still chuckle because Blake had drawn jail duty, where not even the officers carry firearms. He broke up brawls and held down screeching, flailing mental cases until they could be ushered off to safer facilities.

> Cop killer, I know your family's grievin'
> Cop killer, but tonight we get even.

13   By late last year, Blake was itching to get out of the Ada County Jail and onto the street. He was quickly hired by the police department in Nampa, a suburb of Boise and a nice quiet place to settle in with his wife and two young, ballet-dancing daughters.

14   He had been at his new job thirty minutes—half an hour into his very first day—when a call came.

15   A white Mercury Cougar matching the description of one driven by a federal fugitive was flying through town. The driver should be considered armed and dangerous. He had vowed never to return to prison.

16   After a high-speed chase, the suspect high centered his car on the tracks at the railroad yard and ran. Blake was close enough to see that the gun in the man's hand was a .45-caliber semiautomatic, the classic 1911 model Army pistol.

17   Blake drew his Glock .40-caliber and sprinted after the man. The fugitive ran to an old railroad car, and turned. He saw Blake closing on his left, two state troopers on his right. He raised the gun to his right temple. And as Blake watched through the sights of his own weapon, the man killed himself.

18   Later at the hospital, when the physicians had officially declared the fugitive dead and left the room, Blake stayed with him for a few minutes. He wasn't trying to understand why he'd done it. That would be impossible. He wasn't questioning his actions or those of the other officers.

19   He was just trying to take in a little death, he told me later. He wanted to quietly immunize himself, just a bit, against the violence that would become part of his daily life.

20   Then he went home.

21   I stopped the other day at the same record store where my reporter friend had picked up Ice-T's album. A couple of weeks had passed since the state parole board decided that C-BO had violated parole with the anti-law enforcement lyrics in "Til My Casket Drops"— a decision the board swiftly and properly reversed. I wanted to hear the CD.

22   It wasn't selling so well, an employee said, and they had knocked $4 off the price.

23   In the album's liner notes, before he thanks his parents for giving him "the motivation and talent to go after what I want, which is millions," C-BO thanks God for giving him 25 years of life.

24   My brother Blake, who will defend C-BO's right to rap about shooting cops until the day he dies, is just 25 himself.

QUESTIONS FOR THOUGHT

1. The article opens with a comparison of rappers and newspaper writers and ends with a comparison between the author's brother (a police officer) and C-BO (a rapper). Why does Slater choose such an introduction and conclusion?

2. In paragraph 21, Slater states that he bought a copy of C-BO's "Till My Casket Drops." Why does he want to hear the song?

3. In paragraph 23, Slater writes, "In the album's liner notes, before he thanks his parents for giving him 'the motivation and talent to go after what I want, which is millions,' C-BO thanks God for giving him 25 years of life." Why does he include this bit of information? How does this compare with his description of Ice-T in paragraph 11: "a well-paid movie actor with a television sitcom in pre-production"?

4. While there is freedom of speech, you can be arrested for shouting "Fire!" in a crowded theater if, in fact, there is no fire. Should there be other limits on certain speech? What types of speech should have limits? What should those limits be?

READY

Comparison and contrast essays require a close analysis and exploration of your topic. You can, of course, compare and contrast elements that are obvious—colors, shapes, or sizes. But your audience will read for more insight. You must think beyond the superficial traits and pull out elements of your topic that may have never been explored in a particular way before. To get this type of depth, you have to be familiar with your topic, your audience, and your purpose.

Topic, Audience, and Purpose

As I mentioned before, a big difference between comparison and contrast writing strategy and other writing strategies is two topics versus one. The two topics cannot be chosen at random. You need a basis of comparison. I can't compare a citrus fruit and a poorly made car. They may both be lemons, but there is no real basis for comparison. Two music CDs would work wonderfully for a comparison and contrast paper, however. When we compare a Jennifer Lopez CD with a Dave Matthews Band CD, we have immediate points of comparison. Both Jennifer Lopez and Dave Matthews are popular, especially to the college crowd. Both have cutting-edge musical styles. Can we, as thinkers and writers, find even more depth to discuss? When you consider other elements of the performers, such as concerts, lyrics, professional and personal lives, and the fans each attracts, you find more points of comparison for your essay.

Next, consider your audience. What background information do they have about your topics and points of comparison? What is your audience's attitude toward your topics and points of comparison? If, for example, your audience likes Jennifer Lopez but can't see any similarities between her style and that of Dave Matthews's alternative rock style, then you will have to go into much more detail about Dave Matthews. But, if your audience hasn't heard of either entertainer, you must begin with background information on both musicians.

Finally, examine your purpose for writing the paper. Educating your audience is a typical purpose for a comparison and contrast essay. Persuasion can also be a purpose. Soft drink ads are good examples of persuasion. Diet Soda X has fewer calories than Diet Soda Y. Diet Soda Y, however, has an instant winner contest, complete with cash prizes. To encourage people to choose Diet Soda Y, you would highlight the contest and downplay the number of calories it has. If you choose to persuade your audience, make sure that point is clear in your thesis statement. Otherwise, your audience will feel as though you are manipulating them.

Analysis

When you evaluate, you draw conclusions and support those conclusions with detailed information. Let's say you feel your writing instructor is a stronger teacher than your math instructor. Perhaps the writing instructor explains a concept a number of different ways, while the math teacher approaches everything from the same angle. Maybe the writing instructor waits for questions while the math instructor plows ahead from concept to concept. In a comparison and contrast essay, you must explain the ways in which your writing instructor is a stronger teacher, and must also show where your math instructor is weaker.

In "Family Ties Put a Face on the Faceless Issue of Free Speech," Eric Slater sets up the comparisons and contrasts he will explore within the essay. He connects newspaper reporters and rappers such as Shawn Thomas (who recorded "Deadly Game"), whom he calls his "free speech brother." A few paragraphs later, he adds his own brother to the mix, as his brother is a police officer and "Deadly Game" advocates the killing of police officers. By paragraph 9, we can see the elements that Slater will compare and contrast in his essay. We can also see that these comparisons and contrasts are not easy to make. On one hand, Slater champions free speech; he is, after all, a newspaper reporter. On the other hand, that same freedom allows rappers to express rage toward those who are supposed to serve and protect the public but abuse their power. Once Slater establishes these points of comparison and contrast, he moves into a narrative that will help us understand his concerns with free speech.

The Comparison and Contrast Brainstorming Worksheet

This chapter's brainstorming worksheet highlights the points of comparison you will use to evaluate or explain your topics. It also calls on you to explain why you chose those certain points of comparison. After that, you evaluate the topics. At the end of the sheet, you can add information about the topics that wasn't already covered earlier.

Comparison and Contrast Brainstorming Worksheet

Topic: _____

Audience: _____

Purpose: _____

Main Points

Point	Comparison	Contrast

Analysis: _____

_____

_____

_____

Thesis statement: _____

_____

_____

_____

Conclusion: _____

_____

_____

_____

Exercises

1. Select a brother, sister, or close friend and brainstorm similarities and differences in your lifestyles. (Use a copy of the worksheet from this chapter.) Choose three points of comparison and explain why these are appropriate ways to evaluate two human beings.

2. Evaluate two classes you are currently taking. Set up a list of points of comparison for them and explain why these points are appropriate.

3. Look closely at the two photographs that follow. What differences are striking? What similarities? Fill out a Comparison and Contrast Brainstorming Worksheet for an essay comparing and contrasting the way writing was done in the 1930s with the way it is done today.

An office typing pool in the 1930s   *A modern newsroom*

WRITE

Now that you have filled out the Comparison and Contrast Brainstorming Worksheet, you can begin writing your essay. Start by selecting the most appropriate points of comparison. After that, be careful to develop each comparison fully, including enough information so your audience can follow your evaluation.

Select

Suppose you look at your two topics and find twenty or more differences you could develop in your essay. You may use the Comparison and Contrast Brainstorming Worksheet but that may only limit your list to six or seven. How do you choose which to use in a comparison and contrast essay? When you are selecting the points for discussion, focus on those that show the widest contrasts or the closest comparisons. Approaching your writing from this angle will make the draft stronger. Return, briefly, to this chapter's opening discussion comparing high school to college. I didn't talk about similarities such as both have teachers, desks, classrooms, chalkboards, and the like. These things are similarities, but they are not substantial enough for an essay. Instead, I focused on larger elements—athletics, self-motivation, cost—that can be developed more profitably. In the Slater essay, we see comparisons between two "brothers"—one a brother by birth, the other a brother through free speech, each an opposite to the other. Think about opposites and extremes as you create your comparison and contrast paper.

Make Your Homework Help Your Writing

Always do your homework thoroughly. Comparison and contrast essays require reasonable knowledge of your topics. "Reasonable knowledge" includes what you already know; however, you may be compelled to do further research. After all, lack of knowledge about the topics can jeopardize the accuracy of your evaluations. You can't very well say that your writing instructor is a better instructor than your math instructor if you haven't been to each instructor's class. Expanding your knowledge can be as simple as paying more attention or as challenging as reading all the latest research on the subject. Be sensible. Don't go overboard expanding your knowledge of the subjects. In general, reading an article or two about the topics will provide plenty of information.

Structure

Generally speaking, an effective way to organize a comparison and contrast essay is to start with obvious similarities and differences and work your way toward points of comparison that have more depth. Using this approach helps ease your audience into your essay. The paragraphs that constitute the body of this type of essay should focus on one similarity or difference apiece. Devoting an entire paragraph to a single point affords you the space to provide adequate detail for your analysis. Finally, unite your two topics in your conclusion.

Introduction

The opening paragraphs must clearly announce the topics you are going to discuss as well as the points of comparison. Look at the first three paragraphs of "Family Ties Put a Face on the Faceless Issue of Free Speech":

> Newspaper writers and rap stars, it is not widely known, have much in common.
>
> Stereotypically speaking, both groups are almost impossibly bad dressers—rappers opting for gold, gold, Armani and gold; journalists for lightly stained Dockers. Both work with language and, on the rare fine day, spin mere words into music. And most notably, both are frequently saved from a societal whipping behind the woodshed by the protections of the First Amendment.
>
> Brothers of a sort, we are.

Here, Eric Slater establishes that his essay will follow a comparison and contrast writing strategy. Paragraph 2 shows three ways that reporters and rappers are similar: bad clothing, language, and protection under the First Amendment. In the next few paragraphs, Slater introduces yet another element—his brother, who is a police officer—and, with that, a point of contrast.

> What, then, to make of my dilemma with rapper Shawn Thomas? In a song called "Deadly Game," Thomas, my free speech brother, advocates the killing of cops. But I hear his words with new ears because now my real brother is a cop.

> > It's a deadly game of baseball
> > So when they try to pull you over
> > Shoot 'em in the face, ya'll.

These paragraphs set up the essay's point of discussion: defending free speech even when that speech condones violence. As you write your introduction, be sure to highlight your topics and their points of comparison and contrast.

Thesis Statement   Write a straightforward thesis statement in which you give your opinion about the topics and solidify the comparison and contrast nature of the essay. The audience joins the discussion of the topics at the thesis statement, so it must be clear. Paragraph 8 of "Family Ties Put a Face on the Faceless Issue of Free Speech" describes the author's complex thinking about free speech and includes the essay's thesis statement.

> But my younger brother Blake wasn't a cop then, he was a high school kid. And when a group of Texas lawmen threatened to disrupt a Time Warner shareholders meeting if the label didn't drop the Ice-T album, I derided them as simple, predicable reactionaries. I defended the rapper with a simple predictable free speech mantra: art does not beget violence. Today, I defend Shawn Thomas, who records under the name C-BO, with equal fervor but more thought, and—whether art begets violence or not—with the image of my little brother lying by the side of a road, shot in the face.

The first few sentences show Slater's attitude toward free speech before his brother became a police officer. Basically, those officers who called for limits on the Ice-T album were overreacting. However, his cavalier attitude changes after his brother becomes a member of the force. Even though he still supports free speech, Slater recognizes a possible consequence of that speech: his brother's death. This idea is clearly stated in the last sentence, which operates as the thesis statement: "Today, I defend Shawn Thomas, who records under the name C-BO, with equal fervor but more thought, and—whether art begets violence or not—with the image of my little brother lying by the side of a road, shot in the face." Slater gives his point of view in this sentence.

Persuasion presents a slight problem with comparison and contrast essays. In the thesis statement, you are to present your topics and your opinions based on the points of comparison. Be careful not to come down too heavily with your opinion, thus making this a persuasion essay. Just present the contrast or comparison, give your preference, then let the reader decide.

Conclusion   The concluding paragraphs of a comparison and contrast essay should tie the ideas together and return to the differences or similarities mentioned in the introduction. Be sure to keep the conclusions simple, perhaps just a reflection of the thesis statement and the points of comparison made in the essay. Do not add any new comparisons or contrasts. New points won't have enough development if they are added as an afterthought.

In "Family Ties Put a Face on the Faceless Issue of Free Speech," Slater combines two writing strategies to flesh out his conclusion. He begins the conclusion in paragraph 21 with a short narrative:

> I stopped the other day at the same record store where my reporter friend had picked up Ice-T's album. A couple of weeks had passed since the state parole board decided that C-BO had violated parole with the anti-law enforcement lyrics in "Til My Casket Drops"—a decision the board swiftly and properly reversed. I wanted to hear the CD.
>
> It wasn't selling so well, an employee said, and they had knocked $4 off the price.

With the narrative, Slater thematically draws the three principal characters in the story together: himself (who purchased the CD), Shawn Thomas (who recorded the CD), and Blake (the "anti-law enforcement lyrics" bring to mind Slater's concern for his brother's well-being). From here, the conclusion morphs back into a compare and contrast strategy with the last two paragraphs:

> In the album's liner notes, before he thanks his parents for giving him "the motivation and talent to go after what I want, which is millions," C-BO thanks God for giving him 25 years of life.
>
> My brother Blake, who will defend C-BO's right to rap about shooting cops until the day he dies, is just 25 himself.

Slater leaves us with the two important elements of his article, the comparison of the two people he feels connected to in different ways, and his struggle to be comfortable with those connections. This is a shining example of what every good conclusion should do.

Organization

You can organize a comparison and contrast essay two ways. First, you can compare and contrast two subjects. In this arrangement, you must determine the points you want to explore. Each body paragraph focuses on one of the points and is developed with a few sentences about each topic. The other way to organize a comparison and contrast essay is by discussing one topic in its entirety and then discussing the second topic, using the same points of evaluation.

For his article, Slater begins with a strict comparison of newspaper reporters and rap stars. Throughout the piece, however, he intertwines elements of the rapper and the police officer for both comparison and contrast. In one section, for example, Slater writes about not taking the lyrics of the song "Cop Killer" seriously because the song's artist, Ice-T, was more of a performer than a gangster. Within the next paragraph, in contrast, Slater mentions that his laughter "was not as hearty as it might have been" because his brother had just become a police officer. Slater carefully chooses the elements of each topic he is comparing and contrasting to reflect his topic sentence.

Whichever strategy you select for writing your comparison and contrast essay, be sure to be clear. Be clear in comparing the topics. Be clear in showing the contrasts. And always be sure that the comparisons and contrasts reflect the main ideas you are putting forth in your piece of writing.

Exercises

4. Expand the criteria list from either Exercise 1 or 2 into an essay. Be sure to refer to your brainstorming sheets often.

5. Choose two styles of music or two musicians you like and write a comparison and contrast essay. Fill out the brainstorming sheet to be clear on the points of comparison you are using for your evaluation.

6. Using a pen and a notebook, write a short letter to a friend about your writing class. Soon after, compose a second letter, this time using a computer and printer. Take notes on the experience of writing in two different media. Write a paragraph or two on the similarities or differences between composing a letter with a pen and with a computer.

REVISE

You must review your work on a comparison and contrast essay with an eye to development and clarity. Start with the points of comparison. Are these points clearly explained in the essay? From there, move to each body paragraph. Is each evaluation fair? Is sufficient explanation and detail provided for each? Look at your introduction and conclusion. Make sure the ideas mentioned in the introduction are reflected in the conclusion. The heart of the essay should beat smoothly now. At this point, return to the beginning and read the entire essay straight through, looking for general problems in clarity and development. Make awkward passages clear. Highlight or underline any place where the evaluation drifts away from its original idea.

STUDENT SAMPLE

Li was faced with writing a comparison and contrast essay for her English class. She brainstormed a number of topics, all of which centered on her life at home. Li's parents are from Japan, and Li is the first generation in her family to be born in the United States. When she was growing up, Li heard stories and tales about life in Japan. She especially remembers her mother's experiences with the different cultural attitudes toward women. Li hadn't written about the contrasts before and thought this writing project would be a good place to do so.

First, Li needed a good set of criteria. She listed a few on a scrap sheet of paper and then filled out both the TAP Worksheet and the Comparison and Contrast Brainstorming Worksheet.

Comparison and Contrast Brainstorming Worksheet

Topic: _My mother and me_

Audience: _People unfamiliar with the differences between me and my mother_

Purpose: _To educate readers on the differences_

Main Points

Point	Comparison	Contrast
Family Obligations	Mother takes care of everyone first	I take care of myself.
Education	Limited—not a priority in her life	Mother wants me to be educated.
Holidays	Celebrates Chinese holidays	Celebrates Chinese and American holidays.
Freedoms	Didn't have much in her life	I have a lot more than she did.

Analysis: _Our situations have led us to being very different people in terms of family, education, and holidays. I guess things like that can have an impact on who we are._

Thesis statement: _My life is different from my mother's in three basic ways—family, education, and the holidays we celebrate._

Continued

Conclusion: <u>My mother and me are different people when</u>
<u>it comes to family, education, and celebrations.</u>

Li had originally thought to write about the differences of family, education, and holidays, but she realized that holidays would be too general a subject. After all, she was going to educate her audience on the differences between her and her mother, so all three points of comparison should be focused that way as well. She replaced holidays with freedom. Immediately, she knew she could write the paper and created the following rough draft.

My life is different from my mother's in three basic ways. Family, education, and freedom to do what you want when you want to. First of all, family. To my mother, family is everything, to the point where you don't do anything for yourself. You just take care of your family. She served her husband and made sure we had clean clothes and did our homework and all of that stuff. But I don't remember seeing her do anything for herself. She had very limited education. To her, education is for men, not for women. They just need to know the best way to take care of her man. That's why she likes Oprah so much. She gets cooking tips. It is funny. I thought about dropping out of school, but she wouldn't let me. She said that I needed education. Weird! Anyway, freedom is last. Freedom to do what you want to do when you want to do is what I want. My mother doesn't want that. She only goes to the store or to visit a friend. She doesn't do more than that and she doesn't care to, I guess. She hasn't said much if she did. Anyway, my mom is different from me in terms of family, education, and having freedom.

As she reread her draft, she marked areas that had to be improved.

More to introduction   My life is different from my mother's in three basic ways. Family, education, and freedom to do what you want when you want to. First of all, family. To my mother,

I should have a paragraph for each point. family is everything, to the point where you don't do anything for yourself. You just take care of your family. She served her husband and made sure we had clean clothes and did our homework and all of that stuff. But I don't remember seeing her do anything for herself. She had very limited *Talk about the GED conversation here.* education. To her, education is for men, not for women. They just need to know the best way to take care of her man. That's why she likes Oprah so much. She gets cooking tips. It is funny. I thought about dropping out of school, but she wouldn't let me. She said that I needed education. Weird! Anyway, freedom is last. Freedom to do what you want to do when you want to do is what I want. My mother doesn't want that. She only goes to the store or to visit a friend. She doesn't do more than that and she doesn't care to, I guess. She hasn't *This is too much like the beginning.* said much if she did. Anyway, my mom is different from me in terms of family, education, and having freedom.

Is it really weird? That makes Mother sound strange.

Her parents made her this way. Should that go here?

Finally, she wrote this polished draft.

Li X_____

ENGL 101

4/13/00

My Mother and Me

The day I graduated from high school ten years ago, my mother whispered in my ear, "This is the dream I have always wanted for me and for you." We share this dream and very little else. I am my mother's daughter, but we are not alike in many ways, especially with respect to having a family, having an education, and having freedom.

Family is the first way that I am different from my mother. We both believe family is important, but she thinks that all a woman needs to do is serve her family to the point where she won't do anything for herself. She served my father and made sure we had clean clothes and did our homework. I don't remember seeing her do anything for herself. With me, things are different. I feel that family is important but we all work together. In fact, I am waiting to get married until I can find a man who will work with me and not expect me to work for him.

Education is another way that we differ. My mother never finished high school. She dropped out to take care of her mother when she was ill and then met my dad. I encouraged her to get her GED; she won't do that. It doesn't make sense to her to waste her time studying when she has lived her life. But she made sure that I finish my education. Late last year, I thought about quitting school. The pressure was just too great. When I told my mother, she got very sad. "You should finish your education, Li-Li," she said. "You need it."

Freedom is the third way we are different. My mother has very little freedom; I have a lot. My grandparents were strict and made my mother account for every minute she was not at home. Even when she was older, my grandfather forbade her to date until he found the right man for her. I am completely different. I can come and go as I please and have always been allowed to. I can choose who I want to date.

My mother and I both have dark hair, are about the same height, and we share the same smile. But we differ when it comes to family, education, and freedom. And I am glad that we do. I don't think I could live her life, nor could she live mine.

CHAPTER REVIEW

With a comparison and contrast essay, you show similarities (comparisons) or differences (contrasts) between two different but related topics. You shouldn't focus on the surface details, such as size, color, or shape. With a good comparison and contrast essay, you must get below the surface. Seek to compare and contrast elements people haven't realized are present. List all of the possibilities and then choose the traits that are extremes. Make sure these points of comparison are clearly defined before you begin your evaluation. Support evaluation with detailed information, thus creating your body paragraphs. In the introduction, be sure to define the two topics you will evaluate. In the conclusion, summarize the points of comparison.

Final Writing Assignments

1. Compare or contrast your life with that of your parents or grandparents. In what ways do their schooling, travels, and life experiences compare with yours? Write an essay describing your life as compared to theirs. Make sure each point of comparison is clear and that you provide detailed support for each point.

2. Revise your response to Exercise 5 to create a polished essay. As you revise, use the brainstorming sheet and notes on your rough draft. Once you have polished and edited you draft, submit it to your instructor.

3. Write a response to Eric Slater's "Family Ties Put a Face on the Faceless Issue of Free Speech." Reread the essay, highlight the sections you want to discuss in your reading response, and then create your rough draft. Develop your points, add an introduction and conclusion, and then polish your draft. Closely edit and proofread your work. Submit this essay to your instructor.

4. With a partner, brainstorm a list of interests or activities you like. Read over the list carefully. Do you share any interests? How about activities? What are the major differences you two have? Choose similarities or differences and, with your partner, write a comparison or contrast essay.

5. Investigate ways that cultures other than your own celebrate birthdays, holidays, or any other special day. Write an essay that shows their differences or similarities to your customs. Be sure you include an introduction, conclusion, and development for your body paragraphs.

9

CAUSE AND EFFECT

In 1966, *Star Trek* debuted. The science fiction adventure drama documented the journeys of the intrepid crew of the starship *Enterprise*, who searched the galaxy for "new life and new civilizations." The show was canceled three years after it premiered, lasting only seventy-nine episodes. Almost forty years later, the *Star Trek* franchise is still strong and shows no signs of slowing. Most recently, a new series, *Enterprise*, debuted, and yet another feature film has been planned. The show has had far-reaching effects on American culture and our views of the future.

One major effect of *Star Trek* can be seen in the space program. One of the first space shuttles NASA built was named *Enterprise*. When it was unveiled, the cast of the original *Star Trek* show was invited, as was Gene Roddenberry, the show's creator. Many of the astronauts in the space program cite *Star Trek* as the source of their interest in space when they were children.

Star Trek has also had an effect on our vision of the future. When the show first aired, the United States was dealing with racial politics and internal strife. People marched on Washington, riots broke out in the streets, and many wondered if we were ever going to learn to live together. Every week on *Star Trek*, viewers saw Asian, African, Russian, Scottish, American, and even alien people living and working together without regard for color or creed, providing a vision of unity.

As entertainment, *Star Trek* has had the biggest effect on our culture. Consider the slew of movies based on old television shows, like *The Brady Bunch*, *Mission: Impossible*, and *Charlie's Angels*. *Star Trek* started that trend with *Star Trek: The Motion Picture*, released in 1979, ten years after the original show was canceled. Spinoffs were also made popular due to the success of *Star Trek*'s sister series *Star Trek: The Next Generation*, *Star Trek: Deep Space Nine*, *Star Trek: Voyager*, and, currently, *Enterprise*.

Who would have thought that a low-budget science fiction show would have such an impact on American society and entertainment as a whole?

This chapter focuses on writing cause and effect essays. Here, you will learn to connect concepts through their causes and effects. In addition, you will learn to select and develop evidence for your cause and effect theses. After that, you will learn how to structure a cause and effect essay and to present cause and effect relationships with solid evidence and strong transitions.

To continue our discussion of cause and effect, let's move to this chapter's main reading, entitled "Comfortable Energies." This essay focuses on something that many people don't realize may affect them: the arrangement of their living space.

Reading 9 Comfortable Energies

Jenny Liu

BACKSTORY

Imagine you just moved into a house. Weeks later, you can't get a good night's sleep. You feel depressed and moody. Your personal relationships begin to sour. "These things just happen," would be a natural response. But what if there was another explanation? What if the arrangement of your living space or the house itself was causing these problems? In the following essay published in the online magazine *Qi: The Journal of Traditional Eastern Health and Fitness*, Jenny Liu, an architect and designer, argues that we must pay close attention to our living areas, for these physical spaces influence our personal energies.

LEXICON

aura: energy field that surrounds people

catastrophe: major emergency or problem

calamity: major upset or upheaval

feng shui: (pronounced "fun shway") an Eastern philosophy centered on the relationship between physical surroundings and human energies

foreclosure: when a bank assumes the loan on a house due to lack of payment by the owners

malice: evil intent

profusion: a large amount

qi: (pronounced "chee") energy

1   Our body contains energy or "qi" that is sensitive to our surroundings. The shape of our bodies, our facial features, our posture and physical appearance are clues that tell us about the energy we possess. Likewise, a building's form, structure and interior layout reflect the energies that it embodies. Feng shui is a study of the cause and effects that occur from the interaction of various people in different places.

2   When a house's energies match our body's energy, it lets us feel comfortable—there's a sense of security and confidence. Very often when we shop for a house, we tend to settle in houses that have similar energies. However, this does not necessarily mean that the house is good for us. For instance, people with low or negative energy may feel most at home in a house that also has weak energies—unfortunately, this usually causes them trouble or illness. People who have a pattern of money problems may unknowingly chose to live in a house with energies that cause financial instability. The following is a recent case that reflects this:

3   Simon bought a new house and wanted me to check the feng shui. As I drove towards his home, there were several hints that this is a house of money loss and loneliness. The number of his address adds up to one, a symbol of being alone. The house is located by itself on the top of a hill. Although the view is magnificent, this site has no energy because it stands unprotected. There are no mountains or hills around it to shield it from harsh winds or act as a natural container of energy. On all sides, steep slopes let energy or "qi" descend away from the house.

4   The house also has an extremely awkward shape which creates an irregular flow of energy that is conducive to malice and illness. The building's width is greater than the depth and it has a profusion of windows. Both these aspects compounded by the house's shape and site conditions all lead to energy loss. This usually results in catastrophe such as financial difficulties and ultimately, bankruptcy. Simon raised his eyebrows and told me that this house was sold as a foreclosure because the previous owner had gone bankrupt.

5   Although the door opens to the correct direction for Simon's energy field, the entry opens to a driveway overlooking a cliff. There are no bedrooms in the right location for Simon. How did Simon end up buying a house like this? Looking at his aura and his birth chart, his energies are weak and this is an exceptionally bad year for him. Any sort of movement or dramatic change in his life would lead to unforeseen challenges that will cause him much misery and pain. I highly recommended for him not to move this year. He replied that he had to move. Last year, there were four deaths in his family, he was involved in a law suit and suffered severe stress. He wants change.

6   He asked if there was anything he could do to adjust this house's feng shui. I explained to him that it is very difficult because even if the house is dramatically remodeled, the site cannot be changed. The best thing he could do for himself is to postpone moving and use this year to strengthen his own energies through meditation, proper diet, and good deeds. This way, it would be possible for him to release some of his negative energy and try to protect himself through enlightenment and awareness. Looking at Simon's aura, this is not easy because his energy is dark and his life cycle is at a low point—moving into this house may only make things worst.

7   In this type of situation, by reinforcing Simon's energies through deep meditations and positive visualization, as well as taking extra caution in planning, paper work and selecting the best times for any type of construction may help him avoid major calamity. However, I do not recommend long-term residence here. Simon sadly smiled and told me that of all the different houses he saw, this is the one that he felt the best and strongest in, how can this be bad?

8   Sometimes, when we are in times of trouble, our energy is scattered and unfocused—we may not always make the wisest decisions. In the beginning, you may feel comfortable here because the energies are similar to yours and have not affected you yet, but as you live here longer and the house's energy starts to affect you physically, you will find it hard to progress.

9   So, it is important to for us to be aware of how we interact with our surroundings. There are certain patterns that we unknowingly create. Sometimes, we unintentionally walk into a pothole. At times, the only way to success is through failure. However, by opening our minds to understanding the cycles of cause and effect in feng shui, we can intentionally walk into our prosperity.

10   Many times, the best way to know ourselves is through another. From our own perspective, it may be hard to know what is good or bad. Rather than be stuck in a hard situation, peace of mind can be as simple as bringing a set of trained eyes that can see more clearly. In feng shui, by understanding our body's qi and how it responds to surroundings, we can objectively select an environment that is most suitable to enhancing our well being.

QUESTIONS FOR THOUGHT

1. What are your first impressions of feng shui as explained in this article?

2. Reflect on the conditions of your living space, both inside and out. What kind of energy flows around your living area? How does that energy affect you?

3. Feng shui deals primarily with the arrangement of living spaces, since that is where most people spend the majority of their lives. How could feng shui be applied to school buildings or work areas?

READY

You may have heard the adage "Things happen for a reason." Well, in writing terms, that is the basic idea behind cause and effect essays. Event X just doesn't happen; something caused that event to happen. Likewise, Event X will cause Event Y and Event Z to happen. Events X, Y, and Z are connected in some way, and when you write a cause and effect essay, you are writing about those connections.

A deeper discussion of cause and effect is needed before we begin planning and composing. Let's revisit "Comfortable Energies." Feng shui is about the effects of places on people, and the article gives a specific example of this connection. Take a closer look at paragraphs 3 and 4.

Simon bought a new house and wanted me to check the feng shui. As I drove towards his home, there were several hints that this is a house of money loss and loneliness. The number of his address adds up to one, a symbol of being alone. The house is located by itself on the top of a hill. Although the view is magnificent, this site has no energy because it stands unprotected. There are no mountains or hills around it to shield it from harsh winds or act as a natural container or energy. On all sides, steep slopes let energy or "qi" descend away from the house.

The house also has an extremely awkward shape which creates an irregular flow of energy that is conducive of malice and illness. The building's width is greater than the depth and it had a profusion of windows. Both these aspects compounded by the house's shape and site conditions all lead to energy loss. This usually results in catastrophe such as financial difficulties and ultimately, bankruptcy. Simon raised his eyebrows and told me that this house was sold as a foreclosure because the previous owner had gone bankrupt.

Cause is the reason an event occurs. In "Comfortable Energies," the thing that causes or creates problems is the location of the house. On top of the hill, it has no protection. On the other hand, **effect** is the impact or influence an event has on subsequent events. Liu states that the effect of having the house on the hill is that energy ("qi") is drained away, leaving none for Simon.

As you read the essay, it may seem as though cause and effect essays are simply a type of persuasion essay. However, the two writing styles are separate and distinct. Cause and effect essays explore the relationships between events;

often, these relationships are not based on judgments of right or wrong or one point of view versus another. In other words, when writing a cause and effect essay, you are showing the connections for what they are. You are not using the connections as evidence to support a particular point of view.

Topic

Essays on effects usually focus on a single event: the release of a violent movie, voting for X to be student council president, or choosing chemistry as a major. These events could lead to or cause other events. The release of a violent movie could create a backlash against violent movies or inspire some people to violent acts. If Student X becomes student council president, then more international students may participate in student government. Choosing chemistry as a major may eventually lead you to get a Ph.D. These topics inspire thought about what comes after the event.

Essays on cause, however, take a different approach. Suppose a violent movie becomes popular and breaks every box-office record. The movie becomes a phenomenon. You could then analyze the situations that caused the movie to be so popular. Is it just a well-written movie with solid acting and strong plotting, or is there more? What are the social and psychological forces at work that attract people to this type of movie?

Jenny Liu chooses to focus on the effects of feng shui on people. The second paragraph begins with a discussion of how humans are affected by the energies of their living spaces. The following paragraphs show this in motion, as we experience Simon and how the energies of his new house may affect him.

Whether your essay focuses on cause or effect, the idea is to analyze the situation or event. You use the body of the essay to state evidence and support your findings.

Audience

When you are writing a cause and effect essay, analyzing your audience must take place on two levels. First, gather general information about your audience. What is their background on the subject? What would they say are causes or effects in relationship to the topic? What support would be familiar to them or foreign to them? After these questions are answered, you must assess how your audience will react to the points you make. Will the audience be open to your conclusions? Will they take your information as a personal attack? As you analyze your audience, decide how you want to approach information that may be uncomfortable.

The audience for "Comfortable Energies" is readers who are not familiar with feng shui. Liu understands that this audience may be open to the philosophy but uneasy with the concept because it is new. After opening with a definition of feng shui, she gives a more detailed explanation of the cause and effect relationship in paragraph 2:

> When a house's energies match our body's it lets us feel comfortable—there's a sense of security and confidence. Very often when we shop for a house, we tend to settle in houses that have similar energies. However, this does not necessarily mean that the house is good for us. For instance, people with low or nega-

tive energy may feel most at home in a house that also has weak energies—unfortunately, this usually causes them trouble or illness. People who have a pattern of money problems may unknowingly choose to live in a house with energies that cause financial instability.

With the first line, we see the cause and effect relationship between people and place. The rest of the paragraph develops this idea. The audience is now more informed about feng shui and should feel more comfortable with this previously unknown topic.

Purpose

Your primary purpose in writing a cause and effect essay is investigation and analysis. You simply present information, leaving judgment to the reader. Of course, at times you may be tempted to go beyond simply presenting cause and effect information. You may want to use this information to persuade your audience toward a certain point of view. (Turn to Chapter 10 for more information about writing persuasion essays.) Jenny Liu's purpose for writing "Comfortable Energies" is clear. She believes that studying feng shui will help people make better choices about living spaces, which will have a direct and positive affect on their lives.

Causes

Causal essays focus on the reasons a certain event or situation occurred. But how do you analyze an event to find its causes? Select an event or situation. What led to that event? What was taking place locally, nationally, or internationally? On a more personal level, what were you experiencing before the event? Brainstorm ideas that caused this situation to occur. Let's use that fictional violent movie as our topic. What causes a violent movie to become popular? A brainstorming list would look something like this:

Violent movies could be popular because:

People like to see violence in movies.

The stars of the movie are popular.

The storyline is gripping and exciting.

People see violence in movies as entertainment.

No other movies were released that weekend.

The movie reflected a real-life violent situation.

The movie studio spent millions to advertise the movie.

Now we have some ideas about what caused this particular movie to be so popular. Because each of the items on our list relates, in one way or another, to our topic, those relationships are what we will explore in the body of the essay.

Effects

Looking back led us to the cause of a particular event. Looking forward will help us see its effects. In other words, an effect essay analyzes the impact a certain event has or will have on subsequent events. Like cause, effects discussed in the essay have to relate closely to the topic. Effects also have to be reasonable in relation to the event. Suggesting that failing one quiz in a math class will lead to complete academic ruin is exaggeration. Suggesting that failing a quiz will lower your grade in math class is reasonable.

Again, we turn to our violent movie. We find this movie is getting more and more popular, so we decide to analyze the effects it may have on society. This time, our brainstorming list may look like this:

More people will see this movie, making it even more popular.

Sequels and more movies like this one will be made.

More discussions about violence in movies will occur.

Merchandising from the movie will increase.

Although there may be plenty more effects, this is a good beginning. These effects are reasonable and can be supported as you develop your essay.

Combination of Cause and Effect

At times, you may want to discuss both the causes and effects of a topic. The same rule applies: Focus on the relationship of cause and effect. Also, brainstorm toward a balance. Find a similar number of causes and effects so all aspects of the topic are explored equally. Although effect is the focus of "Comfortable Energies," paragraph 5 provides a solid example of how cause and effect are combined.

Although the door opens to the correct direction for Simon's energy field, the entry opens to a driveway overlooking a cliff. There are no bedrooms in the right location for Simon. How did Simon end up buying a house like this? Looking at his aura and his birth chart, his energies are weak and this is an exceptionally bad year for him. Any sort of movement or dramatic change in his life would lead to unforeseen challenges that will cause him much misery and pain. I highly recommend for him not to move this year. He replied that he had to move. Last year, there were four deaths in his family, he was involved in a law suit and suffered severe stress. He wants change.

What caused Simon to choose this certain house? He suffered from weak energy, he experienced tragedy, and he wanted change. What effect will the move have on him? He will experience unforeseen challenges, misery, and pain.

Exercises

1. Read a newspaper or news magazine for an article about a current event. Fill out a TAP Worksheet about the event. On another sheet of paper, brainstorm a list of causes and effects for the event. (Avoid being persuaded by others' thoughts and opinions about the event.)

2. Investigate current events on campus. A good place to begin is with the student activities office or the school newspaper. Make a list of these activities,

choose one, and fill out a TAP Worksheet for it. Brainstorm a short list of causes and effects for the event.

3. Flip through your diary or journal to find a significant point of change in your life, such as starting college. Fill out a TAP Worksheet for this event and then brainstorm a short list of causes for the event and effects this event may have on your life.

Evidence

Cause and effect essays require evidence for support. This evidence must be presented as a connection between the event and the causes or effects you identified in the brainstorming worksheet. To find this evidence, you should do research, seek expert testimony, examine history, and reflect on personal (or human) experiences.

Research   You may not have to work hard to explain a cause or effect relationship; scholars may have beaten you to it. Scan news magazines and scholarly journals for facts and statistics about your topic. Be careful not to go too far with your research, however. You are writing an essay, not a research paper.

Experts   Ask for input from people who know about your topic. Look around your college campus for instructors who have done work in an area that relates to your topic. For example, sociologists, psychologists, and other social scientists study how events are created by or affect society. A botanist or a veterinarian can discuss issues related to plants, animals, and the environment.

History   The past teaches us lessons every day. Past events cause other events. Consider your learning environment. Historically speaking, classes were always taught in a room, complete with desks, chalkboard, and a teacher. But one day, someone thought about teaching classes through the Internet. Now, classrooms are not required. What events in the past caused this new idea for education? How will online classrooms affect the future of education? Ideas like this can lead to great topics. Be careful not to let past information, however, get in the way of new information. History can only speak for the past and guide the present.

Personal (or Human) Experience   Feel free to use your experiences as a basis of cause and effect. Imagine the top-scoring basketball player at your school suddenly quit the team. What would cause that to happen? Maybe you played basketball when you were younger and have experiences that can help you figure out some causes. Personal experience is also fraught with prejudice, which means your evidence may be faulty, so be sure to scrutinize it carefully.

The Cause and Effect Brainstorming Worksheet

Compiling and arranging all of this information can be a challenge; the following worksheet (page 192) should help. Fill it out as completely as possible when planning a cause and effect essay.

Cause and Effect Brainstorming Worksheet

Topic:_____

Audience: _____

Purpose: _____

Causes

1. _____

2. _____

3. _____

4. _____

Effects

1. _____

2. _____

3. _____

4. _____

Thesis Statement:

_____

_____

Evidence
For Point #1:

_____

_____

For Point #2:

_____

_____

For Point #3:

_____

_____

For Point #4:

_____

_____

Conclusion:

_____

_____

Feel free to expand your ideas on another piece of paper.

Exercises

4. Choose a TAP Worksheet from Exercises 1–3. Fill out a Cause and Effect Brainstorming Worksheet to develop your ideas.

5. Reflect on your reasons for attending college. List them and then fill out a TAP Worksheet. After that, complete a Cause and Effect Brainstorming Worksheet.

WRITE

In a perfect world, people would understand your point of view with little effort on your part. You could just present your ideas and move on. In this world, however, presenting your ideas takes a bit more effort, especially with a cause and effect essay. You must explain your point of view and provide evidence or information to support it. The information you need is already on the brainstorming worksheet. You just need to arrange it in such a way that you have an introduction, a thesis statement, body paragraphs (main points and evidence), and a conclusion.

Introduction

A good style of introduction for cause and effect essays is one that immediately connects the audience with the topic at hand. The introduction should also set up the cause and effect tone of the essay. Review the introduction to "Comfortable Energies."

> Our body contains energy or "qi" that is sensitive to our surroundings. The shape of our bodies, our facial features, our posture and physical appearance are clues that tell us about the energy we possess. Likewise, a building's form, structure and interior layout reflect the energies that it embodies. Feng shui is a study of the cause and effects that occur from the interaction of various people in different places.
>
> When a house's energies match our body's it lets us feel comfortable—there's a sense of security and confidence. Very often when we shop for a house, we tend to settle in houses that have similar energies. However, this does not necessarily mean that the house is good for us. For instance, people with low or negative energy may feel most at home in a house that also has weak energies—unfortunately, this usually causes them trouble or illness. People who have a pattern of money problems may unknowingly choose to live in a house with energies that cause financial instability.

The strength of Jenny Liu's introduction lies within the open, informative approach to her topic. Once the topic is introduced, the cause and effect strategy is discussed. The audience is pulled right into the work.

Thesis Statement

The thesis statement for a cause and effect essay should present your perspective on the topic and also mention causes, effects, or both that will be developed within the body paragraphs. While your thesis statement might include a touch of opinion, stay away from heavy persuasion. At the end of the first paragraph of "Comfortable Energies," Jenny Liu states her thesis: "Feng shui is a study of the cause and effects that occur from the interaction of various people in different places." She devotes the rest of the essay to explaining this central point.

Body Paragraphs

Body paragraphs in a cause and effect essay consist of the points (the causes or effects) and evidence that explains and supports those points. Unlike a persuasion essay, in which evidence is presented in hopes of changing audience perceptions, this evidence is presented for purposes of clarification. Each point acts as a topic sentence for a paragraph, with the evidence demonstrated though development, explanation, and detail.

Paragraph 6 of Liu's essay illustrates an effective arrangement of main idea and supporting detail for this writing strategy.

> He asked if there was anything he could do to adjust this house's feng shui. I explained to him that it is very difficult because even if the house is dramatically remodeled, the site can not be changed. The best thing he could do for himself is to postpone moving and use this year to strengthen his own energies through meditation, proper diet, and good deeds. This way, it would be possible for him to release some of his negative energy and try to protect himself through enlightenment and awareness.

Liu offers a few ways that Simon can counteract the house's feng shui. However, as we also see in the paragraph, little can be done because of the location of the house. The details Lui provides help the reader understand the cause and effects better.

Conclusion

Conclusions for cause and effect essays fall into two categories: restatement and reflection. Restating your thesis statement and main points reinforces them. After all, the last thing the reader sees is the conclusion. Placing the main points there will help her retain them. On the other hand, you may want to reflect on the findings in your essay. Reflecting is the act of thinking beyond topic, causes, and effects to find insights. Reflections express your opinion and, in some cases, may even lead you to solutions or to a call to action.

The main idea of "Comfortable Energies" is that feng shui affects the energy of people. Liu used Simon's new house as a case study to illustrate the cause and effect of feng shui on people. In her concluding paragraphs, she ties up the story of Simon and explains the importance of studying feng shui, which she hinted at in the opening.

> So, it is important for us to be aware of how we interact with our surroundings. There are certain patterns that we unknowingly create. Sometimes, we unintentionally walk into a pothole. At times, the only way to success is through failure. However, by opening our minds to understanding the cycles of cause and effect in feng shui, we can intentionally walk into our prosperity.

Many times, the best way to know ourselves is through another. From our own perspective, it may be hard to know what is good or bad. Rather than be stuck in a hard situation, peace of mind can be as simple as bringing a set of trained eyes that can see more clearly. In feng shui, by understanding our body's qi and how it responds to surroundings, we can objectively select an environment that is most suitable to enhancing our well-being.

This ending seems perfect for the essay. No loose ends are left, and Liu expresses her opinion more fully than she was able to in the rest of the essay.

Exercises

6. Using the Cause and Effect Brainstorming Worksheets from Exercise 4 or 5, write a rough draft of a cause and effect essay. Be sure to include an introduction, your thesis statement, the body paragraphs—main points with evidence—and a conclusion.

Select

Even a simple event has many causes and effects. You see a student crying near an elevator. What caused his crying? He left something of importance on the elevator. Maybe his wife just left him. Perhaps he is in severe pain. What are the effects of the situation? Maybe people will just walk by. Maybe someone will stop to help. Perhaps someone will tease him for crying. Because there is an almost unlimited number of causes and effects, you have to choose the causes or effects that you can provide the greatest amount of support for. Your essay will flow better that way.

Liu does a great job of selecting the elements that support her purpose for writing "Comfortable Energies." She wants to show how feng shui affects people and chooses a single case study: Simon and his new house. In paragraph 4, we see a specific example.

The house also has an extremely awkward shape which creates an irregular flow of energy that is conducive of malice and illness. The building's width is greater than the depth and it has a profusion of windows. Both these aspects compounded by the house's shape and site conditions all lead to energy loss. This usually results in catastrophe such as financial difficulties and ultimately, bankruptcy. Simon raised his eyebrows and told me that this house was sold as a foreclosure because the previous owner had gone bankrupt.

Through careful selection, the reader understands how the house's shape (width greater than depth and lots of windows) connects to problems for the homeowners (energy loss, which leads to financial difficulties). No more needs to be said here, so Lui moves on to her next point.

Structure

Cause and effect essays are organized to highlight the causes and effects of an event. After your introduction, clearly state your thesis statement, and then devote one paragraph to each of the causes and effects you are going to discuss throughout the essay. Exhaust the cause or effect in that one paragraph, then move on to the next. Although you can talk about both causes and effects within the same essay and even within the same paragraph, choose this approach carefully. You may find that putting both together creates confusion.

The structure of "Comfortable Energies" reinforces Lui's idea of explaining the causes and effects of feng shui. The reader is introduced to the idea of feng sui and to Simon's energy. At the end of paragraph 7, Simon says, "of all the different houses he saw, this is the one that he felt the best and strongest in; how can this be bad?" Lui answers by going into more detail about energies in the next two paragraphs. Finally, Lui ties everything together in the conclusion. Once again, using this structure, Lui explains feng shui to the reader in a clear and understandable way.

REVISE

In front of you, in rough draft form, sits a list of causes or effects of one event on another. While you have added an introduction and a conclusion, the basic form of the cause and effect essay has not changed. Whatever you are going to discuss in your paper still must be developed through explanation and evidence. As you revise, make sure each point is stated clearly and that the evidence you provide as support does its job. Ask yourself if the evidence you provide is appropriate for your purpose as well as your audience. Also, take a closer look at sections where the presentation of evidence becomes persuasion. Rework areas that seem more centered on changing the mind of your audience than on presenting information. Finally, as you edit your draft, check and recheck the spelling of names and source titles.

STUDENT SAMPLE

Carl was assigned a 500-word cause and effect essay for his English class. The other students seemed to have topics for their papers almost immediately, but Carl struggled to find a topic in which he was interested. He brainstormed a few ideas and then found his topic: math class. During high school, Carl never enjoyed math. The grades for his first math class at college were barely average. However, his second quarter was different. In Dr. Bogswell's algebra course, Carl was inspired, and he excelled. He attended every class, did all of the homework, and passed all of his tests. He even practiced his math skills outside of class. What caused this change, this new awareness of math? That question was going to be answered in his essay.

Carl started with a jot list of things he liked about his math class.

The teacher

Students

Tutoring help before and after class

The building

The textbook

Retaking quizzes if I fail

The time the class is taught

Not as many classes this quarter

    Carl chose the three causes he felt most strongly about: teacher interest, student help, and reduced class load this quarter. The audience was the English teacher, who was familiar with Dr. Bogswell but not did know much about Carl's previous relationship with math or Dr. Bogswell's intervention. Lots of detail was needed. The purpose of writing this essay was to investigate and explain the reasons behind Carl's improvement.

    With all of this in mind, Carl filled out a TAP Worksheet and a Cause and Effect Brainstorming Worksheet.

Cause and Effect Brainstorming Worksheet

Topic: _Math class_

Audience: _other students_

Purpose: _to inform them about changes in my math grades_

Causes

1. _good teacher_
2. _tutoring_
3. _other students_
4. _too many classes_

Effects

1. _went to almost every class_
2. _did all my homework_
3. _passed every test_
4. _did math outside of class_

Thesis Statement

My grade has improved greatly because of Dr. Bogswell's
involvement.

Evidence

For Point #1:

Teacher sat with me and helped me understand
what I missed in class.

Continued

For Point #2:

I got with other students also struggling with math. We studied together and would hang out together. Relaxing.

For Point #3:

I had too many classes before. Now I can concentrate on just two. Relaxing as well.

For Point #4:

_____

_____

Conclusion:

Having a good teacher, other students to lean on, and fewer classes has made a big impact on my math grades.

Feel free to expand your ideas on another piece of paper.

Carl expanded on the information on the worksheets and created this rough draft.

My grade has improved greatly because of Dr. Bogswell's involvement. He is instrumental in getting me to reach my math goals. Math takes up most of my free time. I don't even know why we study math, isn't that why there are calculators? Anyway, Dr. Bogswell at first didn't seem like he was going to help me much. He acted like a regular math instructor and to tell the truth, I was a bit afraid of him. Whatever he did when I asked for help, I don't know. But I liked it because when I went home to do my homework, I knew what I was doing.

People told me college was going to be harder than high school. I didn't know what to expect when I got here, but I never expected something like this. Students were studying together and using old tests. I felt stupid and out of place. But they accepted me and we started hanging out. They are very helpful to me.

I think a big contributing factor to my math downfall was simply too many classes. I had three classes and everything else to keep track of. I was getting stressed, upset, and just didn't want to go on. Having two classes now helps a lot.

Now Carl worked on the introduction. He realized the biggest effect of his new attitude toward math was improved grades, so improved grades became the focus of his introduction.

Introduction

C. C+. C–. These were the grades I had always received in math class. No matter how hard I studied, no matter how many questions I asked in class, no matter how many books I read, I just didn't understand math. I had accepted the fact that I was going to be a math dummy all my life. But all that changed this quarter. Instead of C's, my grades have becomes A's and B's. Now, when I raise my hand in class, I give the right answer. I would like to think that I suddenly got brilliant, but the real causes for my improvement are teacher interest, student help, and a reduced class load. These three things have helped me reach my math potential.

Then Carl worked on the conclusion.

Conclusion

One day, I couldn't do math; the next day, I could. The causes of this sudden turnaround were Dr. Bogswell, the other students in my class, and a reduction in my class load. The three things combined have helped me reach grades I never thought possible. I am very thankful these things came together when they did.

After writing the introduction and conclusion, Carl made notes to revise his essay.

C. C+. C–. These were the grades I had always received in math class. No matter how hard I studied, no matter how many questions I asked in class, no matter how many books I read, I just didn't understand math. I had accepted the fact that I was going to be a math dummy all my life. But all that changed this quarter. Instead of C's, my grades have becomes A's and B's. Now, when I raise my hand in class, I give the right answer. I would like to think that I suddenly got brilliant, but the real causes for my improvement are teacher interest, student help, and

Introduction looks good

a reduced class load. These three things have helped me reach my math potential.

My grade improved greatly because of Dr. Bogswell's involvement. He is instrumental in getting me to reach my math goals. Math takes up most of my free time. I don't even know why we have to study math, isn't that why there are calculators? Anyway, Dr. Bogswell at first didn't seem like he was going to help me much. He acted like a regular math instructor and to tell the truth, I was a little bit afraid of him. Whatever he did when I asked for help, I don't know. But I liked it because when I went home to do my homework, I knew what I was doing.

Is that needed?

Detail—explain what he did

Add more here maybe?

People told me college was going to be harder than high school. I didn't know what to expect when I got here, but I never expected something like this. Students were studying together and using old tests. I felt stupid and out of place. But they accepted me and we started hanging out. They are very helpful to me.

Detail—doesn't make sense

Talk about the movie. That was fun!

I think a big contributing factor to my math downfall was simply too many classes. I had three classes and everything else to keep track of. I was getting stressed, upset, and just didn't want to go on. Having two classes now helps a lot.

I should explain those

One day, I couldn't do math; the next day, I could. The causes of this sudden turnaround were Dr. Bogswell, the other students in my class, and a reduction in my class load. The three things combined have helped me reach grades I never thought possible. I am very thankful these things came together when they did.

I like this. I did a good job here.

With a few minor edits, Carl's final draft looked like this:

Carl J_____

2/22/01

ENGL 100

Thanks, Dr. Bogswell

C. C+. C–. These were the grades I had always received in math class. No matter how hard I studied, no matter how many questions I asked in class, no matter how many books I read, I just didn't understand math. I had accepted the fact that I was going to be a math dummy all my life. But all that changed this quarter. Instead of C's, my grades have becomes A's and B's. Now, when I raise my hand in class, I give the right answer. I would like to think that I suddenly got brilliant, but the real causes for my improvement are teacher interest, student help, and a reduced class load. These three things have helped me reach my math potential.

My grade has improved greatly because of Dr. Bogswell's involvement. He is instrumental in getting me to reach my math goals. I know that I do quite well in writing; I love to write. But math takes up most of my free time. Anyway, Dr. Bogswell at first didn't seem like he was going to help me much. He acted like a regular math instructor and to tell the truth, I was a little bit afraid of him. At the end of the first week of class, I was still struggling with something like addition and Dr. Bogswell asked if I needed help, and I said "Yes!" He sat down with me and went over the hard problems in the book. Whatever he did, I liked it because when I went home to do my homework, I knew how to get the right answer for most of the questions in our assigned homework pages. Now, when I am getting frustrated—and math does get frustrating—I ask for help and things go quite well.

People told me going to college would be a lot harder than high school. I didn't know what to expect when I got here, but I never expected something like this. Many of the students in my math class get together for study time. One even has copies of an old test Dr. Bogswell gave out a few years ago. I felt like an outsider at first, like everyone knew what they were doing except for me. When I saw other students struggling with math too, I thought, "Cool!" The students here were very helpful and friendly. Sometimes we get together to review notes for other classes or just hang out. The other night we all went to see a Jackie Chan movie. It was a good time.

I think a big contributing factor to my math downfall was having too many classes to keep track of. I was taking an English class, a college and career class, a biology class, and trying to keep up with everything else I had to do. There was just too much for one person to do. I was getting stressed, upset, and wanted to drop all of my classes. This quarter, though, I have just two classes: math and English. I can now do all the homework assigned and feel like I am learning math.

One day, I couldn't do math; the next day, I could. The causes of this sudden turnaround were Dr. Bogswell, the other students in my class, and a reduction in my class load. The three things combined have helped me

reach grades I never thought possible. I am very thankful these things came

together when they did.

CHAPTER REVIEW

Through a cause and effect essay, you attempt to explain a situation. With cause, you explain the factors that created or led to a particular event. With effect, you explain the impact a particular event had or will have on subsequent events. As you prepare to write this essay, choose a topic that can be analyzed through cause and effect. Also, analyze your audience for their point of view on the topic, the amount of information about the topic they already possess, and how much explaining will be necessary when you present your information. Finally, your purpose should be to inform your audience of your findings. When writing a cause and effect essay, be sure to develop your points with evidence, information you have gleaned from a number of sources, including research, expert testimony, history, and personal or human experience. In the conclusion, you can either restate the thesis statement and the causes and effects, or you can reflect on the causes and effects you have made within the essay. As you write your essay, select only the causes and effects that you can develop with the body paragraphs of the essay. Structure your essay to highlight your points and to support your thesis statement.

Final Writing Assignments

1. Read the business section of your local newspaper. Find an article about a business that is either closing or laying off employees. Brainstorm factors that caused the closing or layoff, and then write a cause and effect essay. Be sure to support your reasons with information from the article as well as history and other research.

2. Imagine your tuition will be increased by 25 percent next year. List the causes and eventual effects of this increase. Choose either three causes or three effects and write a cause and effect essay. For support of your body paragraphs, consider talking with administrators, teachers, staff, and students at your school.

3. Polish the draft you wrote in Exercise 6. Check the logic of your discussions and argument. Submit the final draft to your instructor.

4. Re-read Jenny Liu's essay "Comfortable Energies" and write a response to it. As you jot down and organize ideas for writing, consider feng shui and its effects on people in general. Write a paper exploring those effects. Perhaps

you might go a different route and write a paper about other causes for people's problems. Either way, be sure to complete a Cause and Effect Brainstorming Worksheet and provide the appropriate evidence to support your insights. Polish your final draft and submit it to your instructor.

5. With a partner, list at least five problems you see around your campus. Next to each problem, write a possible solution to it. Next, list the effects the solution would have beyond solving the problem. Write a cause and effect essay based on your brainstorming.

6. Brainstorm a list of events or situations that affect people in the community, such as layoffs, increased employment, and renovation of abandoned or rundown buildings in your town. Choose one and explore the causes and effects from several cultural viewpoints. For example, how would a business owner feel about laying off employees? How would the employees feel about being laid off? How would a competing business owner feel about those same layoffs? As with other cause and effect essays, be sure to back up your points with evidence.

10

PERSUASION

When people hear the words *martial arts,* they often picture Bruce Lee or Jackie Chan, punching, kicking, chopping, and beating up the bad guys. These Hollywood images do true martial arts practice a great disservice. Martial arts training isn't just about cracking boards or cracking heads; the training is about self-discipline, self-control, and inner peace. Everybody, young and old, should practice martial arts.

First and foremost, martial arts stresses self-discipline. The physical and spiritual training takes a lifetime to master, and every lifetime is made up of single days. Each and every day, one must train, and train hard. Training requires discipline, and training every day helps develop that discipline.

Next, martial arts teaches self-control. When you lose control of yourself, you lose any battle. To be able to fight well, you must have complete control over your body. You must know your strengths and weaknesses. You must get the proper amount of rest and eat well so you are always in top form. Of course, you must also learn to control your spirit so you won't have to physically fight. Holding your temper, releasing your feelings, and walking away when necessary are all examples of spiritual control.

Finally, martial arts is about inner peace. A large part of the training is meditation. Sitting on your knees, hands folded in your lap, eyes closed, you just breathe and listen. When you meditate, you become one with yourself in a way you can't when you are moving through your normal routine. In these moments of meditation, you can be at ease with your life. You get inner peace and continue to draw from it.

Martial arts is an ages-old concept of physical battle. It also focuses on the spirit by helping people develop self-discipline, self-control, and inner peace. Not everyone is able to break concrete blocks with their hands, but we can learn more about our spirits.

The martial arts training just described could be used with writing persuasion essays as well. You don't just grab any topic, write down everything you know, and hope for the best. When writing persuasion essays, you must practice self-discipline in order to focus on your writing task. Next, you must maintain control as you attempt to change people's opinions and not offend or alienate your audience. Last, you should find peace after writing your final draft. You have done what you set out to do, so you can relax and be proud of your writing. Throughout this chapter, we discuss the elements of the persuasion essay, including choosing an effective topic, dealing with a potentially hostile audience, and sticking to your purpose for writing.

Reading "Wise Words from Eminem" by Kathleen Parker is a good way to begin.

Reading 10 | Wise Words from Eminem
Kathleen Parker

BACKSTORY

Popular music has known its share of controversy, from secret messages hidden within lyrics to outrageous performers. One of the most recent controversies focuses on Eminem, a white hip-hop artist. Eminem's fans pack the concerts and buy his CDs by the millions. Opponents claim his music glorifies murder, misogyny, and anarchy. Columnist Kathleen Parker, in a newspaper article, published in 2000, expresses her dislike of Eminem's performances but suggests we as a society should listen carefully to his message.

LEXICON

abhorred: strongly disliked

ergo: therefore; which leads to

loathe: hate

1   As bedfellows go, none could be stranger nor less likely than raunchy rapper champions agreeing on content.

2   If not style.

3   Eminem, for you diehard adults, is a white rapper variously abhorred and adored for his envelope-pushing lyrics.

4   His real ID is Marshall Mathers, ergo Eminem, and his key vocabulary is…reductive.

5   Mathers has never met a multisyllabic word he likes, while body parts and functions say it best.

6   Put it this way: the F-word is to Eminem's world what Om is to Yoga.

7   Which is why parents loathe him while kids are keeping his newest release—*The Marshall Mathers LP*—in the best-seller slot.

8   Parents don't just hate Eminen; many blame him for everything from date rape to school shootings.

9   It's easy to dislike him, I admit.

10   He's excessively profane, offensive to everyone, disrespectful and disgusting.

11   Worse, he's honest.

12   And, unforgivably, he's sometimes right.

13   Some of his worst stuff isn't fit for print, or listening.

14   But he does have a point when he challenges parents to take a hard look at themselves before they flip him the metaphorical bird.

15   In his angry song "Who Knew" on the new album, he asserts surprise over his success and the societal misdeeds for which he gets credit.

16   Imagine a rap beat here and forget everything you know about punctuation, except ellipses, which are mine.

17   The rest are lyrics taken from his "Who Knew" song:

18   "I make fight music, for high school kids I put lives at risk when I drive like this (tires screech) I put wives at risk with a knife like this…I'm sorry, there must be a mix-up. You want me to fix up lyrics while the president…Quit tryin' to censor music, this is for your kids amusement. (The kids!) But don't blame me when lil' Eric jumps off of the terrace You should be watchin him—apparently you ain't parents."

19   I have the uneasy feeling he's referring to Eric Clapton's child, who fell to his death from an apartment window, and I wish he hadn't said that.

20   I wish, too he hadn't said the rest of this, which makes grown-ups squirm for reasons that should be apparent:

21   "I never knew I would get this big I never knew…I'd affect this kid I never knew I'd get him to slit his wrist I never knew…so who's bringin the guns in this country (Hmm?) I couldn't sneak a plastic pellet gun through customs over in London And last week, I seen a Schwarzenegger movie where he's shootin all sorts…and I sees three little kids, up in the front row, screamin, 'Go,' with their 17-year-old uncle I'm like, 'Guidance—ain't they got the same moms and dads who got mad when I asked if they liked violence?' And told me my tape taught 'em to swear. What about the make-up you allow your 12-year-old daughter to wear? (Hmm?)"

22   I'm not recommending Eminem to children, though I commend him to parents who might wish to know what their children are thinkin' and hearin' and what they're sayin' about you behind your back, and consider the possibility that sometimes the words that most offend are the true ones.

23   (Hmm?)

QUESTIONS FOR THOUGHT

1. Suppose a student organization scheduled Eminem to perform at your homecoming. Would you support this decision? Explain your opinion.

2. Why do artists such as Eminem choose popular music as the medium for their messages?

3. Recall a time when you reacted to a medium instead of a message. Why did you react in such a manner?

READY

People want good, strong, well-examined explanations before they consider what you have to say. The President of the United States must persuade Congress to accept a tax cut proposal in much the same way you have to convince your instructor to extend the due date of a writing assignment. Any time you must persuade someone, you must present a strong opinion and then provide equally strong support for that opinion. The opinion and the support are dependent upon topic, audience, and purpose.

Topic

Persuasion essays revolve around controversy, so the topics you choose should be controversial. The topic of Kathleen Parker's essay is Eminem's message within his music. One doesn't have to dig deeply to find the controversy there. Had Parker chosen less controversial artists such as Britney Spears, Eric Clapton, or the Backstreet Boys, her essay may not have had the same effect on her audience.

Self-control should also be a part of choosing your topics. Remember that persuasion essays are informed opinion essays. With an informed opinion essay, you are only writing about a single aspect of a larger topic, using limited research (facts, statistics, and expert testimony) and personal experience to make your point. In other words, this is not a full-blown research paper. You are simply stating your opinion on a topic and supporting that opinion with relevant information. For that reason, your topic should be something about which you have knowledge or can find out about quickly. A persuasion essay on why your school should allow fast-food franchises on campus would be a good topic; chances are you have eaten at a fast-food restaurant, and you attend school. No additional research is necessary. Capital punishment, however, would be off-limits. The amount of research you would have to do would make the task too daunting. Remember your limits and work within them.

Audience

Investigate your audience's concerns and opinions about the topic by asking yourself the following questions:

What does the audience know about the topic?

What is their stance on the issue?

Where do they get their information?

What are some strengths in their line of thinking?

What are some weaknesses in their line of thinking?

The answers to these questions will help you determine your audience's point of view. The answers will also help you evaluate the information on which your audience bases their opinions.

Imagine Kathleen Parker asking herself these evaluation questions as she was preparing to write her column.

- What does the audience know about Eminem and his lyrics?

  Because my column is published in mainstream newspapers, the adult audience is perhaps more mature that the target audience for Eminem's CDs. My readers may not know who he is or know about the content of the music.

- What will be their stance on his lyrics?

  My readers will, most likely, hate his lyrics.

- Where are they getting their information?

They get their information about Eminem from the news and from their children. More involved parents may have actually listened to the CDs.

- What are some strengths in their line of thinking?

Eminem's music is raunchy and vulgar. He seems to exploit women and champion murder and chaos. He uses vulgarity too much, which gets in the way of his message.

- What are some weaknesses?

Eminem does have an important message. Rejecting the message because you don't like the messenger can be dangerous.

Once the audience has been assessed, you must determine if it is friendly, neutral, or unfriendly. Your audience's attitude toward to your topic determines the content of the essay.

Friendly audiences   A friendly audience is one that won't show much resistance to your point of view. These readers already lean your way; they are just looking for more information to support what they believe.

Neutral audiences   These readers sit on the proverbial fence with respect to the issue at hand. They don't have a strong opinion about the topic and seek out other's opinions to help them make decisions.

Unfriendly audiences   An unfriendly audience is staunchly opposed to your point of view. With this type of audience, you must present an extremely compelling argument. Further, you must counter the argument of the opposing side of the controversy.

Parker anticipated an unfriendly audience when she wrote "Wise Words from Eminem." She knew that the mention of Eminem's name would place a barrier between her and the audience. By providing compelling lyrics, Parker hoped to break that barrier and make her audience a little less resistant.

Purpose

Obviously, the purpose in writing a persuasion essay is to persuade your audience to your point of view. Because you are writing a persuasion essay, you must state your purpose clearly in a debatable thesis. A **debatable thesis** is a thesis statement that presents your side of a controversy as the logical, correct side. This type of thesis statement helps the reader understand the focus of your persuasion right up front.

Consider paragraphs 11–14 of Kathleen Parker's essay:

Worse, he's honest.
And, unforgivably, he's sometimes right.
Some of his stuff isn't fit for print, or listening.
But he does have a point when he challenges parents to take a hard look
at themselves before they flip him the metaphorical bird.

In these paragraphs, Parker argues that whether or not you respect him as a performer, Eminem "does have a point when he challenges parents to take a hard look at themselves." Here is her debatable thesis. It is both the heart of the controversy and her point of view.

As you examine your purpose and write your own debatable theses, be clear on your position. While you may be excited and passionate about your topic, your ideas on the controversy may not be clear. As you brainstorm purpose, cut to the center of the controversy and then state your opinion.

Evidence

Imagine a student has told you that your writing class has been canceled for the remainder of the week. Your first reaction may be to celebrate, but afterward, you would probably seek more information to verify this student's claim. Information that verifies claims is called **evidence**.

Evidence is everything in persuasion essays. Presenting solid evidence as support for your point of view is the best way to change people's minds. For our purposes here, evidence is categorized into four groups: authority of experts, facts, statistics, and personal experience.

Expert testimony   Check newspapers, magazines, and television and radio talk shows for expert testimony to support your point. Experts have spent years studying and researching topics, so we tend to rely on their ideas. The authority of experts is useful when dealing with an unfriendly audience because expert testimony makes people take notice. Scrutinize any testimony you may use as support. Check the validity of both the expert and her information. Otherwise, your credibility will be questioned.

Facts   Facts are most often found in reference books, such as dictionaries, encyclopedias, and the like. Basically, any bit of information that is an established truth is a fact. When we say "established truth," we are talking about a statement that is subjective or that can be proved. If I say, "You are now reading a book about writing," you can prove that by looking at the title and flipping through the pages. That is a subjective statement. If a statement cannot be proved, it is considered an objective statement, or one tainted by opinion. If I say "James Bond movies are the best," that is an objective statement because I cannot prove that type of movie is the best. That is just my opinion.

To verify a subjective statement, consult at least three sources. If you find the same information in a number of places, chances are good that the information is a fact. One note, however: Please make sure your sources are distinct. Using three editions of the same newspaper doesn't count. Go to a wide variety of sources to get a broader view of the information.

Both subjective and objective statements can be useful in a persuasion essay. Just be careful to verify facts you present as evidence or support in your essays.

Statistics   Statistics can offer a variety of information for your persuasive essay. Statistics represent research information presented in an easy-to-read and digest format, such as charts or graphs. Statistics can be valuable to your persuasion essay, but be careful. The research used to generate the statistics may not have been done properly. I could conduct a survey revealing that ten students believe that writing class is canceled. If the class has eleven students, that information is useful. If the class has 100, the information is not. Likewise, if I survey only students who often skip class or only students who attend class regularly, then the resulting information will be biased.

Personal experience   For this type of essay, the majority of the evidence you provide will come from your experiences. To help you explore your personal experiences in more detail, use the Self-Reflection Worksheet from Chapter 12 (page 259). A note of caution: Be careful not to base an entire point of view on a single experience. Prejudice, discrimination, even a naïve worldview often centers around limited contact with others.

In "Wise Words from Eminem," Kathleen Parker combines the authority of experts and facts in the evidence she presents to the audience. She speaks of the authority on this topic (in this case, Eminem) and gives the facts (his lyrics) to prove her point. When she quotes lyrics like, "I couldn't sneak a plastic pellet gun through customs over in London. And last week, I seen a Schwarzenegger movie where he's shootin all sorts…" she provides strong evidence, which may persuade her audience to her side of the controversy.

APPEALS

As you prepare to write a persuasive essay, you must consider how you are going to present your information to your audience. A way of presenting information to an audience is called an **appeal**. Being blunt will only scare away your audience or put them on the defensive. You should appeal to your audience's emotions, reason, and values as you plan your presentation.

Appeals to emotion   People often make decisions based on feelings. We buy protection systems for our homes because we are afraid of break-ins. You may sign a petition out of anger that your school tuition is going to increase next semester. Know your audience well if you use this appeal; you want them to have the same emotional response that you do. Otherwise, they will miss the point.

Appeals to reason   We pride ourselves on making sound decisions after we have compared bits of information, done some research, or thought through various aspects of a situation. As you present your point of view, add statistics and factual evidence and let your audience draw their own conclusions. Of course, you can lead your audience to a certain opinion based on the factual evidence you provide.

Appeals to moral code   When you appeal to your audience's moral code, you are appealing to their loyalty to family, friends, country, and lifestyle. People are more likely to consider points of view that will help them maintain their lifestyle. Every society has a moral code, but codes differ from group to group (and even within groups), so approach this aspect of your presentation carefully. The last thing you want is to chase your audience away because you offended them.

For "Wise Words from Eminem," Parker chose to appeal to reason as well as moral code. She states that Eminem has a valid point and offers his lyrics as support. The audience is now forced to consider these lyrics. Parker then appeals to the audience's moral code when she writes, "I'm not recommending Eminem to children, though I commend him to parents who might wish to know what their children are thinkin' and hearin' and what they're sayin' about you behind your back." Understanding children is a large part of the moral code for parents; Parker appeals to that part of the code.

The Persuasion Brainstorming Worksheet

A Persuasion Brainstorming Worksheet is included on the next page to help you collect your thoughts and organize your essay. Be sure to fill it out completely, along with a TAP Worksheet and a Self-Reflection Worksheet. All three can help you create a good foundation for your persuasion essays.

Persuasion Brainstorming Worksheet

Topic:_____

Audience: _____

What does the audience know about the topic?

_____

_____

What is their stance on the issue?

_____

_____

Where are they getting their information?

_____

_____

What are some strengths in their line of thinking?

_____

_____

What are some weaknesses in their line of thinking?

_____

_____

Purpose:

_____

Debatable Thesis:

_____

_____

Evidence:

_____

_____

_____

Appeals:

_____

_____

_____

Exercises

1. Brainstorm a list of topics of controversy in your community or on your campus. Choose one and fill out a Persuasion Brainstorming Worksheet. Why do you think this would be a good topic for a persuasion paper?

2. Read through five letters to the editor published in a local newspaper. Jot down the topic, audience, and purpose for each letter. Reread each letter. Where could the authors have improved their letters in terms of focusing on topic, audience, and purpose?

3. With a partner, brainstorm a list of controversial topics. Place each topic in one of two categories: persuasion essays and research papers. Discuss your choices for each topic. With adjustment, which topics could be placed in both categories?

WRITE

Strategy is the focus of the persuasion writing strategy. You must state your point of view clearly and support it well. To do this, you must carefully choose the information you will use as support. If your support is lacking, you weaken your argument. You also must be sure not to alienate or offend your audience. Your purpose is to influence people to see that your point of view is the most valid. To fulfill this mission, you once again must be careful about what information you provide throughout your discussion.

Select

As you select information for the essay, determine the type of audience you have. If the audience is friendly, then the argument will be fairly easy to make. Select support from your personal experiences and include a few facts. Be sure to appeal to the emotions, especially the positive ones, as your audience is already on your side. A neutral audience will take more convincing, so focus on facts and statistics. Personal experience would also work, but remember that your experience may not be typical and may alienate this audience. Because neutral audiences are willing to consider your point of view, feel free to use any of the appeals. If the audience is unfriendly, be prepared to do a lot of convincing. Focus solely on facts and statistics and stay away from personal experience. Facts and statistics, although they can be manipulated, are not as likely to show the same prejudices or faults as personal experiences are. This audience is looking for weaknesses in your argument, so focus on the appeal to reason. Anything else may appear superficial.

As we established earlier in this chapter, the audience for "Wise Words from Eminem" was probably unfriendly. This audience, made up of parents and older adults, doesn't want to hear that they need to examine their parenting styles or that the dreaded rapper Eminem should be taken seriously. Parker is careful to let the facts speak for themselves and appeals to her audience's reason and moral code. There is one weakness here, however: Parker uses only one song to make her point. The rest of Eminem's music portfolio could be nowhere near as insightful or meaningful as this particular song. But because Parker does appeal to the reason of her audience, they understand that this song represents Eminem on a larger scale. She lets her audience draw their own conclusions.

Structure

Presenting your argument in writing requires explanation. You first must explain your topic through summary in the introduction. From there, you explain your point of view through your debatable thesis and the points you discuss in your essay. You also explain faults in opposing viewpoints. Finally, your conclusion serves as a way to explain, once again, your thesis.

Introduction   An introduction for a persuasive essay should begin with a short bit of background on your topic. Be as neutral as possible when you are talking about the topic; you don't want to alienate your audience within the first few sentences of your essay. Wait until the end of the introduction to include your debatable thesis.

Kathleen Parker begins her essay with this overview of Eminem and his phenomenon:

> As bedfellows go, none could be stranger nor less likely than raunchy rapper champions agreeing on content.
> If not style.
> Eminem, for you diehard adults, is a white rapper variously abhorred and adored for his envelope-pushing lyrics.
> His real ID is Marshall Mathers, ergo Eminem, and his key vocabulary is…reductive.
> Mathers has never met a multisyllabic word he likes, while body parts and functions say it best.
> Put it this way: the F-word is to Eminem's world what Om is to Yoga.
> Which is why parents loathe him while kids are keeping his newest release— "*The Marshall Mathers LP*"—in the best-seller slot.
> Parents don't just hate Eminem; many blame him for everything from date rape to school shootings.

The summary of the Eminem controversy ends at this point and Parker begins to bring in her opinion and leads to her thesis.

> It's easy to dislike him, I admit.
> He's excessively profane, offensive to everyone, disrespectful, and disgusting.
> Worse, he's honest.
> And, unforgivably, he's sometimes right.

Some of his worst stuff isn't fit for print, or listening.

But he does have a point when he challenges parents to take a hard look at themselves before they flip him the metaphorical bird.

Body Paragraphs   A debatable thesis can be developed in two ways. One way is to present your supporting arguments and then offer appropriate evidence, such as facts, statistics, personal experiences, and expert testimony. Another way to develop your thesis is to present opposing arguments and then refute them or demonstrate their faults. Explain the faults clearly, using evidence to support your opinion. If you find a valid point when analyzing the opposing viewpoint, say so.

Kathleen Parker clearly states, in her debatable thesis, that Eminem has a message that adults need to hear. However, she anticipates what her opponents are thinking and admits they have valid points. In paragraphs 9 and 10, she states, "It's easy to dislike him, I admit. He's excessively profane, offensive to everyone, disrespectful, and disgusting." After she quotes lyrics from "Who Knew," she shows that, once again, she agrees with her opponents.

I have an uneasy feeling he's referring to Eric Clapton's child, who fell to his death from an apartment window, and I wish he hadn't said that.

I wish, too, he hadn't said the rest of this, which makes grown-ups squirm for reasons that should be apparent.

Even in the conclusion, Parker states that she would not recommend Eminem's music to children, providing yet another nod to her opponents' point of view.

However, Parker stands by her opinion throughout the essay. In paragraphs 11 and 12, she writes, "Worse, he's honest. And, unforgivably, he's sometimes right." To support her point, she offers lyrics in paragraph 18, which speak for themselves.

Conclusion   In the conclusion, you should wrap up your argument by giving a brief summary of your thesis. It is also a good idea to acknowledge some of the opposing points as well, especially if your audience is unfriendly. This will help the audience focus on your point of view and your reasons for support and will encourage them to stop thinking about the other side of the controversy.

Reread the last two paragraphs of Parker's essay.

I'm not recommending Eminem to children, though I commend him to parents who might wish to know what their children are thinkin' and hearin' and what they're saying' about you behind your back, and consider the possibility that sometimes the words that most offend are the true ones.

(Hmm?)

Parker restates her thesis by suggesting that offensive words are the ones we need to hear. She acknowledges her audiences' unease with her point of view by clarifying that Eminem is not for children, but it is for adults to learn about their children. All other discussion about Eminem's merits is contained in this conclusion.

Exercises

4. Take the Persuasion Brainstorming Worksheet you filled out for Exercise 1 and expand it into a rough draft. Be sure to pay close attention to developing your points.

5. Choose one of the topics you listed as potential persuasion essays in Exercise 3. With a partner, fill out a Persuasion Brainstorming Worksheet and then write a rough draft. Work with the same person with whom you developed the original list of ideas.

REVISE

Normally, when revising a piece of writing, I suggest viewing it as if you were a member of its intended audience. When you revise a persuasion essay, I stress this approach even more. If you are writing to a friendly or neutral audience, critique your points and supporting evidence closely, making sure that each conveys strong support for your point of view. If you are writing for an unfriendly audience, include a critique of the opposing viewpoints and your responses to them. In either case, ask yourself questions, such as,

Are the opposing viewpoints valid as presented?

Are the responses strong enough to change minds?

Am I attacking the messenger and not the message?

In what ways is my argument strong?

In what ways is my argument weak?

Be honest with yourself as you answer these questions. Don't hesitate to make adjustments, for they only make your argument stronger.

Also check the thesis statement and any background information you supply about the topic. Both should be clear and focused. Also make sure your transitions are strong. Remember that transitions show when one idea ends and another begins and they keep the essay flowing between thoughts. You may be juggling a number of ideas, so make sure each one can be clearly identified.

STUDENT SAMPLE

Nini enjoys taking classes at her community college. She had no complaints until she read in the newspaper that the tuition costs at her school were going up. She got upset and angry almost immediately. The new tuition hike, described by an administrator as "minor, really, just an additional five dollars per credit hour," would mean she would have to take fewer classes next quarter. She felt she couldn't be silent, so she wrote about this topic in her English class.

Nini was too angry to focus her thoughts, so she wrote a short paragraph as freewriting:

What are those idiots thinking, raising our tuition like that? To them, it must be easy enough to come up with a few extra dollars here and there. All they have to do is sell a few stocks and boom! They have the money. But students live in the real world. It just isn't easy to get more money. I don't want to get a loan, but working extra hours will put a strain on my study time. And they really aren't thinking about the other side of things either: we don't get more services. We get the same thing but we just pay more for it. That's a point I bet nobody's ever thought of.

Writing out her feelings allowed Nini to focus on the topic more effectively. She read through her paragraph and realized, although much of the language was inflammatory and couldn't be included in the final draft, she did have two good points: working extra hours would affect her study time and the services don't change. With this in mind, she was able to fill out a TAP Worksheet and a Persuasion Brainstorming Worksheet.

Persuasion Brainstorming Worksheet

Topic: Tuition costs at the school

Audience: Administration of the school

What does the audience know about the topic?
They know a lot — they set the policy

What is their stance on the issue?
They will have no problem with the tuition increase

Where are they getting their information?
Reports

What are some strengths in their line of thinking?
Schools don't pay for themselves

Continued

What are some weaknesses in their line of thinking?

Students are going to be hurt by this

Purpose:

To get the administration to change their position

Debatable Thesis:

Raising our tuition at this school isn't

such a good idea.

Evidence:

Students can't pay for school

Appeals:

Emotion and reason

At this point, Nini was ready to write a rough draft.

Raising our tuition at this school isn't such a good idea. It will make people upset and angry with you and your school and I think people will start dropping out and going somewhere else for school.

The first reason you should not increase tuition rates is people have a hard time completing a degree because you have to work harder to make more money so that you can graduate on time. I want to graduate soon, so please don't raise tuition rates.

Next, if we pay more, we should get more. Right now, I get access to the library, free parking, first choice at the stadium when teams play at home, and free peer tutoring. If the tuition rises, will students get more stuff? I don't think so; therefore, we should keep our fees at the rate they are now. I was at the library studying and trying to memorize a lot of words for a test that I was going to have a few days later. I needed a certain book and the computer said the books were in the library system but not at the main campus branch. If our tuition goes up, we won't be able to buy more books and more materials for the library. It will become the butt of jokes for quite some time and members of the school itself will also get laughed at. Do not raise the tuition.

My last point is that a higher tuition rate scares off new people who may have been interested in coming to school here. This school is small, but it serves over 18,000 students each year. Some of those students will be coming straight from high school and haven't had much experience being at a school away from home. It would be better if they could stay home and come to our school. They would do this if the cost were affordable; otherwise, there is no real reason to come to this school.

School is pricey and people need to get an education to make something of themselves in their lives, so they should be able to go to college. They may have been able to pay for it at one time, but no more. Keep college affordable!

She let the essay sit a day and then began revising it. She read it from the point of view of someone in authority at her school (the unfriendly audience) and then she reread from her own point of view. She made these notations as she went.

Should I explain anything before I start?

Raising our tuition at this school isn't such a good idea. It will make people upset and angry with you and your *Too direct.* school and I think people will start dropping out and going somewhere else for school.

I could tell more about my classes.

The first reason you should not increase tuition rates is people have a hard time completing a degree because you have to work harder to make more money so that you can graduate on time. I want to graduate soon, so please don't raise tuition rates.

Next, if we pay more, we should get more. Right now, I get access to the library, free parking, first choice at the stadium when teams play at home, and free peer tutoring. *Are these okay examples?* If the tuition rises, will students get more stuff? I don't think so; therefore, we should keep our fees at the rate they are now. I was at the library studying and trying to memorize a lot of words for a test that I was going to have a few days later. I needed a certain book and the computer said the book was in the library system but not at the main campus branch. If our tuition goes up, we won't be able to buy more books and more materials for the library. It will become the butt of jokes *Maybe getting too extreme here.* for quite some time and members of the school itself will also *Too direct?* get laughed at. Do not raise the tuition.

My last point is that a higher tuition rate scares off new people who may have been interested in coming to school here. *Needs to be more specific. Maybe the second paragraph?* This school is small, but it serves over 18,000 students each year. Some of those students will be coming straight from high school and haven't had much experience being at a school away from home. It would be better if they could stay home and come to our school. They would do this if the cost were affordable; otherwise, there is no real reason to come to this school.

Work on this. School is pricey and people need to get an education to make something of themselves in their lives, so they should be able to go to college. They may have been able to pay for it at one time, but no more. Keep college affordable!

The next night, she wrote her final draft.

Nini G_____

ENGL 100

3/15/00

No Tuition Increases, Please

Jefferson State College has a solid reputation for being one of the best schools in the area. The instructors are knowledgeable and well trained, the staff is always friendly and supportive, and graduates from the school have little trouble finding jobs. What makes the school even better is that it is one of the most affordable schools in the state, which allows students who work full time to pay for a class or two every semester. Recently, the administration announced that tuition will be increased five dollars per credit hour starting next semester. Cutbacks in state funding have contributed to this problem, but students are the ones being punished. The tuition should not be increased at this school.

To begin, an increase in tuition means many students will have to cut back on the classes. This cutback will prolong graduation dates and may discourage many people from finishing their degrees altogether. When I first heard about the tuition hike, I sat down and figured out that I would have one extra quarter of classes before I could graduate. I almost cried. Although I enjoy school, I am here to get a degree to get a better-paying job. I shouldn't have to wait too long to do that.

Next, I think the increase will discourage other students from coming to this school. I mean, why not just pay a few more dollars to attend a bigger university? Sam, a friend from high school, stayed out of school for two years and has just now decided to start college. He was all set to come to Jefferson, but when he heard about the tuition hike, he changed his mind. For about 100 dollars more, he could go to the university and get what he considers a better degree. If too many students do this, the school could lose a lot of business.

Finally, in the real world, if you pay more money for something, you usually get a little something extra. When I go to McDonald's and get my meal supersized, I pay more but I get more fries to eat and more soda to drink. When I pay more at school, what do I get? I get the same instructors, the same classes, the same tutors, the same buildings. Nothing is different but the price tag.

Something is wrong with that.

In conclusion, I encourage the president of the college and all others involved to rethink the new tuition hike. It hurts students' finances, graduation time, and education. College should be available to everyone. Please keep this school affordable.

This draft contains everything Nini was thinking but presents her opinion in a manner that her audience will appreciate. The inflammatory language of the rough draft has been replaced with well-developed, thoughtful writing. Nini's point of view hasn't changed, however.

CHAPTER REVIEW

Persuasion essays involve presenting your opinion on a topic in a way that influences your audience. The topic you choose for your opinion needs to be controversial; otherwise, persuasion is unnecessary. Your audience may have varying points of view on the topic, so you must respond accordingly. If your audience is friendly, then persuasion won't be difficult. If your audience is neutral, they are probably seeking compelling reasons to believe the way you do. If your audience is unfriendly or even hostile, take the hard-sell approach. Present strong arguments with equally strong evidence. Also, acknowledge any valid points your opposition may have. This tactic can help soften resistance to what you are saying. Asking questions about what the audience knows about the topic, their stance on the issue, where they get their information, and strengths and weaknesses in their line of thinking will help you determine your audience's approach to your point of view.

When presenting your case, use a debatable thesis—that is, a thesis statement in which you offer your point of view. From there, make your points and support them with evidence (expert testimony, facts, statistics, and personal experiences). Appeal to your audience through emotions, reason, and codes and values as you present your argument.

As you revise your persuasive essay, consider these questions:

Are the opposing viewpoints valid as presented?

Are the responses strong enough to change minds?

Am I attacking the messenger and not the message?

In what ways is my argument strong?

In what ways is my argument weak?

Finally, make any necessary changes that will strengthen your argument.

Final Writing Assignments

1. Polish one of the drafts you wrote for Exercise 4 or 5. Examine your argument carefully, focusing on the clarity of your points and the strength of your argument. After you have revised, edited, and proofread your paper, submit it to your instructor.

2. Brainstorm a list of all of the people you know and admire, then write a persuasion essay about the one you consider the strongest of all. In your essay, be sure to explain the basis for your decision (overcoming personal tragedy, being a standard for beauty, or helping other people, for example) and then give specific reasons as support.

3. Reread Parker's "Wise Words from Eminem" and then write a reading response to it. Be sure to discuss specific points she makes in her article. Also listen to Eminem's "Who Knew" to get a fresh perspective on the song.

4. With a partner, brainstorm a list of controversial topics. Choose one and then pick a side (pro or con) to support. Write your persuasive essay, and then trade results with your partner. Who had the stronger argument? Why? In what ways could both arguments be improved?

5. Brainstorm a list of common beliefs of your culture. Choose one and write an essay in which you attempt to persuade someone from another culture to believe this way. Because you may be writing to a neutral or unfriendly audience, be sure your points are strong and that you provide valid evidence.

6. Brainstorm a list of common beliefs of your culture. Choose one and write an essay in which you attempt to persuade someone in your culture *not* to believe this common idea. Because you may be writing to a neutral or unfriendly audience, be sure your points are strong and you provide valid evidence.

PART III

Types of Writing: Different Topics, Audiences, and Purposes

Writing process and writing strategies are not limited to the writing you do in the classroom. Letters to the editor, business memos, and even journal writing are also influenced by process and strategy. In this unit, you will learn ways to apply them to your nonacademic writing.

First, we discuss the types of writing needed outside of the classroom. This unit opens with a discussion on reading responses, or writing in relation to something you have read. Next, we discuss self-reflective writing, or pieces of writing that come from you. After that, we move to social consciousness writing, which includes effective ways to speak out through your writing. Writing a research paper follows. Although most research papers you write will be academic in nature, these types of essays have special considerations of topic, audience, and purpose, and so I added them here. Another type of academic writing with special considerations is essay tests, the focus of another chapter in this section. Business writing (memos, job applications, résumés, cover letters, and thank-you letters) rounds out this section.

Writing is writing, whether it is done in the classroom or elsewhere. You still must pay attention to topic, audience, and purpose, and you still must keep in mind any special considerations for the writing task at hand. This unit should help you do just that.

11

READING RESPONSES

Imagine overhearing this discussion between two members of your writing class:

Member #1: Everyone should support our sports teams. They bring in a lot of money to the school and give us a name. People know our school by our sports teams.

Member #2: So we should support them because they put our school on the map, so to speak.

Member #1: Right.

Member #2: Well, aren't you forgetting about the reason the athletes are here? To get an education? Apparently, that is not important to you.

Member #1: Hold up. That's not what I meant. I was just saying...

Member #2: Are you an athlete?

Member #1: Yes, I play on the baseball team.

Member #2: Well, there you go. You are only saying these things because you have a vested interest in school sports. I bet if you were not an athlete and here on scholarship, you wouldn't be saying these things.

Member #1: Listen here, idiot, I was just saying....

Responding to ideas, thoughts, or opinions of others in person can be tricky. During any conversation, you get immediate feedback that influences what you say next. You can see the listener frown, so you may lighten the tone. If you see that person look puzzled, you may restate your point. Or maybe you'll be annoyed. Read the opening dialogue again, and notice how even when two people are talking face to face, misunderstandings can arise.

When you respond to written ideas, the dynamics are different, but sometimes equally tricky. The argument is in writing; you can return to it at any point. You can examine how certain opinions are expressed and supported. You are able to consider and reconsider a point so that your own opinion becomes clearer. Perhaps best of all, you will never be interrupted. Negotiating these dynamics—responding to a reading—is the focus of this chapter. Here, we discuss how to approach a written argument, from discussing the main idea to selecting points for response, as well as the standard structure for writing a response.

Before we go any further, though, let's read the essay "Who'll Stop the Drain?" by Vince Passaro, and then "Goldson's Good Life on a Shoestring," a response to Passaro's essay written by Yonason Goldson.

Reading 11   Who'll Stop the Drain?
Vince Passaro

BACKSTORY

In the United States, just about everyone is in debt. Perhaps you took out a student loan to pay for school, your parents are still paying on the house they "own," or your best friend fights monthly with a creditor about some past-due credit card payment. Being in debt may embarrass us but, according to Vince Passaro, contributing editor of *Harper's Magazine,* it is the American way. He makes $100,000 a year and considers himself "broke." Read his tale of debt and survival and see if you agree with his assessment.

LEXICON

accruing: gathering

alumni: graduates of a school, usually a college or university

basso profundo: big and profound; grand

commiserate: empathize, share similar feelings

conspicuous: noticeable; obvious

dunning: demanding payment of debt

fortnight: fourteen nights; two weeks

prudence: thoughtful consideration

usury: extremely high interest rate

Woody Guthrie: folk singer

1   This is not a story about conspicuous consumption. My wife and I didn't, with one exception, travel; we didn't buy a house or an apartment or expensive furniture we could not afford. Indeed, she will be quick to point out, we didn't buy any home or any furniture, and still live in our same rent-stabilized apartment with three children and such items as we've been able to pick up along the way, such as a secondhand couch and almost 4,000 books. The couch in recent years became too ripped up to bear, leading us finally to buy a nice piece of cloth to hang over it—$50 or so, on a credit card—which cloth now sports its first major tear and has embarked, clearly, down the road toward being as ripped up as the couch beneath it. We spent moderate amounts on clothes, or moderate

amounts for New York City, shopping for our children's apparel and equipment at rummage counters and yard sales; we didn't buy china or jewels or go out to good restaurants. We did go to the movies; in fact, we went to the movies to such a degree that I clearly recall once spending our rent money, which was a very low amount in those days, on a week-and-a-half-long cinema binge. For a period of two or three years I went to bars a lot. That about sums up where we spent our money these last ten years—on such things and on having and raising children in New York, where the upbringing and, particularly, the education of those children has been vastly more expensive than it might have been in most other places.

2   And now we are $63,000 in debt.

3   I think.

4   We owe $6,000 to Citibank Preferred Visa. We owe $4,000 to Discover. We owe $5,000 to BankAmericard Visa, $400 on an old Chase Visa card, $1,700 on a Chase overdraft account (which we may no longer draw on, so that as we pay off the balance we also manage to bounce other checks, written to other creditors). We owe about $3,000 to department stores such as Macy's, Bloomingdale's, Brooks Brothers, The Bon Ton, Ikea, Eddie Bauer, Sears. We each have one of those alumni credit cards, with $8,000 between them. The consumer credit-card debt comes to more than $28,000 overall, the interest rolling on, like Woody Guthrie's Columbia River. A few times, while our standing as debtors still allowed it, we turned some of that debt over with consolidating loans and by getting newer, lower-interest cards and moving our balances. We may have saved a few hundred dollars, but basically these moves gave us an opportunity to build up more debt, so that we cost ourselves more money in the long run. The cards offered at lower interest rates convert to usury-rate cards in three to twelve months. Right now we're averaging 20 percent annual interest, so the interest alone, compounding and compounding, like a fracture, is around $475 per month. At our tax rate, we have to earn $8,500 a year just to service our credit-card debt, never mind pay it back.

5   We are late with every credit-card payment, and the companies call and call and call. They call in the mornings around 8:00; they call in the evenings, between 7:30 and 9:00. They love to call on Saturdays. We have been known to get fifteen calls like these a week, a number somehow in proportion with the enormous number of checks we write per month: often more than forty, sometimes even fifty. Most of these dunning calls are computer generated; some are exclusively electronic. The MovieFone guy, it seems, doubles as a collection agent; that basso profundo voice comes like a foot through the line: "It is important that we speak with you. Please call one of our operators today to discuss your account . . ." Another call starts with an obnoxious trumpet herald: Bah, bah, bah, da-da-da-da-DAH! I always hang up. My wife, much smarter about these things, talks to the agents, tells them how much we want to pay this bill and that she'll send at least something by the end of the week, which, usually, she does. She often hits it off with the agents, laughs at herself and our predicament, gets them to commiserate—people who, given the pay and the turnover in the telemarketing business, probably have money troubles of their own. . . .

6   Any reasonable person might conclude that we've made the wrong choices. Yet most of the time we don't feel that way. In the end, there is no arguing our case; it is something

the gut either tells you to do or not. There is a kind of insanity in accruing debt, as there is in gambling or drinking. Our particular insanity revolves around the cultural and spiritual comfort provided by our children's school. I remember a creeping, decisive horror, when my first two children were still babies, while talking with a very well-paid friend with two children each about a year ahead of our first two. She said, flat out, that she had no intention of spending all her money on her children; she wanted to be able to go out in the evenings, take vacations, live well. It might have been at that moment, by default, that I became someone who did have the intention of spending all his money on his children.

7   I have no greater satisfaction in my life than watching my children learn about music and languages and their world, watching them play and fall and fail and succeed. I like their school and its religious environment; it is a warm, slightly old-fashioned, jargon-free place around the corner from where we live. Our children are eager to get there every day and have missed, the three of them, perhaps six days in five years.

8   Unfortunately, I don't see as much of their lives as I wish to, because I'm either at my office or working at home when they are doing things. All winter, my wife takes the children ice-skating, and in the warm weather she takes them to a pool, while I use the time to work. I would like to have time to do more with my family. I'd like to travel with them; I can see my oldest son in the Uffizi; I can see my middle boy with the horses in the dome of San Marco, my youngest in the Catacombs. My strange role model, I sometimes suspect, is based on what I remember of the slightly insane father of the James family, Henry Sr.—steadily consuming the inheritance, never caring, wanting to give his children not objects so much as the world itself and the mysteries that lie beyond the world. This is not a helpful attitude on a day-to-day basis. . . .

9   My history with money is that it falls out of the sky when you need it. Except that, increasingly, it doesn't. My mother was my sole custodian, and her death when I was eighteen left many unresolved feelings, obviously, but it also left the monthly Social Security benefits that would carry me through my first stint in college. Later, after I'd left school and returned, I found myself without the money to register one semester, until I went to the bursar's office to find out how much I owed them and discovered that a mysterious cash payment of nearly $3,000 had been credited to my account. I told the chief of the office repeatedly that this must have been an error, until on my third visit he produced a copy of the slip written out by the bursar's teller, with my name, my Social Security number, and a payment of $2,800. I never did find out where the money came from. The day after my third child was born, I left the maternity ward and went looking for a bank machine that gave out increments of $10, rather than the usual $20. I had $16 in my account at the time, and needed the ten to buy some food. As it happened, a short story of mine was published in a national magazine that week, and an editor called to see if I was working on a novel. I had about fifty pages of one, and within a few weeks he'd purchased it. The money was just enough to pay all the back bills, and was gone in a fortnight. . . .

10   Now that we are, in fact, broke on $100,000 a year, some will respond that I should have planned better, I should have spent less, I should send my children to schools I can afford. You can't argue with the logic or the morality of prudence. You can only point to a world where so many people find themselves incapable of practicing it. We look at other people we know, with their children in the same schools and living even more expensive lives than ours (better homes, better furniture, vacations, etc.) and the question is—

because in New York the silently mouthed question always is—where's the money coming from? Parents? Grandparents? A trust? The way our parents taught us to live (if we had frugal parents, which many of us didn't) doesn't seem possible. The life they acquired, under a more favorable tax structure and same real estate values, with one wage and a home and summer vacations, doesn't seem possible either.

Reading 12   Goldson's Good Life on a Shoestring
Yonason Goldson

BACKSTORY

In Vince Passaro's "Who Stop the Drain?" debt is viewed as an almost necessary way of life for most Americans. At one point, Passaro states, "the way our parents taught us to live (if we had frugal parents, which many of us didn't) doesn't seem possible." Yet, this more frugal lifestyle can be accomplished, according to Yonason Goldson, an Orthodox rabbi and writer. In this essay originally published online, Goldson explains that a family can live quite well in the United States and be debt-free. Read Goldson's response to Passaro and think about your own financial situation.

LEXICON

deficit: spending when one is already in debt

expenditures: bills, items one must pay for

heresy: ideas that go against established belief

impetuous: impulsive; acting without thinking

incensed: angered

incredulous: unbelieving

lament: a statement of grief or sorrow

martyr: a person who dies for a cause

pervasive: found in many places

1   A long lament by Vince Passaro, published in *Harper's Magazine* (August, 1998) explains how he and his wife have never bought a home, never traveled (except once), and never frequented expensive restaurants. He describes how they have lived with ratty furniture, how he drives a ten-year-old car, and how they have still managed to get themselves $63,000 into debt. More or less.

2   It's a familiar story by now. The major news and lifestyle magazines have all run stories in the last few years about the evils of credit cards, the dangers of deficit spending (both national and domestic), and how Americans seem incapable of exercising restraint when it comes to these two bugaboos. It is not the behavior itself, however, but the attitude underlying the behavior that is so chilling.

3   "Any reasonable person might conclude that we've made the wrong choices," writes Passaro. "Yet most of the time we don't feel that way." Even as Passaro recounts the irrationality of his own behavior, he is emotionally unwilling to accept responsibility for it. We need a place to live, he writes. We need food, and clothes, and private education for our children, and their music lessons, and their sports clubs and, of course, entertainment. And since we need these things, the reasoning goes, we shall have them, income or no.

4   I had no idea just how pervasive this mindset was until I went in to discuss financial aid with an administrator at my own children's private school. He asked how much I earned. I told him the amount, a figure well below $40,000. His eyes narrowed. "How do you live on that?" he asked in a half-whisper.

5   "We get by," I said, uncertain how detailed a report of our family expenditures he really wanted. But the response itself caught me by surprise. I hadn't thought of us as poor, not since the days I received a monthly stipend of $250 and paid $62.50 to rent a 400 square-foot apartment. Now we own a house, my wife drives a '94 minivan, and we hardly ever carry a balance on our three credit cards. Do we know something nobody else knows? Or is everyone else living a much richer life that we are, eating, drinking, and being merry on tomorrow's account?

6   Some people, indeed, might question our way of life. We don't own a TV or a VCR. We eat out—at the pizza place—maybe once in two months. We don't go to movies, although we do have several magazine subscriptions (including *Harper's,* which we plan to replace with *Civilization* when the subscription expires). I am typing this on the antique Macintosh I inherited from my father when he upgraded, but we have no computer games, and I still haven't gotten myself on-line. Our children don't go to summer camp.

7   "What do they do?" incredulous friends or neighbors sometime ask. Well, my eight-year-old daughter loves to read in a way she probably would not if she sat around watching television or playing virtual solitaire every evening. She has a library card, and my wife buys her books at the thrift store for about a quarter each. She rides her bike. (Her birthday present.) She has a fancy new doll she dresses up. (It took almost a year of saving up her allowance to buy it.)

8   My six-year-old son spends a lot of time on his bike. (His birthday present.) He builds Lego a lot, too. (The Lego was on clearance.) He played on a baseball league in the spring. (O.K., we paid full price: $65.) He's also teaching himself to read, because he sees how much his sister likes to do it.

9   Our littlest ones—ages two and three—spend most of their time following their mother around, having stories read to them, doing wooden puzzles, "helping" with the laundry or with the cooking or with the gardening. And we all go to the science museum and the art galleries and the zoo, none of which cost much at all. The children don't seem to mind; they're far more active and social than we were at their age.

10   Is this our implementation of some progressive/traditional child-raising philosophy? I'd like to say that it is, but I suspect that if we had more money we would end up doing a lot of the things we now can't afford—and don't miss.

11   Most professionals these days are well acquainted with the Peter Principle: Work expands to fill the time available. But I think the time has come to broadcast the domestic equivalent: Expenses expand to meet the income available. Or, in many cases, beyond

the income available. What other explanation can there be why we're just as broke after that new raise as we were before it? All of a sudden, there are more things that we need, that we have to have, that we can't live without, even though we were living without them just fine before we decided that now we could afford them.

12   Some things we really do need. Clothes, for instance. A new suit, in particular, since my old one has a hole in one knee and I just split the seat of the pants. But new is a relative term: The suit my wife found for me at the thrift store for $3 looks about as good, after dry-cleaning, as the one I bought for $200 almost five years ago. So does the one she found a month later at our school's rummage sale for $2.50. A Laura Ashley dress for our daughter was 50 cents more.

13   The people at the thrift store know us well by now. They sell toys, as well as clothes. Board games cost a dollar or two. A trike was three. A baby stroller was ten.

14   Some things we want but do without. We haven't added that second story on the house yet, or refinished the basement. We haven't traded in my 1980 Malibu Classic for a new Suburban. I haven't bought a laser printer, or in-line skates, or a new ten-speed. And our children haven't started piano lessons because we have no piano, which I do regret. But there is a lesson—the one my father taught me—in going without: The self-discipline developed by living within one's means is at least as beneficial as the discipline developed by learning to play the Minute Waltz. The benefit to the character is undeniably more profound.

15   I do sympathize with Mr. Passaro. I've been in debt, and I sleep easier and fight less with my wife now that I'm out. But I am incensed that a capable, apparently intelligent adult could go broke, could get himself sunk so deeply, on $100,000 a year—nearly three times my own income. Passaro blames New York City, where he is forced to martyr himself for his children by lavishing on them $36,000 for private education, and which has leeched from him a small fortune in garage fees and parking fines. There are, however, other places to live. (Heresy! screams every true New Yorker.) And there are other solutions to the money problem in general, as there are to most problems in life. They just have to be identified and then implemented.

16   Most alarming is Passaro's lack of willingness to consider any possible solution. Rather, in a style true to the '90s, he seeks to defend his own helplessness and place the blame on the anonymous collective. "You can't argue with the logic or the morality of prudence," he concludes. "You can only point to a world where so many people find themselves incapable of practicing it." The argument is worthy of an average teenager: Everyone else is doing it; why can't I?

17   I would hope that every responsible parent desires to instill in his children a sense of responsibility. But the impetuous nature of children balks at abstract ideology, which doesn't impress this generation's adults very much, either. The best hope for our children is to teach them, through our own example, the rewards of practicing the discipline of self-restraint, the raw pleasure and intense satisfaction of taking control of one's own impulses. We will bestow upon them the richest legacy by providing an environment in which they learn to taste the sweet confidence that comes from looking forward to a future that is theirs for the taking, rather than the bitter hopelessness of a future that has been mortgaged to the excesses of the past.

QUESTIONS FOR THOUGHT

1. Is debt truly necessary to live the kind of life you want to live?

2. Both authors talk about the financial advice they were given by their parents. What financial advice, if any, were you given by your parents? How has that advice helped you?

3. Both authors talk about how their financial situations have affected their children. Passaro says that he spends all his money on his children, while Goldson says that his children are doing fine without all the money. Whose children are in a better environment? Explain your answer.

4. In this society, why is money so important, but something we won't discuss?

READY

We all have strong emotional responses to everyday life situations. Imagine you are cut off in traffic or overlooked when you are next in line at the bookstore. In the car, without thinking, you may feel like honking your horn loudly or gesturing rudely at the driver in the other car. At the bookstore, you might speak up, explaining to the clerk that you were next in line, or you may be tempted to shove the other person out of the way to get service. In either case, we realize that our first response may not be the best response and that we should consider all of our actions.

Responding to a piece of writing falls along the same lines. Often, in college courses, you will be asked to read an essay and respond to it in writing using a persuasion writing strategy. An immediate, knee-jerk reaction is not the best approach. Sure, it may release pent-up feelings momentarily, but a good, solid response to reading requires a different approach. That approach requires starting with topic, audience, and purpose.

Topic

Topic is a special consideration when responding to a reading. On the surface, the topic is the reading to which you are responding. However, you must look deeper than the surface. Before you can formulate a response, you must first decide what parts of the discussion you are going to discuss. Be aware that even though you may not like any ideas the writer presents, you must limit yourself. Consider what you already know. Think about what you can argue and support. Using this approach, you should be able to find specific parts of the essay you can discuss effectively.

Audience

Audience is also tricky when writing a reading response. You must make your point of view clear while trying not to insult or otherwise alienate the author. You also have to be careful to include outside readers (those who may not have read the original article) in your "conversation" with the author. One way to keep everyone on the same page is by acknowledging the essay you are responding to—especially its main point—in the opening of your response. This way, everyone knows exactly what the discussion is about.

Purpose

Are you responding out of anger? Are you in complete agreement with the author and want the world to know? Are you trying to discredit the author? The purpose of your response should be considered before writing begins.

Many times, the purpose behind a response to reading essay is to enlighten the audience of the original essay to other points of view or additional information that may not have been considered before. This is not to say that you (as the one responding to the reading) must disagree with the author. This is only to say that your purpose should be to offer additional information that will persuade the audience to your point of view.

As with any writing situation, be sure to use a TAP Worksheet to pin down topic, audience, and purpose. This worksheet will help you keep those three elements in mind as you begin selecting and structuring your response to reading.

Exercises

1. Read through a number of newspaper and magazine editorials. Choose one or two and list the points you could discuss in a reading response essay. Choose one and fill out a TAP Worksheet as though you were going to write that essay.

2. Read one of the essays in the reading section of this textbook and then fill out a TAP worksheet as though you were going to write a response to that essay.

WRITE

You start with an introduction, you raise ideas for discussion, and you end with a conclusion. What makes a response to reading essay unique is that the product is based on the ideas expressed in another piece of writing. Because of this distinction, certain concerns arise, including discussing your point of view on specific points and giving the response an effective format or structure.

Select

Whether you write a paragraph, or an essay, or even a book in response to a reading, you can't discuss every point. You have to pick and choose your areas of discussion carefully. First, after you read the essay, read it a second time with a pen or pencil in hand. As you come across sections you want to address, underline them. Organize these points in order of importance and then choose the top few points for your essay.

Main Points in the Reading   The heart of a response to a reading is responding to individual points made in the reading. First, you must select those points, keeping your purpose in mind. As mentioned earlier, it would be easy to simply react to the first five or six sentences, but you may be missing the important part of the reading. Always keep in mind that you must have something to say, a point of view, as a basis for your discussion.

With your purpose in mind, go through the article point by point, choosing those that hit you most strongly. Write each of the points on a sheet of paper; then, across from each point, write your opinion of it. Ignore the temptation to attack the person (the ad hominen fallacy) or to make fun of grammar or sentence structure. Focus only on ideas. Each of these points will serve as a separate part, perhaps a paragraph, of your essay, giving your response an organizational pattern.

When selecting points to discuss from "Who'll Stop the Drain?" for his response, Yonason Goldson seems to have focused on three areas: how Passaro got himself into debt, steps Passaro could take to get out of debt, and Passaro's attitude about debt in general. These points frame Goldson's argument and he quotes Passaro directly in connection with them. They are also broad enough to incorporate other concerns Goldson has with Passaro's essay.

Quotations   As you can see, you must decide when and how to use material directly quoted from the original essay. You might choose a "quote and response" approach, placing a quotation at the beginning of a paragraph and then responding with your own point of view. Alternatively you might incorporate quotations within your response. This approach is less formal and more conversational. Whichever way you decide to use quotes, be sure to represent their meanings accurately. You don't "win" the argument if you misquote your source. You simply make your response look weak and lose credibility.

Discussions in response to reading essays require quotes, but go easy on their use. Use only one or two for each section of the body of the response. Limit the size of the quote used as well. Three to five sentences per section are enough, as long as you have stated your opinion and then offered information to support it.

The Reading Response Worksheet

To help you keep track of the points you are going to discuss and your responses to them, use the Reading Response Worksheet.

Reading Response Worksheet

Title of reading: _____

Author's name: _____

Overall impression of reading:

_____

_____

Audience: _____

Purpose: _____

Point To Be Discussed	My Response

Additional notes:

_____

_____

_____

Thesis statement:

_____

_____

_____

Your Thesis Statement   Notice that the worksheet asks, first, for your overall impression and then for your selection of points from the reading. When you have filled in that much, review what you have written. What is the main point? Draft this main point as your thesis statement.

Exercises

3. Look over your TAP Worksheets from Exercises 1 and 3 and decide which has the best prospects for an essay. Fill out a Reading Response Worksheet for your choice.

4. Reread the editorials you chose in Exercise 1. Search for letters to the editor about those editorials. Analyze the letters for strengths and weaknesses in the arguments presented.

Structure

You want your readers to be able to follow your discussion with ease. To achieve this, structure your response in standard essay format. Begin with an introduction, analyze specific points of the reading in several body paragraphs, and conclude with a strong statement of your overall opinion. Remember that some members of your audience may not have read the essay to which you are responding, so make sure you begin with the original work and then move on to your ideas.

Introduction   Your reader should know from the start that you are responding to a reading. Make sure to mention the title of the article and its author within the first few lines. The introduction should set the tone for the entire paper as well. Make sure that your thesis statement reflects the tone of the paper.

Read the introduction to "Goldson's Good Life on a Shoestring" and you will see the connection to "Who'll Stop the Drain?"

A long lament by Vince Passaro, published in *Harper's Magazine* (August 1998) explains how he and his wife have never bought a home, never traveled (except once), and never frequented expensive restaurants. He describes how they have lived with ratty furniture, how he drives a ten-year-old car, and how they have still managed to get themselves $63,000 into debt. More or less.

It is a familiar story by now. The major news and lifestyle magazines have all run stories in the last few years about the evils of credit cards, the dangers of deficit spending (both national and domestic), and how Americans seem incapable of exercising restraint when it comes to these two bugaboos. It is not the behavior itself, however, but the attitude underlying the behavior that is so chilling.

Body Paragraphs   Body paragraphs for a reading response are also similar to those used in a persuasion essay—that is to say, an idea is presented and then the remaining sentences in the paragraph are used to support or refute the idea. In a reading response essay, the idea presented will, most likely, be one from the reading. Quote the original idea word for word to be respectful to the original text. After that, explain your point of view about the idea in the quotations. As always, be sure to develop your point with detail, explanation, and example.

Goldson makes good use of Passaro's points, as illustrated in paragraph 15 below.

> I do sympathize with Mr. Passaro. I've been in debt, and I sleep easier and fight less with my wife now that I'm out. But I am incensed that a capable, apparently intelligent adult could go broke, could get himself sunk so deeply, on $100,000 a year—nearly three times my own income. Passaro blames New York City, where he is forced to martyr himself for his children by lavishing on them $36,000 for private education, and which has leeched from him a small fortune in garage fees and parking fines. There are, however, other places to live. (Heresy! screams every true New Yorker.) And there are other solutions to the money problem in general, as there are to most problems in life. They just have to be identified and then implemented.

Goldson does well in pointing out the details Passaro mentions in his essay ($36,000 for private education, garage fees, parking fines). He then goes on to make his own statements about these details. He says he is incensed, and his anger is clearly expressed.

Not every paragraph in a reading response essay has to be directed toward a specific idea found in the original reading. At times, you will need a paragraph or two to make your own point of view clear. In Goldson's case, he wanted to clarify a point not raised by Passaro in "Who'll Stop the Drain?" For that, he used a complete paragraph.

> Most professionals these days are well acquainted with the Peter Principle: Work expands to fill the time available. But I think the time has come to broadcast the domestic equivalent: Expenses expand to meet the income available. Or, in many cases, beyond the income available. What other explanation can there be why we're just as broke after that new raise as we were before it? All of a sudden, there are more things that we need, that we have to have, that we can't live without, even though we were living without them just fine before we decided that now we could afford them.

Here is where unity and coherence come into play. Primarily, you are presenting your opinion on the thoughts expressed by another person in writing; you are also presenting your idea on the same topic. Be sure every paragraph and sentence is directed toward fulfilling one of those two intents.

Conclusion   The conclusion of your essay is the place to pull together your views and refocus on your opinion of the topic. At this point, further discussion of the reading isn't necessary. Your audience knows how you feel about certain points that were made. Now you must convey to them how you feel about the topic as a whole.

In this concluding paragraph to "Goldson's Good Life on a String," Goldson reflects on the overall problems with the accumulation of debt as a way of life.

> I would hope that every responsible parent desires to instill in his children a sense of responsibility. But the impetuous nature of children balks at abstract ideology, which doesn't impress this generation's adults very much, either. The best hope for our children is to teach them, through our own example, the rewards of practicing the discipline of self-restraint, the raw pleasure and intense satisfaction of taking control of one's own impulses. We will bestow upon them the richest legacy by providing an environment in which they learn to taste the sweet confidence that comes from looking forward to a future that is theirs for the taking, rather than the bitter hopelessness of a future that has been mortgaged to the excesses of the past.

He leaves the reader with his point of view; no reference to the original essay is required.

Exercises

5. Draft the reading response you outlined in the Reading Response Worksheet for Exercise 3.

6. Return to the letters to the editor you studied in Exercise 4. Outline a few of them and then discuss the strengths and weaknesses of their organization and structure.

7. Working backward from Yonason Goldson's essay, fill out the Reading Response Worksheet as he might have completed it and prepare a detailed outline of his essay.

Writing With Others

READING RESPONSE

On first thought, writing a response to reading with another person may seem an unusual struggle. Opinions are often personal, and for a group to come up with a set of opinions everyone agrees with may seem impossible. However, with a little negotiation and compromise from all parties involved, responding to a reading as a group won't be as difficult as you might think.

First, know your position on the topic and the reading. Often, student writers are frustrated that their points are not being heard when, in fact, they haven't truly expressed any points. The group can help you clarify your ideas so they *are* heard. Do your homework. Read the article. Fill out a TAP Worksheet. Fill out a Response to Reading Worksheet. Then present your ideas to the group. You will feel better about the outcome, and the group will like hearing actual ideas, not just rambling.

Continued

Second, be willing to compromise. Opinions are tricky; we hold them tightly for fear that, if we let them go, we will somehow look ignorant or uncertain about what we think. While it is important to have opinions and express them, it is equally important to listen to other opinions and open our minds to them. As different points of view are expressed, sit back and contemplate one question: What is best for the project? Maybe Jane's first idea is a strong way to open the essay, while your first point would make a good, solid follow-up to hers as a second point. While compromise is important, keep in mind that "giving in" to everyone else is not productive at all. If a weak point is presented, make a case for a stronger point to be used. Other members of the group will respect you and listen to you when they feel you are actually working toward the good of the writing project and not leaving the real work to everyone else.

Third, revise the rough draft individually and then come together as a group to discuss the recommended changes. If time permits, make copies of the rough draft for all the members of the group. Each person can then make suggestions for revision and present them to the group. This strategy allows for involvement from everyone. If time is too short, have each member of the group read through the draft and suggest changes. Begin with the revision of content and ideas first, then move to editing and proofreading.

Remember: Always keep the assignment in focus. Push personal feelings for other members of the group or the topic itself aside after decisions are made. Nothing slows a group project more than people who continue to argue a point after the group has decided to move on. You may always feel as though the points you brainstormed for the response were stronger than someone else's. Once you present your ideas to the group and the decision to proceed is made, file those thoughts away and finish the assignment. Perhaps you can write your own response presenting your points your way.

With a little patience and a lot of work, writing a response to reading with a group can yield an effective essay. Simply keep focused on the writing project and focus on the ideas and insights of all members of the group.

REVISE

When you revise a reading response, focus on unity and coherence. The essay must flow from point to point with ease. You must also focus on checking quotes from the original essay carefully, as accuracy is a major part of a reading response essay.

Unity and Coherence First, examine your topic and your thesis statement. Make sure the ideas you posited here are strong. Next, reexamine the points from the essay you are responding to. Each point you address should be clearly stated and follow the spirit of the original. Even unintentional misrepresentation of the author's work will look like disrespect. After that, look at the body paragraphs. Each should have a topic sentence, an explanation, and enough information to persuade your audience toward your point of view. When all that is done, look at mechanics and grammar.

Quotation Check   When you refer to any outside source, you must remain faithful to the wording and the intent of that source. One of the surest ways to cast doubt on the validity of your point of view is to purposefully misrepresent someone else's. Because some members of your audience may be familiar with the original piece, you have even more reason to be accurate. This may sound intimidating, but it isn't meant to. When you revise, simply take a few more minutes and check the wording and the intent of the sections of the essay from which you are quoting and make changes, if necessary.

STUDENT SAMPLE

Gary, a member of the school's football team, has been active in sports since he was a small child. He is also a strong student with a B average. During a discussion of "Send Your Children to the Libraries," by Arthur Ashe, many of the students in Gary's writing course expressed the opinion that children should be steered toward academic careers rather than sports. Gary was frustrated because he had an opposing viewpoint—that students should be encouraged to play sports *as well as* study, as the two go together. Gary was going to keep his thoughts in his journal but decided to write a reading response instead.

Reading 13 Send Your Children to the Libraries
Arthur Ashe

BACKSTORY

Arthur Ashe was one of the most prominent professional tennis players of his day. Among his many distinctions, Ashe was the first and only African-American man to win the U.S. Open and Wimbledon, the supreme tennis championship. A college graduate, Ashe always taught that everyone needed a good education. In fact, in his hometown of Richmond, VA, a statue of Ashe shows him carrying books in one hand and a tennis racket in the other. In the following essay, originally published in the New York Times in 1977, Ashe warns of the dangers of pushing children to be star athletes instead of encouraging them to be scholars.

LEXICON

cashmere: an expensive, high quality fabric
dubious: questionable; doubtful
emulate: model; pattern one's self after
pretentious: claiming too-great self-importance

1   Since my sophomore year at University of California, Los Angeles, I have become convinced that we blacks spend too much time on the playing fields and too little time in the libraries.

2   Please don't think of this attitude as being pretentious just because I am a black, single, professional athlete.

3   I don't have children, but I can make observations. I strongly believe the black culture expends too much time, energy and effort raising, praising and teasing our black children as to the dubious glories of professional sports.

4   All children need models to emulate—parents, relatives or friends. But when the child starts school, the influence of the parent is shared by teachers and classmates, by the lure of books, movies, ministers and newspapers, but most of all by television.

5   Which televised events have the greatest number of viewers? Sports—the Olympics, Super Bowl, Masters, World Series, pro basketball playoffs, Forest Hills. ABC-TV even has sports on Monday night prime time from April to December.

6   So your child gets a massive dose of O. J. Simpson, Kareem Abdul-Jabbar, Muhammad Ali, Reggie Jackson, Dr. J. and Lee Elder and other pro athletes. And it is only natural that your child will dream of being a pro athlete himself.

7   But consider these facts: For the major professional sports of hockey, football, basketball, baseball, golf, tennis and boxing, there are roughly only 3,170 major league positions available (attributing 200 positions to golf, 200 to tennis and 100 to boxing). And the annual turnover is small.

8   We blacks are a subculture of about 28 million. Of the 13½ million men, 5–6 million are under twenty years of age, so your son has less than one chance in a thousand of becoming a pro. Less than one in a thousand. Would you bet your son's future on something with odds of 999 to 1 against you? I wouldn't.

9   Unless a child is exceptionally gifted, you should know by the time he enters high school whether he has a future as an athlete. But what is more important is what happens if he doesn't graduate or doesn't land a college scholarship and doesn't have a viable alternative job career. Our high school dropout rate is several times the national average, which contributes to our unemployment rate of roughly twice the national average.

10   And how do you fight the figures in the newspapers every day? Ali has earned more than $30 million boxing, O. J. just signed for $2½ million, Dr. J. for almost $3 million, Reggie Jackson for $2.8 million, Nate Archibald for $400,000 a year. All that money, recognition, attention, free cars, girls, jobs in the off-season—no wonder there is Pop Warner football, Little League baseball, National Junior League tennis, hockey practice at 5 A.M. and pickup basketball games in any center city at any hour.

11   There must be some way to assure that the 999 who try but don't make it to pro sports don't wind up on the street corners or in the unemployment lines. Unfortunately, our most widely recognized role models are athletes and entertainers—"runnin'" and "jumpin'" and "singin'" and "dancin'." While we are 60 percent of the National Basketball Association, we are less than 4 percent of the doctors and lawyers. While we are about 35 percent of major league baseball, we are less than 2 percent of the engineers. While we are about 40 percent of the National Football League, we are less than 11 percent of construction workers such as carpenters and bricklayers.

12   Our greatest heroes of the century have been athletes—Jack Johnson, Joe Louis and Muhammad Ali. Racial and economic discrimination forced us to channel our energies into athletics and entertainment. These were the ways out of the ghetto, the ways to that Cadillac, those alligator shoes, that cashmere sport coat.

13   Somehow, parents must instill a desire for learning alongside the desire to be Walt Frazier. Why not start by sending black professional athletes to high schools to explain the facts of life.

14   I have often addressed high school audiences and my message is always the same. For every hour you spend on the athletic field, spend two in the library. Even if you make it as a pro athlete, your career will be over by the time you are thirty-five. So you will need that diploma.

15   Have these pro athletes explain what happens if you break a leg, get a sore arm, have one bad year or don't make the cut for five or six tournaments. Explain to them the star system, wherein for every O.J. earning millions there are six or seven others making $15,000 or $20,000 or $30,000 a year.

16   But don't just have Walt Frazier or O.J. or Abdul-Jabbar address your class. Invite a benchwarmer or a guy who didn't make it. Ask him if he sleeps every night. Ask him whether he was graduated. Ask him what he would do if he became disabled tomorrow. Ask him where his old high school athletic buddies are.

17   We have been on the same roads—sports and entertainment—too long. We need to pull over, fill up at the library and speed away to Congress and the Supreme Court, the unions and the business world. We need more Barbara Jordans, Andrew Youngs, union cardholders, Nikki Giovannis and Earl Graveses. Don't worry: We will still be able to sing and dance and run and jump better than anybody else.

18   I'll never forget how proud my grandmother was when I graduated from UCLA in 1966. Never mind the Davis Cup in 1968, 1969, and 1970. Never mind the Wimbledon title, Forest Hills, etc. To this day, she still doesn't know what those names mean.

19   What mattered to her was that of her more than thirty children and grandchildren, I was the first to be graduated from college, and a famous college at that. Somehow, that made up for all those floors she scrubbed all those years.

Although Gary understood Ashe's argument, he wanted to address a few points in his essay. He jotted them down.

"We blacks spend too much time on the playing fields and not enough time in the books." (paragraph 1)

"Don't worry; we will still be able to sing and dance and jump and run better than everyone else" (paragraph 17)

Ashe seems to be condemning sports in general.

It is important to get an education and not gamble on sports.

Away from the text, Gary puzzled out what he wanted to say about each point. He filled out a Reading Response Worksheet to get focused.

Reading Response Worksheet

Title of reading: _Send Your Children to the Libraries_

Author's name: _Arthur Ashe_

Overall impression of reading: _I liked the reading, but I didn't agree with all of his ideas._

Audience: _Student athletes_

Purpose: _To give the student athlete point of view_

Point To Be Discussed	My Response
Blacks spend too much time on the playing fields and not enough time in the books	Sports can help keep you healthy
It is important to get an education and not gamble on sports	The two can go hand in hand—this helped in my math class
Don't worry—we will still be able to sing and dance and jump and run better than everyone else	Student athletes have the best of both worlds

Additional notes: _____

Thesis statement: _Kids should be both students and athletes_

From here, Gary was ready to write his rough draft. He wasn't worried about the details or anything else; he simply wanted to discuss his point of view in relation to Ashe's. Here's what he wrote:

In "Send Your Children to the Libraries," tennis professional Authur Ashe says that he wants parents to encourage their children to study and go to college and not worry about sports. The way he tells it, sports is a very damaging thing for young people. I found this point of view strange coming from a professional athlete. I thought maybe Ashe just didn't want the competition of the younger crowd. But when I gave it some more thought, I found that he had a point. Kids should be students and athletes. That gives them a good chance of doing well in both areas.

Sports can be used for your health. It can also be used to make you smarter. Example: I figured out this algebra problem by connecting it to some plays I had just learned in football practice. When I saw the numbers and made the connection, everything made sense to me. Math and sports go hand in hand.

You have to know plays or the coach won't let you play. I knew this guy who was dropped from the team after the second game last season because he was always late, he drank after practice, and he refused to memorize the plays. Memorizing helps you learn your plays and keeps you mentally prepared for the game. It's like giving your brain a mental workout while giving your body a physical workout. I mean, just like on the field, you have to produce in class. You just can't walk in and hope to do well; you have to prepare. Mentally visualizing every step you are going to take to either score, or get an "A."

I will have to agree with Ashe here. Being a student athlete has its ups and downs. He says, "Don't worry." To me, this says that even if you don't do as well on the field or in the books, you are still at an advantage for being in both worlds. More practice or book time will take care of that problem quickly. The two go hand in hand. It gives the student-athlete more to look forward to or strive for than just the plain old book work.

At first, I believed that Ashe was condemning sports in general. But then I thought about it and realized that him condemning sports would be contradicting his whole way of earning money. But he is just bringing to our attention that having an education is not a bad thing; it is a good thing. That is an idea you hear a lot.

After two days and another discussion about the essay, Gary sat down to revise his draft. He was pleased that he had gotten his feelings off his chest. But, it seemed, he still had a lot of work to do.

In "Send Your Children to the Libraries," tennis professional Authur Ashe says that he wants parents to encourage their children to study and go to college and not worry about sports. The way he tells it, sports is a very damaging thing for young people. I found this point of view strange coming from a professional athlete. I thought maybe Ashe just didn't want the competition of the younger crowd. But when I gave it some more thought, I found that he had a point. Kids should be students and athletes. That gives them a good chance of doing well in both areas.

"For example..." My teacher will want more detail.

Sports can be used for your health. It can also be used to make your smarter. Example: I figured out this algebra problem by connecting it to some plays I had just learned in football practice. When I saw the numbers and made the connection, everything made sense to me. Math and sports go hand in hand.

How does this connect to school?

May have to rearrange a few things here.

You have to know plays or the coach won't let you play. I knew this guy who was dropped from the team after the second game last season because he was always late, he drank after practice, and he refused to memorize the plays. Memorizing helps you learn your plays and keeps you mentally prepared for the game. It's like giving your brain a mental workout while giving your body a physical workout. I mean, just like on the field, you have to produce in class. You just can't walk in and hope to do well; you have to prepare. Mentally visualizing every step you are going to take to either score, or get an "A."

On what point?

I will have to agree with Ashe here. Being a student athlete has its ups and downs. He says, "Don't worry." To

me, this says that even if you don't do as well on the field or
in the books, you are still at an advantage for being in both
worlds. More practice or book time will take care of that
problem quickly. The two go hand in hand. It gives the
student-athlete more to look forward to or strive for than just
the plain old book work.

At first, I believed that Ashe was condemning sports in
general. But then I thought about it and realized that him

Is this enough for the conclusion? condemning sports would be contradicting his whole way of
earning money. But he is just bringing to our attention that
having an education is not a bad thing; it is a good thing.
That is an idea you hear a lot.

Gary polished the draft with some severe revising and editing and then proof-read his final product.

Gary M_____

ENGL 101

10/24/00

Athletics vs. Academics

Arthur Ashe spoke strong and inspiring words in his essay "Send Your
Children to the Libraries." Some words that were brought to my attention were,
"We blacks spend too much time on the playing fields and too little time in the
libraries." Even though he said "blacks," we know that it applies to all of our
society. The subject Ashe speaks of is one of the most controversial topics in the
sports world today. We always hear of people preaching to the young about how

important it is to maintain a good educational background. It is just as important to achieve and maintain a good balance by pursuing extracurricular activities that teach life skills. Sports is one of the most intellectually stimulating activities that you can perform outside of the classroom. A sport can teach us discipline and trust and can also be a metaphor for your studies.

To use sports for your physical well-being is one thing; to use it to expand your mind in multiple ways while achieving in the sport is what it's all about. Sports can help students out in the classroom. For example, say you have this problem in your math class that you can't solve. Say the problem is 11–2+3 squared. You take a football defense, which has 11 players. I hurt 2 players, so now we have 9. I kick 3 field goals on that same starting defense. 3 squared equals 9. Add the 3 field goals that I scored to the 9 starting defensive players and you get the answer to the equation. It's all in what you want out of the sport. If you tell yourself that this is going to be an educational experience, then that's what it's going to be. And to be a successful student-athlete, that's what you have to do.

Being a student-athlete has its ups and downs. Excelling both on and off the field is the reward for being a good student-athlete. Mr. Ashe said, "Don't worry; we will still be able to sing and dance and jump and run better than anyone else." To me, that's saying that even if you don't do as well on the field or in the books, you still are at an advantage for being in both worlds. More practice or book time will take care of that problem quickly. The two go hand in hand. You have to maintain an above-average grade to keep playing sports to begin with. This will make you want to thrive in the classroom as well as on the field. It gives the student-athlete more to look forward to or strive for than just the plain old bookwork. To touch on the academic side of things, if sports were so bad for the students, then why would colleges like Harvard, Yale, and Princeton have athletic teams?

You cannot play the game unless you study the plays. You have to know the game like your own underwear. Studying anything is good for your brain. Memorizing skills are needed a lot in the world today. Studying plays is a good brain exercise that helps prepare your brain for more memorization, like for a test or a paper. It's giving your brain a mental workout while you are giving your body a physical workout. The brain is the most productive muscle in your body. You also have to produce on the field and in the classroom. You have to know what you are doing before you do it. Mentally visualizing every step you are going to take to either score or get an "A" is important. Preparation for life is largely what you learn with these two things.

In conclusion, I believe that Arthur Ashe was saying that we need kids who are more intellectually inclined than athletically inclined. At first, I believed that Ashe was condemning sports in general. But then I realized that condemning sports would be contradicting his whole way of earning money. Even though he had a college degree from UCLA, his livelihood was a professional sport; therefore, he weakens his argument on the importance of a good education. No teacher or instructional video can ever teach the skills that you learn from sports. These two important values are good life skills to have when you venture out into the world of "reality." It's a reel eye-opener for the one who is not prepared.

Arthur Ashe just wanted to bring to our attention that having an education is not

a bad thing; it is a good thing. Not having these two things together would seem

unnatural, and I know no other way. As the saying goes, "Crafty men condemn

studies, simple men admire them, and wise men use them."

CHAPTER REVIEW

One type of writing situation you will encounter in college is the reading response. A response to reading essay is a type of persuasion essay in which you analyze a piece of writing and present your point of view about the issues it discusses. First, decide what sections of the piece of writing you are going to respond to. After that, jot down your responses to each of those points. Then, put these lists into essay format. Start with an introduction that includes the title and author of the original essay and your thesis statement. Move to the body paragraphs of the essay. Each should include a point from the writing and then your detailed response to it. In the conclusion, express your point of view clearly so your audience is left with how you responded to the original article.

Final Writing Assignments

1. Revise the rough draft you wrote for Exercise 5. Be sure to check for problems with grammar and mechanics. Check all quotations, proofread, and submit your finished reading response to your instructor.

2. Select a reading from Part 4 of this textbook and write a response to it following the process described in this chapter.

3. Find a partner in your class who will write a response to the same reading you selected for Writing Assignment 2. Compare responses when you are finished.

4. Choose one the readings from this chapter ("Who'll Stop The Drain?" "Goldson's Guide to Good Living on a Shoestring," "Send Your Children to the Libraries"). Reread the essay carefully, highlighting points you would like to discuss in your own essay. Fill out a Reading Response Worksheet and then write a rough draft. Revise it and polish it to make it a final draft. Submit the final draft to your instructor.

12

SELF-REFLECTION:
Looking In

Stress can do weird things to people, like make eyes twitch or stomachs do flip-flops. For humorist and filmmaker Woody Allen, it causes nightmares.

> Getting through the night is becoming harder and harder. Last evening, I had the uneasy feeling that some men were trying to break into my room to shampoo me. But why? I kept imagining I saw shadowy forms, and at 3 a.m. the underwear I had draped over a chair resembled the Kaiser on roller skates. When I finally did fall asleep, I had that same hideous nightmare in which a woodchuck is trying to claim my prize at a raffle. Despair.

Woody Allen, "Selections from the Allen Notebooks"

Almost everything you experience or think can be written about. Strange dreams and nightmares become humorous tidbits. Heartbreak leads to poetry. The frustrations of parenting can lead to an advice column. A crazy weekend becomes a narrative for a writing class. A disagreement you have with a political view expressed in a magazine editorial becomes a letter to the editor. These dreams, nightmares, frustrations, and disagreements often start as writing that is not to be shared. In fact, some of the most insightful writing comes from personal diaries and journals. The idea here is that, by looking inside yourself, you can find ideas and thoughts to write about.

I realize that, for some students, sharing a personal situation with others can be unnerving. You may feel as though you didn't handle yourself well when a problem arose or that writing about a personal achievement or failure will open you up to ridicule. However, personal experiences fuel some of the greatest writing of our time and allow for a great deal of self-expression. Also, sharing personal experiences with others can help them face down the demons and fears in their own lives. Reading about how others deal with a similar situation can empower and impress people. You may have stumbled across a piece of writing that helped you during a rough time in your life, and now you have a chance to return the favor. Finally, personal experiences can add credibility to your work. Adding a personal experience that relates to the topic helps make your point of view more believable. Your audience will respond to that sincerity. In my introduction to this book, I talked about my teaching experiences. As a reader, you will have more trust in what I say about writing because you know I also teach it. Please don't be hesitant to try your hand at self-reflection.

This chapter focuses on ways to get what is inside you out on the page. Self-reflection sources, such as personal experiences, journals, and diaries, open the chapter. In this type of personal writing, the audience is you. When you decide to turn a self-reflection into writing for others, all the elements of thinking about topic, audience, and purpose kick in. Figuring out what details to select and the right tone for presenting them are vital in writing self-reflective essays. From there, we move to the structure of self-reflection writing and then to an example of a bit of self-reflection that becomes the basis for a larger piece of writing.

The reading for this chapter is "On Books and Beginnings," by Maurice Sendak.

Reading 14 On Books and Beginnings
Maurice Sendak

BACKSTORY

Have you ever wondered what inspires people to choose certain professions? Did an architect see a picture of the pyramids of ancient Egypt and think, "I want to design and build something like that?" Did your school nurse have a near-death experience that impacted his life so deeply that now all he wants to do is heal others? For that matter, what would inspire anyone to become a writer? This question was posed to Maurice Sendak, author and illustrator of such books as *Where the Wild Things Are* and *In the Night Kitchen*. In the following essay, originally published in the anthology *3 Minutes or Less: Life Lessons from America's Greatest Authors*, Sendak takes us on a personal journey of what inspired him to create children's books for a living.

LEXICON

brevity: shortness

collaboration: two or more people or groups working together

interminable: without end

kosher: appropriate; permissible

naïve: unaware, lacking knowledge

unison: togetherness; joint action or voice

1   It probably began on my grandmother's lap in Brooklyn way back when us thirty kids were always, it seems, recovering from one interminable disease after another. To keep me amused, my grandmother would pull the window shade up and down to reveal a series of real moving pictures. First up, and to my joy I watched my brother and sister making a sooty snowman in the backyard. Then down, a breathless pause, and up again and they were gone! It was all like turning pages of a picture book.

2   My first proper book, Twain's *The Prince and the Pauper*, was given to me by my older sister. It had marvelous illustrations by Robert Lawson. The fresh new book smelled divine and felt even better, all shiny and smooth with a brilliant inlaid picture on the dark red front cover. Thus began my passion for books. Not reading, but smelling, fondling, biting and luxuriously caressing. It felt and smelled so much better, classier, than the cheap paper books I had up till then—that funky sour stink issuing out of comic and big little books. I still like that smell and I still treasure that copy of *The Prince and the Pauper*. That experience directly led, or so it must for the sake of brevity, into creating books with my brother, Jack. Our collaboration began when I was seven and he was twelve. He wrote the stories and I illustrated them on shirt cardboard. Our masterpiece and swan song was the dramatic tale, *They Were Inseparable*. We were both in love with our sister, who was sixteen, and this story had to do with that dark passion. The plot, in brief: the brother and sister are madly in love and decide to get married. We were either very stupid or very naïve but, as I recollect, this tale was a great family favorite and when read aloud to the relatives my parents positively glowed. Anyway, somewhere deep in my brother's unconscious something finally warned him that the situation wasn't strictly kosher because, immediately preceding the wedding, the brother is in a terrible accident and as he lies dying and bandaged from head to foot (my favorite picture) the sister bursts into the hospital room, pushes aside nurses and doctors who attempt to stop her, leaps onto the dying brother, clasps the bundle of bandages and before anyone can stop them, they cry out in unison, "We are inseparable" and leap from the fourteenth floor of the Brooklyn Jewish Hospital—SPLAT! At this point, I would proudly hold up my shirt-cardboard depiction of that terrific death. So, it seems that as a small boy, I pasted and clipped my bits of books together and hoped only for a life that would permit me to earn my bread by pasting and clipping more bits of books. And here I am, all grown-up, at least physically, and still in the same old business.

QUESTIONS FOR THOUGHT

1. Recall some imaginative games or projects that you and your brothers, sisters, and friends created when you were younger. Do any make you cringe now? How does your recollection of those experiences compare to Sendak's?

2. A defining moment in Sendak's life was receiving the book *The Prince and the Pauper*. What gifts have you been given that helped shape your life?

3. If you had experienced the events described in Sendak's story, would you have shared them with strangers? Why or why not?

READY

Self-reflection begins before you begin to write, before you even know you are going to write. It begins with experience. Each of us, in living every day, has an abundance of experiences that are at once universal and unique. We have fallen in love and have faced heartache. We have stayed up too late eating junk food and talking with old friends. We have held jobs, fought with friends, given in to temptation, and failed to live up to expectations. It is the richness of these experiences that makes them worth writing about.

The moment you put your thoughts on a sheet of paper, you are, in essence, clarifying what you think. Your ideas can be triggered by a number of sources. Perhaps you have been struggling for weeks in a math class. You have to take the class; it is required for your major. The problem is you are on the verge of failing. You have studied, gotten a tutor, attended every class, asked the instructor for additional help, but you still don't understand the material. By next week, you have to make a major decision: to stay in the class and hope you pass or withdraw from the class and take it next semester. This situation is a perfect time for self-reflection. You could write down your feelings about the math class. You could write about what options you have tried and brainstorm some more. You could write a future scenario about what will happen if you withdraw from the class. You could write a letter to the instructor about the situation. In all of these cases, self-reflection helps you get clear on what the problem is and how you can solve it. Of course, not all self-reflection writing is geared toward problem solving. Personal writing should not be synonymous with problems and painful memories. Writing about positive experiences is also an option. Just keep in mind that self-reflection is personal writing.

Personal, inward writing can take many forms, including **journals** and **diaries**, where you can record personal experiences and personal values and beliefs.

Writing for Yourself

Writing for yourself starts with calendars and day planners, in which you record your daily activities. From there, you move to a journal or diary. As children, many of us had those little books for private thoughts kept safe under lock and key or stashed in a shoebox under a bed. Many explorers kept written logs—records of their day-to-day explorations—or journals—written reflections on those explorations. Maybe for a writing class you have been instructed to keep a journal of some sort. Whatever reason journals and diaries are kept, they serve the same purpose: to hold our thoughts about daily occurrences. Journals and diaries are comments on our lives. Even if you write down what you have for breakfast every day or keep track of the long distance phone calls your brother makes this month, you are, in essence, writing.

Tips

Make Self-Reflection Writing Flow

When you write for yourself, don't be a critic. Just write. For a boost, follow these tips.

▶▶▶▶ **Write at least a few sentences every day.** If you don't write a little bit every day (even for five or ten minutes), you miss an opportunity to record what may become a good topic later on. Of course, there will be days that you can't write in the journal. Don't worry about that, either. Self-reflection should be a fun, enjoyable, and educational experience, not a chore.

▶▶▶▶ **Do not set out to create topics. Let life reveal topics to you.** Simply write about what is going on around you. Searching for topics may freeze your creativity. But be open to discovering recurring concerns or themes in what you write.

▶▶▶▶ **Don't worry about grammar, spelling, and punctuation.** As with writing process and other writing situations, you can address technical detail if you decide to turn a journal entry into a piece you write for others.

▶▶▶▶ **Be honest with yourself.** A journal or diary is of no use to you whatsoever if everything you write focuses on someone or something else. Be true to what you feel and think. If you hate writing in journals, write about that. If you have a wonderful day simply because you got a hug from your daughter, write about that. Write about one particular problem you are experiencing every day for a week. Write about completely different aspects of your life in every entry. Explore different moods and how your language changes with these different moods. Remember to keep yourself and your life at the center of the writing.

▶▶▶▶ **Choose a special notebook for your journal and write with a favorite pen or pencil.** This advice may sound odd, but considering that your journal is a record of your life, it does make sense. You want to be comfortable and relaxed when you write, so your writing tools should be comfortable to you as well.

▶▶▶▶ **Try to write at the same time each day.** For one week, get up twenty minutes earlier than normal to write in your journal. The following week, get up at your normal time, but stay awake twenty minutes later to write in the journal. Whichever time seems the best for you is the time you should always write

Continued

in your journal. (If neither time works, try to find twenty minutes within your day to take a break and write.)

▶▶▶▶ **Do not write under the influence.** Rumors and myths abound about Hemingway drinking hard whiskey while writing *The Old Man and the Sea*. William Burrows, author of the cult classic *Naked Lunch*, is said to have taken many types of drugs while writing the book. While these stories and others have some truth to them, writing under the influence does not create great insights or great writing. You can't get to your inner thoughts if you can't think straight. Even too much caffeine or sugar can affect your thinking. I don't mean to sound like a public service announcement, but your best bet is to stay clean and sober when you are writing.

Exercises

1. In a journal or diary, record your dreams for one week. Record what you can remember about the dreams themselves, as well as any thoughts you have right after you wake.

2. Sit in a crowded place (a restaurant during mealtime or a shopping mall on a Saturday afternoon, for example) and record the things you see and hear. Don't attempt to describe or write about everything or everyone you see. Simply look around you and begin writing.

3. Create a list of ten or more ideas that you can refer to as you develop your journal writing skills. Make these ideas as personal as you possibly can. What makes you happy? Sad? In ten years, where do you hope to be? What accomplishment are you most proud of at this moment? What one thing do you hope to accomplish before you die? What scares you the most? Refer to the list of ideas and write about one at a time. And be honest with yourself in your journal entries.

4. Brainstorm a list of people or situations (sickness, divorce, etc.) that concern you. Select one and write a series of entries about it. These entries may take the form of letters, dialogue, or even prayers. Make the conflict clear and then offer solutions.

5. Brainstorm a list of people or situations (your child or children, a recent promotion at work, a good grade on a difficult test, etc.) that bring you joy and happiness. Select one and write a series of entries about it. These entries may take the form of letters, dialogues, or prayers. Explain the situation or who the person is and then explain your joy and happiness.

The Self-Reflection Worksheet

To help you with your self-reflection, use the following Self-Reflection Worksheet. Like the other worksheets in this book, the point is not to tell you what to write but to help you write it productively.

The Self-Reflection Worksheet

Name: _____

Date: _____

Topic of self-reflection (optional):_____

Reflection: _____

_____

_____

_____

_____

_____

_____

Other ideas:_____

_____

_____

_____

_____

_____

_____

Source of reflection: _____

_____

To be shared?   Yes   No

Explain: _____

_____

_____

_____

_____

_____

Exercises

6. At the end of the week, read through the dreams you recorded for Exercise 1. Write about any patterns or meanings you can glean from the entries.

7. Find copies of published diaries and journals and read some of the entries. What did those authors write about? How did they communicate on paper? Pick a topic from the variety offered within those pages and write about it.

8. Brainstorm a list of important events in your life. Write down the details of one event and then explain why it was important to you.

Writing with Computers

SELF-REFLECTION

Often, when we think of the big, heavy desktop computers in our libraries, offices, and classrooms, we don't see much that can help us get personal in our writing. However, computers can be useful for self-reflection writing. First, consider using a laptop or other portable computer as a journal or diary. The option of taking these machines just about anywhere allows you to be comfortable when you type and to write when you have time (such as in the library or cafeteria between classes). Next, computers have virtually unlimited amounts of storage (through diskettes and CD-ROMs). Finally, most word processing programs are equipped with keyword search capability, which can be useful if you decide to use your personal writing as a resource for writing for others. Keyword searches scan each entry for certain words, much like a search engine on the Internet seeks websites about a particular topic. Click on the Find command, type in a keyword, and read through the results. By using keyword searches, you will be able to find entries related to a theme with little problem.

Writing with Others

SELF-REFLECTION

At first glance, a "Writing with Others" section seems out of place in a chapter on personal writing. Take another look. Just because the writing is personal doesn't mean that it can't develop as part of a group writing session. Get together with a friend or two and write in your journals simultaneously. The act of writing together lends support to members of the group. Feel free to share what you have written. This sharing helps you learn what issues and concerns others are writing about and builds a writing community. By writing and reading together, writers can often help each other find entries that can be useful in other writing situations. An entry you didn't consider interesting may strike someone else as useful for an assignment. Whatever approach you take, just keep in mind that, while the thoughts and ideas may be personal, writing itself can be an enjoyable group activity.

Topic, Audience, Purpose

Self-reflection begins as personal writing geared toward you. You may already have a journal or diary that you write in daily, or every once in a while you may jot down personal feelings, values, or beliefs and examine them. You may not have intended to show anyone these entries, which is fine. But when you begin to think of expanding your self-reflection into writing for others, you need to think about topic, audience, and purpose. Use this chapter's reading as an example. Sendak's essay focuses on his start as a writer and illustrator of children's books. That is the topic. The audience is the people who read and admire his work and his sense of humor. His purpose is twofold: to educate his audience and to entertain them. He is successful on both counts.

WRITE

As with every piece of writing, you have to consider your audience and the form of the essay when you begin opening personal pieces to others. Letting someone read a personal piece of writing without reworking it first is rarely a good idea. You may not have had sharing in mind, and you may want what you wrote in your journal or diary to remain private. When you deliberately share it with others, though, you can tweak it through selection and organization.

Select

Selecting material from your self-reflection writing to use in a piece of public writing can be both difficult and easy. On one hand, you are close to the events, and some feelings you don't want to expose may come out in your public writing. That part would be tough. On the other hand, because you know the subject matter well, recounting details, expressing feelings, and developing the piece of writing overall would be easy. The two main aspects of selection you have to be aware of are comfort level and criticism.

Comfort Level A truly unique aspect of self-reflection is attention to comfort level. In writing that starts from the outside, you can be objective. But with self-reflection, you can become tense and begin having trouble writing. Your comfort level is shaken because you may feel as though you yourself are being judged along with what you are saying and how you are saying it. In other words, to find fault with your words is to find fault with you.

Understand this basic idea surrounding comfort level: You are allowed to keep some of your experiences, thoughts, and feelings to yourself. Select only what you want to reveal. In fact, putting too much self-reflection into a piece of writing can lead to self-absorption, and that may embarrass your reader.

Criticism Occasional criticism, even rejection, is inevitable in writing for others. Even famous authors have received rejection letters. Stephen King is said to have gotten hundreds of rejection letters before he published his first novel.

And not-so-famous writers learn to take rejection as a matter of course. I received a call from an editor stating that the idea behind this textbook was a good one, but my style of writing wasn't appropriate for a textbook and I had to rework sample chapters. As writers, we all need to keep in mind that, once the words are on the page, they no longer reside in us. People are going to read and comment on them; get used to that experience, but do not take it personally. Recall "Confrontations, Common Bonds," the main reading in Chapter 1. In that account, discussions of student work quickly degenerated into hurt feelings and defensive attitudes, all because students took the criticism to heart.

Structure

Appropriate essay structure is important in personal writing that is shared with others. *You* may understand the seemingly random nature of your thoughts, but your audience won't. Stick to the basic structure of introduction, body, and conclusion. Make sure you present a main idea and that your words support it.

Sendak's essay begins with a snippet of memory about his first picture book: his grandmother sliding a blind up and down. From there, the essay moves into a detailed memory about working with his brother on a book when they were children. To tie it all together, Sendak offers the main idea.

> So, it seems that as a small boy, I pasted and clipped my bits of books together and hoped only for a life that would permit me to earn my bread by pasting and clipping more bits of books. And here I am, all grown-up, at least physically, and still in the same old business.

Every part of the essay moves smoothly toward these last lines, which means the structure of the essay is perfect.

Exercises

9. Have you ever cheated an employer by secretly spending time on personal projects while pretending to work? What if one day you caught an employee of yours doing this? Write a journal entry about the incident. Then fill out the Self-Reflection Worksheet to turn your reflections into writing for others.

10. If you knew that all racial and ethnic discrimination in the country would disappear in twenty-five years, would you be pleased by the rapidity of the change or upset by its slowness? Give at least three reasons explaining your response. Trade your responses with members of the class and discuss the answers.

11. Select one of the journal entries you have written for this chapter or an idea for a self-reflective essay the exercises suggest to you. Prepare a TAP Worksheet and a Self-Reflection Worksheet for it and then write a draft.

REVISE

Once you decide to make a personal piece of writing public, revise it the same way you would any other piece of writing—that is to say, identify topic, audience, and purpose, and adapt the writing to fit each one. As you revise this once-personal reflection, consider the distance and tone of the work. Be open to using humor to help pull your ego away from your reflection.

Distance and Tone

Make sure you have the distance from the piece you need to revise it effectively. Having distance from an event simply means that enough time (and healing) has passed so you are able to recount the event and control your emotional response. For example, at age eight, you may have thought your parents horribly mean and unfair when they wouldn't let you stay up past your bedtime on a school night to watch monster movies. Perhaps you even refused to eat dinner that night and threatened to run away if they didn't change their minds. Ten years later, with distance between you and the event, you can understand your reaction. You were angry. You can also understand your parents' reasoning: *The Creature from the Black Lagoon* would be on again, and you needed your rest to do well in school the next day.

Distance allows you insight. Pay close attention to the tone of your piece. You may have mixed emotions in certain situations, which may be transferred into the writing. The revision stage is the time to straighten out those emotions.

Take a look at Sendak's essay once again. His reflection focuses on the joys of being a kid who loves to tell stories. Almost every childhood has painful moments, and Sendak may have written about one or two of his own in the original reflection. But when it came time to revise the essay for publication, Sendak focused on the fun and excitement of that particular point in his life. Distance helped him put the events into perspective and helped him focus on their fun and wonder.

Humor

With distance comes embarrassment. At age ten, you may have thought that refusing to eat dinner was a good way to get your parents to change their minds, but all that happened was you went to bed hungry that night. When you tell the story, you may laugh at your hunger strike. It wasn't funny then, but now, it can be a scream. Laughing at yourself or finding something funny in an event makes us human and can be a good way to turn a personal piece of writing into a public one.

Consider Maurice Sendak's childhood attraction to his sister. Some people would be embarrassed to admit having a crush on an older sibling, but Sendak has distance from the experience and sees it as funny. His humor allows us to laugh with him.

STUDENT SAMPLE

Jill is 38 years old and graduated from high school 20 years ago. She decided to pursue a degree in business last year. After two weeks in college, Jill wrote a journal entry about returning to school:

How does it feel after going back to school...That is a big question and one I don't know if I can answer right now. School has just started and it seems overwhelming to me right now. A lot of people here. I guess I didn't expect to see so many people here. The age thing doesn't really bother me. I grew up as the youngest member of seven children in the family and so I guess that being out of place as far as age goes doesn't bother me at all. But the fashions get to me. Kids are wearing stuff that looks so strange and unnatural. How do the teachers take these kids serious when they don't take themselves seriously? Maybe they do take themselves seriously and I just don't get it. That happened the other day. I was waiting for the shuttle to take me to the parking lot when this guy came over to me. He was wearing torn jeans and a leather jacket. I was scared at first. He was the perfect picture of the hoods you see in the movies and I was sure that he was going to grab my purse. But he didn't. He offered me a cigarette and then started reading a book for his English class. As it turned out, he was just hanging out waiting for a shuttle too. I had misjudged him. Maybe I do have a problem with age.

As the example illustrates, journal or diary entries do not stay on one track very often. Your mind jumps from idea to idea, and your pencil or pen follows. Still, just about any entry will yield a bumper crop of potential ideas for writing assignments or ways that the entry can be revised or changed for a certain writing situation. For instance, let's imagine Jill being given the following writing assignment:

Personal experiences help define and shape who we are and our outlook on life. This is especially true for how we interact with each other. While many of our experiences with other people are positive, negative ones also happen. Write a paragraph or essay about a personal experience you had with another person where you learned something about people and about yourself. First, tell about the experience you had and then tell what you learned.

Jill thought her earlier journal entry would be a good one for this assignment, but she had to be selective in what she could use and what needed to be revised. First, she filled out the Self-Reflection Worksheet and then reviewed her entry.

The Self-Reflection Worksheet

Name: _Jill_____

Date: _____

Topic of self-reflection (optional): _Prejudice_____

Reflection: _I judged a young man who looked different._
He looked like a thug, but he wasn't. I knew I
needed to adjust my way of thinking.
_____
_____
_____
_____

Other ideas: _I judge on many different levels._
_____
_____
_____
_____
_____

Source of reflection: _Journal_____
_____

To be shared?   (Yes)   No

Explain: _I want to write about how I judge and what I need to change about me._
_____
_____
_____
_____

How does it feel after going back to school…That is a big

But isn't that the point—to answer this question?

question and one I don't know if I can answer right now. School has just started and it seems overwhelming to me right now. A lot of people here. I guess I didn't expect to see so many people here. The age thing doesn't really bother me.

Why not? What did I expect?

I grew up as the youngest member of seven children in the

I feel like the oldest now—a different perspective.

family and so I guess that being out of place as far as age goes doesn't bother me at all. But the fashions get to me. Kids are wearing stuff that looks so strange and unnatural. How do

Like what?

the teachers take these kids serious when they don't take themselves seriously? Maybe they do take themselves seriously and I just don't get it. That happened the other day. I was waiting for the shuttle to take me to the parking lot when this guy came over to me. He was wearing torn jeans and a leather jacket. I was scared at first. He was the perfect picture of the hoods you see in the movies and I was sure that he was

Which ones?

going to grab my purse. But he didn't. He offered me a cigarette and then started reading a book for his English class. As it turned out, he was just hanging out waiting for a shuttle

What about his clothing? Other things?

too. I had misjudged him. Maybe I do have a problem with age.

After reviewing her notes and examining the writing assignment again, Jill realized the best section to use was the actual incident involving the other student. That section showed she misjudges people and that the way they dress has nothing to do with whether they take themselves seriously as students or not. She recopied that section to another sheet of paper and then pulled out a TAP Worksheet to begin forming and shaping the journal entry into a good response to the assignment.

After she examined the topic, audience, and purpose for the assignment, her TAP Worksheet looked like this:

TAP Worksheet

Topic: What is the topic of the writing project? _Personal experience where I learned something about myself._

Continued

What type of topic is it? (Academic) Self-reflection Outside source

Audience: Who are the members of my audience?
Instructors—classmates—people who don't know me

What is the educational level or levels of my audience?
College educated—taking college classes

What does my audience know about my topic?
Probably something about self-discovery but nothing about me.

What has been their reaction to topics like this before?
Seem okay with this type of writing.

What has been their reaction to my previous writing?
Liked it a lot.

Purpose: Why am I writing this particular piece?
Explain why I judge people at times.

Why is the audience reading this particular piece?
To find out more about me.

Strategy: List the writing strategy or strategies or strategies that may be used in this writing project. Discuss reasons for using these selected strategies.
Narrative and description will be a big part of this piece or writing—the story will reveal my judging and I need to describe the person.

Style: What approach are you going to take with this topic? Discuss your choices.
Straightforward—perhaps some humor—I want the reader to be surprised by the person like I was.

Time: Estimate the amount of time needed for this writing project. (Consider the type of topic when estimating.) _1–2 weeks_

Resources: Jot down any outside resources that will be required for this writing project.
None—but I will want some peer review.

Now the point of the essay was starting to take form. The incident revealed a few of Jill's prejudices, but it also showed how she learned from the experience. All of that would be reflected in the writing. Given her audience (the instructor of the class, who knew very little about her) and the purpose (to discuss the nature of prejudice), she knew she had to provide background about the source of her judgments. She had never really asked herself this question before. Where did her prejudices come from? Where do anyone's judgments begin?

Turning to her journal, she reread the entry and saw something she hadn't noticed before: age and dress. She mentioned them as concerns when she wrote about her recent college experience. Perhaps those were issues that helped create the image in her head. She still needed something else, another point that helped her get to what she felt about the other students at the time. She turned to a blank page in her journal and wrote the following entry focused on answering the question on judgments and how they were created.

This time, I am talking about judging people and where I got it from. My parents were always judged so we never judged anyone. They each had trouble in school and were made fun of. My mother couldn't afford makeup, so she never wore any and she told me that a lot of kids teased her about it. Even today, she doesn't wear a lot of makeup. Maybe some lipstick if she is going somewhere. But they both told me never to judge others because it makes people hurt inside. You may not see it, but they do hurt. I know all kinds of people...what was it that shook me up about this guy? He looked like bad news. Like something bad on television. Maybe television created this image in my head and I bought into it. He did look like something out of *Boston Public,* but that isn't fair to him. I got scared because of something on t.v. Wonder how many more images we carry around from t.v. and don't realize it?

Taking a break to read through what she had written so far, Jill saw she had identified three areas for judgment: family, television, and dress. As she thought more about these points, she became uncomfortable. Television and dress were okay to write about, but family wasn't. She simply didn't want to go into that in this essay, so she brainstormed another idea: age. Because the man was young, she made a snap judgment about him. It was mentioned in the original entry. Perhaps she needed to reconsider it now as a basis for her judgments. Now her work was taking structure. The thesis statement would reflect how she misjudges people. From there, she would move into the story itself (as that was a big part of the assignment). The body paragraphs would consist of the three aspects of her judgments. (Additional brainstorming would be needed to flesh out each point.) Finally, she decided to add a conclusion that would tie everything together. Once the outline was in place, she wrote the following rough draft.

After an incident at the campus shuttle stop, I realized that I judge people unfairly. The other day I was waiting for the shuttle to take me to the parking lot when this guy came over to me. He was wearing torn jeans and a leather jacket. I was scared at first. He was the picture perfect of the hoods you see in the movies and I was sure that he was going to grab my purse. But he didn't. He offered me a cigarette and then started reading a book for his English class. As it turned out, he was just hanging out waiting for a shuttle too. First, although I consider myself open-minded, I guess I found out that maybe the way a person dressed reflected on how serious they took themselves as students. I mean how can teachers take these kids serious when they don't take themselves seriously? I realized, though, that maybe they do take themselves seriously and I just don't get it. Finally, I judge people based on images I get from television and movies. I thought that this guy was going to act like one of the "bad students" you see on shows like *Boston Public* or *Dangerous Minds*. I just watch too much television. I need to get out more. In conclusion, this experience has taught me, above all else, to pay closer attention to what I immediately think about people when I first meet them. Judgments based on appearance, age, and the media are not fair at all. I hope that man that I misjudged did not judge me too harshly for misjudging him.

Satisfied with her progress so far, Jill took the draft to class for peer editing. Rakim, her peer editing partner, gave solid feedback on the draft. After a few more adjustments in content and mechanics, Jill wrote this essay.

Jill H_____

ENGL 100

Assignment #2

10/10/2001

Personal Judgments, Personal Insights

Every day, we unconsciously judge people. If someone we don't know walks towards us, we speed up, thinking that this person may try to hurt us. When we walk into a place of business, we look for the man in the suit or a woman in business attire because we automatically think they are the ones in charge. Well, after an incident at a campus shuttle stop, I realized that I judge people unfairly.

Last Tuesday, I was waiting for the shuttle. This young man walked over to the stop. He was wearing torn jeans and a leather jacket. He was the picture-perfect image of the hoods seen in movies such as *Dangerous Minds* and *Stand and Deliver* and the television show *Boston Public*. I was sure he was going to grab my purse. But he didn't. Instead, he offered me a cigarette and then began reading a book for his English class. I was stunned. And then I was embarrassed. Here I was, ready to run, and all he wanted to do was read.

This event told me a great deal about how I interact with others. First, I found out that I have a problem with age. He was young, nineteen or so, and I judged him on that. I automatically suspected him of something because he was so young. To be honest, I don't know how old he really is. I had no way of finding out, but I still made the judgment.

Next, I used to think that a person's clothing reflected how seriously they took themselves. If you wear a suit or a nice dress, you are a professional. If you wear torn jeans and a leather jacket, you don't think much of yourself and are looking for trouble. Clothes, I found out, are just clothes. He is a student; he should dress in a comfortable way so he can learn.

The last thing I realized was my basis for these judgments were images from television and movies. Interestingly enough, I got many of my images about college life from the media. *Animal House* and the other kids in college movies teach you that guys in college are just jerks trying to dodge the realities of the real world. I guess I need to get out more.

In conclusion, this experience has taught me, above all else, to pay closer attention to what I immediately think about people when I first meet them. Sometimes, it is good to be cautious but that shouldn't be the only way I see the world. I hope the student I misjudged did not judge me too harshly.

Jill effectively took an embarrassing moment and turned it into a learning situation. For the purposes of the assignment, she had enough distance from the event to make some good points about her actions.

CHAPTER REVIEW

Self-reflection writing is writing generated by self-examination. In journals or diaries, people record everyday events, describe personal experiences of the past, and challenge personal values and beliefs. Self-reflection should remain personal and private; however, some writing situations call for personal points of view, and a diary or journal is a good source of these. When considering using an entry in a piece of public writing, examine topic, audience, and purpose of the writing situation as well as what type of writing strategy will be used (narrative, process, description, definition and classification, persuasion, comparison/contrast, or cause and effect). Some entries will lend themselves better than others to certain writing strategies. When exploring topics for self-reflection, keep in mind your comfort level. If you are not comfortable with other people reading (and possibly peer-reviewing or grading) the contents of certain entries in your journal or diary, don't use them. At any rate, use journals and diaries to help expand your knowledge of yourself and enhance your writing abilities.

Final Writing Assignments

1. Revise the draft you wrote for Exercise 11. Discuss it with your collaborative group. Then revise again, proofread, and format the essay, and then submit it to your instructor.

2. Read the writing assignments below and then match one of your own journal entries with one them. Develop the assignment into a paragraph or essay. Be sure to a the TAP Worksheet and a Self-Reflection Worksheet.

   a. Personal experiences help define and shape who we are and our outlook on life. This is especially true with our interactions with others. While many of our experiences with other people are positive, negative ones also happen. Write a paragraph or essay about a personal experience you had with another person where you learned something about people and about yourself. First, tell about the experience you had and then tell what you learned.

   b. Some writers view keeping a journal or diary as therapy. In other words, writing down problems helps people work through them, much the same way talking about these problems with a professional counselor or therapist would help. In a paragraph or essay, give your point of view on this idea. Use specific examples from your journal to support your opinion.

3. Reread Sendak's essay and then reflect on a personal memory from your childhood. Fill out a Self-Reflection Worksheet about the memory. Revise the reflection to make it a piece of public writing.

4. Find a photograph of yourself as a child or a drawing of yourself you did as a child. What do you see when you look at the picture? What did you imagine yourself to be when you get older? Write about your ideas and feelings.

SOCIAL CONSCIENCE:
Speaking Out

13

This town lost another bookstore last week.

More and more, small independent bookstores are going out of business around this town. I love bookstores, so I get sad when I see that yet another one has closed down. What bothers me even more is that the larger bookstore chains are coming in to replace the smaller stores. It isn't that the town can't support bookstores; the big chain stores stay open forever. But, for some reason, we just won't support the independent stores.

This seems to be the way of the retail world. Bigger is better. Put a small clothing store downtown, and it will fold in five years. Put that same clothing store in a mall housing 20 other stores on the outskirts of town and it will thrive for ten years. Why do we as consumers do that to small businesses?

Somebody ought to write a letter.

When faced with an issue like the one above, you might get angry or frustrated at first. You may be tempted to speak out—to say something to others about the situation. But later on, at your computer, you might shy away from the idea. You might think, "What is so important about my opinion?" Understand that cultures consist of individual members, each with their own views on a subject. Your concerns are just as valid as the next person's. Consider one of the largest cultures of which you are a member: the college community. Within this group are administrators, instructors, students, and others all involved with the same focus: education. The student body president may feel that students would benefit from three dances every semester and suggests channeling student funds to that end. You, on the other hand, may feel that dances are a waste of your money and that student activities funds could be better spent helping students with emergencies. If you don't make your opinion known, the student body president won't be able to consider your ideas and will go with the three dances as planned. Being a citizen or member of any group means you must speak out when necessary. Exercising your **social conscience**—your concern for issues and events that affect your community—helps clarify your thoughts and ideas on an issue and may effect change.

Of course, you may also need to do this type of writing in your college courses. With the informed opinion essay, you voice your opinion on a topic. You won't be expected to spend weeks in the library getting information; that is primarily reserved for writing research papers (see Chapter 14). However, you will be expected to give your opinion and then support it with facts and other information. At any rate, the important thing is that you learn to voice your opinion effectively. This chapter provides guidelines for putting your private concerns into public domains, such as letters to the editor. We begin our discussion by examining worldview and the influences that create it, such as values and beliefs, background, friends and family, personal experience, and education. From there, we move to gathering information from various sources, including the Internet. Audience and purpose of social conscience writings are also discussed.

Before we begin, take a look at this article about rap music. Rap is often dismissed as an art form, but this author argues in its favor, stating it is a type of poetry.

Reading 15 | The Live (Not Jive) Poets' Society: How Rap Has Rescued Rhythm and Rhyme from the Undead
Kalamu ya Salaam

BACKSTORY

One of the most celebrated styles of music is rap music. Once limited to the streets of the inner cities, rap has become a multibillion-dollar industry. Like many types of music, rap has its share of controversy. Many critics of rap music find it difficult to listen to and think the musicians' lifestyles (sometimes referred to as *gangsta*) offensive. In this essay, published in *Black Issues Book Review*, writer and critic Kalamu ya Salaam suggests that rap is an art form to be reckoned with, an art form that will have positive influences on poetry in the future.

LEXICON
cerebral: mental
Eurocentric: focusing on a European point of view
laud: praise
nascent: beginning to develop
portends: is an omen of a future occurrence
proliferation: increasing abundance
replete: full
rhetoric: use of language
vernacular: speech pattern

1   From slams to open mikes, from *Love Jones*-style movies to a slew of recent spoken word CDs, listening to and writing poetry is one of the most popular activities among young adults. Some critics are calling the phenomenon simply a trendy fad that is producing a big sound of little substance. One argument such critics give is that the absence of form in contemporary poetry has led to slipshod work by young poets who never learned the expert use of meter and traditional poetic forms such as the sonnet. However, in a rush to dismiss the excesses of free verse, many critics are completely overlooking rap.

2   In terms of utilizing the four major poetic techniques (figurative language, rhyme, meter, controlled line length) rap and spoken word are the major poetry of our time. Figurative language is the use of association to help explain or to make an expression vivid and compelling; usually the association is a comparison (simile: "my love is like a red, red rose") or an identification (metaphor: "my love is a red, red rose in the garden of my heart"). Rhyme is the use of the same or similar sounds; "hot fun / in the summer sun." Meter is the cadence of words measured by syllables and inflections, or stresses, on the syllables; "we laughed, we cried, we nearly died." Controlled line length is the author determining based on form and preference where the lines of a poem end. Of these four building blocks of poetry, only controlled line length is sometimes inaudible. Poetry started off as an oral art form and, even at its most academic, continues to utilize "sound techniques."

3   The most common and popular form of poetry in America today is rap. Rap meets all the basic criteria of poetry. Or as the rapper Rakim proclaims: Rap is a mixture of "rhythm and poetry plus created sound effects."

4   Rap lyricists reintroduced and innovated the use of rhyming and meter in modern poetry. Before rap, meter was virtually extinct and rhyme was discredited as old-fashioned. There are rules for rhyming, when two sounds conform to the basic rules of exactly the same sound in the same sequence beginning with a vowel sound and preceded by different consonant sounds (in the dark / on a lark; dark and lark are a true rhyme). Iambic pentameter is a specific measure of meter; an iamb is a two syllabic unit, or foot, that is an unstressed syllable followed by a stressed syllable, and pentameter means five feet to the line, thus iambic pentameter is a line that contains five iambs. Although it doesn't use iambic pentameter, rap nevertheless does make strong use of both rhyme and meter.

5   Because both rap and spoken word are performance oriented rather than text oriented, there has been a shift in stylistic emphasis away from controlled line length with complex and/or subtle uses of figurative language and a shift toward an emphasis on meter and rhyme with clever and/or ironic uses of figurative language. This shift is reflective of the so-called "stage versus page" debate, which is not really a contradiction of mutually exclusive techniques but rather simply a choice of one set of poetic techniques over another. Once one strips away the so-called sophistication of free verse and actually looks at the substance of what is offered, it is easy to comprehend that most free verse confuses cerebral gymnastics with being deep and socially relevant. In reality, the majority of free verse is no more deep than is the majority of rap, which just focuses on different concerns and uses different poetic conventions.

6   It is true that if one judged solely from commercial top-40 rap or the proliferation of open mike offerings, it would be difficult to laud rap's poetic content or the seriousness of the majority of spoken word. But there is more than initially meets the ear. Over

the next four or five years we will see the flowering of young poets who grew up on rap and who are simultaneously well-schooled in traditional textual poetry; from this group we can expect poetic innovations of major import.

7   *S/HE*, the new book by Saul Williams, the star of the movie *Slam*, is a good example of new directions in poetry. The book includes a CD of Saul reciting some of the interlocking, untitled poems that compose the book. *S/HE* is structured like jazz with themes and improvisations on the theme. The variations make liberal use of irony and homonyms and are replete with witty wordplays. Particularly striking is the non-narrative orientation of much of the poetry in *S/HE*.

8   Narrative poetry is the poetry of story-telling, the form most often employed in slams and open mikes. That Williams investigates surrealism and a variation of lyric poetry almost romantic in its' references is an exciting development that portends a successful search for new directions. While the book is not an unqualified success, it is an opening salvo indicating the shape of poetry to come.

9   Young writers such as Asha Bandele, Willie Perdomo, Ruth Forman, and Thomas Sayers Ellis are each in their own way seeking ways to extend the literary tradition while incorporating black musical influences, influences which include heavy dosages of rap. Because rap predisposes them toward rhyme and meter, I expect that as this generation of young writers matures, some of them will use (and may even create) formal poetic forms as vehicles for their self-expression.

10   Moreover, as today's young poets grow beyond their 20s, other concerns besides sex, self-confession, and rhetoric will come to the forefront of their consciousness as is always the case when angry young lions and lionesses become middle-aged parents and adults who find themselves supplanted by a new generation of young people, some of whom will be rebelling against those who are today's rebels. Within the next decade, look for the more serious among this current crop to craft a poetry that will be every bit as innovative as Hughes's blues or Baraka's bebop (and please remember it only takes one to get a movement started).

11   Our literary history has always consisted of two trains running, one emulative of traditional Eurocentric literary forms and the other innovative in the black vernacular tradition, a tradition that poetically always follows, rather than precedes, major shifts in the development of black music. Rap is the latest major development in black music and now that rap is maturing, it is a sure bet that a new literary form is forthcoming. We are in the nascent stage now, the shell is broken, in a minute the new poetic Blackbird will be in flight.

QUESTIONS FOR THOUGHT

1. What is your view of rap music as an innovative art form? (If you are unfamiliar with rap, go to your local music store or library and sample some of the more current CDs, or find a rap station on the radio.)

2. Salaam's discussion of rap music uses an academic tone. How does this approach legitimize his view of rap music?

3. In paragraph 6, the author states, "It is true that if one judges solely from commercial top-40 rap or the proliferation of open mike offerings, it would

be difficult to laud rap's poetic content or the seriousness of the majority of spoken word." Listen to some popular rap songs. What is the content of the songs? Is Salaam correct in his sentiment?

READY

When preparing to speak out on paper, it is best to know how you are going to approach the situation. Jumping in head first is rarely a good idea, and doing it in writing can cause you a lot of trouble. Finding your worldview and focusing on how you feel and what you think about a situation will help you be clear on how to express your concerns.

Discovering Your Worldview

A **worldview** is a set of personal, political, or religious guidelines through which we interpret our surroundings. The most challenging part of making your voice heard on any issue is having a clear idea of what you feel about that issue. This is where the self-reflective writing described in the previous chapter can help. When we reflect, we can look at the influences that help shape our worldview, such as values and beliefs, background, friends and family, personal experiences, and education.

Values and Beliefs   Among the most substantial influences on our worldview is our value and belief system. Our religious texts provide guidelines for how we should live. These religious and spiritual guides influence our worldview. For example, one reason you may support a dress code is that your religious text states people should dress in a manner that shows respect for both themselves and for a higher power.

Background   During a discussion of an issue, we might hear someone say, 'Well, I know this may sound bad, but this is just the way I was raised." Family traditions, marriages, divorce, employment, unemployment, and even relocations can all contribute to the formation of our worldview. Perhaps you don't mind having a dress code on campus because you were taught that, in public, you should also wear long pants and dress shirts.

Friends and Family   Many of our decisions in life are based on what our associates do. Because friends and family are people we care about, it seems natural that their influence would be a part of our worldview. As we think through ideas, however, we must be sure to recognize their influence and keep it to a minimum if it is getting in the way.

Personal Experience   Perhaps the largest influence on your worldview is your own experience. Personal experiences are a driving force behind many of our actions and reactions. Like it or not, in order to think clearly about a point of view on a topic, you must examine your experiences, seeing which ones are helpful in this situation and which ones are not. Maybe the reason you are against the idea of a dress code is that your parents forbade you to wear what you wanted when you were younger, and this new code sounds like the same sort of confinement.

Education   Education exposes us to a variety of thoughts, ideas, objects, and views from other people. This wide range of knowledge helps us understand and examine a topic and our own worldview more effectively. Possibly one argument for having a dress code can be supported by recent research that suggests uniforms help students focus on studies rather than trying to fit in.

The Personal Perspectives Worksheet

For help in clarifying your views and discovering where they come from, fill out the Personal Perspectives Worksheet. Along with the categories already mentioned, others, such as travel and outside influences, are included.

Personal Perspectives Worksheet

Topic: _____

Background How many people are in your immediate family? How many males and females? What memories of your childhood affect your view?	
Age How old are you? In what ways does your age affect your outlook?	
Locations Where do you live? In what part of the city or town do you live? How does your location affect your view?	
Friends and Family Who are your closest friends? Which family members are you closest to? How do their opinions influence yours?	
Travel Where have you traveled? Who have you met during your travels? How have they influenced you?	
Religious Beliefs Describe your beliefs in a higher power (if you have such beliefs). How do these beliefs affect your opinions of this subject?	
Education What schools did you attend when you were younger? What type of education did you receive? How does your education influence your opinions?	
Other Influences What books, television programs, movies, plays, lectures (and so on) have influenced your worldview? How do these other influences affect your view?	

Write your opinion of the topic on a separate sheet of paper.

Caution: Never get so caught up in one source of influence that you ignore other influences and information. Challenging the view of a member of one political party just because your family has always belonged to another is narrow-minded. Think through your views, considering all information and influences as you go. Also, be aware that worldviews are not permanent. What we think about a subject today may change by the end of the week, month, or year, depending on our influences. Further, worldviews are neither right nor wrong. They are simply a culmination of influences. Thinking people constantly reexamine their views and opinions, sometimes trading in one opinion for another. Worldviews change as you grow, so be prepared.

Exercises

1. List five current events from a newspaper or news magazine. Choose one and fill out a Personal Perspective Worksheet about the topic. Write a short paragraph explaining your views on the topic. Did you find any surprises or areas where you didn't expect you believed as you do?

*2. As a class or with a partner, choose a current event. Have each student fill out a Personal Perspectives Worksheet. In small groups, discuss the worksheets. How are they similar? How are they different?

3. Select a letter to the editor of a newspaper or magazine. Find the original article on which the letter is based. Fill out a Personal Perspectives Worksheet exploring the letter writer's point of view, then fill out a Personal Perspectives Worksheet exploring your own point of view. Finally, write a short response to the topic.

4. Record a television news program. List the topics discussed in the program. Write a Personal Perspectives Worksheet on one of the topics. Write a short paragraph giving your opinion of the topic.

5. Find a recent article in a newspaper or magazine and fill out a Personal Perspectives Worksheet. Next, watch a segment on a news program about the same topic. Fill out another Personal Perspectives Worksheet for the news program. What kind of detail did you get from the article? What kind did you get from the news program? Which did you find more useful?

Becoming Informed

Being in touch with yourself and your worldview is the first step in speaking out. You must also look outside yourself and squarely at the issue that has engaged you enough to write about it. Gather the information you need to be knowledgeable about it. Be informed.

The Source of the Problem   Where do you begin? The best place to get information is from the original source, the situation or speech or article or discussion that got you interested in the issue in the first place. Check the newspaper or magazine article for details and then look in back issues to see if more about the topic has been written. Check the byline, that little caption under the headline of an article stating who wrote it, call the editorial department of the publication, and ask to speak with the reporter. As you read the article itself, look to see who is quoted or used as source material and contact that person for more detail. Be sure to give the author of the article credit within your essay.

Interviews   Don't worry about bothering people if you need information. If you approach people in a professional manner, more often than not they will respond quite favorably to your questions. Set up a time when you can talk at length about the topic with your contact person. Have a set of questions ready so you don't ramble or repeat yourself. When you attend your meeting, dress appropriately and be on time. After you have talked, be sure to thank your contact person for his/her time. Even if the information you gather for the session terns out to be useless to you or you disagree with what the person said during the interview, remain professional. You may have to contact this person later. When you write your essay, be sure to acknowledge the interviewee.

Whether your research includes articles or interviews, you are expanding your background on the topic. Immediately after gathering your information, jot down what you think or feel about it. What bits of information will be useful to you? What bits of information won't be? How does this new information affect your point of view on this subject? Be prepared to make adjustments to your Personal Perspectives Worksheet in light of new information.

Writing with Others
SOCIAL CONSCIENCE

When you are writing to express a point of view on an issue, remember that many other people probably share your feelings. Getting others involved is part of what social conscience writing is all about. Three ways to get others involved are surveys, petitions, and letter-writing campaigns.

Surveys: Before you set out to write a letter to the editor or the president of your campus, consider finding out what others think and feel about the topic by taking a survey. A good survey consists of a number of questions directed at the topic that can be easily answered in a yes-or-no format. Keeping the questions short and to the point encourages people to respond. A good first step with your survey is to ask a friend or two to read through it and give you feedback. These readers may even have a question or two to add. A note about administering the survey: Be sure to survey a large cross-section of the population most affected by the issue. At times, you may want to question only African-American women, white males, or college administrators because those are the groups most directly affected. However, if your target is the entire student body, then make sure you are including everyone. The results of your survey will then be much more credible.

Petitions: Unlike surveys, in which you attempt to find out other people's opinions, petitions are circulated in order to get people to support a predetermined position. Well-written petitions

Continued

explain the reason for the petition and then ask for support. Generally, a social security number or student identification number must accompany each signature to prove the signer's authenticity. Make sure that the petition is addressed to a specific target person or group. Saying that your petition is directed to "the people in charge of running things on campus" is too vague. Saying your petition is directed to "the President and the Board of Regents" is clearer and will add credibility to your cause. Also try to present the signed petition at a formal meeting.

Letter-Writing Campaigns: Writing a letter to a manager or a school principal can be an effective way to make your thoughts known. However, remember the adage regarding strength in numbers. After you have written a letter stating your position on a topic and you are clear about to whom and where the letter should be sent, make a copy of it. Send the original letter and use the copy to persuade others to speak out as you did. If they seem hesitant, show them the letter you sent and allow them to use your letter as a guide for the one they will send.

The Internet When you speak out on a topic, having access to current information about that topic is vital. The Internet is a perfect place to get current information. Sites such as MSN.com and search engines such as Google.com constantly update their information sections (sometimes even hourly) and provide access to numerous articles and a wealth of background material. When using the Internet for this type of research, be careful. Searching from news sites and databases will turn up reliable information. Other types of websites, those written by disgruntled or misinformed people, should be scrutinized closely. Whatever site you choose, make sure the data are current, that the author of the information has credentials that reflect authority on the subject, and that background or related information is provided. In fact, you should use this approach with any information you may consider using in an essay. In short, evaluate before you quote.

Writing with Computers

SOCIAL CONSCIENCE

Computers are helpful when you are working on a social conscience piece of writing. A computer allows you the opportunity to save every letter you write so you can keep a file on the progress of the project. A typed letter looks professional and is easier to read than a handwritten note, which means people are more apt to take your views seriously. Be sure to put your name, address, phone number, and e-mail address on each page of the letter (many word processing programs include a section for creating letterhead) so people can contact you in response.

Computers with Internet access are even more helpful. You can use e-mail to send your letter instantly or create your own website to get your voice heard. The rules for printed letters apply

Continued

to e-mail and websites as well. Be clear in what you are saying. Always give your e-mail address along with a mailing address and a phone number so people have several ways to contact you. Be patient as you wait for a reply. Regardless of how emotional the topic may be for you, refrain from spamming (sending unsolicited copies of your letter to hundreds or thousands of people whether they have any connection to the topic or not) and flaming (sending nasty e-mail messages).

With technology and social conscience comes great responsibility. Use technology wisely as you make your voice heard.

Topic

You have a topic—a problem on campus, in your neighborhood, in society, with a state law, or with a government policy. You examined your opinion on the topic when you filled out the Personal Perspectives Worksheet. You gathered information about the topic, so you are informed. As you get ready to work, you must pay close attention to audience and purpose. For example, refer to this chapter's opening essay "The Live (Not Jive) Poets' Society." Here, the author focused on the audience (academics) and the purpose (to inform the reader that there is poetry in rap music and that the new generation of rap artists is moving that poetry into a new art form).

Audience

When writing to effect change, you start at a slight disadvantage. The audience the writing is intended for will not, most likely, be sympathetic to your point of view. Your congressional representative has taken many hours to decide how she will vote on an issue. The manager at the bookstore has a lot of other problems to deal with and will not enjoy reading your letter of complaint. School administrators report to many people (such as the Board of Regents) and, often, decisions they make are influenced by those other people. These situations work against you from the beginning, but you can overcome them if you know your audience and attack the problem, not the people.

Know Your Audience   Whether you get the type of feedback you want or not, people are listening to what you say. Look at the situation from your audience's point of view. Examine their opinions and respond to each on its own merits. Imagine, too, how your audience will react, and devise ways to counteract these reactions. Also, respect your audience for who they are, not for their opinions. Use titles when addressing people, refrain from insults, and direct your comments to the appropriate person.

Attack the Problem, Not the People   Sometimes, personalities get in the way of our speaking out on an issue. When we attack the person and not the message, we are committing an ad hominen fallacy. Focus on the problem at all times.

Salaam's audience for "The Live (Not Jive) Poets' Society" is academic; after all, the article was published in *Black Issues Book Review* magazine. The author had to present rap music as an art form worthy of the name poetry. To do this, he opened the article with a discussion on traditional forms of poetry and how rap fits into these traditional forms. By doing this, Salaam shows respect for his audience but still gets his point across.

Purpose

Why are you writing the letter you are writing? Do you want to get something off your chest, or do you want to see immediate change? Having a clear purpose in mind allows your writing to be clear because you will understand your angle on the situation. Kalamu Salaam wants to share his opinion with us and make us aware of the powerful new voices in rap music.

Salaam's purpose in writing the essay, however, could have been a call to arms. A call to arms is directing the audience to act on the topic. Salaam could have told us to grab every new *S/HE* book and CD we could find. As an action by itself, buying a book or CD is harmless. Other kinds of actions can be dangerous, so when you use a call to arms, be careful. When we are knee-deep in frustration or anger over a situation, a call to action may be our first response. Take care, however, to remember the responsibilities that go along with a call to arms. Present information in such a way that your audience can decide for themselves if they want to take your requested course of action. Also, take care to limit the action. Writing letters to a member of Congress is one thing; in most situations, telling readers to kidnap one of them is taking matters too far. Remember: Moderation in all things.

Exercises

6. Read five letters to the editor of a local newspaper. Jot down topic, audience, and purpose for each one. Were the letters published in an appropriate newspaper? Explain your answers.

7. Discuss the ideas presented in "The Live (Not Jive) Poets' Society," and then formulate your own opinion on the subject. Jot down topic, audience, and purpose for your opinion essay.

WRITE

Once you have thought through your point of view on an issue, it is time to write your essay. Examining your worldview will help guide you as you work, but don't restrain your passions in the first drafts. Speaking out requires that you actually speak out—that is, that you actually say what is on your mind—and your audience will accept deep feelings about the topic. Put your feelings into the writing and make your voice heard.

Select

Face it: No matter how hard you try, you can't take on the entire world. Speaking out about every situation you feel strongly about or about every aspect of one situation can't be done. You would be worn out in no time, and you may come across as a crank. Focus your discussion on one specific part of the topic. For your audience to understand what you are speaking out against, you must summarize or paraphrase the topic before you give your point of view.

Summarize   A summary is a short version of a larger work. When you summarize a topic, you tell your audience the main points of the larger work in your own words. By nature, a summary is short, leaving out all unnecessary information.

In paragraph 7 of this chapter's opening essay, Salaam writes,

> *S/HE*, the new book by Saul Williams, the star of the movie *Slam*, is a good example of new directions in poetry. The book includes a CD of Saul reciting some of the interlocking, untitled poems that compose the book. *S/HE* is structured like jazz with themes and improvisations on the theme. The variations make liberal use of irony and homonyms and are replete with witty wordplays. Particularly striking is the non-narrative orientation of much of the poetry in *S/HE*.

This paragraph summarizes Saul Williams's book. It gives a brief overview of the contents of the book as well as Salaam's insights on that content.

Paraphrase   Much like a summary, a paraphrase is a short version of a larger work. The difference is in the wording. When you paraphrase, you take actual sentences from the essay to create a smaller work. You must avoid opinions and insights when you paraphrase because you are just presenting the essence of a work to your audience.

A paraphrase of Salaam's article would look like this:

> The article "The Live (Not Jive) Poets' Society: How Rap Has Rescued Rhythm and Rhyme from the Undead," written by Kalamu ya Salaam, is a study of rap music and traditional forms of poetry. Salaam's position is that rap is a form of poetry with roots in iambic pentameter and free verse, with a mixture of figurative language, meter, rhyme, and controlled line length with free verse. Salaam states that rap will mature into an innovative poetic form within five years and offers rapper Saul Williams's new book *S/HE* as proof. Rap will remain a form of rebellion, says Salaam, but as its artists grow, so will the art form.

Here, Salaam's article is condensed into its basic parts or the main ideas. Word choice is critical; I wanted only to present Salaam's ideas, not critique them or misinterpret them.

Whether you summarize or paraphrase, you must be sure to include the main ideas of the work you are writing about. Otherwise, your audience will not be able to fully understand your reasons for using this outside information in your work.

Structure

When you are expressing concern or outrage, it doesn't help to just start yelling. People who may otherwise agree with you or help you find a solution will be turned away immediately. This is true in writing as well. You have to first set up or explain the situation, discuss your point of view, and then offer solutions or give a call to arms. This organizational structure can be used in a variety of ways when speaking out in writing, including the traditional opinion essay and the letter to the editor.

Opinion Essays   In an opinion essay, you express your point of view on a given topic. You should start with a short explanation of the topic. You should then move to your thesis statement, which should include the main points to be discussed in your essay. The next paragraphs will be the body of the essay, each paragraph devoted to a particular point. Once the body paragraphs are completed, you should end your essay with a restatement of your thesis statement—and, possibly, a call to arms. Salaam's article is a good example of an opinion essay.

Letters to the Editor   A popular form of speaking out is the letter to the editor of a newspaper or magazine. Although you are speaking out just like you would in an opinion essay, you have some structural differences to consider. Instead of a formal introduction, start your letter with a short summary of the topic. If your letter is in response to a specific article, be sure to give the headline and publication date of the story. From there, explain your main idea and give it specific support. Finally, wrap up your letter with a short conclusion. Because space is at a premium for most newspapers and magazines, tighten whenever possible.

REVISE

When speaking out in writing, you should first follow standard revision advice. Clean up problems in content. Check spelling and grammar. Be sure you maintain a professional tone. Always be respectful in address and language. Slang and poorly edited writing doesn't just make you look bad; it trivializes the subject. Be sure to follow format as well. For example, the appropriate greetings and salutations must be included in letters to the editor, along with the date. Follow word limits and other requirements or considerations, usually found on the opinion pages of most newspapers and magazines. For websites, you can usually e-mail the editor for guidelines, or find the Frequently Asked Questions. All of these points will help your audience listen to your message and not focus on the medium.

Exercises

8. Choose one of the topics from Exercise 1 or 2 and expand it into a draft. Be sure to develop your opinion with appropriate support.

9. Brainstorm ways that student life on campus could be improved. Fill out the TAP and Outline Worksheets and then write an opinion essay. Be sure to call on appropriate support in developing your opinion.

10. Select an article from a newspaper or magazine and write a letter to the editor. Fill out the TAP and Outline Worksheets for the letter before you write it. As you edit, refer to the publication's guidelines for length and any other format considerations. Closely proofread your letter and submit it to the editor.

STUDENT SAMPLE

A recent trend at colleges and universities is that corporations are giving money to build sports arenas. In return, the school names the new arena after the corporation that supplied the money. When Joi found out this was happening at her school, she was outraged. To her, school and corporations shouldn't mix, and naming a sports arena after a company didn't sound like a good idea. She decided to speak out.

At first, the only thing she could think to write down was "I don't think this is a good idea," so she filled out a Personal Perspectives Worksheet.

Personal Perspectives Worksheet

Topic: _Corporations buying arenas._

Background How many people are in your immediate family? How many males and females? What memories of your childhood affect your view?	*4 people in the family—2 men/2 female—men were really into sports*
Age How old are you? In what ways does your age affect your outlook?	*20—not much influence here.*
Locations Where do you live? In what part of the city or town do you live? How does your location affect your view?	*I live on campus.*
Friends and Family Who are your closest friends? Which family members are you closest to? How do their opinions influence yours?	*Most of my friends don't care either way—a few people I know don't like the idea.*

Continued

Travel	
Where have you traveled? Who have you met during your travels? How have they influenced you?	Travels haven't affected this topic.
Religious Beliefs	
Describe your beliefs in a higher power (if you have such beliefs). How do these beliefs affect your opinions of this subject?	No influence here.
Education	
What schools did you attend when you were younger? What type of education did you receive? How does your education influence your opinions?	When younger, I enjoyed sports at school. I don't like it as much now at college—seems too professional.
Other Influences	
What books, television programs, movies, plays, lectures (and so on) have influenced your worldview? How do these other influences affect your view?	I've read a few articles about this happening at other schools—wasn't all good for them—afraid it won't be all good for us—

Opinion on the topic: The school should not take the money for the

new corporate sports arena

The worksheet helped Joi clarify her thinking. Her brother would be a good source of information; he played basketball in college and coaches Little League. He may understand the politics behind the decision. Joi also realized that her school might need the money that sports brings in, thus influencing the decision. That point was also going to influence her approach to the writing.

A trip to the school library revealed information Joi thought would be useful to her cause. One article in a previous edition of her school paper explained that the president of the college had appointed a committee to review the new arena and name change. Through this article, she was able to get a complete list of names, titles, and campus addresses of the committee members. The article included the names and office locations of those members of the committee from the corporation. Joi decided to write a letter geared toward the committee and to send each member a copy. She also planned to send a letter to the editor of the school paper as a way to gauge student feeling on this matter. She also discovered that using corporate names for sports facilities was a growing trend. She wasn't sure if that bit of news would help her, but she tucked it away for later consideration.

When she returned from the library, Joi called her brother. He told her that money ruled when it came to sports facilities. "The games are profitable enough and selling merchandise brings in some money," he said, "but the big dollars for state-of-the-art sporting arenas has to come from somewhere else. The companies are more than willing to shell out the money, so let them have their names up there." She made a mental note: Any solution she offered would have to include funding.

Now she was ready to compose the rough draft for the letter to the committee. Taking all of the pieces from her worksheets, her research, and the interview with her brother, she came up with this rough draft.

To Whom It May Concern:

Recently, you made the wrong decision. Your group decided to go ahead and sell out our college by placing the name of a company over the name of our school. This really stinks.

I attend the school and have for a year now. I feel a great pride when my school teams win, especially when we play at home. I get just a bit happier knowing that our school name and colors are the last thing the losers see when they leave our town. That will all change, though, now that you and your group have decided to vote on a name change. Now, the last thing the team will see is a large sign advertising a company.

I just don't get it. Aren't you proud of your school? Does money mean that much to you that you would have to sell our new stadium? I have been told that this is happening all over the country, that new stadiums are being built with company names plastered across the front. That is all right for them, but not okay with me. We should be proud of our school.

Consider changing your minds on this issue. Perhaps an athlete's name could go in the front of the building instead. Who knows? Just don't let this decision go by the way it is. You may even want to remove certain members of the committee and start again.

Thanks for your time. Do the right thing.

Once the draft was finished, Joi set out to revise it. While keeping in mind topic, audience, and purpose, she also made notes for style and tone, her goals, and the expected outcome.

Need to get names.   To Whom It May Concern:

Recently, you made the wrong decision. Your group decided to go ahead and sell out our college by placing *Slang—needs respect.* the name of a company over the name of our school. This really stinks.

I attend the school and have for a year now. I feel a great pride when my school teams win, especially when we play at home. I get just a bit happier knowing that our school name and colors are the last thing the losers see when they leave our town. That will all change, though, now that you and your group have decided to vote on a name change. Now, the last thing the team will see is a large sign advertising a company.

I just don't get it. Aren't you proud of your school? Does *Does this seem a bit angry? I am angry, but this may be too much.* money mean that much to you that you would have to sell our new stadium? I have been told that this is happening all over the country, that new stadiums are being built with company names plastered across the front. That is all right for them, but not okay with me. We should be proud of our school.

Need to explain this solution if I want them to change their minds. Consider changing your minds on this issue. Perhaps an athlete's name could go in the front of the building instead. Who knows? Just don't let this decision go by the way it is. You may even want to remove certain members of the committee and start again.

Thanks for your time. Do the right thing.   *Should that stay?*

Joi

She saw that she had gone off on a tangent and slipped into slang. She also adjusted her goal. Originally, she had demanded that the name change not take place and that the committee be disbanded. After some thought, however, she simply asked for an audience with the committee to talk about the matter. That approach seemed much more realistic. She revised her draft yet again, taking all of the changes into consideration, and came up with this final draft.

Dr. Steven Tomes

President, Little College

Little Town, OH 23333

Dear Dr. Tomes:

Recently, a committee you appointed to oversee the creation of the new basketball arena suggested naming the new facility the Fizzie Pop Arena, replacing our school name. I think this is a mistake and would like to talk to you about it.

School pride means a great deal to the students who attend this place. They pack the arena every game and show up wearing the school colors. It feels great when we win a home game. I get even happier knowing that the last thing the losing team will see as they drive away will be our school colors and our name on the side of the arena. That will all change, though, when the name changes. The last thing the losers will see is a big sign advertising Fizzie Pop, not our school.

Many schools are getting funding for their facilities from companies and then putting the company name on those facilities. I understand the need for money to build a new sports arena and that money has to come from somewhere. I also understand that companies should get recognition for their generous donations. However, I don't understand why our school name has taken a back seat to the company's name. Put the company's name on the scoreboards, on the programs, or on a plaque or statue on the front of the building. But please don't rename the arena.

I have shared some of my concerns with other students and, even though I have written this letter to you, I would like to request a meeting between students and members of your committee.

I look forward to your reply. Thanks for your time.

Sincerely,

Joi

Before she sent that letter off, she wrote another one, this time directed to the students and faculty of the school. She wanted to raise awareness of the situation and urge others to write to the committee. Using the notes and the first letter as a basis, she composed the following letter.

To the Editor:

I don't know how many students and faculty members are aware of this, but a terrible thing has happened on this campus. The Fizzie Pop Bottling Company has taken over. The new arena has been renamed the Fizzie Pop Arena. Why on earth would the president and his committee rename our arena after a company? I am sure they donated a lot of money to build the arena, but enough to have their names above our school name? That seems ridiculous to me.

People, we need to wake up and start paying attention to what is going on. If we don't, we might find ourselves going to the Fizzie Pop University. I for one don't like the sound of that. How about you?

Get involved!

Joi

Rereading the new letter, Joi felt that it attacked the committee too much and that people weren't being encouraged to get involved. She also felt as though some of her words were too stiff; these were students she was addressing, after all. She was asking them to sign a petition against the name change. They would appreciate a more casual tone as long as she remained on track. Her revised draft is below.

To the Editor:

I read your article about the recent decision to rename our arena the Fizzie Pop Arena and I almost screamed. I think that move is crazy. Buildings like that sports arena cost millions and that money has to come from somewhere. I also understand that people want recognition for their donations to our school. However, I don't think money or recognition should come before pride in our school. When we win home games, I want the last thing the losers see on their way out of town is our names on the side of the arena. I have written a letter of concern to the president and suggest that others do the same. In my letter, I asked for a meeting between the students and the committee that made the decision. Please do the same. Together, we can change things, or at least open some discussions.

Thanks for your time.

Joi

She proofread each letter carefully, being sure to recheck the spelling of everyone's name and title. The letters were ready to go.

A few days later, her letter to the editor appeared in the paper. Joi noticed that students were beginning to question the name change and write letters to the editor themselves. A few days after her letter was published, she was sent e-mail from the director of the athletic department asking if she could attend the next committee meeting and share her concerns about the name change.

Joi spoke out and made an impact. She didn't worry about immediate change or whether or not she would get her way. She wanted to have a discussion about the name change, and she eventually got it. When you find topics and issues you feel strongly about, speak out. Write a letter and let people know how you feel. Get involved—and put your writing skills to good use.

CHAPTER REVIEW

You should exercise your social conscience and speak out in writing when necessary. Defining your worldview is the best way to start. Examine the events and influences that have helped shape your opinions, such as values and beliefs, background, friends and family, personal experiences, and education. By using a Personal Perspectives Worksheet, you can determine what part of your worldview is affected by the situation at hand. Once you have determined your point of view, research your topic. Go to the library, ask people who are involved in the situation, or go online for information. When you have researched the topic, then choose a form for your voice: the opinion essay or the letter to the editor. Either way, be sure to add information about the topic to your discussion in the form of a summary or paraphrase. A summary is a brief overview that may contain your opinion. A paraphrase is also a brief overview, but it focuses on the main points of an argument and contains little, if any, bias.

Final Writing Assignments

1. Read through your local newspaper or your campus paper to find an issue that concerns you. Write a letter to the appropriate government official or administrator expressing your concerns. To find the name and title of the appropriate person, check with your local library or look in the blue pages section of your local phone book.

2. Consider issues that affect our country as a whole—poverty, racism, health care, etc.—and write a letter to a government official expressing your concerns. For more information on issues affecting the entire country, go to your campus library or check the Internet.

3. Revise one of the drafts you wrote for Exercises 8–10. Submit it to your instructor.

4. Write a response to Kalamu ya Salaam's essay "The Live (Not Jive) Poets' Society." Highlight the main points of the essay and them complete a TAP and Personal Perspectives Worksheet to help focus your point of view on the topic. From there, write your essay. Submit the final draft to your instructor.

14

ACADEMIC WRITING:
Using Research

When I first decided to write this textbook, I thought it would be a breeze. After all, I had been teaching writing for six years and had been writing for many years before that. Writing this thing should have been a simple matter of sitting down and writing out my thoughts and ideas on how students should learn to write for an academic audience.

After the first few pages, though, reality set in. I found myself exhausted of ideas. I didn't know everything that needed to be included in a textbook and had to look at other sources for information and inspiration. I looked at other textbooks, I read through numerous magazines, books, and websites, and I talked with colleagues. Of course, my editor also added her years of experience to my project. All of this collected information was research. This book could, in fact, be thought of as a research project, not unlike the research papers discussed in this chapter.

Research papers require gathering information and sharing that information with an audience. For our discussion of academic writing, we start with appropriate topics and then move into research, outside sources, how to think critically about these sources, and how to use them in our own work. The chapter concludes with a brief look at the Modern Language Association (MLA) style of documenting source material and formatting research papers.

We begin our discussion with a research paper focusing on selecting a good college entitled "The Best Four-Year College for Me."

Reading 16 | The Best Four-Year College for Me
Erica Gates

BACKSTORY

Major decisions, such as selecting the college you will attend, should never be made lightly. How did you choose the school you now attend? What factors were important in your decision? Friends? Finances? Sports? In the following reading, posted on the Internet, student Erica Gates accesses a variety of resources for help in finding the best four-year college for her. Compare your search for a school with hers.

LEXICON

commute: travel from one place to another regularly

determining: controlling or deciding

Research Question: What is the best four-year college for me to attend to get a degree in accounting?

Audience: myself, my family, and anyone else interested in the same colleges and the same degree.

Erica Gates

ENG 111-07

December 10, 1996

INTRODUCTION

1   Ever since I took accounting classes in high school, I have wanted to be an accountant. I really liked math and I caught on to the accounting techniques quickly. It has always been important to me that I go to college. I know that I will have a better shot of becoming a well-known accountant if I have a degree in accounting.

2   I am currently going to Germanna Community College (GCC) and I want to transfer to a four-year college and get a bachelor's degree. I have a 13-month-old son and I have to find a college that fits both of our needs. I decided to carry out a research project so I could determine which college to attend to get a degree in accounting. The cost of tuition and living expenses, such as housing, is a major factor. Child care, financial aid and scholarships, location, and whether my credits will transfer are also important factors. I picked George Mason University (GMU) and Mary Washington College (MWC) because they are the closest four-year colleges to my house. I wanted to be close to home because of my family. I did not know if I had to commute or not so it would be easier if I was closer.

METHOD

3   The first thing I did was go to the Fauquier Library in Warrenton to see what kind of references I could find. I found a book on colleges that I thought would help me. The name of the book was *The Big Book of Colleges* by Edward T. Custard. I looked at this book because it told me a lot about the different colleges and what each college offers. It had all of the basic things I needed to know such as the housing costs, student services, admissions and cost of tuition. The library also had the college catalogs there which were very helpful. They told me everything from cost and facilities to schedules of classes. The catalogs that I had were *Mary Washington College 1993–1995 Academic Catalog* by James B. Gouger and Mary I. Kemp and *George Mason University 1996–1997 Undergraduate Catalog* by Colleen Kearney Thornberg.

4   I called Mary Washington College and spoke to Mrs. Caroline Columbia, Counselor in the Dean of Admissions Office. I asked her about the classes that I was currently taking and asked whether they would transfer or not. I asked about the housing facilities and financial aid and scholarships. Mrs. Caroline Columbia also sent me a transfer guide

from the college and general information pamphlets. I also called George Mason University and spoke to Mrs. Patricia Riordan, Counselor in the Dean of Admissions Office. She told me about my classes transferring. She also gave me a lot of information about the housing and what numbers to call if I needed to speak to someone in the future. Then I went to George Mason University for an "Open House" on November 3, 1996. I had a tour of the campus and got a lot of information about financial aid, housing, classes, costs of living and a lot more.

FINDINGS

Cost

Tuition

5   The most important factor for me when I was deciding what college to transfer to was the cost. I used Edward T. Custard's *Big Book of Colleges 1996 Edition* to find out how much the tuition was at George Mason University and then at Mary Washington College (MWC). Tuition was $4,212 a year at George Mason and was $2,026 at Mary Washington (Custard 380 and 587). I set a limit of $5,000 per year and I was glad that both colleges that I picked were under that amount. Mary Washington was obviously the better choice when it came to comparing prices, George Mason was twice as much a year. I decided that MWC was my choice when tuition was a factor.

Housing Costs

6   I really needed to know how much it would cost to live on campus. At George Mason room and board was $4,930 per year and Mary Washington was $4,942 (Custard 380 and 587). I also wanted to find out how much it would cost to live in an apartment or townhouse. When I talked to Mrs. Columbia from Mary Washington, she said, "There aren't any apartments or townhouses on campus." I looked in the *George Mason University 1996–97 Undergraduate Catalog* and I found that they have apartments and townhouses available on campus. They are $1,950–2,100 per semester (Thornberg 24). When I talked to Mrs. Riordan from George Mason, I asked her if I could live on campus with my son in an apartment or townhouse and she said, "There aren't any young children allowed to live on campus. There are apartments close by and we have an apartment locating service available to students." I really wanted to live on campus because it would be a lot more convenient for me to go there. I know that if I go to a four-year school soon I will have to either commute or get an apartment or townhouse near the college.

Child Care

7   I did not think that child care was going to be a determining factor in choosing a college because I thought I would have to take my son to a public daycare nearby. When I was talking to Mrs. Riordan from George Mason, she told me that child care was available on campus to students, faculty and advisors. I could not believe it! That would help me out a lot because I could have my son right there with me at school and it was free. If I went to MWC, I would have to find a daycare and I would have to pay for it. George Mason was definitely the better choice when child care was a factor.

Financial Aid and Scholarships

8   I really wanted to know if there was financial aid and scholarships available to me. In Edward T. Custard's *Big Book of Colleges 1996 Edition*, I found out that financial aid was available at George Mason and Mary Washington. There are a variety of types of aid and scholarships available at both colleges. At George Mason "freshman scholarships and grants average $3,132. Individual awards range from $100 to $18,630" (380). At MWC "freshman scholarships and grants average $1,800. Individual awards range from $50 to $5,000" (587). I was glad that a lot of aid was available at each college and it was at least enough to pay for more than half of a year's tuition. Every little bit helps. Both colleges had aid available so financial aid and scholarships did not affect my decision.

Location

9   I wanted to go to a college that was in-state. Both George Mason and Mary Washington are nearby. George Mason is in Fairfax and is about 1 hour away from my house. MWC is in Fredricksburg and is about 1 hour and 45 minutes away from my house. George Mason is located in an urban area and MWC is located in a rural area (Custard 380 and 587). When I went to George Mason to visit the college I really liked it. I liked it because it was near a lot of things but it was not really crowded. It was a huge campus. I did not like the fact that I have to drive on a major interstate because traffic could be a problem. MWC is a lot further and there would be traffic also because it is located in downtown Fredricksburg. They both seem to be nice places to live in. I would not mind commuting for an hour, but I do not want to commute for almost 2 hours. George Mason is a lot closer and I would rather be closer if I had to commute. GMU would definitely be my choice based on the factor of location.

Transfer Credits

10   I am presently going to Germanna Community College and I wanted to make sure the classes that I am taking would transfer. When I talked to Mrs. Riordan from George Mason, she told me that the college would send me a list of all the credits that they would take after I was accepted. I found the general requirements for my degree in accounting in the *George Mason University 1996–97 Undergraduate Catalog* (56–57). It also had a list of the different classes I should take so I know what should transfer.

11   When I talked to Mrs. Columbia of MWC, she said she would send me a transfer guide in the mail. I looked at it and it was really helpful. It told me what business classes I should take before I transfer and it also had the community college classes, the section, and what it was equivalent to at MWC. Most of the classes I have taken and plan to take will transfer (*Mary Washington* 13–28).

12   I think George Mason should come up with one instead of waiting to submit me a list after I am accepted. It seemed to be a lot easier for me to transfer to MWC because I knew what classes they would accept. Therefore, MWC would be my choice based on the factor of transfer credits.

CONCLUSION

13   When I first was deciding what college to go to, I thought the cost of tuition and living costs were the most important factors. When I finished my research I realized that child care and location were the most important. I decided that George Mason University would be the best college for me to transfer to. I like the location and if I have to commute, it is a lot closer than MWC. They have daycare on campus so it will be a lot easier for me to drop my son off and pick him up. If I go there I won't have to worry about finding a good daycare or having to pay for it. George Mason is more expensive than MWC, but I might make the difference up in cost with daycare expenses if I went to MWC. In comparing both colleges, George Mason seems to be the best choice for me and my son.

WORKS CITED

Columbia, Caroline. Telephone interview. 13 Nov. 1996.

Custard, Edward T. *The Big Book of Colleges 1996 Edition.* New York: Random House, 1996.

Mary Washington College Transfer Guide for the Virginia Community College System and Richard Bland College 1995–96. Fredricksburg, Virginia: Mary Washington College in-house publication, 1995.

Riordan, Patricia. Telephone interview. 14 Nov. 1996.

Thornberg, Colleen Kearney. *George Mason University 1996–97 Undergraduate Catalog.* Princeton: Graphic Image, 1996.

QUESTIONS FOR THOUGHT

1. What type of research did you do to determine where you would attend college?
2. What additional resources could Erica have used?
3. What other major decisions can be made through writing research papers?

READY

When writing a research paper, your job is to present expert opinion from a variety of sources on a topic as well as your own point of view. Background information is required, along with source material that supports various aspects of the topic.

Topic, Audience, and Purpose

When choosing a topic, brainstorm a list of subjects that interest or intrigue you. Choose one and jot down what you already know about the topic. This jotting shows you what you *don't* know, which will help when you gather information. From here, create a research question to answer as you research the topic. Next, generate a list of sources that will provide both background information and expert opinion. Erica's topic was a good school near her home that would serve her needs. She created the research question "What is the best four-year college for me to attend to get a degree in accounting?" She knew she had a number of considerations when choosing a college (tuition, housing, child care, location, and transfer credits). These concerns became the basis of her paper.

As you review your source material and expand your knowledge, keep in mind your audience's level of knowledge of the subject. Analyze what your audience may already know. Include any background information that will be useful to your audience. Likewise, always remember your purpose for writing your research paper. In many cases, you are educating your audience on many facets of your chosen topic. All of the information in the paper should go toward that end.

Consider Erica's paper once again. She must transfer to a four-year school in order to become an accountant. She also states that she has a thirteen-month-old son, which will affect her choice of college. Throughout the paper, she provides information that informs the audience and focuses the paper on the purpose.

The purpose of a research paper is to present aspects of the topic to the audience. Be careful not to confuse this purpose with the thesis statement or the main idea behind your research paper. Erica's purpose is to present research on two schools—George Mason University and Mary Washington College—in the areas of tuition, housing, child care, financial aid, location, and transfer credits. The thesis statement (or what she hopes to accomplish with this research paper) will answer the question of which school is best for her. The purpose, however, is to present information about both schools, as well as her decision-making process, to her audience.

Research

Once you have established topic, audience, and purpose, be sure to fill out a TAP Worksheet. After that, you will need to consult strong **outside sources**— that is, you will need to collect information from sources other than yourself. Generally speaking, you will consult magazines and newspapers, scholarly books and journals, television, radio, reference works, and experts in the field. It is not necessary to read through every book and magazine or log on to every website devoted to your topic. You need only refer to those sources that will help with the purpose of the research paper.

Magazines and Newspapers   For many topics, magazines are the best place to begin, for magazine articles often provide background information, extensive research, and charts and graphs to help explain difficult material. Like magazines, newspapers are written for a general audience, but the information may be much more current. Articles in newspapers generally lack the detailed background you may find in magazine articles on the same topic. Check *The Guide to Periodicals and Publications* for a listing of magazine articles by topic. Information on newspaper articles can be found in newspaper indexes available at your library or online. If you are interested in editorials or other people' opinions about a topic, check *Editorials on File*, a listing of newspaper editorials separated by topic. Also check for online and CD-ROM–based newspaper and magazine listings.

Scholarly Books and Journals   Scholarly works are important to research papers; including these works shows you have gone to a higher level in your research than the general public may expect. However, be aware that the writing in many books and journals is dense. Terms, background information, and even references to other research may not be explained; the author expects the audience to come equipped with this information. Keep in mind that you should understand the information you cite in your research paper. A lack of understanding will show in your writing. Quoting an expert or citing a groundbreaking study won't impress your audience if you don't have a real reason for using the information.

Television   Television viewers can watch talk shows, news magazines, public television shows, CNN, CNN Headline News, C-SPAN, CNBC, and MSNBC, all of which provide around-the-clock coverage of national and international events as well as press conferences, trials, and government sessions. Be sure to take notes as you watch or get transcripts of programs, usually available through the station's website.

The Internet   One readily available research tool is the Internet. Many times, we gather information from the Internet without realizing we are doing research. When you log on to a search engine, type in your topic and press Enter, you will get an abundance of results, so you have to choose carefully which you will pursue. Focus on your research question to weed out sites that may provide useless information. Then look at the information itself, followed by the credentials of the author and the most recent date that the website and its material were updated. If the material seems useful, the author credible, and the site recent, bookmark or print that information for possible future use. Otherwise, keep looking.

Radio   Radio can be a good source for information. Many AM stations broadcast talk shows and other news programs that offer in-depth reports on a variety of topics, especially local issues. For more national coverage, National Public Radio has a vast offering of programming that can provide researchers with good information. Like television, radio broadcasts aren't likely to be repeated when you need the information, so tape the programs or get transcripts from the broadcasting station. Also, check with your local library to see if tapes of the broadcasts are available.

Reference Works   Reference works are sources that can be accessed for specific information on a topic, such as definitions of terms. Good reference materials are a great way to begin your research. Unabridged dictionaries list the meanings of unfamiliar words. Encyclopedias give a basic overview of your topic and include related ideas for further research. Check your library for more specific reference material, such as technology dictionaries and almanacs.

Critical Thinking

Sifting through points of view to find information requires **critical thinking,** which is in-depth thinking that goes beyond accepting the information at face value. This type of thinking includes evaluating the information for both accuracy and relevance to your needs as well as making connections between bits of seemingly unconnected statements.

Tips

Make Yourself Think Critically

You need to glean the important information from your source material and leave out trivial, nonessential, or opinionated rhetoric. Here are a few tips:

▸▸▸▸ **Look for the most recent information.** Hundreds (possibly thousands) of books, articles, and websites exist for just about every topic. If you look at the most recent information, your choices slim considerably. You can now focus on information necessary for your writing project or at least have a clearer direction for your research.

▸▸▸▸ **Check a variety of sources if you get stuck.** Rarely do we get all of our information from a single source, such as the Internet or our local newspapers. Different sources provide different depths of information, reveal different perspectives, and are necessary for balance in your paper. Seek out a range of sources as you research your topic.

▸▸▸▸ **Use sources that are credible and that your audience will respect.** Movies such as *Titanic* and *Pearl Harbor* deal with historical events and would be useful sources for a research paper about, say, media perceptions of historical events. However, serious historians would most likely object to your citing these in a paper about causes of either event. Just as with any other writing situation, you want to reach your audience. You don't want them to doubt your choice of source material and miss the message behind the writing.

▸▸▸▸ **Focus exclusively on the information you need to complete your research.** If you are like me, passing up a good book or an interesting article is difficult. Research exposes you to a vast amount of information. Try not to get distracted and lose focus. Return to the paper's outline for the purpose of your writing. Jot down additional ideas, books, magazine articles, and other bits of information so you can come back to them later, but keep your attention on the goal of completing your paper. Be aware that within articles, writers can purposefully lead you astray. Apply focus in all aspects of your reading.

Writing with Computers

RESEARCH ON THE INTERNET

Effective use of the Internet for research begins with the search engine and the keyword you use to initiate your searches. A search engine is a program that scours the Internet for information

Continued

based on the keywords or topics you provide. For example, AltaVista is a search engine. If I type "space ship" into the engine, it retrieves links to hundreds of thousands of websites that have something to do with space shuttles. Here is where the headaches begin. A search engine looks for sites that include the keyword you provided; it does not discriminate in any other way. NASA's official website may appear alongside a site advertising a game about space ships or a fan page devoted to drawings of space ships from *Star Wars*. Rather than visiting each site, you should use more keywords. Instead of "space shuttle," try "space shuttle fuel" or "space shuttle" plus "hydrogen." Narrowing your search in this way will yield fewer but more useful results and, therefore, more time to actually do the research.

Consider also that all sites are not created equal. The domain (usually the three letters after the dot in the Internet address) tells what type of site you are viewing. A *.com* is a business site, or one that is financed through advertisements. A *.gov* means the site is sponsored by a government agency. Sites created for organizations use the *.org* suffix. Finally, *.net* means the site is part of a computer network. General information can be found on .com sites, but more specific information may be found on some of the others.

When using the Internet, be careful not to get lazy. You should scrutinize the information in a website just as you would information from a print source. You should also print out information you may consider using and make notes from the hard copy instead of the computer screen. Resist the urge to simply copy and paste sections of information from a website to your paper. This practice could lead to plagiarism, whether you intend it to or not.

Along with the Internet, many other computer-based research tools are available. Many encyclopedias are recorded on CD-ROM, as are many ethnic newspapers and databases. Ask your librarian for more information about computerized source material. Be sure to scrutinize this material just as you would any other.

Exercises

1. Read an article from a section of a newspaper or magazine you seldom (if ever) read. List five related topics you would consider exploring. In a few sentences under each of the topics, explain why you chose this particular topic and whether it would be better as a topic for an opinion piece or a research paper.

2. Brainstorm a list of reasons you chose the college that you attend. Write a brief paragraph about how you could turn these reasons into a research paper.

3. Brainstorm a list of college majors you might like to pursue. How could you turn that list into a research paper?

Note Taking

Effective note taking requires good organization. The one statistic or quote that supports your thesis statement perfectly will do you no good if you cannot locate it when you need it. In order to combat this problem, start with a stack of index cards. When you access a source, grab a card and make a bibliography card out of it; be sure to include all the information you will need for your Works Cited page, including author, title of publication, date of publication, place of publication, and page numbers of the information. A sample card for Erica's paper would look like this:

Bibliography Card

Custard, Edward T. The Big Book of Colleges 1996 Edition.

New York: Random House, 1996.

After you make the bibliography card, organize information from that source material in three levels: general (or background), specific (statistic), and must-have. General information includes history or background material that may appear in a number of sources and would be known by your audience. Summarize this information as you take notes.

General Information Card

Tuition—

George Mason University: $4,212.00

Mary Washington: $2,026.00

—Custard, pages 380 and 587

The second level, specific information, comprises specific data that may come in handy when clarifying a point. Write this down in your own words, paying particular attention to exact statistics and other facts.

Specific Information Card

> Child care was available on campus to students, faculty, and advisors
>
> and it was free!
>
> —Riordan, interview

Finally, at the third level, the must-have level, is information that is vital to your paper and strikes you as perhaps the best way to say what needs to be said. These statements should be used in your paper verbatim (word for word). This is not to say that your own writing is subpar; however, to add power or flavor to your research paper, directly quoting a relevant source is appropriate. Plus, direct quotes add credibility to your work.

Must-Have Information Card

> "There aren't any young children allowed to live on campus.
>
> There are apartments close by and we have an apartment
>
> locating service available to students."
>
> —Riordan, interview

Index cards may seem unwieldy, a bit awkward, and somewhat archaic at first, but they force you to think about what you are using as research information. The cards curb the temptation to simply cut and paste information without reading it thoroughly. Also, the cards force you to make sure you have all of the important information for your Works Cited page.

Exercises

4. Take notes on the following readings as though you were doing research. Create a bibliography card, a general information card, a specific information card, and a must-have information card for each reading. Share and discuss your notes with your classmates.
   a. "Learning What Team Really Means" (pages 370–372)
   b. "How Scott Weiland Got Sober" (pages 383–386)
   c. "Underhanded Achievement" (pages 399–401)
5. Choose a topic from Exercise 2 or 3 and research it. Fill out a TAP Worksheet and then create a research question. After that, gather information and take notes. Be sure to check a variety of sources. Also, make sure you have at least one bibliography card, one general information card, one specific information card, and one must-have information card for each source. Write a short paragraph about your research experiences and share it with your classmates.

WRITE

After your research is complete, you can begin writing your paper. As with all other writing assignments, you should have an introduction, body paragraphs, and a conclusion. The big difference with this writing project, however, is that as you write, you must work in your research. That requires paying close attention to selection and documentation to avoid plagiarism.

Select

Audience and purpose will guide your selection process when it comes to research papers. Information necessary for your audience to understand concepts behind the topic must be included in the paper. Information that provides a balance of opinions and insights must also be included. Reconsider information that is well stated or comes from an interesting source but doesn't help your audience or serve your purpose. Whatever information you choose must support the thesis statement or the main ideas within the body of the paper.

Thesis Statement   The thesis statement is the controlling idea behind your essay. Some thesis statements dictate the internal information in the essay. In an opinion essay, for example, you state your opinion up front and then devote the rest of the essay to supporting this opinion. However, a research paper is different. The thesis is reflected in the research question you establish at the beginning of the writing process. Information you include in your paper must help answer this question.

For example, Erica's thesis focused on the best college for her based on a certain set of criteria. She did not include any information that moved her discussion away from this thesis.

Main Points   Main points dictate the information that should be included in each of the body paragraphs. (Note that conclusions drawn from the research are discussed later.) Return to Erica's research paper for examples. She stated the criteria, or main points, for her discussion: tuition, housing, child care, financial aid, location, and transfer credits. Irrelevant information—for example, the size of the student population or the number of buildings on the campus—was thrown out.

Structure

As you arrange your information, put yourself in your audience's position. What would make learning about this topic and taking in the information easier? First, provide background information that helps your audience learn about the topic in general and then move into your research question. From there, discuss the details of the topic. Devote each body paragraph to a different aspect of the topic, developing each point through statistics, expert points of view, and other information. Finally, review the information you presented and state any conclusions you have made about the topic. Generally speaking, the structure of a research paper is **introduction**, **method**, **findings**, **conclusion**, and **references**.

Introduction   In the introduction, grab the reader's attention, provide background information about the topic, and then discuss the research question and main ideas you explore through your research. Look at Erica's introduction. Right at the beginning of the paper, she explains how her goal of becoming an accountant led her to choose a four-year college to attend. Having established that, she lists the major points she discusses in the paper: tuition, housing, child care, financial aid, location, and transfer credits. From this, the reader knows the topic and the purpose of the paper.

Method   In the next section of your research paper, you must explain how you did your research. This includes listing the people you contacted, the sources you consulted, and any experiments you did to obtain information, such as surveys. Stating your methods here helps familiarize the audience with the nature and depth of your research. Erica consulted books on colleges, received college catalogs, talked to admissions counselors, gathered pamphlets and other handouts, and even toured one of the schools. She was thorough in her research.

Findings   Once you have stated how you got your information, you must discuss the information itself. Refer to the introduction and let it guide you as you select and organize the information for your paper. For example, look at the paragraph on tuition in Erica's paper. She states the tuition costs for each school and then explains which school is a better choice if tuition only is considered. She presents information about the other points in the other paragraphs.

Conclusion   The conclusion of the research paper summarizes the findings of the research and states your interpretation of the information. When formulating this interpretation, be sure to focus only on the information gathered during the research stage of the paper. Erica's research led her to conclude that George Mason University is the best choice for her. She states this clearly in her conclusion. Thus, her research paper served its purpose.

References   The last page of your paper is the Works Cited page, the list of sources you referred to in the paper itself. Be sure to follow MLA style carefully or ask your instructor for the format he or she prefers. Erica's Works Cited page, as well as the Works Cited page information found in this chapter, are good examples of how the page should be formatted.

The Research Outline Worksheet

The Research Outline Worksheet on the next page will help you organize your information well. Sort your index cards and any other bits of information you have written down according to the following categories: introduction, methods, findings, conclusion, and reference. Then transfer the information from the cards to the outline page. Granted, some of the information may be lengthy, so don't copy the entire passage. Just make a note on the outline worksheet stating where the information should go and then work it in when you write your draft. If you see a weak section, now is the time to strengthen it through more research.

Research Outline Worksheet

Topic: _____

Audience: _____

Purpose: _____

Research question: _____

_____

_____

Introduction: _____

_____

_____

Method: _____

_____

_____

Findings: _____

_____

_____

_____

_____

_____

Conclusion: _____

_____

_____

References: _____

_____

_____

_____

Additional comments: _____

_____

_____

_____

Summarizing and Paraphrasing Source Material

A **summary** is a condensation of a large amount of information. When you summarize, you are zeroing in on the main idea of the work. With a **paraphrase**, you are also condensing information by restating ideas and information from a source in your own words. With a **quote**, you are putting information from a source into your paper. Quotes come in several forms. A **line quote** is a single sentence or two taken from a source, while a **block quote** is a paragraph or two taken from a source. A **direct quote** is information borrowed word for word from a source. An **indirect quote** is a quote borrowed from a source but restated in your own words.

Because referencing source material is important when writing a research paper, let's look at an example of direct and indirect quotation. Refer back to Erica's research paper, particularly paragraphs seven and eight. Paragraph eight states,

> At George Mason "freshman scholarships and grants average $3,132. Individual awards range from $100 to $18,630" (380). At MWC "freshman scholarships and grants average $1,800. Individual awards range from $50 to $5,000" (587).

This is a good example of direct quotation. If we were to read pages 380 and 587 of *The Big Book of Colleges 1996 Edition*, we would find the tuition information exactly as Erica was written it in her paper. In other words, the wording of the information came directly from the source.

In paragraph seven, Erica takes a different approach.

> When I was talking to Mrs. Riordan from George Mason, she told me that child care was available on campus to students, faculty and advisors. I could not believe it! That would help me out a lot because I could have my son right there with me at school and it was free.

Erica wanted to use the information about the free child care on campus, but she didn't want to use the wording that Mrs. Riordan used, so Erica rephrased the information. This is a good example of indirect quotation. Please note that the only thing that is changed is the phrasing of the information, not the information itself.

Transitions are also a consideration when writing a lengthy work such as a research paper. **Transitions** are words or phrases that move the reader smoothly from one thought to another. To introduce new points, you can simply write "First," "Second," "Next," and "Finally." When introducing a point of research, consider transitions such as "According to the author,…" "This idea is well supported in an article by [author's name here] when she states that…," or "[Author's name] also goes on to say that…." Keep in mind that you can, however, create just about any sort of transition that fits your needs.

STUDENT SAMPLE

Let's turn our attention to Stephanie, a student who chose to research the connection between cellular phone use and traffic accidents. Stephanie found that cellular phones were being blamed for driving hazards and health hazards but were also good tools for drivers to have. She arranged her paper this way:

Research Outline Worksheet

Topic: _Cellular phones_

Audience: _Those who use cell phones or criticize cell phone users_

Purpose: _To explore the dangers of cell phone use_

Research question: _What are the dangers of cell phone use?_

Introduction: _In this ever-changing world there is controversy over the use of cell phones_

Method: _Readings from journals_
Interviews with professionals

Findings: _Three areas of controversy—_
Driving hazards—Accidents—weaving from lane to lane, dialing and answering the phone
Driving Positives–Helpful to emergency vehicles—helpful when breakdowns
or accidents occur—video imaging for rescue vehicles
Health hazards—Radio frequency—antennas—pacemakers—cancer

Conclusion: _I find that cellular phone usage demonstrates_
more positives than negatives

Continued

References: _I'll start with Consumer Digest article about_
cell phones, then check the Internet for ideas.

Additional comments: _____

Her research went well so far; she accessed a number of print resources and interviewed an expert. She filled out her index cards and, ready to write her paper, determined how to present the information she found: summary, paraphrase, and quote. Her rough draft looked like this:

Cellular Phones: Are They a Help or a Hazard?

You are sitting at a busy intersection on your way home from work. You look to your left and your right, and the drivers of both cars are talking on a cellular phone. In today's ever-changing world, there is controversy over the use of cellular phones. Are they really that much of a hazard? I feel this fear is truly exaggerated.

Cellular technology has been around a lot longer than most people realize. According to Kathleen Kocks, in her article in *Journal of Electronic Devices*, cellular technology began in 1947 when Bell Laboratories (now part of Lucent Technologies) developed the analog cellular concept. The technology lay dormant until the early 1980s, when commercial cellular services were launched in Washington, D.C., and Chicago, Illinois. Since then, there has been a cellular phone revolution. Usage has skyrocketed, growing more than 50 percent each year and now incorporating over 300 million users worldwide. Working for a cellular phone company, I find out firsthand how important people's cellular phones are to them. For the most part, they find themselves totally disconnected from the world without them.

With the market growing so rapidly, this means more people use their phones while driving on busy freeways. In Joseph Palenchar's article in *Twice*, he informs us that in more than thirty studies conducted by the Harvard Center for Risk Analysis, they came up with the calculations that a driver's risk of being killed while driving and talking on a phone is 6.4 in a million per year, or 80 percent less than their risk of dying while driving with a blood alcohol content of 0.1 percent (which is defined as legally drunk in most states) twelve times per year for one half-hour each time. Palenchar also tells us that the risk of a motorist being killed by a driver who is talking on a cellular phone is 1.5 in a million per year, or 92 percent less than the risk of being killed by a driver with any level of alcohol in his or her blood. Looking at these statistics, I feel that we need to worry more about our drunk drivers than about our cellular phone users.

A crash that killed a two-year-old led to a proposed law called Morgan's Bill. This federal bill would make it illegal for drivers to use cellular phones while driving. An article in *Workforce* states that, according to Todd Raphael and the National Council of State Legislatures, at the time this article was published, there were twenty-four states considering bans on cellular phone use while driving. A couple of the cities that have already incorporated the ban are Brooklyn, Ohio, and New York City. In Brooklyn, Ohio, all drivers were banned from using phones while driving and, in New York City, they have banned all cab drivers from using them while driving.

Someone can reach over and change a radio station or CD and swerve between lanes just as easily as if he were answering a cellular phone. Or how many times have you seen someone smoking and they drop their cigarette. That's definitely a road hazard.

I do feel that if you have someone with you who can dial the number for you or answer it, then that is the safest way, but like myself, many of us usually travel alone. It is important for users to know when to use the phone and when not to. If there are road hazards such as snow, ice, heavy fog, or even just heavy rains, then they should know not to use the phone until they are stopped somewhere safe. But this is just using common sense.

As with anything, a lot of the people are so busy addressing the negative things of a product that they have a tendency to overlook the good things they do. Between January 1996 and June 1997, it is reported by Simon Chapman in *The Lancelet*, 3,975,154 calls were made to the 000 emergency services (174,405—4.3 percent—were made from mobiles, with 59 percent to police, 31.5 percent to ambulances, and 9.5 percent to fire services.) To me, the statistics show a definite positive side to cellular phones.

You're driving along and notice a drunk driver. You take out your cellular phone and call 1-800-GRAB-DUI. You let them know where the driver is and which way he is going. The police then stop him, arrest him, and get him off the road before he injures or kills himself or someone else. Or, the scenario that you were driving along by yourself and you start having severe chest pains. You are not near any businesses or houses that could see you and passersby just think you are lost. You pull over and call 911 and an ambulance is then able to get to you and possibly save your life. If you had not had a cellular phone with you, or not been able to use it, then you probably would have sat on the side of the road and died.

In *American Medical News*, Tracy Binius tells of three Maryland Express care ambulances that are outfitted with digital cellular phones that send real-time images to a neurologist at the University of Maryland Medical Center so they know what to expect when they get to the facility.

Not only are there driving concerns with cellular phones. Along with that also come the health hazards. Though it is important to note, there are also health hazards associated with cellular phones. As we know, cellular phones work on frequencies. In *Popular Mechanics*, they tell us that the range of frequencies making up the electromagnetic spectrum is broad. It goes from AM radio broadcasts, which begin around 500,000 cps (cycles per second) to microwave ovens, which cook at a rate of 2.8 billion cps. In this range, cellular phones come in at a lower rate of 840–880 million cps. You don't see anyone trying to get microwave ovens banned.

A gentleman in Florida tried to sue the cellular industry when his wife died of a brain tumor. He went on several talk shows about the issue. There was no way to prove that it was incurred because of a cellular phone.

There are so many opinions in this angle as well. Christine Kuehn Kelly reports on both sides in "Are Cell Phones Dangerous to Your Health?" Some say research has connected cellular phone use to changes in the structure of the brain. The interaction can alter the brain's perception and judgment. There may also be some long-term concerns linking to cancer and possibly leukemia. Dr. Adey also says that cellular phone transmissions open the blood-brain barrier. This is a protective shield that keeps toxins away from brain tissues. When this protective shield is not intact, you end up with headaches. That is because substances that normally remain in the blood then can reach the pain-sensitive tissue covering the brain.

Kelly also reports that John Moulder, Ph.D., an expert on radio frequency radiation safety at the Medical Center of Wisconsin, states he doesn't believe any negative health effects have been demonstrated from cellular phone usage. Moulder states, "Studies haven't seen any increased risk in brain tissue in mobile phone users and, from what's available now, show no need to suspect a problem." I think that at this time there is not enough evidence of health to show whether they are safe or not. If they do cause brain cancer, it will take a really long time to happen.

Although no health risks in radio frequency have been determined, the Cellular Telecommunications Industry Association has volunteered to finance new studies to be performed by the federal government.

Certain types of cellular phones have been found to temporarily inhibit or turn off a user's heart pacemaker or cause the pacemaker to pace the heart at an inappropriately fast rate. This is very dangerous. It has been found that the analog phones rarely cause any interference. If someone has a pacemaker and needs to use a cellular phone, they just need to make sure they use it on the opposite side and keep a distance of 6 inches from the antenna.

There are several other suggestions on preventions that cellular users can consider. Use the longest extensible antenna and keep it far away from the head as much as possible. Only use the cellular phone for ten minutes at a time and then wait about one hour in between calls, when possible. Children should be prohibited from using cellular phones because their cells are more susceptible to damage. These would obviously cut down on any suspicion anyone would have.

In my opinion, we can find so much to worry about in the world today. I think that we are pondering the health issues associated with cellular phones too much. If we are going to eliminate them because of the frequencies they emit then we should also eliminate our microwave ovens, hair dryers, and electronic clocks and shavers that all operate within the same range of frequencies. And in the aspect of driving, I feel that by banning cellular phones you are only going to have people trying to sneak and use them, which is only going to cause more driving hazards.

If asked the question if I thought cellular phones were help or hazard, I would have to answer, HELP!

From here, Stephanie was ready to work on her revised draft.

Exercises

6. Choose one of the topics you've researched and prepare to write about it. Use the Research Outline Worksheet. Expand the ideas into a rough draft.

REVISE

Revising a research paper can be daunting. You may have eight, ten, fourteen, or more pages of writing waiting to be polished. Following a few guidelines should help make the revising process go better.

First, polish your draft for content. Address the issues of topic, audience, and purpose throughout your paper and have appropriate support, examples, and details. Quote source material correctly and provide credit throughout your work.

From there, polish the grammar and mechanics. It may help to develop a strategy for polishing longer works, such as reading the document in reverse order. Allow plenty of time for this part of the revision process.

Finally, polish with MLA style in mind. Make sure that each of the entries on the Works Cited page is complete and punctuated correctly. For entries in question, ask for your instructor's help or refer to the most recent edition of the *MLA Handbook for Writers of Research Papers,* by Joseph Gibaldi.

Documentation and Plagiarism

When you write a research paper, you share information you have collected from others. Documentation provides a record of your research and allows the reader to see where and how the research is being used. In addition, documentation separates your words from the words of your sources. Without documentation, you run a good chance of committing **plagiarism**, or passing off someone else's thoughts, words, or ideas as your own. In academia, plagiarism is considered theft and carries with it serious consequences (including expulsion from school). The bottom line is this: If you use information from another source, credit the source.

A Brief Guide to MLA Documentation

The most effective way to avoid plagiarism is to properly document information gleaned from sources and to provide a list of sources to the readers. Modern Language Association (MLA) style helps us do just that. **MLA style** is commonly used in English classes and provides a consistent way to present information about source material both within the text of the research paper and at the end in the form of a Works Cited page. For MLA documentation, you must refer to the source within the text of the paper itself and in the bibliography. This is commonly known as internal and external documentation.

Internal Documentation   **Internal documentation** marks a source used within the paper. This type of documentation allows the reader to see exactly where the information came from as it is presented. In MLA style, the source author's last name and the page number of the source material are placed at the end of the sentence containing the information.

Return to paragraph six of Erica's research paper. In this paragraph, she writes, "I looked in the *George Mason University 1996–97 Undergraduate Catalog* and I found that they have apartments and townhouses available on campus. They are $1,950–2,100 per semester (Thornberg 24)." "Thornberg 24" tells us that the information within the previous sentence came from Colleen Thornberg and can be found on page 24 of the undergraduate catalog.

External Documentation   A list of references placed at the end of your research paper is considered **external documentation**. The two basic types of external documentation are the bibliography and the Words Cited Page. A **bibliography** is a list of all the sources you consulted as you researched your topic. A **Works Cited** page is a listing of every source you actually refer to—or cite—within the paper. Both bibliographies and Works Cited Pages include author, publisher, and publication date of the sources and follow MLA format.

Sample Works Cited Page

Blundo, Joe. "'Pocket Monsters' Are Busy Emptying Mom's and Dad's." <u>Columbus Dispatch</u> 28 Aug. 1999: D1.

Clark, Judy. "Quench Your Real Thirst." <u>Women Today</u>. 25 Aug. 1999. 26 Mar. 2003 <http://www.womentodaymagazine.com/selfesteem/quenchthirst.html>.

"It Can Happen in an Instant." <u>Parent News</u>. Columbus: United Services for Effective

Parenting of Ohio, 1999.

Laughlin, Thomas. "Teaching in the Yard: Student Inmates and the Policy of Silence."

<u>Teaching English in the Two-Year College</u> 23 (1996): 284-90.

Zinsser, William. <u>Writing to Learn</u>. New York: Harper and Row, 1988.

MLA Style Documentation Guide

MLA style documentation may look overwhelming at first glance, but it isn't once you learn how it works. Regardless of the source, you need to include the author of the source, the place and date of publication of the source, and page number of the source material. If you are using a book as a source, that is no problem. But sources such as websites and artwork can prove challenging. The following is a short guide to MLA style documentation designed to get you started with appropriate format. For more information please refer to Joseph Gibaldi's *MLA Handbook for Writers of Research Papers*.

Art Work   Use this format for artwork found in another publication.

Kirby, Jack. <u>Within This Tortured Land</u>. Illus. in <u>How to Draw and Sell Comic Strips</u>

<u>for Newspapers and Comic Books</u>. Alan Mckenzie. Cincinnati, Ohio: North

Light Books, 1987. 79.

To cite the original work or pieces found in galleries or museums, list author first, then title of the piece, the place of display, and the city and state of display.

Books   With one author:

Zinsser, William. <u>Writing to Learn</u>. New York: Harper and Row, 1988.

Same author, different source:

— <u>On Writing Well</u>. New York: Harper Collins, 1995.

With two authors:

Yeager, Chuck, and Leo Janos. <u>Yeager</u>. New York: Bantam Books, 1985.

With more than two authors:

Lass, Abraham H., David Kiremidjian, and Ruth M. Goldstein. <u>The Wadsworth</u>

<u>Dictionary of Classical and Literary Allusions</u>. Hertfordshire, England:

Wadsworth, 1994.

A publisher outside the United States would be listed in the same format as a publisher inside the United States. You must state the country of publication for sake of clarity.

With an editor:

Zinsser, William, ed. <u>Inventing the Truth: The Art and Craft of Memoir</u>. Boston:

Houghton Mifflin, 1995.

Computer and Online Documentation   Website:

<u>Mark Twain</u>. Ed. James Zwick. 2003. 13 Dec. 2002 <http://www.boondocksnet.com/

twainwww/>.

Article from a website:

Clark, Judy. "Quench Your Real Thirst." <u>Women Today</u>. 25 Aug. 1999. 26 Mar. 2003

<http://www.womentodaymagazine.com/selfesteem/quenchthirst.html>.

Computer software with author:

McClure, Randall, and Suzanne Dixon. <u>Writer's Toolkit</u>. CD-ROM. New York: Addison

Wesley Longman, 1999.

Computer software without author:

<u>WordPerfect Suite 8</u>. CD-ROM. Corel Corporation, 1997.

Encyclopedia   Entry with author:

Currell, David. "Puppets." <u>Grolier Encyclopedia</u>. 1997 ed.

Entry without author:

"Rancho Palos Verdes." <u>Grolier Encyclopedia</u>. 1997 ed.

Film   With film entries, you must have title, director (since this is considered the "author" of the piece), distribution company, and release date. If it is important to your paper, you should also include actor names.

<u>Halloween H20.</u> Dir. Steve Miner. Perf. Jamie Lee Curtis and Adam Arkin. Dimension

Films, 1998.

Magazine Articles   With one author:

Wallace, David Foster. "Brief Interviews with Hideous Men." <u>Harper's</u> Oct. 1998:

41-56.

With more than one author:

McDonough, William, and Michael Braungart. "The Next Industrial Revolution."

<u>Atlantic Monthly</u> Oct. 1998: 82-92.

Without author:

"Should You Get an Affinity Card?" <u>Consumer Reports</u> Sept. 1999: 5.

Newspaper Articles   With author:

Blundo, Joe. "'Pocket Monsters' Are Busy Emptying Mom's and Dad's." <u>Columbus</u>

   <u>Dispatch</u> 28 Aug. 1999: D1.

   Without author:

"Police Report Rush of Car Thefts." <u>Northland News</u> 25 Aug. 1999.

Pamphlets

"It Can Happen in an Instant." <u>Parent News</u>. Columbus: United Services for Effective

   Parenting of Ohio, 1999.

Scholarly Journals   Scholarly journals add another dimension to the standard entry: the volume and the continuous page numbering system from issue to issue. Each single issue is designed to be collected into a larger volume year later on. Simply make sure you use the volume number of the publication and the page numbers as they appear in the article. Notice too that the title of the article is in quotation marks while the title of the publication is underlined.
   With one author:

Laughlin, Thomas. "Teaching in the Yard: Student Inmates and the Policy of Silence."

   <u>Teaching English in the Two-Year College</u> 23 (1996). 284-90.

   With more than one author:

Lunsford, Andrea A., and Susan West. "Intellectual Property and Composition

   Studies." <u>College Composition and Communication</u> 47 (1996). 383-411.

STUDENT SAMPLE

Here we see Stephanie hard at work revising her research paper.

Cellular Phones: Are They a Help or a Hazard?

You are sitting at a busy intersection on your way home

from work, you look to your left and your right, and the

What is the problem? drivers of both cars are talking on a cellular phone. In today's

ever-changing world, there is controversy over the use of

cellular phones. Are they really that much of a hazard? I feel

this fear is truly exaggerated.

Cellular technology has been around a lot longer than

most people realize. According to Kathleen Kocks, in her

Jargon—I need to explain article in <u>Journal of Electronic Devices</u>, cellular technology began in 1947 when Bell Laboratories (now part of Lucent Technologies) developed the analog cellular concept. The technology lay dormant until the early 1980s when commercial cellular services were launched in Washington, D.C., and Chicago, Illinois. Since then, there has been a cellular phone revolution. Usage has skyrocketed, growing more than 50 percent each year and now incorporating over 300 million users worldwide. Working for a cellular phone company, I find out firsthand how important people's cellular *Don't think this fits here* phones are to them. For the most part, they find themselves totally disconnected from the world without them.

With the market growing so rapidly, this means more people use their phones while driving on busy freeways. In Joseph Palenchar's article in <u>Twice</u>, he informs us that in *??* more than thirty studies conducted by the Harvard Center for Risk Analysis, they came up with the calculations that a driver's risk of being killed while driving and talking on a phone is 6.4 in a million per year, or 80 percent less than their risk of dying while driving with a blood alcohol content of 0.1 percent (which is defined as legally drunk in most states) twelve times per year for one half-hour each time. Palenchar also tells us that the risk of a motorist being killed by a driver who is talking on a cellular phone is 1.5 in a million per year, or 92 percent less than the risk of being killed by a driver with any level of alcohol in his or her blood. Looking at these statistics, I feel that we need to worry more *I can add more here.* about our drunk drivers than about our cellular phone users.

A crash that killed a two-year-old led to a proposed law *I should explain* called Morgan's Bill. This federal bill would make it illegal for *this more.*

drivers to use cellular phones while driving. An article in *Workforce* states that, according to Todd Raphael and the National Council of State Legislatures, at the time this article was published, there were twenty-four states considering bans on cellular phone use while driving. A couple of the cities that have already incorporated the ban are Brooklyn, Ohio, and New York City. In Brooklyn, Ohio, all drivers were banned from using phones while driving and, in New York City, they have banned all cab drivers from using them while driving.

Someone can reach over and change a radio station or CD and swerve between lanes just as easily as if he were answering a cellular phone. Or how many times have you *[Explain this, maybe?]* seen someone smoking and they drop their cigarette? That's definitely a road hazard.

I do feel that if you have someone with you who can dial the number for you or answer it, then that is the safest way, *[I wrote that and even I have a hard time reading it.]* but like myself, many of us usually travel alone. It is important for users to know when to use the phone and when not to. If there are road hazards such as snow, ice, heavy fog, or even just heavy rains, then they should know not to use the phone until they are stopped somewhere safe. But this *[?]* is just using common sense.

As with anything, a lot of the people are so busy addressing the negative things of a product that they have a tendency to overlook the good things they do. Between January 1996 and June 1997, it is reported by Simon Chapman in <u>The Lancelet</u>, 3,975,154 calls were made to the 000 emergency services (174,405—4.3 percent—were made from mobiles, with 59 percent to police, 31.5 percent to

I should explain how that isn't clear — ambulances, and 9.5 percent to fire services.) To me, the statistics show a definite positive side to cellular phones..

You're driving along and notice a drunk driver. You take out your cellular phone and call 1-800-GRAB-DUI. You let them know where the driver is and which way he is going. The police then stop him, arrest him, and get him off the road before he injures or kills himself or someone else. Or, the *Only part of a sentence* scenario that you were driving along by yourself and you start having severe chest pains. You are not near any businesses or houses that could see you and passersby just think you are lost. You pull over and call 911 and an ambulance is then able to get to you and possibly save your life. If you had not had a cellular phone with you, or not been able to use it, then you probably would have sat on the side of the road and died.

In <u>American Medical News</u>, Tracy Binius tells of three Maryland Express care ambulances that are outfitted with digital cellular phones that send real-time images to a neurologist at the University of Maryland Medical Center so they know what to expect when they get to the facility.

Not only are there driving concerns with cellular phones. Along with that also come the health hazards. Though it is important to note, there are also health hazards associated with cellular phones. As we know, cellular phones work on frequencies. In <u>Popular Mechanics</u>, they tell us that the range of frequencies making up the electromagnetic spectrum is broad. It goes from AM radio broadcasts, which begin around 500,000 cps (cycles per second) to microwave ovens, which cook at a rate of 2.8 billion cps. In this range, cellular phones come in at a lower rate of 840–880 million cps. You don't see anyone trying to get microwave ovens banned.

Does this go too far?

A gentleman in Florida tried to sue the cellular industry when his wife died of a brain tumor. He went on several talk shows about the issue. There was no way to prove that it was incurred because of a cellular phone.

The paper slows down here.

There are so many opinions in this angle as well. Christine Kuehn Kelly reports on both sides in "Are Cell Phones Dangerous to Your Health?" Some say research has connected cellular phone use to changes in the structure of the brain. The interaction can alter the brain's perception and judgment. There may also be some long-term concerns linking to cancer and possibly leukemia. Dr. Adey also says that cellular phone transmissions open the blood-brain barrier. This is a protective shield that keeps toxins away from brain tissues. When this protective shield is not intact, you end up with headaches. That is because substances that normally remain in the blood then can reach the pain-sensitive tissue covering the brain.

I need to tell who he is

He is an expert on safety, not a safety at the medical center.

Kelly also reports that John Moulder, Ph.D., radio frequency radiation safety at the Medical Center of Wisconsin, states he doesn't believe any negative health effects have been demonstrated from cellular phone usage. Moulder states, "Studies haven't seen any increased risk in brain tissue in mobile phone users and, from what's available now, show no need to suspect a problem." I think that at this time there is not enough evidence of health to show whether they are safe or not. If they do cause brain cancer, it will take a really long time to happen.

Although no health risks in radio frequency have been determined, the Cellular Telecommunications Industry Association has volunteered to finance new studies to be performed by the federal government.

Certain types of cellular phones have been found to temporarily inhibit or turn off a user's heart pacemaker or cause the pacemaker to pace the heart at an inappropriately fast rate. This is very dangerous. It has been found that the analog phones rarely cause any interference. If someone has a pacemaker and needs to use a cellular phone, they just need to make sure they use it on the opposite side and keep a distance of 6 inches from the antenna.

There are several other suggestions on preventions that cellular users can consider. Use the longest extensible antenna and keep it far away from the head as much as possible. Only use the cellular phone for ten minutes at a time and then wait about one hour in between calls, when possible. Children should be prohibited from using cellular phones because their cells are more susceptible to damage. These would obviously cut down on any suspicion anyone would have.

I should probably take this out.

In my opinion, we can find so much to worry about in the world today. I think that we are pondering the health issues associated with cellular phones too much. If we are going to eliminate them because of the frequencies they emit then we should also eliminate our microwave ovens, hair dryers, and electronic clocks and shavers that all operate within the same range of frequencies. And in the aspect of driving, I feel that by banning cellular phones you are only going to have people trying to sneak and use them, which

is only going to cause more driving hazards.

Long enough for a conclusion?   If asked the question if I thought cellular phones were

help or hazard, I would have to answer, HELP!

Works Cited

Binius, Tracy. "Wireless Enhances Emergency Runs." <u>American Medical News</u> 42.12

(1999): 28.

"Cellular Phone Disturbs Pacemakers." <u>Consumers Digest</u> 35.5: 79.

Kocks, Kathleen. "Who's Afraid of Cellular Phones?" <u>Journal of Electronic Devices</u>

22.4 (1999): 39-45.

Palenchar, Joseph. "Study: Driving While Wireless Slightly Riskier." <u>Twice</u> 15.20

(2000): 47.

<u>Popular Mechanics</u>. "Invisible Rays, Hidden Hazards." 170.5 (1993): 33.

Raphael, Todd. "Are Car Phone Bans Coming?" <u>Workforce</u> 79.5 (2000): 14–16.

Chapman, Simon. "Emergency Use of Cellular (Mobile) Telephones." <u>The Lancelet</u>

351.9103 (1998): 650.

Finally, she revised and proofread what she had created and then produced
her final draft.

Stephanie C____

10/5/01

ENGL 102

Cellular Phones: Are They a Help or a Hazard?

You are sitting at a busy intersection on your way home from work. You

look to your left and your right, and the drivers of both cars are talking on

cellular phones. In today's ever-changing world, there is increasing controversy

over the use of cellular phones. Are they really that much of a hazard? I feel this fear is truly exaggerated. The dispute of more accidents occurring because of the use of cellular phones, as well as the potential health risks, are unsubstantiated.

Cellular technology has been around a lot longer than most people realize. According to Kathleen Kocks, in her article in <u>Journal of Electronic Devices</u> (39), cellular technology began in 1947 when Bell Laboratories (now part of Lucent Technologies) developed the analog cellular concept. The technology lay dormant until the early 1980s, when commercial cellular services were launched in Washington, D.C., and Chicago, Illinois. Since then, there has been a cellular phone revolution the world over. Usage of cellular phones has skyrocketed, growing more than 50 percent each year and now incorporating over 300 million users worldwide.

With the market growing so rapidly, this means more people may in fact be communicating by cellular phone while driving on busy freeways and during other everyday tasks. In Joseph Palenchar's article in <u>Twice</u> (47), he informs us that in more than thirty studies conducted by the Harvard Center for Risk Analysis, the focus groups came up with the calculations that a driver's risk of being killed while driving and talking on a phone is 6.4 in a million per year. This can also be seen as 80 percent less than the risk of dying while driving with a blood alcohol content of 0.1 percent (which is defined as legally drunk in most states) twelve times per year for one half-hour each time. Palenchar also tells us that the risk of a motorist being killed by a driver who is talking on a cellular phone is 1.5 in a million per year, or 92 percent less than the risk of being killed by a driver with any level of alcohol in his or her blood. Looking at these statistics, I feel that we need to worry more about our drunk drivers than about our cellular phone users.

In 1999, a car accident involving the death of a two-year-old and cellular phone usage prompted a law called Morgan's Bill. This federal bill would make it illegal for drivers to use cellular phones while driving. An article in <u>Workforce</u> states that, according to Todd Raphael and the National Council of State Legislatures, at the time this article was published, there were twenty-four states considering bans on cellular phone use while driving. (Raphael, 14) Two of the cities that have already incorporated the ban are Brooklyn, Ohio, and New York City. In Brooklyn, Ohio, all drivers were banned from using the phones while driving and, in New York City, they have banned all cab drivers from using them while driving. I don't feel the ban is necessary. It is just as likely that someone could swerve between lanes or be unaware while on the road just by reaching over to change a radio station or CD. I do feel that if you have someone with you who can dial the number for you or answer the phone, then that is the safest way, but like myself, many of us usually travel alone. How many times have you seen someone smoking in the car and they drop their cigarette? That's definitely a road hazard.

It is important for users to know when to use the phone and when not to. If there are road hazards such as rain, snow, ice, heavy fog, or even just heavy rains, then they should know not to use the phone until they are stopped somewhere safe. This same reasoning would apply in many situations in which a person wouldn't hesitate to act in a sensible manner.

As with anything, people focus mainly on the nagative aspects of a product, and they have a tendency to overlook the good things the product provides us. Between January 1996 and June 1997, it is reported by Simon Chapman in

The Lancelet, 3,975,154 calls were made to the 000 emergency services (174,405—

4.3 percent—were made from mobiles, with 59 percent to police, 31.5 percent to

ambulances, and 9.5 percent to fire services) (Chapman, 650). These numbers

illustrate that cellular users are utilizing their phones for life-saving tasks, not

just common conversation.

Let me provide an example: You're driving along and notice a drunk driver.

You take out your cellular phone and call 1-800-GRAB-DUI. You let them know

where the driver is and which way he is going. The police then stop him, arrest

him, and get him off the road before he injures or kills himself or someone else.

Here is another scenario: You are driving by yourself and you start having severe

chest pains. What should you do? You are not near any businesses or houses that

could see you and passersby just think you are lost. You pull over and call 911,

and an ambulance is then able to get to you and possibly save your life. If you had

not had a cellular phone with you or not been able to use it, then you probably

would have sat on the side of the road and died. In American Medical News, Tracy

Binius tells of three Maryland Express care ambulances that are outfitted with

digital cellular phones that send real-time images to a neurologist at the

University of Maryland Medical Center so they know what to expect when they

get to the facility (28). This point alone shows just how critical a mobile

communications device can be, despite the assumed risks.

It is important to note, however, that there are also health hazards associated

with cellular phones. As we know, cellular phones work on radio frequencies. In

Popular Mechanics, researchers point out that the range of frequencies making up the electromagnetic spectrum is broad (34). It goes from AM radio broadcasts, which begin around 500,000 cps (cycles per second) to microwave ovens, which cook at a rate of 2.8 billion cps. Within this range, cellular phones come in at a lower rate of 840–880 million cps. There is a fear that cellular phones may contribute to sickness based on this information. A gentleman in Florida tried to sue the cellular industry when his wife died of a brain tumor he felt was attributable to heavy cellular use. He went on several talk shows about the issue, but there was no evidence that her tumor had resulted from the cellular phone usage.

Christine Kuehn Kelly reports on both sides in "Are Cell Phones Dangerous to Your Health?" (2) Some reports find that research has connected cellular phone use to changes in the structure of the brain. According to Ross Adey, M.D., professor of biochemistry at the University of California at Riverside, fields from cellular phones interact with tissues in the brain. The interaction can alter the brain's perception and judgment. There may also be some long-term concerns linking cellular phone usage to cancer and leukemia. Dr. Adey also says that cellular phone transmissions open the blood-brain barrier; this pertains to a protective shield that keeps toxins away from brain tissues. When this protective shield is not intact, you end up with headaches because substances that normally remain in the blood then can reach the pain-sensitive tissue covering the brain directly.

Kelly also reports that John Moulder, Ph.D., an expert on radio frequency radiation safety at the Medical Center of Wisconsin, states that he doesn't believe any negative health effects have been demonstrated from cellular phone usage. Moulder states, "Studies haven't seen any increased risk in brain tissue in mobile phone users and, from what's available now, show no need to suspect a problem." (3) I think that at this time there is not enough evidence of health detriments to show whether cellular phones are safe or not. If they do cause brain cancer, it would take a really long time and large amounts of exposure to happen. Despite there being no health risks from radio frequency determined, the Cellular Telecommunications Industry Association has volunteered to finance new studies to be performed by the federal government.

According to an anonymous writer in <u>Consumers Digest</u>, certain types of cellular phones have been found to temporarily inhibit or turn off a user's heart pacemaker or cause the pacemaker to pace the heart at an inappropriately fast rate. (79) This is very dangerous. It is speculated that the analog phones rarely cause any interference. If someone has a pacemaker and needs to use a cellular phone, they just need to make sure they use it on the opposite side than the pacemaker and keep a distance of 6 inches from the antenna to be safe.

Although there is no need for concern, there are several other suggestions for prevention that cellular users can consider. (1) Use the longest extensible antenna and keep it far away from the head as much as possible. (2) Only use the cellular phone for ten minutes at a time and then wait about one hour in between calls, when possible. (3) Children should be prohibited from using cellular phones because their cells are more susceptible to damage. These methods should cut down on any suspicion or risk that anyone would have.

It is my opinion that we are pondering on the health issues associated with cellular phones too much. If we are going to eliminate them because of the frequencies they emit, then we should also eliminate our microwave ovens, hair dryers, and electronic clocks and shavers, which all operate within the same range of frequencies. In the aspect of driving, I feel that by banning cellular phones, this will only result in people trying to use them illegally, which will only cause more driving hazards on already dangerous roads.

I find that cellular phone usage demonstrates more positives than negatives. One strong example is the use of mobile communications in ambulances, allowing the doctors to prepare for incoming patients. As for the argument of cellular phone usage being a driving hazard, I believe that the real issue at hand is that of irresponsible motorists and not the cellular phone industry.

[New page]   Works Cited

Binius, Tracy. "Wireless Enhances Emergency Runs." <u>American Medical News</u> 42.12
        (1999): 28.

"Cellular Phone Disturbs Pacemakers." <u>Consumers Digest</u> 35.5 (1996): 79.

Chapman, Simon. "Emergency Use of Cellular (Mobile) Telephones." <u>The Lancelet</u>
        351.9103 (1998): 650.

Kelly, Christine Kuehn. "Are Cell Phones Dangerous to Your Health?"
        <http://cbshealthwatch.com>.

Kocks, Kathleen. "Who's Afraid of Cellular Phones?" <u>Journal of Electronic Devices</u>
        22.4 (1999): 39-45.

Palenchar, Joseph. "Study: Driving While Wireless Slightly Riskier." <u>Twice</u> 15.20
        (2000): 47.

<u>Popular Mechanics</u>. "Invisible Rays, Hidden Hazards." 170.5 (1993): 33.

Raphael, Todd. "Are Car Phone Bans Coming?" <u>Workforce</u> 79.5 (2000): 14-16.

CHAPTER REVIEW

When writing a research paper, you gather information from a variety of sources and integrate that information into a discussion on your topic. You must analyze your audience's level of knowledge about the topic in order to identify the type of information that should be included in the paper. Because your purpose is to educate your audience on various aspects of the topic, only information directed to that focus should be used. The type of information you may use in a research paper can vary from general to must-have, and it all must be documented to avoid plagiarism.

Whatever type of information you use, it must be of good quality, and choosing quality information requires critical thinking skills. You must check the author's background, the publication date of the source, and the references that the author uses for his/her own research to make sure the source is appropriate for your paper.

Integrating your research into your paper takes work. Use summary, paraphrase, and quotation to do so. Also, be sure to avoid plagiarism, which is passing off someone else's work as your own. When you want to use someone else's ideas, simply give him or her credit using MLA documentation. Documentation takes place on two levels: internal (occurring inside the text of the paper itself) and external (occurring as a Works Cited page at the end of the paper).

Although a variety of new elements come along with writing a research paper, you still must rely on the writing process to complete the project. Once the outline and rough draft are finished, revise the paper carefully. As you revise, keep in mind the demands of the audience as well as your purpose for writing the paper.

Final Writing Assignments

1. Revise the research paper you began in Exercise 6 to a final draft. Along with following the general rules of revision, make sure you give appropriate credit to your sources and that you follow the MLA style of documentation.

*2. With a partner, brainstorm a list of features of your school you didn't know about or realize before you started attending. Turn this list into a research paper. Fill out a TAP Worksheet and then start your research. For balance and detail, choose at least five sources for this paper and create a working bibliography or Works Cited page. Keep track of the information on index cards, separating general, specific, and must-have information. Outline your paper and then write a rough draft. Revise it, making sure to incorporate your research results into your discussion. Edit the research paper and then proofread it.

15

ESSAY TESTS

The scene is always the same: a classroom with desks like the ones in grade school. The room is large, almost the size of a warehouse, and the teacher sits on the desk. All of my friends sit still, not moving a muscle. They all stare at the large clock on the wall, its hands flirting with 8:00 AM. I rush into the room, shake my friends, try to get the teacher's attention, but everyone ignores me. Finally, the clock strikes eight, the bell peals, the teacher says, "Begin," and my friends open their test booklets in unison. They scribble furiously at their desks. I take my seat, which seems unusually small. My test book glares at me and, when I try to open it, remains shut. I try to pry it open with my pencil, but the pencil breaks. I try to tear it with my teeth and cut my lip instead. Suddenly, the bell peals once more. It is now 9:00 AM. The other students, single file, march to the teacher and hand in their completed tests. I am the last one in the room with a test. The teacher walks over and snatches it from my hand.

"I see, Mr. Hall," she says, "that you didn't get your test done in time. Looks like you will have to repeat grade school once again." As she laughs, I wake up.

I have got to do something about this test anxiety.

Whether you major in computer science, English literature, or early childhood development, you encounter the same headache: tests. Tests are designed to assess or measure how much you know about the material covered in a class. For some tests, you must fill in blanks with correct answers or match a word in one column with its definition in a parallel column. For others, you must write essays. As essay test requires you to write a paragraph or, more likely, several paragraphs that are appropriately structured, well written, and completed in the time allotted. Writing an answer to an essay question is not difficult once you realize that you are following a familiar process—the writing process—through Ready, Write, and Revise. You are simply condensing it, using the skills you have learned about writing in an abbreviated way. Reading and understanding essay questions, writing a good, solid response to them, and being well prepared for a test are all covered in this chapter.

Many of the readings in this book are by professional writers, but this time we are going to read "I'd Like to Use Essay Tests, But..." by educator Marilla Svinicki. The teacher's perspective on tests is valuable to you as a student.

Reading 17 I'd Like to Use Essay Tests, But...

Marilla Svinicki

BACKSTORY

Discussions of testing and test anxiety are usually focused on the student. After all, they are the ones taking these tests. However, instructors also wrestle with testing issues. Is the test a fair measure of skills? How many points should be deducted for this small mistake? Which type of test should be used: multiple choice or essay? Marilla Svinicki, an instructor from the University of Texas at Austin, offers insight on the teacher's perspective on tests.

LEXICON

algorithms: formulas

curriculum: coursework; group of studies

exhorting: strongly urging

extant: still in existence

integrative: leading to connections

parceling: measuring and dividing

sic: so; used when a direct quote contains errors or mistakes

spewed: spit out rapidly or vigorously

spontaneous: without planning

stymied: baffled

Essay question: Discuss the importance of the nature/nurture controversy in the shaping of current developmental theory.

Student answer: The nature/nuture (sic) controversy was very impotent (sic) in shaping current developmental theory because (sic) it was needed to help people who were doing work in that area to come up with their current theories....... (Huh?)

1   Do you cringe when you read the kind of tortured prose and fractured thinking that is represented by the above example? Or plow through paragraph after paragraph of detail in a student's answer in hopes of finding an original thought somewhere in the pile? Or find yourself subconsciously reading more into an answer than is really there as you try to interpret the meaning of a student's essay?

2   Most instructors who venture into using essay tests will experience one or more of these phenomena somewhere along the line. It has been our habit in the past to blame the students, the school system and the English department for not teaching our students how to write a solidly argued, concisely worded essay answer, but we must face the fact that we are as much to blame for their imprecise prose as those other entities. The

"Writing Across the Curriculum" movement of several years ago urged instructors in all departments to help their students learn to write more coherent prose, whether it be in papers or essay tests, not just to improve student writing but to encourage more complex thinking. Having to explain an answer in prose format requires more from the student in the way of deep processing of the material than is usually the case on objectively scorable exam questions.

3   Many instructors across campus subscribed to these ideas enthusiastically, but were stymied when it came to putting them into practice in their classes. They increased the use of essay questions, but didn't know how to help their students improve other than exhorting them to do better.

4   Part of the problem may lie in the way instructors help (or fail to help) students prepare for writing essay tests. Learning specialists have known for a long time that the kind of preparation needed for responding to essay questions is different from that needed for objective tests. Unfortunately, many of our students are unaware of that difference. They prepare for all exams with the same learning strategies, and then are ill-equipped to tackle the kind of thinking needed during essay tests. In fact, they may be surprised to learn that they might need to actually think through and construct an answer for a test rather than being able to quickly search their memory for an already extant answer which can then be simply spewed out on the test.

5   If we want the students to be able to deal with the complex nature of essay tests and other forms of spontaneous writing, there are some things we can do in our instruction that will prepare them more adequately. The following list of suggestions is by no means exhaustive, but it should serve as a stimulus for your own thinking about how your students might best prepare for your tests.

HELP THEM THINK DIFFERENTLY ABOUT THE MATERIAL.

6   Students are conditioned from an early age to think in terms of discrete facts and "correct" answers rather than looking for the relationships which are characteristic of essay answers. One of the first steps toward improved essay answers is to adopt a different perspective on the nature of what is to be learned from the material presented and read. To help students think about the material differently, the instructor can:

a. encourage them to integrate material from class to class and unit to unit. For example, you can give them a set of integrative questions to ask themselves each time they begin a new topic, questions like

> *How does this topic compare with/relate to what has gone before?*
>
> *How is it different? How is it similar?*
>
> *Why is it included in the course? Why at this point?*
>
> *What are its main points, its strengths, its weaknesses?*
>
> *How does it apply to the overall goal of the course?*

b. have them write their own sample essay questions for each lecture or reading assignment and then in class, discuss those that most closely parallel what you would ask.

c. explain the levels of cognitive complexity (such as Bloom's taxonomy) which might be expected of them in the course and differentiate between knowledge of facts and ability to analyze and critique material.

d. emphasize process during classtime itself, so that the students begin to understand how conclusions are reached rather than focusing on the conclusions alone.

HELP THEM STUDY THE MATERIAL DIFFERENTLY.

7   Studying for essay exams is much different from studying for objectively scorable exams. Instructors should encourage students to:

a. create outlines of readings and lecture notes which emphasize the relationships among the ideas.

b. draw concept maps, which are visual diagrams of how terms, principles, and ideas interconnect.

c. paraphrase or create an executive summary for each reading or lecture.

HELP THEM WRITE STRUCTURALLY SOUND ANSWERS.

8   To help students compile the information they have learned into answers which are written more effectively and efficiently, an instructor can:

a. provide a list of key words used in essay questions and what they imply in terms of answer content and structure.

b. give students opportunities to practice writing essay answers in class and discussing the structure of the answers.

c. assign brief out-of-class essay questions with which to practice and provide individual feedback on the writing. You may wish to develop a feedback phrase sheet, which lists your most commonly used comments and an extended description of what that comment means. Then the feedback on the answer itself can be written using the key phrase instead of the entire comment. (To get really efficient, just use a set of numbered phrases.)

d. give the students an opportunity to grade an essay answer using the system you normally use so that they will understand how they are being evaluated.

e. provide examples of good and poor answers to essay questions with an explanation of why they are evaluated that way.

f. show students how to use algorithms for answering typical question types. For example, a prototype answer for a "compare and contrast" item might always include two points of similarity between the two concepts and two points of difference. Help them develop generic outlines or concept maps for common types of questions into which they can plug the specifics of the topic.

g. help them learn time management techniques for essay writing. For example, scanning all the items and parceling out an appropriate amount of time to spend on each according to weight or importance; spending a few minutes outlining an answer before writing, possibly even giving some credit in grading for content which appears on an outline, but was not included in the answer due to time constraints; having a checklist for quickly evaluating answers before completing the exam (such as "did you answer the question?" "are the transitions clear?" "is evidence provided for each assertion?" and so on).

WHY SHOULD WE BOTHER?

9   There is actually an additional selfish motive for improving students' essay writing skills: it makes the grading process much easier. When students learn how to read an essay question and from the structure of the question, select an answer protocol that insures that all parts of the answer are present and well-organized, the task of grading those answers becomes less one of interpretation and more one of evaluation.

10   When students can write well-argued essays in clear and concise prose, it actually can be a pleasure to grade their work. It certainly will take less time and mental effort. In the long run, both parties benefit.

11   Unfortunately there is no guarantee that all students will be able to use these strategies to improve their essay writing, but at least they would be aware that integrative essay questions require a different type of preparation than they may have used in the past. That awareness may be the first step on the developmental path to the higher level thinking characteristic of college-level work.

QUESTIONS FOR THOUGHT

1. Should a student's final grade in a class depend on tests? If so, what types of tests? Why?
2. Consider the various tests you have taken over the years. Which types of test are you most comfortable with? Why?
3. What test-taking strategies have you used over the years?
4. Teachers, doctors, and lawyers all have to pass tests in order to practice in their field. In what other professions should tests be required? Why?

READY

All the knowledge in the world won't do you any good if you show up late for a test or forget your supplies. Being prepared for a test is the most important part of taking it. Preparation is more than writing down the dates and times for each exam on a master schedule or calendar (although that is a good place to start). Preparation includes everything from studying and taking good notes to examining previous tests and joining a study group.

Study

Preparation for a test can begin weeks before the scheduled test day. In fact, if done right, preparation for a test begins the first day of class. While you won't have to sit and memorize your notes or pages in a textbook every day, certain practices can help you retain the material better and help you do better on the test.

Take Good Notes   When you take notes, you are writing a study guide for the course. For this reason, note taking is a valuable skill. Begin note taking by having pen or pencil and paper ready before class begins. At the top of each page, put the date and topic of the lecture. Leave a wide margin on the left-hand side of the page so you can make additional notes to yourself later. As you take notes, do not write every word that is said. Instead, write the information the instructor writes on the board. Listen for references to page numbers in the textbook and jot those down as well. Feel free to jot notes on handouts distributed during a class session. (Remember that handouts are notes, also, so read them carefully.) After class, review the notes you have taken. Rewrite sloppy sections, because you want to be able to read these notes later. In the left-hand margin, add notes from reading the textbook or from group discussions. When you are finished, your note page should be a clearly written capsule of the day's information to which you can quickly and easily refer.

Review As You Go Along   With lecture notes, textbook reading, and class discussions to review, you can be overwhelmed a few days before the test. The trick with reviewing is to not wait to begin. Find time every day after class to go through your notes or to reread passages in the textbook that were mentioned in class. Jot down questions and ask them at your next class meeting. This type of ongoing review process keeps the material fresh in your mind, helps you make connections, and allows you to measure what you think you know about the material versus what you actually know. When the days just before the test roll around, studying will be much less overwhelming.

Use Textbook Aids   Textbooks often come with their own study aids. Study questions at the beginning or at the end of each chapter can help you learn the main idea and pieces of key information for that chapter. Many books (including this one) also have summaries at the end of each chapter, giving you a way to review the main idea. Exercises sprinkled throughout chapters can also help you learn information and give you an idea of the type of test questions you may encounter.

Predict Questions   When you take a test, you are answering questions designed to measure what you know about the material. A good review strategy is to predict what questions will be on the test. For example, your history professor discussed three events that had major influences on modern medicine. A possible test question is "What three major events influenced modern medicine?" Another is "Choose one of the three major influences on modern medicine and illustrate the impact of this event."

The point of predicting is not to create a test that you think will be the real thing. Instead, this exercise is designed to train your brain to think about connections within the material.

Examine Past Exams   Often, instructors revise tests from quarter to quarter or semester to semester. Perhaps new information in the field prompts new test questions, or a test was used too often and change became necessary. At any rate, some instructors are happy to give you copies of older tests to study from or at least indicate what the tests will be like in terms of structure and type of questions. Students who took the class before may also have quizzes and tests you can review. Remember: These previous tests are study aids and not answers for your upcoming test.

Join a Study Group   Schedule times to meet with other students to review material. Perhaps a passage in the textbook isn't clear to you and someone in your study group can decipher it for you. Maybe you have learned an easy way to memorize material that is giving other people fits. Any exchange of information can be priceless to the group's members.

Just keep in mind that you have come together to study. Every now and then, members of the group might need to vent about how difficult the class is. Allow time for venting, but stay focused. Hours of complaining won't help anyone be prepared for the test.

Prepare

The hours immediately before you take a test can have a major impact on your performance at test time. Studying should occur over a period of weeks, and you may feel completely confident in your mastery of the material. However, you should take into consideration a few other factors when test day rolls around.

Eat Right; Eat Smart   Cigarettes and black coffee may give you a sudden burst of energy or at least get you going. They do not constitute a good thinking diet, however. Start your test day by eating breakfast and by taking your time while you eat. The proper food—a sandwich, eggs and bacon, cereal and toast with juice—gives you energy that will last through your test and allow you to think clearly. Eating slowly allows you time to digest your food and sets a proper pace for taking the test. In other words, if you start your day in a rush, you will take your test in a hurry, increasing your chances of making careless mistakes.

Sleep Well   The glorified image that most people have about studying is the all-nighter. They see themselves surrounded by friends, pizza, soda, black coffee, and piles of books in the wee hours of the night, cramming for a final the next day. Granted, school schedules, along with work and family demands, can eat up lots of our time, but studying all night isn't the best way to prepare for a test. In fact, in many ways, staying up all night can do more harm than good. When you break a pattern of sleep, you throw off your body's natural schedule, and it has to make accommodations. One type of compensation is a reduction in reflexes and comprehension. In trying to keep up with the new demand, your mind won't retain information efficiently. You will be sluggish for at least part of the next day, and that feeling will affect your test-taking ability.

Decide early on that you will study only until a certain hour the night before a test, then stick to your decision. At deadline time, relax. Take a shower or go for a long walk, then get some sleep. Your body will then be your friend, not an obstacle to deal with at test time.

Gather Your Materials   Set out what you will need for the test: paper, pens, pencils, and watch. Chances are, you won't need that extra pencil or pen or those few extra sheets of scrap paper while taking the test—but you never know. Valuable time can get eaten up while you search through a book bag for another pen, and your concentration will be thrown off. Just make sure of the materials that you will need for the test and then pack extras.

Arrive Early   Think back to a time when you thought you were going to be late for class or an appointment. You rushed about, trying to gather your things at the last minute, and then worked yourself into a frenzy trying to get to your destination. Once there, you had to take a few minutes to compose yourself. This behavior can cause a person to lose focus on the test, which may result in a lower grade. Arrive early for the test in order to get a good seat and to be relaxed.

WRITE AND REVISE

Once the test is in front of you, your first impulse may be to follow the writing process from prewriting to proofreading. If you were writing a paper, this would be the perfect approach. However, you are writing an answer to an essay question and you have limited time, so you have to make some adjustments. You will follow the writing process, but it will be condensed. To make the most of your time, you will have to write and revise as you go. To do this effectively, get a good overview of the essay questions, look for specific wording, sketch an outline, and then write your response. As you write, review each sentence for clarity.

Overview

Read through the test and make sure you understand what is being asked. If you need clarification, be sure to ask your instructor about the question—but don't ask for the answer. There is a difference, and your instructor can spot which type of question you are asking.

Once you are clear about each question, decide which ones you are going to answer first. Often, elements of a test carry different point values. The true-false questions may be worth only two points each, while each essay question may be worth five or ten. The goal is to complete the test (and most times you will), but keep in mind that you may run out of time. Answering the questions worth the most points first will help you make the best use of time. If points are not a factor, then consider the degree of difficulty for each question. Naturally, some questions will be easier for you to answer than others. To reduce stress and keep your energy flowing, answers the easy ones first. Those answers will come quickly and with confidence, which can carry you along as you tackle the more difficult ones. Do not spend too much time deciding your strategy here. Just choose one and go; you can always make adjustments later.

Specific Questions

To answer an essay question effectively, you must go beyond simply regurgitating information from class lectures or your textbook. Your instructor expects you to show your understanding of the material. To do this, you must first utilize your reading skills, particularly in terms of deciphering verbs and understanding the limits of each essay question.

Pay Attention to Verbs. The key to any essay test question is the **verb.** Verbs show action, and the verb in an essay test question directs you to the best approach to your answer. Examine the following Verb Direction Chart:

Verb Direction Chart

If you see this verb...	*you need to...*
Describe	Give detail in your explanation.
Discuss, state	State your opinion, then give specific support.
Compare, contrast	Show how two things are similar (compare) or different (contrast).
Illustrate, prove, or explain	Write a persuasion essay with emphasis on support.
Outline, list, or summarize	Arrange the information to follow an expository format where main points are clearly defined and supported.
Evaluate, choose, criticize	Show critical thinking skills. Follow up main points with a well-written explanation that has detail and support.

Imagine, for example, that you found the following question on a language and communications test: "Compare the role of television in the 1996 presidential election to the 2000 presidential election. Choose three main ideas as the focus for your response. Explain and support your answer." The directional verb "compare" means to show similarities, so you would have to write about three ways the two presidential elections were alike in relation to television. The verbs "explain" and "support" simply tell you that you need to provide detail in your response.

Pay Attention to Parameters Read each question carefully and note the parameters or limits of each question. Understanding the parameters of the questions allows you to include only the information that is necessary, keeping you on track as you write your answer. Refer to the essay question above. Notice that it asks for information about television and two presidential elections. Talking about television in any other way will detract from your answer.

Select and Structure

Writing and revising as you answer your essay questions means you are also selecting what information to include and working out a structure as you go. Working with a sketch outline will help you select only the pertinent information quickly. The outline will also help you arrange this material quickly. When I say sketch, I mean sketch. Do not waste time writing a formal outline or sweating every detail in it. Just jot down a few words or phrases that will help your mind focus on the information and organizational pattern of your answer.

Make the Question into a Thesis Statement   Rework the question into a thesis statement. This way, you are sure to be focused on what the question asks. Selecting what to say next can be done mentally. Organizing your ideas for the answer to the question can be done as a sketch outline on scrap paper.

Refer to the beginning of "I'd Like to Use Essay Tests, But..." and examine the student's response to the essay question. The student is asked to discuss the importance of the nature/nurture controversy, so the response should focus on the concept of nature and the concept of nurture. Instead, the student simply began writing, with no regard for the verb within the question or any type of essay structure. The student ends up talking in circles instead of answering the question.

Pace Yourself   As time allows, read back through the test to check your work. Look closely and carefully to catch spelling errors, bad grammar, and awkward phrasing. Be careful not to make massive changes to an answer. You are checking your work for accuracy and clarity; you don't have time for rewrites.

Exercise

1. Write an essay question focusing on the advice given in this chapter. Be sure to pick your words—especially the verbs—carefully. Trade questions with a classmate and write a response to the question you receive. Return the question and your answer and then discuss the strategies you used to write the response.

STUDENT SAMPLE

Rob had always had a problem taking tests; he became nervous and lost focus. This time, however, he was prepared. He had studied with a group of students a few days ago, had reviewed his notes last night, and he had arrived a few minutes early after eating a good breakfast. He had all his materials ready when the instructor handed out question sheets. Rob chose the first question.

Throughout the essay "Learning What 'Team' Really Means," author Mariah Burton Nelson discusses ways that women athletes can be sources of inspiration and education to young girls. Write an essay in which you discuss at least three ways that young boys can also be inspired by women athletes. Explain your answer.

On back of the question sheet, Rob scribbled this quick outline:

Boys can learn a lot from women athletes—

Role models and heroes

    Williams sisters are heroes

Strength

Breaking stereotypes

    Girls can't play sports and girls sports don't matter

Anyone can do anything

    Women in other roles

Rob glanced at the outline. Role models and heroes could be developed, as could stereotypes. Strength seemed the weakest. He was hard pressed to come up with support, so he abandoned that idea. Women in other roles was a better way to phrase his third point, so he decided to go with that instead. Armed with his three points, he created this thesis statement for the opening of his answer.

In "Learning What 'Team' Really Means," Mariah Burton Nelson does an excellent job explaining the impact of women's sports on girls. I think women's sports can also teach young boys a few things.

He then planned his strategy. He was going to start with the topic sentence, write a sentence or two about each and then he would end the essay. He checked his watch—twenty minutes to go. He went to work.

With five minutes left, he had written the following answer:

In "Learning What 'Team' Really Means," Mariah Burton Nelson does an excellent job explaining the impact of women's sports on girls. I think women's sports can also teach young boys a few things. First, boys can see women as heroes. Mia Hamm or the Williams sisters can be cool with boys just like Michael Jordan is because they are winners. Next, boys can learn to challenge the stereotypes they have about girls. When I was younger, I used to tease my males friends by saying, "You punch like a girl." Had I seen Laila Ali box, I never would have said that in a bad way. Finally, women's sports show women in roles other than moms and teachers. Boys can see women coaches, fans, athletes, managers, and announcers. I feel all of these factors would have a big impact on boys today.

Tips

Make Tests Real Learning Experiences

The end of the test doesn't necessarily mean the end of the learning process. Consider a few of the following ideas after you have taken a test. These strategies can help you gain insight on how well you did on the test and help you prepare for the next test—and the final exam.

▶▶▶▶ **Review the material on the test.**

Within a day of taking a test, go back through your notes and study materials and consider your test answers. Looking back over material you were just tested on doesn't seem like much fun, but it does have its rewards. First, reviewing the material helps you retain it. Second, it helps you gauge the strength of your answers, giving you a general idea of your grade on the test.

▶▶▶▶ **Go back to the study group.**

Study groups are great for test preparations; they can also be good for test debriefing. Going over questions and answers with members of the group can help you gain perspective on how well you did on the test. This practice can also help the group lay the groundwork for future study group meetings.

▶▶▶▶ **Discuss your test results with the instructor.**

From early on, we are trained to accept test results as they are presented. "I thought I had the right answer for question 3, but I guess not, because I missed it. That just proves I'm not good in biology," we might say. When you do not understand why you received a certain grade, simply ask the instructor. Please keep in mind that asking the instructor for clarification about a grade is much different then confronting the instructor about the test grade. Approach the situation as though you are getting help, not looking for a grade change.

Continued

▶▶▶▶ ·**Make notes of any problem areas.**

Many instructors duplicate the structure of their tests. If a midterm had ten matching questions, five true false questions, and three essay questions, the final exam will probably have matching, true-false, and essay questions as well. When you receive your grade on the test, look over the type of questions you had problems with and focus on that type when you study for the next test in that class.

▶▶▶▶ **Celebrate.**

Don't lose sight of the idea that taking a test is an achievement. Whether you do well or not, you worked hard and ought to celebrate the end of the hard work. Treat yourself to a favorite snack or go out for pizza with your study group after the final exam. Even if your celebration means a nap after class or an extra hour of television this weekend, take some time for yourself. You deserve it.

CHAPTER REVIEW

Every college student has to take essay tests. Answering essay questions effectively relies on reading them carefully and understanding what is being asked. Consider the verb used in the question, as it directs the approach you should take in your answer. Also consider the parameters of the question itself; in other words, be sure to answer only what the question asks. When preparing for a test, follow these study tips: Get previous exams, review the material throughout the semester, take good notes, predict the questions that may appear in the test, and join a study group. Before you actually take the test, get a good night's sleep, eat a good breakfast, and have all of your supplies handy. During the test, focus on getting the most points possible; answer the easier questions first, check your work when you are done, and get clarification on any question you don't understand. When the test is over, review the material, get feedback from your study group, make notes of any problem areas you encountered, discuss the test results with your instructor, and reward yourself for a job well done. Following these steps should make taking essay tests—and any other test, for that matter—much easier.

Final Writing Assignments

Answer each of the following essay questions as though they appear on an actual essay test. Set up your work area as though you are taking the test, keeping supplies at hand and a clock nearby. Give yourself only 30–45 minutes to create your answer. Ask your instructor to critique your responses.

1. After reading Garry Kasparov's article "The Day That I Sensed a New Kind of Intelligence" (page 58), describe *intelligence*. Use examples from the reading to support your answer.

2. Read Allan Bloom's essay on music (page 379). Summarize Bloom's argument and evaluate it.

3. Find essay questions in your other textbooks, such as the review questions often found at the end of each chapter. (If your textbooks don't have any, create your own based on your notes.) Choose one question and answer it. Have a student read your answer and evaluate it.

4. Write an essay responding to Marilla Svinicki's comments about essay tests. You will of course, express the student's point of view. Fill out a TAP Worksheet, choose a writing strategy, and develop your essay according to that structure. Edit and proofread your essay carefully, then submit your final draft to your instructor.

16

BUSINESS WRITING

When Juanita graduated from high school, she was excited to get out into the working world and not worry about all that writing she did in school. Juanita wrote her résumé and cover letters and then applied to a number of local businesses, filling out an application for each one. Then, when she was hired, she found she had to write memos to her boss to request vacation days. There were weekly and monthly meetings where she had to take notes and then write short reports. When a new computer system was proposed for the company, Juanita was asked for her input via a memo. After the new system was installed, Juanita wrote a thank-you note to the trainer for helping her learn the new system.

Yes, Juanita was happy to be out of school and away from all those writing assignments.

Opportunities for students to become involved in businesses and professional organizations abound. Perhaps you have an internship with a local business. Maybe you have (or are looking for) a part-time job on campus to offset the cost of tuition. Maybe you are active in a professional organization. Because students are involved in business and business-related activities, they should hone their business writing skills, the focus of this chapter.

Business writing is the type of writing that is centered on business or professional organizations. As in all types of writing, it involves communicating with an audience. In the case of business writing, your audience is an employer, other employees, and people from other businesses and organizations. Consequently, new considerations are in store. You must follow rules for the content and structure of your business writing, and you have to work a bit faster than you would for a class assignment. Throughout this chapter, we discuss these factors in terms of three basic areas: **letters** (including **cover letters** and **thank-you letters**), **memos**, and **résumés**.

Reading 18 Memo from Davidson College President
Robert F. Vagt

BACKSTORY

In 1998, a group of female students at Davidson College proposed creating a sorority on campus. The college's president, Robert Vagt, vetoed the idea. In his opinion, sororities would work against the mission of the college. As you read the memo he wrote explaining his position, see if you agree with his point of view.

LEXICON

constituent: a member of the group a leader serves or reports to

admonition: critical advice; warning

buttressed: supported

imprudently: unwisely

caliber: quality

To The Davidson College Community
From President Robert F. Vagt
January 12, 1998

1   Apologizing in advance for the excessive use of pronouns in the first person, I would like to explain why I will not invite at this time sororities to come to this campus.

2   I hold the fundamental belief that the right of any group to organize on this campus is not solely a function of popularity, for sentiment about such an issue, while always interesting and informative, should not be determinative. Rather, the only basis for denial is a judgment that the group or its activities may violate the noble aims or the best interests of this institution and its constituent community.

3   After careful consideration of the many points and counterpoints put forward by students, parents, staff and faculty, it is my judgment that the presence of sororities at Davidson could put at risk one of this institution's great strengths—that is, the unsurpassed quality, the breadth and depth, of the female applicants for admission. Clear expressions of concern were voiced by the Admissions Office about the potentially negative effect on applications, and this admonition was buttressed by a number of high school guidance counselors who were on this campus several weeks ago. Further, the overwhelming majority of the hundreds of female students, both current and graduated, who made themselves heard, vigorously asserted that the presence of sororities on this campus would have acted as a strong depressant on their interest in attending Davidson. Absent these facts, simple equity would have dictated inviting sororities to organize here. However, we cannot and will not jeopardize imprudently something as vital to Davidson as the caliber of its students.

4   Please allow me also to note what this decision is not. It is not a reflection of a lack of confidence in the ability of the women on this campus to make judgments for themselves. There was an assertion made that with the introduction of sororities, women would somehow come under the sway of a well-organized force that would move onto this campus. The truth is, woe betide anyone who underestimates the clear vision and strong will of the women at Davidson.

5   This is also not a judgment about Greek societies in general, nor about fraternities and eating houses at Davidson in particular. While there was considerable expression of heartfelt sentiment about Patterson Court, this decision is not in response to several negative assertions, for which there was produced little or no substantiation particular to this campus.

6   This decision does leave me quite uncomfortable in one notable aspect. There had been a strong case made in a self study of less than two years ago that Davidson "should continue its receptivity to initiatives from African-American students who wish to pursue the establishment of a traditionally black fraternity and/or sorority," in order to meet a need perceived by African-American students which does not seem to be met by any part of the current system. To the extent that this situation continues to exist, we must work to make it better.

7   This is a decision which will not be pleasing to all. There is an important group of women who articulately endorsed the invitation of sororities to the campus. They and their views are important to this community, and it is with great reluctance that I take a stance inconsistent with their request. In an effort to express this more fully, I would invite those of you who wish to respond to this decision to meet with me in the 900 Room of the College Union on Tuesday, January 13, at 8 p.m.

8   This campus has participated in active debate on an important issue about which there were strong, opposing views. This is clearly not the first such occurrence in Davidson's history and certainly—even hopefully—not the last. During the course of this exchange, I was aided immeasurably by letters, phone calls, e-mail messages, and notes captured in frost on my office and car windows. While each had a point of view, and most were strongly held, they were identical in one respect—each was sent in a spirit of expression of what is best for Davidson College. This institution is fortunate to command such support. Please accept my thanks for your insight and assistance.

QUESTIONS FOR THOUGHT

1. In paragraph 2, Vagt writes, "It is my judgment that the presence of sororities at Davidson could put at risk one of this institution's great strengths—that is, the unsurpassed quality, the breath and depth, of the female applicants for admission." Why does he choose to phrase his statement this way?

2. Reread the entire memo. Highlight passages where Vagt praises female students. Because his purpose in writing the memo is to explain why Davidson will not have sororities, what is the purpose of this praise?

3. Imagine you are a member of the "important group of women who articulately endorsed the invitation of sororities to the campus." What would your reaction to this memo be?

4. Does any college campus need sororities or fraternities?

MEMOS

A **memo**, or memorandum, is a short note or letter that provides information to those within a company's structure; typical subjects are a request for sick leave, a reorganization notice, and a suggestion for donations for the next holiday party. While the structure of a memo can vary, you must specify your audience, the topic of the memo and the date. The body of the memo takes an essay format, with an introduction, explanation, and a conclusion.

Make Your Memos Effective

Here are some tips to follow when writing a memo.

▸▸▸ **Keep the content of the memo concise and focused.** Memos are generally used to convey specific information. Keep content short and to the point.

Continued

Extraneous information comes across as idle chatter and can cloud the message. Vagt is good at staying on track with his memo to Davidson College. Every word in every paragraph concerns his decision about sororities on campus.

▶▶▶ **Be clear and forthright with the information in the memo.** Don't try to bury bad news or show off good news. Be straightforward. Consider the opening line from Vagt's memo: "I would like to explain why I would not invite at this time sororities to come to this campus." The position of the author and the purpose for the memo are clear.

▶▶▶ **Explain the new information; don't rehash old information.** The purpose of a memo is to relay new information to others in the organization who do not need background. Going over old news wastes time. Vagt gives the reasons for his decisions and refers to ideas from previous debates, but he does not recount the history of the debate over sororities on campus.

▶▶▶ **Send the memo to the appropriate people.** Be aware of who needs the information, who is in charge of what areas, and target your memos to the appropriate department and person. Vagt's memo was addressed to the Davidson community at large because the topic involved so many people.

▶▶▶ **Check details carefully.** All business communication requires a close eye directed toward detail, and memos are no exception. Make sure names and titles are accurate and that spelling and punctuation are correct. Remember, your professional image is created and reflected in your memos.

Exercises

1. Bring samples of memos you have received at work to class. Remove information like names and addresses and then make copies of the memo for the class to evaluate. How well do the memos effectively communicate their main points? How could they be improved?

2. Rewrite the following information as a company-wide memo generated by the president's office. Please feel free to add any missing information.

   Bil-Der's Tile and Roofing, a company in business over thirty years, has solved roofing and flooring problems for businesses all over the city. Their most recent (and most important, they might add) job has been fixing the roofs of city hall and the mayor's house. This week, it was decided that this great company will fix the roof in the cafeteria of our company.

   People have complained for years that the roof in this area needs work. They have noticed water damaged spots and, just last week, someone complained about cracks in the ceiling. These complaints (all on file) were finally acted on at the last board meeting when the president, Don S. Theleader, moved funds from one account (business travel) to repairs and maintenance with the board's approval. The president's office is 101. The telephone number is 555-5467. His email address is leaderboss@company.org.

When most roofing construction is done, some businesses have to close. The smell and the noise is simply too much. In our case, this won't happen. Bil-Der's Tile and Roofing promise that everything from construction to clean up will take place in a reasonable amount of time and will cause as little discomfort as possible. The biggest problem will be parking. Due to the large trucks that will need prime access to the cafeteria roof, the west wing of the parking lot will be closed for about two weeks. Carpooling and taking the bus to work will be alternatives to driving. During the heaviest part of the construction, the cafeteria will be closed.

The whole project begins Monday.

JOB APPLICATIONS

Almost every employer requires potential employees to fill out a job application. This is usually a one- or two-page form that asks for information such as full name, birth date, social security number, and educational background. These forms do not take the place of résumés; they are used primarily for immediate evaluation of applicants. When filling out job applications, write neatly, fill in all appropriate spaces, and be honest. Do not offer any information that is not asked for on the application; if the employer wants to know more, you will be interviewed.

Résumés

A **résumé** is a valuable tool, for it presents vital information about you to a possible employer. Résumés aren't written in paragraph or essay format; rather, the important information is listed for quick access. Generally speaking, a résumé should be only a page or two long. This space limitation requires you to be highly selective with the information you put in your résumé. Most résumés include contact information, your objectives or reasons for submitting the résumé, your work history, any job-related skills you have, your education, interests that relate to the job for which you are applying and, finally, references.

Contact Information   At the top of your résumé, post the most important information: your name, address, phone number, and email address. This information should be on all the documents you send to the company or organization, but it is especially important here as this is the document that represents you. A potential employer may want to get in touch with you immediately; offering your contact information in a prominent place is an advantage.

Objective   In one sentence, explain your reasons for submitting a résumé. Many times, you will be dealing with a large company with quite a few positions available, so you must cite the position, organization, or career goal that you have in mind. Be as specific as possible. Stating your objective clearly will help get your résumé to the correct people.

Work History   List the places you have worked and the dates you worked at those places, beginning with the most recent and working backward chronologically. Even if your work experience comprises part-time jobs bagging groceries, babysitting, or working as a student assistant in the Humanities Department of your school, include this information on your résumé. Employers seem to have more confidence in people who have had previous job experience, regardless of the particulars of the job. Do not attempt to explain any gaps in your work history on the résumé. Information of that nature (which may or may not be important) can be discussed at the interview.

Job-Related Skills   Prominently display skills that your potential employer is seeking, such as customer service or proficiency with Microsoft Office applications. Don't list irrelevant skills.

Education   List your education history, degrees, and training in reverse chronological order, beginning with the most recent experience and working your way backward. If you don't have a degree or formal training, feel free to list coursework on your résumé. Make sure, though, that the coursework is pertinent to the job you want. Also, in this section, include special certifications or other merits that show you go out of your way to improve yourself.

Interests and Other Personal Information   Outside interests such as hobbies can make you stand out or they can be used against you. One boss may think your comic book collection shows organizational skills, while another might think you haven't quite grown up yet. If the job you are seeking is in the field of illustration or design, that comic book collection may work in your favor. To be safe, mention only hobbies and interests that connect with the job you are seeking. While interests and hobbies can appear on a résumé, other personal information such as marital status or physical appearance should not. Who cares if you are single and have blue eyes? Just focus on information that represents your professional side.

References   At the end of your résumé, list your references—people who will vouch for your abilities. Limit the list to three people and do not include friends or members of your family. Be sure to get permission before you use someone as a reference.

The Résumé Worksheet

Gathering and keeping track of all the information you might want to include on a résumé is easier if you fill out the Résumé Worksheet, which follows.

The Résumé Worksheet

Contact Information

Name: _____

Address:_____

Phone number: _____

Email address:_____

Fax number: _____

Objective: _____

_____

_____

Work History

Place of employment:_____

Address:_____

Title of job: _____

Dates of employment: _____

Duties of the job: _____

Place of employment:_____

Address:_____

Title of job: _____

Dates of employment: _____

Duties of the job: _____

Place of employment:_____

Address:_____

Title of job: _____

Dates of employment: _____

Duties of the job: _____

Continued

Job-related skills:

_____

_____

_____

Education

School: _____

Dates of attendance: _____

Diploma or degree: _____

School: _____

Dates of attendance: _____

Diploma or degree: _____

Interests:

_____

_____

References

Contact person: _____

Relationship: _____

Phone number: _____

Email address: _____

Contact person: _____

Relationship: _____

Phone number: _____

Email address: _____

Contact person: _____

Relationship: _____

Phone number: _____

Email address: _____

Make Your Résumé Memorable

You want your résumé to stand out. Here are some pointers.

▶▶▶ **Open with your strengths**. There is no one correct way to create a résumé. Many people open with their strongest section, such as employment or education. By opening the body of the résumé with your strengths, you are showing off your talent, and that will attract the employer's attention quickly.

▶▶▶ **Type your résumé in an easy-to-read, professional font.** Be careful not to overpower your audience with bold graphics and numerous fonts and typefaces just because you have access to them through your computer. Even if you are applying for a part-time job in the art or computer science department on campus, stick with a simple, straightforward résumé design where the sections (objective, employment history, and so on) are highlighted in bold. A simple design that is easy to read will give the impression that you are a professional.

▶▶▶ **Use off-white or light gray résumé paper.** The paper your résumé is printed on also reflects on you. If the paper is too thin, it can be ripped too easily; if it is too thick, it can become unmanageable. If the paper has designs on it, beware. Except for well-placed bullets or underlining, graphics can make the page look too busy. No one will want to read it. Your safest bet is plain résumé paper, in off-white or light gray, found at most printing shops, stationery stores, computer supply companies, and copy centers.

Exercises

3. Create a résumé or redesign an old one. Include all of the parts mentioned, but keep it simple. Once done, show the résumé to the instructor or to other members of the class for comparison.

4. Collect some résumés from your campus career counselors. Compare these to your own. What are the similarities and differences?

STUDENT SAMPLE

Mike, a college freshmen, wants to work for a landscape company during the summer. He has done some previous landscaping work and has three references. He sat down and filled out a Résumé Worksheet and then turned the information into a résumé tailored to the summer job he hoped to get.

The Résumé Worksheet

Contact Information

Name: _Mike J. Public_

Address: _1101 E. Broadlake Court_

Phone number: _614-555-1717_

Email address: _mjp@email.com_

Fax number: _—_

Objective: _Part-time manager in landscaping_

Work History

Place of employment: _Census 2002_

Address: _Columbus, OH_

Title of job: _—_

Dates of employment: _May–June 2000_

Duties of the job: _lead team, organized roster, took care of problems, collected info for census_

Place of employment: _Nationwide Insurance_

Address: _Columbus, OH_

Title of job: _customer assistance_

Dates of employment: _May–September 1999_

Duties of the job: _customer assistance, filing_

Place of employment: _Wonderland Arcade and Cinema_

Address: _Parkersburg, WV_

Title of job: _Clerk_

Dates of employment: _January 1998–May 1999_

Duties of the job: _clerk, ticket taker, made concessions, cleaned_

Continued

Job-related skills:

_____

_____

_____

Education

School: _Columbus State Community College_____

Dates of attendance: _September 2001 to present_____

Diploma or degree: _Business Management_____

School: _Parkersburg South High School_____

Dates of attendance: _September 1997—May 2001_____

Diploma or degree: _Diploma_____

Interests:

_____

_____

References

Contact person: _Julie Sims_____

Relationship: _Manager—National Insurance_____

Phone number: _614-555-0001_____

Email address:_____

Contact person: _Paul Stevens_____

Relationship: _Instructor_____

Phone number: _614-555-0102_____

Email address:_____

Contact person: _Gary Thomas_____

Relationship: _Instructor_____

Phone number: _614-555-00210_____

Email address:_____

Michael J. Public

1101 E. Broadlake Court

Columbus, OH 00000

Phone: (614) 555-1717   Email: mjp@email.com

Objective: To become a part-time manager at a landscaping business

Work History

Census 2002   Columbus, OH   May–June 2000

Duties included managing a team of three census takers, organizing their routes, assisting with problems, and collecting and returning information to the National Census Board

National Insurance   Columbus, OH   May–September 1999

Duties included customer assistance, filing, and organizing past claims

Wonderland Arcade and Cinema   Parkersburg, WV   January 1998–May 1999

Duties included assisting customers, preparing concessions, operating a cash register, and scheduling employee workdays and breaks

Education

September 2001–Present

Columbus State Community College   Columbus, OH

Major: Business Management

September 1997–May 2001

Parkersburg South High School   Parkersburg, WV

Graduated with diploma in May 2001

References

Available upon request

Business Letters

To make the best impression when applying for a job, send your résumé with a strong cover letter; if you get an interview, send a solid thank-you letter afterward. These letters are written presentations of your skills and abilities, so pay close attention to the **elements**, **form**, and **tone** of each one.

Cover Letters   An employer's first written contact with you is your résumé's **cover letter**. This letter functions as a sort of introduction from you to your potential employer. It should include information about who you are, what you can offer the company or organization, and how you can be contacted for an interview. Your writing should reflect the politeness you would give on the job.

The format of a cover letter mirrors that of a traditional essay. You begin with an **opening** or introduction. In this case, the opening introduces you and your interest in the position for which you are applying. As you write your opening, avoid being either too casual or too formal. The best approach is to be clear and to the point and to always consider your audience expectations.

In the **body** of the letter, discuss your work-related strengths. These items may be listed on your résumé, but do not assume your audience has read your résumé. Flesh out the strengths that enhance your application. If the job posting asked for friendly, helpful people, then stress that you were honored as employee of the month at your last job and won an award for outstanding public service. If computer skills are a requirement for the internship, highlight the software programs with which you are proficient. If you don't have the work experience, think about related experiences you do have that could meet the requirements. Perhaps you volunteer at a shelter and have been honored for your professionalism and enthusiasm. Those software programs you are learning in computer science class can be listed as limited computer skills. Be sure not to ramble, though; you only have a page or two to work with. Stick with information that relates to the job itself.

Finally, your cover letter needs to have a strong **closing**. Closings can be tricky. You want the reader to respond favorably to your letter and call you for an interview, but you cannot demand a phone call at a precise date and time. Remind the reader of the position you are interested in and then explain how you can be contacted. You might also add a sentence saying you will call the employer after a week if you are not otherwise contacted—and be sure to follow through.

STUDENT SAMPLE

For an example of a cover letter, let's turn to Mike and his application for a summer internship at a local landscaping firm. The job consists of heavy lifting, lots of detailed gardening work, long hours in the sun, dealing with the public, and learning the basics of running a landscaping business. Mike already has an appropriate résumé, and he is confident that he has the skills and abilities for the job. He just has to write a cover letter that will get him an interview.

Dear Mr. Richards:

I read your ad in the Sunday, April 13th edition of the *Gazette* for the part-time landscaping manager position with great interest. Currently, I am working toward my B.A. in Business Management, and the job sounds like it would give me a good opportunity to grow. I believe I can handle the demands of the job quite well. I am submitting the attached résumé for your consideration.

Management has always interested me. Most recently, I managed a small team of census takers for Census 2000. Last summer, I had an internship with National Insurance, assisting customers with problems and learning the basics of the business. I am sure the skills I have acquired will greatly benefit your company.

Mr. Richards, I look forward to meeting with you to discuss possible employment opportunities. Feel free to give me a call at 555-1717 day or night. I will contact you in a week to set up an interview. Thanks for your time.

Yours,

Michael Public

Michael Public

Thank-You Letters   The cover letter and résumé get you an interview. After the interview, send a **thank-you letter** as a gesture of professionalism and goodwill. If you do get the job, the thank-you letter shows that you follow through on the contacts you make. If you don't get the job, the letter shows that you harbor no hard feelings and keeps the door open for future employment with that company or organization.

The opening of the thank-you letter should include a brief mention of who you are and where and when the interview took place. You may have been one of many candidates for the position, so the employer may not immediately remember you or your interview. The body of the letter also should be brief. Simply thank the interviewer for the time you spent together. If a particular point of discussion sticks out in your mind, mention it as well. In the conclusion, be sure to again thank the interviewer and add a reminder of where you can be reached if he or she has further questions. You may also want to include a sentence stating your continued interest in the company, just in case another opportunity presents itself

Perhaps the most important aspect of a thank-you letter is politeness. If you get the job, boasting about how great you are will only alienate your boss. Being mean and spiteful if you don't get the job makes you look petty. Just convey a polite, professional tone, just as you did in the cover letter and résumé.

STUDENT SAMPLE

Return to Mike and his quest for a summer internship. The résumé and cover letter looked good, and the interview went well. Now he has written a thank-you letter to send to the interviewer.

Dear Mr. Richards:

I thank you for your time during our April 24th interview. I especially liked our discussion on the future of ecommerce and business ethics. I have to admit that these topics aren't covered in my textbooks, so the insight was eye-opening.

I look forward to hearing from you once all the interviews have been conducted.

Thanks once again for your time and consideration.

Yours,

Michael Public

Michael Public

Exercises

5. Gather samples of cover letters and thank-you letters from your school's library or student activities office. What are some of the strengths of these letters? What are some of the weaknesses? Compare your notes with those of other member of the class.

6. Read through the following want ads. First determine what skills and education would be necessary for the job and then write mock cover letters as though you were applying for each job. Compare notes and cover letters with those of other members of your class.

   a. Gutter Installers: Wanted now: self-starters for gutter installation business. Qualified candidate should have 1-2 years experience and valid driver's license. 14-year-old company will provide $30,000-$40,000 annually for year-round work, depending on experience. Paid vacations, 401(K), medical/dental ins. and uniforms also provided. Call for appt. Acme Roofing: 555-1234.

   b. Modeling Agency: Stars of Tomorrow seeks talent scout for new fall fashion show. Must have strong sales and communication experience. Experience preferred but not a must. $40,000 annual starting salary. Contact Paul at 555-1243.

c. Caregiver: Immediate opening for in-home caregiver to elderly woman. Experience and solid references required. Also need valid driver's license. Good pay and full time benefits. Call Tuesday-Friday 9:30 am–4:30 pm only. 555-2134.

d. Customer Service: Rayne's Floral Shoppe seeking full time customer service representative. Strong data entry skills and communication skills a must. Competitive salary and health ins. package. Apply in person or send résumé to Rayne's Floral Shoppe, 1000 Bluebell Ave., Austin, OH 00000.

7. Write a cover letter based on your skills for a job you found in the want ads of your local newspaper. (You may also want to look for job postings in the career counseling center at your school.) Find the want ad and then write your résumé and the cover letter. Have your instructor or peers review the cover letter; then (if you choose), mail out the résumé and the cover letter.

8. Using the cover letters from previous exercises, write thank-you letters for those interviews.

Writing with Computers

BUSINESS WRITING

Word processing programs have forever changed the face of business writing. Many programs offer templates and tutorials for creating business letters and résumés—but, sadly, many of these templates are worthless. Some templates are decorated with flowers or other artwork that is distracting, while others use unusual fonts or are difficult to edit. Computers are useful, though, when you have to store a business letter. Make a hard copy of every business letter you send out (just for safekeeping). After this, open an electronic folder and place the file containing the letter in it. Accessing it will be no problem next time.

You may also use computers to store and update your résumé. After you finish creating your résumé, save a copy on the hard drive or a diskette. This way, if you need a copy of your résumé, all you have to do is print one. You may be asked to submit a résumé via email. Some people have their résumés posted on a website for easy access. Keep in mind that you must keep your résumé current, especially if it is posted on a website. Through the use of computers, updating the résumé is fairly simple. Just open the file, make the changes, then save.

CHAPTER REVIEW

Business writing, or the writing done to get a job or writing on the job, includes memos, résumés, cover letters, and thank-you letters. Memos are the way most information travels within an organization or business. A memo should be concise, focused on the issue at hand, and include just the information that is necessary. Résumés outline a person's skills and abilities with respect to a certain job. Résumés must be short (one page maximum) but still include job-related information, educational background, work history, and references. The cover letter is sent with the résumé and tells of a person's interest in employment. Traditional cover letters introduce the applicant, display his or her strengths and talents, and invite the employer to request an interview. After the interview, a thank-you letter is sent to show appreciation for the interviewer's time and continued interest in the business or organization.

Final Writing Assignments

1. Create a résumé of your current skills, experiences, and educational background, and then visit your school's job placement center. Have a specialist critique your résumé for its strengths and weaknesses. Ask about the types of jobs you could apply for.

*2. With a few members of your class, collect a variety of job applications. (Be sure to include applications from your school.) Compare the applications for the information asked and then discuss the most effective ways of filling them out. (If you would like to be considered for employment, return the completed applications to the respective employers.)

*3. Being a student can be a full-time job, so treat it as such. Write a cover letter and résumé for someone applying for the job of student in your class. (Creating a want ad for the job would be a good place to start.) Have other members of your class critique your work.

4. Write a want ad, cover letter, and résumé for several "professions," such as writer, parent, child, adult, or member of your family.

PART IV

Reading and Writing About Popular Culture

Take a quick quiz: in a short phrase, describe each of the characters below and tell why they are famous.

- Sherlock Holmes
- Mike Tyson
- Austin Powers
- Madonna
- Superman
- Yoda

Chances are, that was one quiz you had no trouble taking because each of the people are so popular that they have influenced nearly all parts of American society. Whether you have ever been to a Madonna concert or read a Superman comic book or not, you still know who these people are. They have become pop culture figures. Popular or pop culture is a culture shared by almost everyone, regardless of race, gender, or socio-economic status. In this course, you have been writing about various areas of popular culture. Here, you will read about them.

When reading and thinking about popular culture, it isn't enough simply to make references. You should go beyond what it presented and look at the influences that aspect of pop culture has on our society. Studying what is popular and how it got that way can help us find out more about our society and ourselves.

The readings in these sections cover seven different aspects of pop culture: sports, music, television, science and technology, movies, cartoons, and advertising. These readings suggest how popular culture shapes our society and has helped to shape each of us. You will encounter familiar areas and areas that may be new to you. Each reading, however, offers new perspectives.

To enhance your understanding of the material, each selection is arranged in the manner in which you should approach reading a paragraph or essay. You encountered backstory, lexicon, and questions for thought earlier in the book. In this section, you will discover questions for discussion, questions of style, questions for strategy, and questions for writing.

- **Questions for Discussion:** Once you have read a selection, discuss your opinions, thoughts, and feelings about it. The questions provided for each reading help guide you.

- **Questions of Style:** These questions help you explore the way language is used in the reading.

- **Questions of Strategy:** These questions help you analyze how each author uses writing strategies to meet the demands of topic, audience, and purpose.

- **Questions for Writing:** Prompts for writing paragraphs and essays round out each reading.

To make your reading time as productive as possible, consider these reading strategies:

- **Get a good dictionary and thesaurus and use them sparingly.** To find a dictionary or thesaurus that fits your needs, go to your campus bookstore or another bookstore and select two or three dictionaries you might use. Look up the same word in each dictionary and compare definitions. The definition that is most concise indicates the dictionary you should buy. When reading, be sure to highlight, underline, or circle any words you have to look up in a dictionary, but wait until you have finished the selection before you consult a dictionary. In most cases, you can get the gist of the meaning from the context, and your concentration may be broken if you pause in midsentence to look up a word.

- **Look for the main idea or controlling thought in each reading and in each paragraph.** Just as you have a main idea in mind as you write, so does the writer of each reading selection. Look for the main idea. Discover how the author uses writing strategies to support it and evaluate the quality of what you are reading. Make notes in the book's margins or in a separate notebook to help with the discovery and evaluation process as you read.

- **Talk back as you read.** Readers come in two types: those who sit by, hand in lap, eyes scanning the words (passive readers); and those who write in the margins of their books, asking questions, making comments about what they are reading (active readers). Strive to be an active reader. Keep in mind that reading is like listening to someone talk. At times, you will agree with what is said. At other times, however, you will disagree and want to say something in response. Jotting down your thoughts is your way of responding to what you are reading. Some questions to ask yourself as you talk back include:

What is the background of the author?

What part of this discussion do I agree with? Why?

What part of this discussion do I disagree with? Why?

What experiences in this piece can I relate to?

What is the main idea? How well is it supported?

- **Take breaks.** Marathon reading sessions help no one when it comes to academic material. Stopping every half-hour or so just to stretch or reflect on what you have read will help you retain the information.

- **Form a reading group.** Many people read a great deal because they use a buddy system whereby they meet with others who have similar reading interests and together they read and discuss the same books. This reading community can be a wonderful way to enjoy reading. In college, reading communities can be an invaluable aid to learning as well. Your reading community could get together to read and discuss difficult passages in, say, a chemistry text or a history book. The additional feedback can help you see points of view you may not have considered before.

- **Read every day.** Reading is like every other muscle or skill that you have: You get better at it when you practice. Get into the habit of reading at least twenty minutes every day (at the same time, if possible). Read articles from the newspaper. Read cereal boxes in the grocery store. Read a page or two from a good mystery novel while you are waiting at the bus stop. Read the health pamphlets in the dentist's office. Read comic books to your children or for your own pleasure. Soon, you will see an improvement in your reading skills. Also, the more you read, the more you will enjoy reading.

Remember that reading is vital to improving your writing. If you don't read, you sacrifice command of your language. If you do read, your choices when using language increases. Worlds open up for you!

17

SPORTS

Sports invade almost every part of our lives, whether we are players, fans, or simply have a casual interest in the games. Sports figures become heroes for what they can accomplish on the court or field. Tiger Woods is a strong example. He is the first player in the history of golf to hold all four major titles, and he is the idol of millions. Somehow, certain athletes like Woods are able to outshine not only the average person but other athletes as well. In most cases, though, an athlete doesn't have to be outstanding to gain a degree of awe from people. We just seem to respond to people who find time and energy for physical activity. If someone mentions playing racquetball or shooting hoops or swimming in their spare time, we might feel guilty for not finding more time for physical activity ourselves. Finally, we hold athletes to a higher moral standard than other people. We are shocked when an athlete commits crimes or goes against society. "If he has that talent," we think to ourselves, "why would he get involved with criminal activity?"

Not only are athletes elevated in our society but also sports themselves are treated with respect and honor. Like music, sports bridge racial and ethnic gaps, bringing people together. Sports can be a way to release frustration as well as help younger children develop of sense of purpose, team play, and sportsmanship. Sports are also responsible for large amounts of revenue. Professionals, of course, are paid to play. Those professionals have agents, who are paid. Cities that host professional sporting events add millions of dollars to their coffers every year. Advertisers have found that having an athlete pitch products increases sales dramatically. It is safe to say that, without sports as a large part of our culture, our society would be different, for good or for bad.

We often seek writing about sports in the sports section of our local or national newspaper. Articles on players' performances, team rankings, and team changes are important. However, writing about sports can and should go below the surface of any game. Sports is a big part of American culture, and its importance demands that writers take a close look at the games people play and why they choose to play them.

The two readings in this section, "Learning What 'Team' Really Means" and "Gravity's Rainbow," discuss different aspects of sports and American culture. In "Learning," author Mariah Burton Nelson analyzes the importance of women's team sports and the impact that team sports can have on women. The second reading, "Gravity's Rainbow," written by New York City reporter Guy Trebay, describes the world of street skating and the way of life that has been created from this extreme sport. While some may shake their head at young people doing flips on skateboards, Trebay shows a human side to the people who skate and their reasons for skating. Consider your own experiences playing and watching sports as you read each essay.

Reading 19 Learning What "Team" Really Means
Mariah Burton Nelson

BACKSTORY

In the past few years, women's team sports have gathered more fans and more respect than ever before. While it is true the players play well, author Mariah Burton Nelson asserts that these team sports are having a larger impact on women—and society—as a whole. In the following essay from *Newsweek*, Nelson explores the reasons these teams are having such influence.

LEXICON

adoration: admiration; looking up to

divisive: leading to separation

enthusiasm: excitement

recriminations: responses to a negative action with a negative action

1   What's going on here? over 90,000 people flocked to the final game of the Women's World Cup. The Women's National Basketball Association averaged almost 11,000 fans per game last year, and that's up 12 percent this season. Even the Women's Pro Softball League recently got better TV ratings than a (men's) Major League Soccer game shown during the same time slot. How come American sports fans' fascination with female athletes has shifted from skirted skaters (Dorothy Hamill, Michelle Kwan) and tiny teenage tumblers (Mary Lou Retton, Kerri Strug) to rough, muscular women in their 20s and 30s who grunt, grimace and heave each other aside with their hips? Are we simply wild over their athletic brilliance? Or does the popularity of women's team sports tell us something deeper about how female athletes and fans are redefining themselves, what they really want and who they might become?

2   One obvious reason for our adoration is that American women are the best team athletes in the world. They rock. They rule. What's not to love? They're good sports, too, apparently unpolluted by the violence and greed that plague men's sports. Then there's the role-model thing: "Little girls need big girls to look up to," said basketball star Teresa Edwards.

3   But there's something else underlying all the hype and hoopla. I know I learned about more than hook shots and rebounds when I played basketball at Stanford back in the late

'70s and later as a professional, here and in Europe. Now, as millions of girls grow up playing team sports, they, too, are discovering how to embrace victory unapologetically and other essential life lessons. Older women watching the Mia Hamm generation sense this, and want to get in on the action. Here's some of what team-sport athletes know:

4   **They know who their teammates really are.** Most women are good at friendships, but how many have *teammates* who don't just sympathize, but help us achieve success? A friend might say, "I don't want to start a business with you because it might hurt our relationship." A teammate says, "Of course I'll do it with you: we share the same vision and passion, so we'll be successful."

5   **They know how to compete.** Nonathletes tend to avoid competition and believe friends shouldn't compete, according to a survey in my book "Embracing Victory." Athletes don't see competition as divisive; they use it to connect. They play hard in practice, knowing their best efforts help teammates improve. They shake hands with opponents, grateful for the challenge.

6   **They know how to lead.** One day when I was 12, the girls on the playground circled around me, asking, "Can we play softball? Can I pitch?" I wondered: "Why are they asking me?" But I decided: "If people are going to look up to me, I ought to become the sort of person who's worth looking up to." Later, as captain and leading scorer at Stanford, I tried to bring hope and enthusiasm to the team each day. That's how people become leaders: they practice.

7   **They know how to bond.** When I speak to women's business groups, the complaint I hear most often is, "The women in my office don't support each other." Girls who learn to compete only over beauty and boyfriends grow up to be women who don't bond in the workplace, don't share information, don't mentor. Team athletes support other women. "Walking side by side over many miles of tough terrain, it brings you closer," says soccer's Michelle Akers. "It's a shared vision of who we are."

8   **They know how to take risks.** When we needed to score, my teammates used to pass me the ball—even though I sometimes dribbled off my foot instead. Athletes don't always succeed, but they're willing to take public risks, which inspires women whose fears of looking foolish keep them safely seated on the sidelines.

9   **They know how to ask for help.** In basketball, athletes on defense need to yell "HELP!" Such public pleas are humbling, and debunk the Superwoman myth. We really don't have to be the perfect worker, mother, partner, friend. We can and must ask for help—in life, as in sports.

10   **They know how to forgive themselves.** When girls start playing sports, they say "I'm sorry" a lot. But eventually they stop apologizing and focus on their next achievement. How appealing to those of us who torture ourselves with self-recriminations!

11   **They know that women are strong, successful and free.** With their high-fives, hugs and aggressive, competitive play, female team athletes represent who many of us want to be, or want our daughters to be. By pursuing victory in a context of friendship, support, respect and celebration, team-sport athletes are redefining what it means to be an athlete, and what it means to be female. No wonder we love them. They show us our future: female bonding, and female excellence, at its best.

Once we loved tiny skaters and tumblers; now it's muscle we admire.

QUESTIONS FOR THOUGHT

1. Think back through your childhood and describe in writing team sports you participated in. Be sure to jot down your age at the time and how long you played each sport. Why did you play those sports? Why were you on those teams (if you were)? What lessons did those sports teach you?

2. Title XI states that colleges and universities must provide sports for women when sports for men are offered. What are some of the arguments in favor of this idea? What are some of the arguments against it?

3. Should men's and women's sports teams compete against each other? Why or why not?

QUESTIONS OF STYLE

1. Through the essay, the author uses the pronouns "we" and "us" ("Are we simply wild over their athletic brilliance?" "No wonder we love them."). Who do the pronouns represent? Why do you think she chose to use these pronouns?

2. Why does the author start the essay with statistics? How does this color the effectiveness of the introduction?

QUESTIONS OF STRATEGY

1. A mixture of strategies is used in this essay. Find one, explain it, and then explain why it was used.

2. The main strategy in this piece is persuasion. Reread the review of chapter 10, "Persuasion" (page 223) then compare those ideas to this reading. Where is the persuasion effort strongest? What makes it strong? Where is it weakest? What makes it weak?

3. Nelson describes eight lessons that team sports teach women, but she does not support all of the lessons in the same way. How does this affect the overall essay?

QUESTIONS FOR WRITING

1. Consider other facets of society (business, education, entertainment, and so on) and reflect on the skills that women bring to them. Choose one and write an essay on how women have and continue to influence that aspect of society. Be sure to follow your points with details and examples.

2. Other than role modeling, how can young girls be encouraged to achieve their goals? Write an essay in which you define three or four ways that young girls can be encouraged and how each way will help them. Be sure to add an introduction and conclusion to your essay and to develop your points with details, explanations, and examples.

3. Throughout her essay, Nelson discusses ways that women athletes can be sources of inspiration and education to young girls. Write an essay in which you discuss at least three ways that young boys can also be inspired by women athletes. Be sure to add an introduction and conclusion to your essay and to develop your points with details, explanations, and examples.

4. Write a response to Mariah Burton Nelson's "Learning What 'Team' Really Means." Define *team* for yourself and then compare and contrast your definition with Nelson's. Be sure to include specific examples, as Nelson does, to support your point of view.

*5. With a partner, contact your school's athletic department and ask about scholarships available for men and women. Write an essay comparing or contrasting the results. Address the types of scholarships available, the monetary value of each scholarship, and the application requirements for each scholarship.

6. Research types of sports played in countries other than the United States, such as soccer or cricket. Write an essay focusing on one of these sports. Give background information about the history of the sport, who plays it, and how it is played. Submit your polished essay to your instructor.

Reading 20 Gravity's Rainbow
Guy Trebay

BACKSTORY

In 1996, a section of an old city park became Skate Park, a place where skaters could go to perfect their skateboarding techniques. Guy Trebay, a reporter for the New York publication *Village Voice*, wrote about the park from the point of view of the skaters. Do you consider skateboarding a sport? Would you support the creation of a "Skate Park" in your town? As you read Trebay's article, see if your definition of *sports* and *athletes* is challenged.

LEXICON

aerials: skate tricks executed in the air

break: create waves high and long enough for surfing

carve: turn

diss: speak with disrespect

grinds: skate tricks where the body of the skateboard touches the ground

half-pipe: a semicircular ramp that resembles a tube or pipe cut in half lengthwise

inverts: stunts in which the skaters go upside down

lip tricks: stunts performed at the edge of a skateboard ramp

maquette: mockup, model

rapt: enthralled; giving full attention

shred: perform intense skateboard maneuvers

side-airs: skateboard moves performed in the air

1   Rahmaan Mazone stands poised at the lip, contemplating his doom. Below him is a 10-foot drop into a steel-plated half-pipe. The arc looks even deeper when you factor in Rahmaan's own six-foot height and the wheels of his in-line skates. Only a handful of local skaters have mastered the knack. Rahmaan wants to be one. "I just love heights to death," he says.

2   "Go!" a skateboarder urges as Rahmaan pauses, hovers, seems to cantilever his bulk out over a volume of empty air.

3   He's ready. He is about to let go. He's almost there and then . . . "Aargh!" Rahmaan groans, collapsing in a heap on the platform. "I don't want to die!"

4   We are in Skate Park, a very recently constructed rectangle of asphalt at 108th Street in Riverside Park. For some time, this place was known as Tuberculosis Park, principally because numerous homeless people were encamped here. Many still inhabit an enclosed arcade beneath the park walkway, and also the park itself, and the Penn Central tunnels where the so-called Mole People live.

5   Skate Park opened just a month ago; already close to 80 skaters arrive each day. The concept originated with 20 local adolescents guided by the Salvadori Educational Center on the Built Environment. It was realized with a $50,000 grant from the National Parks Service's Innovations in Recreation Program, matched by an equivalent sum from the Department of Parks and other contributors. "We were eager to meet the needs of teens in Riverside Park," explains Riverside Park administrator Charles McKinney. "And we were searching for a project that would allow kids to design their own place. It was just lucky for us that this place was standing here derelict."

6   Crackheads had taken over. Consequently, "there was very little controversy" about reuse of the park. The project was designed with the help of four teachers who conducted a group visit to a skate park in Shimmersville, Pennsylvania, the creation of scale models, and also of a clay maquette depicting the riverside terrain. Construction took just under five weeks. That, too, was accomplished by students. The yield, besides a huge plywood hulk, was "an enormous jump in these kids' self-esteem," says McKinney. There was something else. "We've designated this area from 100th Street to 111th Street as a place to explore prototypes" for specifically adolescent park use, since "urban park environments frequently deny that the needs of some age groups and cultures exist."

7   The kids in the Salvadori program were considered "at risk," as Andy Kessler points out. "One of the teachers involved said that's ridiculous, because all kids are at risk. People think that they can shelter their kids and keep their kids from getting into all sorts of shit. But these kids already know everything. The best thing you can do is give them something to focus on."

8   Daniel Horowitz, for one, is rapt. The skinny Dalton junior is dressed geeky slacker style. He has his own blue helmet and his brother's oversize board. Wobbling up and down the half-pipe, Horowitz works up almost enough speed to reach the rim of the half-pipe, then falters and skids to his knees. "This is only my second time," Horowitz says, as an expert skater prepares to drop into the pipe.

9   "You know, the good thing here," Rahmaan Mazone remarks, "is, instead of getting dissed, people support you. The advanced people share equally with the newcomers." They flame out equally, too.

10   The guy doing aerials rockets above the lip and his board keeps going. Suddenly he's Wile E. Coyote hanging in midair. When he crashes and skids in a painful heap to the bottom of the tube, Mazone lets out a whistle. "That is mad worse than getting body-slammed."

11   Next up is Gil Boyd, a compact and muscular 24-year-old. Using his leg strength and unusually low center of gravity, Boyd carves a precise path through the pipe. He resembles a surfer and, as Andy Kessler explains, "in its purest form, skateboarding's very close to surfing, although there's not much surfing in these parts, since the Hudson doesn't break too well."

12   Boyd's aggressive approach brings to mind the new technical dynamics of skate, surf, and snowboard, and people who don't so much ride as carve and shred. "I've been doing this since 1978," Boyd explains when his own ride is ended. "And what people are doing a lot of now is aerials and lip tricks. It all looks treacherous, but the danger is overrated. There's an art to falling. I've never personally seen a broken neck."

13   Even before the Parks Department had hung a sign on Skate Park, the private sector began applying muscle: Nike, Blades, and others offered to "sponsor" the brand-new park. "I was pleased I was on the Parks Department's side with that one," says Kessler, whose salary as the park's full-time supervisor is provided in part, at least through November, by the $3 daily use fee. Kessler was among those who lobbied to forego big corporate subsidies in favor of one-day events. That way there are no permanent banners to disfigure the park. "Keep the parks as parks," he says.

14   And let them evolve. Except for a single half-pipe in the South Bronx, Skate Park is about the only legal place in all five boroughs where, at about three o'clock every afternoon, you'll find intense bands of skaters (both sexes) caught up in the kind of back side-airs, inverts, lip tricks, and grinds that won't necessarily send their parents reaching for Prozac. "It's a great sport," says Kessler. "There is no one best part about it. It just feels great riding. There's really just nothing like it when you drop into that tube."

QUESTIONS FOR THOUGHT

1. Define the term *sports*. Is skateboarding a sport according to your definition? Why or why not?

2. In paragraph 7, Trebay writes, "The kids in the Salvadori program were considered 'at risk,' as Andy Kessler points out. One of the teachers involved said that's ridiculous, because all kids are at risk." In what ways are all children at risk? What activities other than sports give students "something to focus on"?

3. Trebay presents a positive picture of skate parks. What would be some of the negatives about these places? Why do you think Trebay doesn't highlight these negative aspects in his article?

QUESTIONS OF STRATEGY

1. Usually, authors are encouraged to avoid jargon, or terms familiar to a certain group of people that are meaningless to others. Trebay chooses to sprinkle skateboard jargon (carve, shred, aerial, and so on) throughout his essay. Why? How does his use of jargon affect the reader's appreciation for the skateboarding culture?

2. Trebay opens his essay with the experience of one of the skaters, Rahmann Mazone, as he prepares to skate. Three paragraphs later, Trebay pulls the scene back to show the reader where the event is taking place: a skate park in New York City. Why does Trebay choose to begin his essay this way? How does this approach reflect the tone and organizational pattern of the remainder of the essay?

3. In paragraph 13, Trebay writes, "Even before the Parks Department had hung a sign on Skate Park, the private sector began applying muscle: Nike, Blades, and others offered to 'sponsor' the brand-new park." Look up the word *muscle*

in a dictionary and see which meaning is the most appropriate for this sentence. Why does Trebay use this term? Does it seem out of place or perfect for the essay? Explain your answer.

QUESTIONS FOR WRITING

1. Compare extreme skating to another sport, such as baseball or basketball. Describe each sport in terms of its basic rules, the number of players involved, where each takes place, and so on. Interview a few athletes at your school about why they participate in sports. As you write your comparison and contrast essay, be sure to maintain balance and not show preference for one sport over another.

2. Research the number and location of parks, youth centers, and other recreational areas designed for young people in your town. Are these facilities adequate for the populations they are designed to serve? Make a list of criteria for your evaluation, and then visit the sites. Afterward, write a persuasion essay arguing for or against the creation of a new center.

3. Attend a sporting event as a reporter. Observe athletes and fans in these surroundings and jot down sights, smells, language, and anything else that catches your attention. Also, interview the people and capture their dialogue as they talk. Finally, write a complete descriptive essay on the topic.

4. Write a response to the article "Gravity's Rainbow," by Guy Trebay. Read through the essay again, highlighting sections for discussion as you go. Write your thoughts about these sections and then develop this writing into a complete response to reading essay.

18

MUSIC

Music, as the cliché goes, is the universal language. We wake up to early morning music programs, we carry music with us throughout our days via portable sound systems, and we relax to soothing music at the end of the day. You have a favorite song, as does every person in your classroom and at your school. Every country has a national anthem that rouses pride in its citizens. Yes, music is truly universal and music is the focus of this chapter.

On a basic level, there are three reasons we love music. One, music is fun to listen to. Try sitting still when a snappy, energetic song comes on the radio. Try not to sing along with a favorite CD. Both are extremely difficult because the rhythm and beat invite us to join in. We also enjoy the portability of music. We can listen to music in the car, at home, walking to and from class, while sitting at our computers, and even while we are in the shower. You can't do that with other art forms. Finally, music connects people emotionally. Imagine hosting a birthday party for your best friend. You would probably play upbeat, lively music to set the tone. Likewise, you would expect to hear somber, classical music at a wake. In almost every situation, music becomes an essential part of the mood.

On another level, music has a much greater influence on our lives. Musical groups like the Beatles and Public Enemy have used music to express political views. Benefit concerts are held to raise money for starving people or out-of-luck farmers. Even today, in some places, steady drumbeats signal war or other emergencies. Rock and roll is a call to rebellion, while a dirge means a death has occurred. Music can enhance our emotional connections; on the other hand, battles are waged over music, both as an art form and as commerce. Some lyrics are considered too controversial, so many songs aren't played over the airwaves. Music even became a large issue on the Internet. Music fans traded music files through websites like Napster for free. Music companies saw this as a threat to their profits and rallied to shut the site down. As a compromise, many music companies now allow fans access to music files (often before a CD is released), for a fee.

Music is many things to many people, and it touches most lives in some way. The pair of readings in this chapter deals with a few of those touches and connections. First, the age-old debate about the effects of rock and pop (and, more recently, rap and hip-hop) on youth continues with Allan Bloom's "Is Rock Music Rotting Our Kids' Minds?" The second article, "How Scott Weiland Got Sober," is a character study of Buddy Arnold, a former drug addict and musician who, at age seventy-five, helps other musicians overcome their addictions. Feel free to listen to your favorite music as you read these essays. You might gain some new understanding of it.

Reading 21 Is Rock Music Rotting Our Kids' Minds?
Allan Bloom

BACKSTORY

Music made popular by teenagers and young adults has always created controversy with the older crowd. Young people flocked to Chuck Berry, Little Richard, and others in the early days of rock and roll. The fans wore t-shirts, jeans, let their hair grow, and challenged authority, all in the name of this music. The trend continues today, with young Eminem or P. Diddy fans adopting fashions and language from music videos and also challenging authority. Are these young people rebelling because that is what young people do, or is the music influencing them to fight back? In this selection from his book *The Closing of the American Mind,* Allan Bloom, a respected sociologist, claims that rock and roll music (and, by extension, rap, hip-hop, and pop music) corrupts young minds. As you read, think about the music you like and the reasons you are attracted to it. How does it influence you?

LEXICON

assiduously: with dedication

consecrated: made sacred or holy

countervailing: opposing

culminate: reach a high point

encapsulates: summarizes

esthetic: art form

martyrs: people who die for a cause

masturbatorial: self-stimulating

nascent: starting to develop

onanism: self-gratification

philosophic: based on ideas or philosophies

pubescent: reaching puberty or a maturing state

sublimation: raising to a higher level

1   Picture a thirteen-year-old boy sitting in the living room of his family home doing his math assignment while wearing his Walkman headphones or watching MTV. He enjoys the liberties hard won over centuries by the alliance of philosophic genius and political

heroism, consecrated by the blood of martyrs; he is provided with comfort and leisure by the most productive economy ever known to mankind; science has penetrated the secrets of nature in order to provide him with the marvelous, lifelike electronic sound and image reproduction he is enjoying. And in what does progress culminate? A pubescent child whose body throbs with orgasmic rhythms; whose feelings are made articulate in hymns to the joys of onanism or the killing of parents; whose ambition is to win fame and wealth in imitating the drag-queen who makes the music. In short, life is made into a nonstop, commercially prepackaged masturbational fantasy.

2   This description may seem exaggerated, but only because some would prefer to regard it as such. The continuing exposure to rock music is a reality, not one confined to a particular class or type of child. One need only ask first-year university students what music they listen to, how much of it and what it means to them, in order to discover that the phenomenon is universal in America, that it begins in adolescence or a bit before and continues through the college years. It is *the* youth culture and, as I have so often insisted, there is now no other countervailing nourishment for the spirit. Some of this culture's power comes from the fact that it is so loud. It makes conversation impossible, so that much of friendship must be without the shared speech that Aristotle asserts is the essence of friendship and the only true common ground. With rock, illusions of shared feelings, bodily contact and grunted formulas, which are supposed to contain so much meaning beyond speech, are the basis of association. None of this contradicts going about the business of life, attending classes and doing the assignments for them. But the meaningful inner life is with the music . . . .

3   My concern here is not with the moral effects of this music—whether it leads to sex, violence or drugs. The issue here is its effect on education, and I believe it ruins the imagination of young people and makes it very difficult for them to have a passionate relationship to the art and thought that are the substance of liberal education. The first sensuous experiences are decisive in determining the taste for the whole of life, and they are the link between the animal and spiritual in us. The period of nascent sensuality has always been used for sublimation, in the sense of making sublime, for attaching youthful inclinations and longings to music, pictures and stories that provide the transition to the fulfillment of the human duties and the enjoyment of the human pleasures. Lessing, speaking of Greek sculpture, said "beautiful men made beautiful statues, and the city had beautiful statues in part to thank for beautiful citizens." This formula encapsulates the fundamental principle of the esthetic education of man. Young men and women were attracted by the beauty of heroes whose very bodies expressed their nobility. The deeper understanding of the meaning of nobility comes later, but is prepared for by the sensuous experience and is actually contained in it. What the senses long for as well as what reason later sees as good are thereby not at tension with one another. Education is not sermonizing to children against their instincts and pleasures, but providing a natural continuity between what they feel and what they can and should be. But this is a lost art. Now we have come to exactly the opposite point. Rock music encourages passions and provides models that have no relation to any life the young people who go to universities can possibly lead, or to the kinds of admiration encouraged by liberal studies. Without the cooperation of the sentiments, anything other than technical education is a dead letter.

Joan Jett at the Showbar, Seattle. Making music or rotting minds?

4   Rock music provides premature ecstasy and, in this respect, is like the drugs with which it is allied. It artificially induces the exaltation naturally attached to the completion of the greatest endeavors—victory in a just war, consummated love, artistic creation, religious devotion and discovery of the truth. Without effort, without talent, without virtue, without exercise of the faculties, anyone and everyone is accorded the equal right to the enjoyment of their fruits. In my experience, students who have had a serious fling with drugs—and gotten over it—find it difficult to have enthusiasms or great expectations. It is as though the color has been drained out of their lives and they see everything in black and white. The pleasure they experienced in the beginning was so intense that they no longer look for it at the end, or as the end. They may function perfectly well, but dryly, routinely. Their energy has been sapped, and they do not expect their life's activity to produce anything but a living, whereas liberal education is supposed to encourage the belief that the good life is the pleasant life and that the best life is the most pleasant life. I suspect that the rock addiction, particularly in the absence of strong counterattractions, has an effect similar to that of drugs. The students will get over this music, or at least the exclusive passion for it. But they will do so in the same way Freud says that men accept the reality principle—as something harsh, grim and essentially unattractive, a mere necessity. These students will assiduously study economics or the professions and the Michael Jackson costume will slip off to reveal a Brooks Brothers suit beneath. They will want to get ahead and live comfortably. But this life is as

empty and false as the one they left behind. The choice is not between quick fixes and dull calculation. This is what liberal education is meant to show them. But as long as they have the Walkman on, they cannot hear what the great tradition has to say. And, after its prolonged use, when they take it off, they find they are deaf.

QUESTIONS FOR THOUGHT

1. Is rock music (or other types of music marketed to youth) rotting our kids' minds? In what ways does this type of music have negative effects on the listener?

2. In what ways can rock music have positive effects on the listener?

3. Bloom writes, "Liberal education is supposed to encourage the belief that the good life is the pleasant life and that the best life is the most pleasant life." Examine your life in terms of school. How will your education help you reach "the most pleasant life"? What do you consider "the most pleasant life?"

QUESTIONS OF STYLE

1. Bloom opens his piece with an example of a thirteen-year-old listening to music and doing homework. At the beginning of the second paragraph, he admits that the example is exaggerated for effect. Why does Bloom choose to open his piece in this way?

2. The essay ends with these two lines: "But as long as they have the Walkman on, they cannot hear what the great tradition has to say. And, after its prolonged use, when they take it off, they find they are deaf." What do these lines mean literally and metaphorically? Why does Bloom choose to end the essay this way?

QUESTIONS OF STRATEGY

1. Bloom uses description to illustrate his points. Find examples of description throughout the essay. How effective are they?

2. Persuasion is another strategy Bloom uses. Find his main idea and then examine the support he employs to prove his point. Where is his argument the strongest? Why? Where is the argument the weakest? Why?

QUESTIONS FOR WRITING

1. Find the lyrics to a controversial song and analyze them in an essay. Give a line-by-line explanation of the meaning of the song and then explain why the song is so popular. (Consider reading Kathleen Parker's essay about rapper Enimem on page 206 for more information.)

*2. With a partner or two other people, brainstorm a list of problems in the world today and then write a song about one problem. (If a member of the group is musically inclined, set the lyrics to music.) In an essay, discuss the meaning behind your song and then discuss the process of writing it. Include any emotional release you may have gotten out of writing the song.

3. Write an essay illustrating ways music is used in cultures other than your own. Begin your search for information at your school's international student office, or search the Internet for "international music."

Reading 22   How Scott Weiland Got Sober
Greg Kot

BACKSTORY

Musicians are on the road year-round, making money and gaining fame through concerts and appearances. To keep the pace, more than a few musicians have turned to alcohol and drugs. Buddy Arnold, a jazz saxaphonist, was one of those musicians. Fortunately, Buddy overcame his addiction to heroin and began helping other musicians deal with their lifestyles and problems. The story of his survival and work is the subject of the following article, written by *Rolling Stone* journalist Greg Kot.

LEXICON

austere: deliberately simple

flourishing: increasing, blooming

unabashedly: without shame

1   Buddy Arnold remembers he was once so desperate for a fix that he broke into Billie Holiday's apartment to use her "works," street slang for the equipment heroin junkies use to shoot up. He soon found himself on his knees, trembling with anticipation, fear and sickness, fumbling underneath her bathroom sink like a kid in search of an illicit prize. "Something's here!" he thought. "Suddenly I feel a sharp point sticking me in the middle of my back. 'Who are you, m-----f-----? What are you doing in my pad?' "

2   It was Holiday, wielding a knife. But after the fast-talking Arnold explained who he was—a jazz saxophonist she'd once met on the New York club circuit—she took pity, and they shot up together. Arnold shared smack with Charlie Parker and gigged with the likes of the Tommy Dorsey Band and Stan Kenton when he wasn't doing time in federal prison.

3   Now, Arnold, 75, has been clean for twenty years and has devoted his life to helping musicians kick the habit that nearly killed him. He runs the ten-city Musicians' Assistance Program out of a Hollywood office with his wife, Carole Fields, and he's worked with everyone from Kurt Cobain to John Frusciante of Red Hot Chili Peppers, as well as hundreds of less high-profile musicians.

4   "He's been through hell, and he wants to help other people avoid it," says Everclear guitarist Art Alexakis. "I was a junkie for ten years, and Buddy for thirty, so we know how

to scam and scheme our way into anything. But he and his wife are straight, honorable people, and they're all about getting people in [rehab] programs—not just musicians but their girlfriends, crew guys. His attitude is, 'If someone calls me, I'm going to help.' I'd do anything for the guy because he's 100 percent real."

5   Arnold's growing reputation in the rock community is due to two factors: He gets results, claiming that sixty percent of the more than 850 clients he has helped at MAP since 1992 have remained clean; and he runs a financially austere nonprofit operation. He pays himself $85,000 a year and Fields $90,000, out of a $1.2 million annual budget—which means the vast majority of funds go to helping musicians find treatment.

6   Despite the low overhead, MAP finds itself in a constant struggle to stay afloat. Over the years, the organization has survived thanks in large measure to contributions from the recording industry, an indication of the high esteem in which Arnold is held. Hilary Rosen, president of the Recording Industry Association of America, which represents the major labels, calls him "God's gift to humanity." Gary LeMel, president of worldwide music for Warner Bros., is another Arnold advocate and a MAP trustee. LeMel's daughter Tal is a rock guitarist who tried to kick a heroin habit for years before she met Arnold. "Buddy was someone my wife and I could call anytime and get advice," LeMel says. "We dealt with so many counselors, but Buddy's approach was different, more human. He could live to be 100 and still be the hippest guy in the room. He relates to musicians on that level, and my daughter responded. She loves Buddy and has great rapport with him, as does almost everyone."

"You can't ever tell who's going to make it," says MAP founder Buddy Arnold, with Scott Weiland.

7   Arnold participates in weekly MAP counseling sessions, but his primary work is hooking up musicians with affordable rehab programs and putting them in touch with other musicians on the road to recovery. His connections in the rehab world, gleaned from years of low-paying work in that field in the eighties, have made him a lifeline for hundreds of rock & roll junkies.

8   Daryl Johnson, bassist for Daniel Lanois and Emmylou Harris, among others, made the weekly trek to Hollywood from San Diego after his release from prison in 1999 just to attend counseling sessions with Arnold. "I was hooked on drugs, money, women—you name it," Johnson says. "And this guy looked at me, and he knew—he told me all about me. This cat knows what it means to be down, and he knows what it takes to get back up."

9   "He didn't jive with me," says Earth, Wind and Fire drummer Freddie White. "I had a coke-snorting problem that I didn't know was a problem until Buddy set me straight. Last year I received one of the greatest gifts in my career, which was being inducted into the Rock & Roll Hall of Fame, and the person I called was Buddy, to thank him."

10   Still, Arnold is saddened about the ones who got away. "Failure and death are built into what I do," he says. "Kurt Cobain—he was a nice kid. Very soft-spoken, warm, no pretensions. Kurt said to me once, 'Buddy, I play all the wrong notes. All I do is turn up the distortion level.' I never understood that, but now I think I do. He wasn't dealing with a melodic or harmonic line. He was dealing with some kind of emotional impact. That's what that music was about. That's what his life was about. I've learned you can't ever tell who's going to make it, or who won't."

11   Arnold has the same attitude toward his organization. "Bottom line is, we have no guarantee of money coming in the rest of this year," he says. Last year, the major record companies pressured the National Academy of Recording Arts and Sciences to share twenty-five percent of the profit from the academy's annual Grammy nominees album with MAP, bringing $742,000 to Arnold's organization.

12   "We were flabbergasted," Fields says. But academy president Michael Greene says the profit-sharing deal won't be renewed this year. "The labels were really ardent about helping them last year because MAP was near bankruptcy, but that deal really chopped into some of the children's charities we support," Greene says. "That said, if MAP at any moment runs into fundamental financing issues about programs they're doing, I am always here."

13   Previously, Arnold had rebuffed Greene's offers to merge the financially strapped MAP into the academy's own health and drug-assistance charity, MusiCares. But Greene says he bears no ill will toward MAP, and he praises the organization as an invaluable ally. "I have several friends who owe their lives to the work of MusiCares and MAP," he says.

14   But Arnold says all the good will in the world won't help his organization pay the bills, with record-breaking numbers of drug addicts and alcoholics in the musicians' community calling MAP offices for help. At the current pace, more than 300 clients will seek MAP's help this year, but the organization is living off savings. "We know somehow we're going to continue," Arnold says, "but it's a hell of a way to run a store." The organization hopes to replenish the coffers with its annual fund-raiser, to be held this year on November 7th in Los Angeles, which will honor Bonnie Raitt and the Red Hot Chili Peppers.

15   As MAP struggles, drug use is flourishing within the music industry. "There seemed to be a growing enlightenment a few years ago," Greene says, "but I'm running into a lot of very young musicians now who seem to start recreationally and can't quit." Heroin in

particular is roaring back into vogue, Arnold says. "It never goes away, because it protects you against the world, like a wet suit," he says. "It solves all problems, or at least puts you in a state where you aren't thinking about your problems."

16   All of which suggests that Arnold's drug-intervention efforts are more necessary than ever. As Alexakis says, "There was a period in the early nineties when the sex-drugs-rock & roll stereotype subsided, but I think it's coming back. There are a lot more bands out there who are pretty unabashedly pro-drug. I don't necessarily think that just because we're musicians we deserve an organization like Buddy's. But I think we should be thankful because it's there."

QUESTIONS FOR THOUGHT

1. What would motivate someone to help people who are addicted to alcohol and drugs? Does Buddy sound sincere about his work?

2. Why do so many musicians turn to drugs and alcohol? How do those who stay clean and sober cope with these factors?

3. Should anyone addicted to drugs and alcohol get free rehabilitation? Should the government fund all rehab programs? Explain your answers.

QUESTIONS OF STYLE

1. Readers are introduced to Buddy Arnold not as he is now (clean and sober) but how he was years ago (breaking into apartments to feed his drug habit). Why does Kot choose this way to tell the story?

2. The only negative view of Arnold's program is expressed by Arnold himself, in paragraph 10: "Failure and death are built into what I do." Do you believe everyone who knows about the program supports it? Why does Kot choose not to include other negative viewpoints?

3. Kot uses a number of references to musicians ranging from Billie Holiday and Tommy Dorsey to Kurt Cobain and the Red Hot Chili Peppers. For the most part, he doesn't explain who these musicians are. Why not? How does the range of musicians reflect on Arnold's life and program?

QUESTIONS OF STRATEGY

1. In paragraph 15, Kot writes: "Heroin in particular is roaring back into vogue, Arnold says. 'It never goes away, because it protects you against the world, like a wet suit,' he says. 'It solves all problems, or at least puts you in a state where you aren't thinking about your problems.'" How does this passage reflect Arnold's character?

2. When writing a narrative, one way to describe a person is by having other people talk about them. Reread the article and jot down what is said about Arnold. What type of person do you think he is based on what others say about him?

QUESTIONS FOR WRITING

1. Write an essay profiling someone you admire. Interview this person. Talk with the person's family and friends. Include some of your own insights. When you have completed this essay, present it to the person you profiled as a token of your appreciation.

*2. With a partner, write a persuasive essay about whether or not a young person should seek a career as a musician. List the pros and the cons and then write an essay explaining your feelings on this issue. Be sure to include strong evidence and support for your point of view.

3. Write about a time where you had to overcome a problem. First, describe the problem; then, discuss how you dealt with it. What advice would you give someone in a similar situation?

4. Write a response to "How Scott Weiland Got Sober." Choose the points from the essay you find most appealing and write about them. Be sure to include examples and details to support your point of view.

19

TELEVISION

Television has a hold on American society like no other device has before or since its creation. You could argue that the automobile, which allows us to travel just about anywhere whenever we want, has had a larger impact than television. While the automobile is important, there are barriers to owning the machine, such as cost, license, and maintenance. You might argue that the personal computer is much more important that television will ever be. We now have the expertise and the machinery to connect people globally, to send and receive information instantly, and to visit places via the Internet that we may never be able to get to physically. This is true, but computers cost money, require at least a little bit of user knowledge, and the Internet has many traps and pitfalls for the novice user. Television remains the single most influential part of our culture.

First off, televisions are cheap. In fact, unless it is a digital model, if you pay more than $200–$300 for one, you may have been cheated. Next, televisions require absolutely no expertise to use. When was the last time you saw a shelf of books dedicated to operating a television set? Once you plug the thing in and find the On button, you have mastered the machine. Even a two-year-old can operate one. Finally, television has affected every other area of our lives. When Americans get together, one of the first things they discuss is television shows they have seen recently. Television has even influenced other types of entertainment. Some of the most popular movies in recent years have been based on old televisions shows, such as *Charlie's Angels*, the *Star Trek* movie series, *The Brady Bunch*, and *Mission: Impossible*.

Like it or not, television showed up at our collective doorstep, and it has become the guest that won't leave. We turn it on for background noise, get angry at what it has to offer, despise how much of our time it eats up, and even schedule our evenings around it (every Wednesday evening, I took a break from working on this manuscript to watch *Star Trek: Voyager*). Perhaps analyzing and writing about television will help us understand its hypnotic influence.

Many aspects of television are ripe for discussion. Some people write reviews of the shows they watch; others talk about the evils that television brings to our society. The readings in this section address the effects of television on people. In "Television Changed My Family Forever," Linda Ellerbee reflects on how different her family life became because of television. Peter Hamill's essay "Crack and the Box" compares heavy television viewing with drug addiction and identifies some surprising similarities. Reflect on the role of television in your life as you read these selections.

Reading 23 | Television Changed My Family Forever
Linda Ellerbee

BACKSTORY

Let's take a little journey into the past. Can you remember the first time you used the Internet? The first time you used a personal computer? The first time you used a cellular phone? The first time you drove a car? Each of these devices changed your life in some way, whether you are aware of it or not. Even if you don't use it regularly, for example, the Internet has changed the way you gather information or send letters to friends. Decades ago, television was a new device that eventually made a lasting impact of society. In this essay from her book *Move On*, former television reporter Linda Ellerbee discusses the first time her family encountered television and how it affected them.

LEXICON

accommodate: make allowance for

ambrosia: fruit dish including orange sections and coconut

cadence: rhythmic flow; musical beat

Ed Sullivan: variety show host in the 1950s and 1960s

Uncle Milty: Milton Berle, television comedian

commie pinko: slang for Communist

inconsequential: having little meaning, substance, or effect

1   Santa Claus brought us a television for Christmas. See, said my parents, television doesn't eat people. Maybe not. But television changed people. Television changed my family forever. We stopped eating dinner at the dining-room table after my mother found out about TV trays. We kept the TV trays behind the kitchen door and served ourselves from pots on the stove. Setting and clearing the dining-room table used to be my job; now, setting and clearing meant unfolding and wiping out TV trays, then, when we'd finished, wiping and folding our TV trays. Dinner was served in time for one program and finished in time for another. During dinner we used to talk to one another. Now television talked to us. If you had something you absolutely had to say, you waited until the commercial, which is, I suspect, where I learned to speak in thirty-second bursts. As a future writer, it was good practice in editing my thoughts. As a little girl, it was lonely as hell. Once in a while, I'd pass our dining-room table and stop, thinking I heard our ghosts sitting around talking to one another, saying stuff.

2   Before television, I would lie in bed at night listening to my parents come upstairs, enter their bedroom and say things to one another that I couldn't hear, but it didn't matter, their voices rocked me to sleep. My first memory, the first one ever, was of my parents and their friends talking me to sleep when we were living in Bryan and my bedroom was right next to the kitchen. I was still in my crib then. From the kitchen I could hear them, hear the rolling cadence of their speech, the rising and falling of their voices and the sound of chips.

3   "Two pair showing."

4   "Call?"

5   "Check."

6   "Call?"

7   "Call." *Clink.*

8   "I raise." *Clink clink.*

9   "See your raise and raise you back." *Clink clink clink.*

10   "Call." *Clink clink.*

11   "I'm in." *Clink.*

12   "I'm out."

13   "Let's see 'em."

14   It was a song to me, a lullaby. Now Daddy went to bed right after the weather and Mama stayed up to see Jack Paar (later she stayed up to see Steve Allen and Johnny Carson and even Joey Bishop, but not David Letterman). I went to sleep alone, listening to voices in my memory.

15   Daddy stopped buying Perry Mason books. Perry was on television and that was so much easier for him, Daddy said, because he could never remember which Perry Mason books he'd read and was always buying the wrong ones by mistake, then reading them all the way to the end before he realized he'd already read them. Television fixed that, he said, because although the stories weren't as good as the stories in the books, at least he knew he hadn't already read them. But it had been Daddy and Perry who'd taught me how fine it could be to read something you liked twice, especially if you didn't know the second time wasn't the first time. My mother used to laugh at Daddy. She would never buy or read the same book again and again. She had her own library card. She subscribed to magazines and belonged to the Book-of-the-Month Club. Also, she hated mystery stories. Her favorite books were about doctors who found God and women who found doctors. Her most favorite book ever was *Gone with the Wind*, which she'd read before I was born. Read it while she vacuumed the floor, she said. Read it while she'd ironed shirts. Read it while she'd fixed dinner and read it while she'd washed up. Mama sure loved that book. She dropped Book-of-the-Month after she discovered *As the World Turns*. Later, she stopped her magazine subscriptions. Except for *TV Guide*. I don't know what she did with her library card. I know what she didn't do with it.

16   Mom quit taking me to the movies about this time, not that she'd ever take me to the movies very often after Mr. Disney let Bambi's mother get killed, which she said showed a lack of imagination. She and Daddy stopped going to movies, period. Daddy claimed it was because movies weren't as much fun after Martin broke up with Lewis, but that wasn't it. Most movies he cared about seeing would one day show up on television, he said. Maybe even Martin & Lewis movies. All you had to do was wait. And watch.

17   After a while, we didn't play baseball anymore, my daddy and me. We didn't go to baseball games together, either, but we watched more baseball than ever. That's how Daddy per-

fected The Art of Dozing to Baseball. He would sit down in his big chair, turn on the game and fall asleep within five minutes. That is, he appeared to be asleep. His eyes were shut. He snored. But if you shook him and said, Daddy, you're asleep, he'd open his eyes and tell you what the score was, who was up and what the pitcher ought to throw next. The Art of Dozing to Baseball. I've worked at it myself, but have never been able to get beyond waking up in time to see the instant replay. Daddy never needed instant replay and, no, I don't know how he did it; he was a talented man and he had his secrets.

18   Our lives began to seem centered around, and somehow measured by, television. My family believed in television. If it was on TV, it must be so. Calendars were tricky and church bells might fool you, but if you heard Ed Sullivan's voice you knew it was Sunday night. When four men in uniforms sang that they were the men from Texaco who worked from Maine to Mexico, you knew it was Tuesday night. Depending on which verse they were singing, you knew whether it was seven o'clock or eight o'clock on Tuesday night. It was the only night of the week I got to stay up until eight o'clock. My parents allowed this for purely patriotic reasons. If you didn't watch Uncle Milty on Tuesday nights, on Wednesday mornings you might have trouble persuading people you were a real American and not some commie pinko foreigner from Dallas. I wasn't crazy about Milton Berle, but I pretended I was; an extra hour is an extra hour, and if the best way to get your daddy's attention is to watch TV with him, then it was worth every joke Berle could steal.

19   Television was taking my parents away from me, not all the time, but enough, I believed. When it was on, they didn't see me, I thought. Take holidays. Although I was an only child, there were always grandparents, aunts, uncles and cousins enough to fill the biggest holiday. They were the best times. White linen and old silver and pretty china. Platters of turkey and ham, bowls of cornbread dressing and sweet potatoes and ambrosia. Homemade rolls. Glass cake stands holding pineapple, coconut, angel food and devil's food cakes, all with good boiled icing. There was apple pie with cheese. There were little silver dishes with dividers for watermelon pickles, black olives and sliced cranberry jelly. There was all the iced tea you'd ever want. Lord, it was grand. We kids always finished first (we weren't one of those families where they make the kids eat last and you never get a drumstick). After we ate, we'd be excused to go outside, where we'd play. When we decided the grown-ups had spent enough time sitting around the table after they'd already finished eating, which was real boring, we'd go back in and make as much noise as we could, until finally four or five grown-ups would come outside and play with us because it was just easier, that's all. We played hide-and-seek or baseball or football or dodge ball. Sometimes we just played *ball*. Sometimes we just played. Once in a while, there would be fireworks, which were always exciting ever since the Christmas Uncle Buck shot off a Roman candle and set the neighbor's yard on fire, but that was before we had a television.

20   Now, holiday dinners began to be timed to accommodate the kickoff, or once in a while the halftime, depending on how many games there were to watch; but on Thanksgiving or New Year's there were always games so important they absolutely could not be missed under any circumstances, certainly not for something as inconsequential as being "it" and counting to ten while you pretended not to see six children climb into the back seat of your car.

21   "Ssshhh, not now, Linda Jane. The Aggies have the ball."

22   "But you said…you promised…."

23   "Linda Jane, didn't your daddy just tell you to hush up? We can't hear the television for you talking."

QUESTIONS FOR THOUGHT

1. In what ways does television change Linda Ellerbee's family? Consider how you use television. How does it affect your life?

2. Ellerbee talks about a device to which most Americans have access: television. Think about a device you use regularly but to which you haven't had access all of your life, such as a computer, the Internet, or a cell phone. Describe your life before the device and then describe your life now. How did the device become a large part of your life?

3. Linda Ellerbee was a television journalist for many years and now hosts *Nick News,* a news television program for teenagers. After reading this essay, would you have thought Ellerbee would choose working in the television industry? Why or why not?

QUESTIONS OF STYLE

1. At the end of the first paragraph, Ellerbee writes, "Once in a while, I'd pass our dining-room table and stop, thinking I heard our ghosts sitting around talking to one another, saying stuff." Why does Ellerbee choose the image of ghosts to make her point? How does the sentence apply to the overall tone of the paragraph?

2. Paragraphs 3 through 13 are simply bits of dialogue that have occurred during a card game. What is the significance of these ten paragraphs?

3. In paragraph 18, Ellerbee writes,

> My family believed in television. If it was on TV, it must be so. Calendars were tricky and church bells might fool you, but if you heard Ed Sullivan's voice you knew it was Sunday night. When four men in uniforms sang that they were the men from Texaco who worked from Maine to Mexico, you knew it was Tuesday night. Depending on which verse they were singing, you knew whether it was seven o'clock or eight o'clock on Tuesday night.

> Why does Ellerbee choose to use such detail in the paragraph instead of simply telling the reader which shows and commercials were broadcast at that time? What does this type of detail add to the overall tone of the essay?

QUESTIONS FOR STRATEGY

1. "Television Changed My Family Forever" is a narrative. Examine the elements that make the essay a narrative. Why does Ellerbee choose this personal approach to make her point about television?

2. Paragraghs 15 and 16 illustrate how television affected Ellerbee's mother and father. What type of people were her parents before television came into the house? Develop your response with examples from these paragraphs.

3. Ellerbee uses a cause and effect strategy within her narrative. What was her family's lifestyle before television? How were their lives affected by the advent of television?

QUESTIONS FOR WRITING

1. Write an essay about something that changed your family life, or your life, forever. Outline Ellerbee's essay if you need a guide. Be sure to explain life before and after the change. Also, remember to develop your points through explanation, details, and examples. Be sure to add an introduction and conclusion to your essay as well.

2. Write an essay about the impact of television on your life. First, do a little research. Chart the number of hours your watch television and what you watch on television. Make note of any television viewing you do outside your home (for example, watching it in the school lounge or at a friend's house). Also, make note of discussions about television you have throughout your day. Next, organize your notes into categories that can be used as the basis for the body paragraphs of your essay. Finally, write and revise the essay, adding an introduction and conclusion and developing each point with explanation, details, and examples.

3. Write a response to Linda Ellerbee's essay. Highlight the points she makes that stand out for you and then give your opinion of each. Be sure you support your point of view with specific detail and examples.

*4. How much influence does television have on your campus? With a partner, survey students on your campus to find out how much television they watch per day and what types of shows they watch. Ask for reasons why the students watch television. Write an essay about your findings and give the class a report.

5. How do American television shows differ from shows in other parts of the world? Watch the International Channel or find videotaped television shows from other countries in your school's library. Write an essay that compares and contrasts American television shows and those from another country.

Reading 24 Crack and the Box

Pete Hamill

BACKSTORY

If a friend says that she watches three hours of television every day, what would your reaction be? To many people, this would not be unusual. But what if that friend watched five, six, or more hours every day? What if that person started to schedule class, doctor's appointments, or social commitments around their television viewing? According to author Pete Hamill, constant television viewing has all the signs of television addiction and should be treated as such. As you read, see if you agree with his point of view.

LEXICON

asocial: withdrawing from society

Manuel Noriega: former ruler of Panama; said to have been a drug lord

Medellin cartel: Columbian drug ring

obliterate: remove completely

psychoactive: affecting mind and thought

1   One sad, rainy morning last winter I talked to a woman who was addicted to crack cocaine. She was twenty-two, stiletto-thin, with eyes as old as tombs. She was living in two rooms in a welfare hotel with her children, who were two, three, and five years of age. Her story was the usual tangle of human woe: early pregnancy, dropping out of school, vanished men, smack and then crack, tricks with johns in parked cars to pay for the dope. I asked her why she did drugs. She shrugged in an empty way and couldn't really answer beyond "makes me feel good." While we talked, . . . the children ignored us. They were watching television. . . .

2   Television, like drugs, dominates the lives of its addicts. And though some lonely Americans leave their sets on without watching them, using them as electronic companions, television usually absorbs its viewers the way drugs absorb their users. Viewers can't work or play while watching television; they can't read; they can't be out on the streets, falling in love with the wrong people, learning how to quarrel and compromise with other human beings. In short, they are asocial. So are drug addicts.

3   One Michigan State University study in the early eighties offered a group of four-and five-year-olds the choice of giving up television or giving up their fathers. Fully one-third said they would give up Daddy. Given a similar choice (between cocaine or heroin and father, mother, brother, sister, wife, husband, children, job), almost every stone junkie would do the same.

4   There are other disturbing similarities. Television itself is a consciousness-altering instrument. With the touch of a button, it takes you out of the "real" world in which you reside and can place you at a basketball game, the back alleys of Miami, the streets of Bucharest, or the cartoony living rooms of Sitcom Land. Each move from channel to channel alters mood, usually with music or a laugh track. On any given evening, you can laugh, be frightened, feel tension, thump with excitement. You can even tune in *MacNeil/Lehrer* [a public television program, called now *The NewsHour with Jim Lehrer*] and feel sober.

5   But none of these abrupt shifts in mood is earned. They are attained as easily as popping a pill. Getting news from television, for example, is simply not the same experience as reading it in a newspaper. Reading is active. The reader must decode little symbols called words, then create images or ideas and make them connect; at its most basic level, reading is an act of the imagination. But the television viewer doesn't go through that process.

The words are spoken to him or her by Dan Rather or Tom Brokaw or Peter Jennings. There isn't much decoding to do when watching television, no time to think or ponder before the next set of images and spoken words appears to displace the present one. The reader, being active, works at his or her own pace; the viewer, being passive, proceeds at a pace determined by the show. Except at the highest levels, television never demands that its audience take part in an act of imagination. Reading always does.

6   In short, television works on the same imaginative and intellectual level as psychoactive drugs. If prolonged television viewing makes the young passive (dozens of studies indicate that it does), then moving to drugs has a certain coherence. Drugs provide an unearned high (in contrast to the earned rush that comes from a feat accomplished, a human breakthrough earned by sweat or thought or love).

7   And because the television addict and the drug addict are alienated from the hard and scary world, they also feel they make no difference in its complicated events. For the junkie, the world is reduced to him or her and the needle, pipe, or vial; the self is absolutely isolated, with no desire for choice. The television addict lives the same way. Many Americans who fail to vote in presidential elections must believe they have no more control over such a choice than they do over the casting of *L.A. Law*.

8   The drug plague also coincides with the unspoken assumption of most television shows: Life should be easy. The most complicated events are summarized on TV news in a minute or less. Cops confront murder, chase the criminals, and bring them to justice (usually violently) within an hour. In commercials, you drink the right beer and you get the girl. Easy! So why should real life be a grind? Why should any American have to spend years mastering a skill or craft, or work eight hours a day at an unpleasant job, or endure the compromises and crises of a marriage?

9   The doper always whines about how he or she feels; drugs are used to enhance feelings or obliterate them, and in this the doper is very American. No other people on earth spend so much time talking about their feelings; hundreds of thousands go to shrinks, they buy self-help books by the millions, they pour out intimate confessions to virtual strangers in bars or discos. Our political campaigns are about emotional issues now, stated in the simplicities of adolescence. Even alleged statesmen can start a sentence, "I feel that. . . ." when they once might have said, "I *think*. . . ." I'm convinced that this exaltation of cheap emotions over logic and reason is one by-product of hundreds of thousands of hours of television.

10   Most Americans under the age of fifty have now spent their lives absorbing television; that is, they've had the structures of drama pounded into them. Drama is always about conflict. So news shows, politics, and advertising are now all shaped by those structures. Nobody will pay attention to anything as complicated as the part played by Third World debt in the expanding production of cocaine; it's much easier to focus on Manuel Noriega, a character right out of *Miami Vice*, and believe that even in real life there's a Mister Big.

11   What is to be done? Television is certainly not going away, but its addictive qualities can be controlled. It's a lot easier to "just say no" to television than to heroin or crack. As a beginning, parents must take immediate control of the sets, teaching children to watch specific television *programs*, not "television," to get out of the house and play with other

kids. Elementary and high schools must begin teaching television as a subject, the way literature is taught, showing children how shows are made, how to distinguish between the true and the false, how to recognize cheap emotional manipulation. All Americans should spend more time reading. And thinking.

12   For years, the defenders of television have argued that the networks are only giving the people what they want. That might be true. But so is the Medellin Cartel.

QUESTIONS FOR THOUGHT

1. Make a schedule of the times you watch television. Would you say you are addicted to television as a whole or to a specific show? Explain your answer.

2. Medicine is designed to heal people. When it is misused, it can become a drug habit. In what ways can watching television be viewed as a "habit"?

3. What other seemingly harmless "addictions" in our society could lead to drug addiction? Explain your answer.

QUESTIONS OF STYLE

1. In paragraph 5, Hamill writes, "Except at the highest levels, television never demands that its audience take part in an act of imagination." In your opinion, what would those "highest levels" be? Why does Hamill not include examples, as he does in paragraph 4?

2. Notice the examples of television shows that Hamill offers: *The NewsHour with Jim Lehrer, L.A. Law,* and *Miami Vice.* Examine the context in which each specific television show is mentioned. Why does Hamill choose these particular shows to make his point?

3. Throughout the essay, longer sentences are offset with shorter ones—even one-word sentences. Why does Hamill use the shorter sentences and fragments? How do these sentence lengths affect the overall flow of the essay?

QUESTIONS FOR STRATEGY

1. Hamill opens his essay with a description of a crack addict. Why does he use this image? What effect does it have on the overall tone of the reading?

2. For the structure of his essay, Hamill created a persuasive argument using comparison/contrast techniques. Examine the persuasive points in the essay and then examine the compare/contrast points. Is enough appropriate support given in every case?

QUESTIONS FOR WRITING

1. Consider the amount of time you watch television during a week. For the most accurate reflection of your viewing time, keep a log of the hours you

watch and the programs you watch. At the end of the week, assess your viewing habits and write an essay about them. In the essay, discuss how many hours you watched television, what programs you watched, and any activities you rescheduled or ignored completely because of television.

*2. Hamill's essay was written before the Internet became popular. Could an argument be made that some people are addicted to the Internet? Get a partner and poll students and professors on your campus on how many hours they surf the Internet and why they do so. With your partner, write an essay about the idea of Internet addiction as it relates to your college campus.

3. Write a response to this reading countering Hamill's assertion that television has a negative impact on American society. In your essay, discuss the positive effects television has had or can have on American society. Be sure to support your ideas with specific illustrations and examples.

4. Imagine your friend confides that she has an addiction problem and wants you to help. Write an essay in which you outline several methods for combating an addiction. Be as specific as possible as you develop your methods. (For further insight on addiction, refer to "How Scott Weiland Got Sober" on page 383.)

20

SCIENCE AND TECHNOLOGY

You have at your disposal one of the most advanced information processors available today. This tool is compact, versatile, and inexpensive. It is sleek and thin, small enough to fit comfortably in one's hands, in a jacket pocket, or behind an ear. No need to worry about upgrades or compatibility with other machines. This little tool comes loaded with all the software you need: word processing, sketching and drawing, and even math and science software. Whenever you need something written, sketched, or calculated, simply grab this tool and a few sheets of plain white paper, and you are off. Perhaps the most attractive feature is the availability and cost. These revolutionary word processors are available in drugstores, bookstores, art supply stores, and arts and crafts stores. For as little as ten to fifteen cents apiece, you can become more productive, write better letters, do many quick calculations, and draw. And when you are done, you can dispose of it and get another one.

Of course, I am talking about a pencil here—not exactly what one pictures during a discussion of science and technology, but a good example of what they are designed to do. Science and technology provide ideas and machinery for our convenience. Years ago, people walked or rode horses to get around. Now we think nothing of getting in a car and zooming down the street, across the state, or even across the country. Planes take us to other continents in a fraction of the time steamships used to make the same journeys. Perhaps the biggest area of impact technology has on our society is information. We used to wait hours or even days to get information about world events. Now, through the use of telecommunication networks, we receive a constant stream of images and information from all over the world as these events take place.

Many people are convinced that science and technology have greatly improved our lives and, often, that is true. In "Underhanded Achievement," author Curtis Rist discusses how scientific principles can improve a basketball player's chances of sinking foul shots. And, as you will read in "The Dyslexic CEO," computing and word processing technology have made living with dyslexia much easier. In these articles, we see the wonders of science and technology. However, we run the risk of losing ourselves and our souls to machines as we become more and more dependent on them.

Technology can be wonderful, as long as we keep our perspective. As you read these articles, jot down your insights about technology. And use a pencil.

Reading 25 Underhanded Achievement

Curtis Rist

BACKSTORY

Scientific principles and sports often go hand in hand. For example, professional pool players use geometry to improve their games. In the following article originally published in *Discover* magazine, science is applied to a basic element of basketball: the free throw. For the players, the results are both amazing and embarrassing.

LEXICON

ellipse: oval

velocity: speed

1   As a boy in Elizabeth, New Jersey, in the 1950s, basketball legend Rick Barry got some painful coaching lessons from his father, a semipro. While the youngster's friends liked to shoot their foul shots, or "free throws," in the respectable overhand style, the old man wanted Barry to toss them just as he did—underhand. "That's the way little kids shoot, and it didn't help that everybody calls it the 'granny shot,' " Barry says. "I didn't want any part of it, but my father drove me nuts until I tried it. And amazingly, it worked." Barry's average from the free-throw line bounced from 70 to 80 percent and kept on climbing when he became a pro. "Nobody ever teased me, but then it's hard to tease somebody when the ball keeps going in."

2   Judging by mechanics alone, this should be the case with just about every foul shot. "There's nothing simpler in basketball, because you can take all the time you want to make it, and there's nobody waving their arms in front of you trying to block you," says Peter Brancazio, a physics professor emeritus from Brooklyn College and author of *SportsScience*. "It's like bowling. You do exactly the same thing over and over and over again." Yet while Barry can easily sink nine out of 10 shots, others fall far short. The late Wilt Chamberlain, for instance, could shoot a basket from just about anywhere on the court—except when he toed up to the line 15 feet from the hoop. There, the legendary "Big Dipper" sank barely five out of 10 shots, although he got plenty of practice: 11,862 attempted free throws, a National Basketball Association record that still stands.

3   Sports columnists gripe about the bad free-throw techniques of modern players like Shaquille O'Neal, but no one has suffered more public humiliation at the free-throw line than the Knicks' Chris Dudley. One year, he made only three out of every 10 shots, and last season, when he managed to sink two free throws in a row during post-season play-offs, he made headlines ("Chris No Dud at Foul Line!" screamed the New York *Daily News*). "I'm convinced that from a physics standpoint, if everyone learned to throw underhand you'd see these statistics rise dramatically," says Brancazio.

4   The key to a successful foul shot lies in the arc of the ball—in general, the higher the better. While an official-sized basket is 18 inches in diameter, the basketball itself is

It's All in the Arc

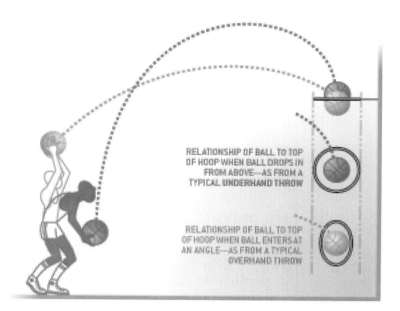

RELATIONSHIP OF BALL TO TOP
OF HOOP WHEN BALL DROPS IN
FROM ABOVE—AS FROM A
TYPICAL UNDERHAND THROW

RELATIONSHIP OF BALL TO TOP
OF HOOP WHEN BALL ENTERS AT
AN ANGLE—AS FROM A TYPICAL
OVERHAND THROW

only about 9.5 inches, which gives a margin of 8.5 inches. But when the ball is thrown nearly straight at the basket—in the style of Shaquille O'Neal—the margin disappears because the rim of the basket, from the perspective of the ball, resembles a tight ellipse. "That's why these guys miss so much," says Brancazio. "Because of the sharp angle of the typical overhand throw, there ends up being a much smaller window for the ball to go in." If the ball comes down at the basket from a steeper angle—the way it does if tossed up in the high arc characteristic of an underhand throw—the margin reappears. "That means there's a far greater chance of making the basket," he says.

5   Using lots of trigonometry, Brancazio calculated the optimal angle of the arc from the free-throw line. If tossed at 32 degrees or less, the ball will likely hit the back of the rim. "That doesn't mean it won't go in, but it will certainly bounce off the metal and reduce the chance of success," he says. At angles greater than that, the ball has a chance of making a nice *swish.* The optimum angle, he calculated, is 45 degrees—plus half the angle from the top of the player's hand to the rim. "The shorter you are, the steeper that angle has to get to give you the best chance of making the shot," he says. Of course, lobbing a ball very high so that it comes down nearly straight into the basket would be the most efficient technique, but a shot like that "is almost impossible to aim," says Brancazio. Instead, he says, his formula makes it possible for a player to shoot with the largest possible margin for error.

6   Another factor of the granny shot also helps a free throw win cheers rather than jeers: a backward spin added to the ball. If a ball with backspin happens to hit the metal rim of the basket, the friction of contact suddenly reduces its forward velocity. "It's like a drop shot in tennis—the ball bounces, but it doesn't have a forward motion on it," says Brancazio. This effect tends to freeze the ball at the rim and greatly increases the chance that it will tip into the basket rather than ricochet off.

7   The underhand throw can also minimize the drift of the ball. "A little sideward movement at the start of the throw will translate into a big movement toward the end," says Tom

Steiger, an assistant professor at the University of Washington in Seattle who teaches basketball physics in a sports science class. The trick to keeping the ball moving along a single plane toward the basket lies in "minimizing the x-axis motion," he says. "In other words, you have to keep your elbows tucked in." If they're sticking out, that can easily add an unwanted nudge to the ball, which results in a missed shot. The underhand throw provides better stability than the overhand "because you're holding the ball with both hands," Steiger says. This helps players balance the subtle motor muscles in the hands, and keeps them more relaxed. The movement of the underhand throw is a simple, easy-to-control upward pendulum motion. By contrast, the more conventional overhand free-throw shot involves separate movements of the wrist, elbow, and shoulder that can add errors. "If the ball ends up rolling off one side of your hand even a little bit, you'll miss," he says.

8   Despite the logic of a granny approach to foul shooting, no NBA player has used it since Barry retired in 1980. "That baffles me," Barry says. "With the underhand shot, I could make 80 percent of my throws with my eyes closed. And I do mean closed." Over the years he has tried to convert everyone from four of his sons who have played professionally to O'Neal to Chris Dudley—but nobody paid any attention. "A lot of guys who are lousy at the free throw would be prime candidates for this, but they just won't do it," says Barry, who for the last five years coached a minor-league team called the Florida Sea Dragons. "I mean, how can guys call themselves professionals when they can't even make 60 percent of their free throws? Where's their sense of pride?"

9   Perhaps that's the problem. "As good as it is," Steiger says, "it does look kind of stupid."

QUESTIONS FOR THOUGHT

1. In what ways would science and mathematics affect professional sports such as baseball or bowling?

2. According to the article, shooting free throws granny-style greatly improves the player's chances of making them, yet almost no professional uses this technique. Why do people in general reject new policies and procedures that can improve their lives? Should we automatically change our procedures when new (and possibly better) ways come along? (For more insight, refer to "The Good E-book" on page 32.)

QUESTIONS OF STYLE

1. Many of the paragraphs at the beginning of the essay highlight pro basketball players who have had trouble making free throws. Why does Rist choose to arrange the essay in this manner?

2. The article opens with a discussion of Rick Barry learning to shoot underhanded free throws and ends with Barry discussing his disbelief that nobody uses this technique. Why does Rist choose this bookend style to open and close the essay?

3. Rist sets off technical information with statements of explanation, such as:

> Using lots of trigonometry, Brancazio calculated the optimal angle of
> the arc from the free-throw line. If tossed at 32 degrees or less, the ball will

likely hit the back of the rim. "That doesn't mean it won't go in, but it will certainly bounce off the metal and reduce the chance of success," he says. At angles greater than that, the ball has a chance of making a nice swish.

Why does Rist choose this approach to the more complex information? What does this structure suggest about the audience of this essay?

QUESTIONS OF STRATEGY

1. Rist gives a clear argument supporting the use of the underhanded free throw within the essay itself. Outline this section. Are the reasons supporting his argument valid?

2. This essay is sprinkled with comparisons between the overhand and the underhand free-throw shots. List or highlight a few of those comparisons. Are they used effectively?

QUESTIONS FOR WRITING

1. Write an essay about the science involved in an everyday activity, such as walking a dog or baking a cake. Jot down notes about the process and then include scientific information about it. For example, you could research how the muscles in the human foot work together when you walk or discuss the chemical reactions that occur when baking a chocolate cake. For information about the science behind the procedure, surf the Internet, scan a few basic science texts, or ask a professor who teaches in a science field like biology or physics.

2. Interview an athlete or a coach, along with a science professor, and write about the scientific properties in a sport other than basketball. Combine these two culturally different points of view and explain how science affects the sport.

3. Write a response to "Underhanded Achievement." Discuss your point of view on the topic and the main points Rist makes in his essay. Be sure to include a strong thesis statement as well as specific examples in your essay.

*4. With a partner, try to make free throws as described in Rist's article. First, shoot some free throws overhand and note your results. Next, throw the ball underhanded and note those results. Have your partner do the same thing and compare notes. Together with your partner, write an essay about the experience and the outcome.

Reading 26 The Dyslexic CEO
James Mathewson

BACKSTORY

When composing essays on a computer, some of us take the spell-checker for granted. When the program detects an unfamiliar word, we choose another word or simply ignore the suggestion and move to the next word. For writers with dyslexia, a disability in which words and letters are transposed or move on the page, spell-check programs help in more ways than just highlighting unfamiliar words. In the following essay written for a computer user newsletter, James Mathewson talks about the importance of these programs.

LEXICON

coherent: understandable

consummate: ultimate

DOS: Disc Operating System (an early format for computer programs)

impediment: block

IT: information technology

oxymoron: two terms used together that seem to contradict one another

plethora: abundance

repercussions: backlash

rudimentary: basic; primitive

1   On May 16, Cisco CEO John Chambers made a startling admission in the *New York Times* "The Boss" feature—he's dyslexic. He first made the admission to his daughter's class on bring-your-parent-to-school day, when one of her classmates tried to ask a question but stumbled over her words and was embarrassed by her dyslexia. "Take your time," he said, "I'm disabled too."

2   This revelation should have amazing repercussions throughout the IT industry. If the CEO of one of the largest tech firms on the planet can fight through his disability, anyone can. At least that's what a lot of kids in that class—and *New York Times* readers—came away with. As I edit our annual Training issue, I have a strong urge to amplify Chambers's admission and motivate the folks in IT who have struggled, for whatever reason, with language skills.

3   I have a theory about dyslexia: It's a lot more common than people think. In fact, I think most people have mild dyslexia. Think about all the times you have unintentionally inverted letters or mispronounced words, especially when under pressure. Most people can overcome their disabilities and have successful careers through extra study. But many struggle with language skills—especially English skills—and this keeps them from achieving the success their intelligence warrants. Technology can help, but years of focusing on what you do best and avoiding what you struggle with can turn a disability into a lack of necessary skills.

4   Chambers' admission struck a chord with me because it reawakened a lot of my own struggles with dyslexia. The idea of a dyslexic editor may seem like an oxymoron, but it is not a contradiction in terms in my case. I remember all those years of working with my mom after school on spelling—an hour a day for five years—without appreciable improvement in what were horrible spelling grades. Most of my struggles were based on my brain's natural tendency to invert letters on tests. I could recite the proper spelling in our after-school sessions, but it never translated into testing success.

5   The biggest challenge was not the disability, but overcoming the frustration associated with working so hard and still failing. For me, the natural inclination was to pay attention to math and science and not even try in English. Why put so much effort into something without hope for success?

6   Mom claimed it was genetic. She was the word person and Dad was the math person. The only impediment to my success in math and science was boredom. English was another story altogether. Mom said that I had Dad's brain. He was an excellent engineer who made himself the consummate communicator. But he couldn't spell *cat* if you put him to the test. He knew enough to hire a secretary who could spell, and he had a knack for conveying ideas verbally and for the format of business letters and memos. This was enough in those days.

7   Nowadays, even the most highly trained programmers and analysts need to be able to write well. You can have the best ideas in your business and they will never be taken seriously if you can't put them down in a coherent and clean document. When I first figured this out, it was like looking up at a mountain and knowing I simply had to climb it to get where I needed to go. That was back in college, when the PC was new and the most popular word processor at school was PC Write—a DOS-based shareware program with a rudimentary spell checker.

8   The technology liberated me because I no longer had to check every word in my term papers. I only had to look up the words that the spell checker found. But, unlike current spell checkers, it didn't suggest alternatives. I had to look up all the misspelled words in a paper dictionary and retype them in the document. Through the process of looking up all those words on all those term papers for several years in college and graduate school, I slowly gained confidence in my language skills. At some point, I got such a kick out of succeeding where I had failed my whole life that I decided to make writing and editing my profession.

9   Before I started climbing the mountain, I never would have believed that I could be a published author, let alone the editor of a publication. I've read that the brain is a very adaptable organ. Stroke victims, for example, relearn language skills by training other parts of their brains. Perhaps a similar thing happened to me. All that repetition allowed me to train another part of my brain, and I no longer show any signs of my disability. I spent so much time and effort overcoming my disability that I became better at language skills than any of the subject matter I had studied for a decade.

10   One thing I have learned in my climb is that you're judged more on how you deal with adversity than on your successes. And so I have been richly rewarded for conquering the mountain.

11   I can say I would never have gotten anywhere without office technology to provide me with a safety net—even a rudimentary one. Today, there is a plethora of assistive technologies to help disabled people. Lots of hardware has been developed to let those with physical disabilities use computers. Special speech technologies allow those with sight impediments to be productive. Dyslexia is also overcome with speech recognition; those with written language barriers often are excellent speakers. I could go on and on about the products for disabled learners, but I'll let you do the research at Dyslexic.com <www.dyslexic.com/software>.

12   My hope is that for those of you struggling with language-based disabilities, John Chambers's story combined with my own will inspire you to overcome your difficulties. Society will still demand that you learn to communicate well. But with the help of some readily available technology, you can turn language barriers into skills worth boasting about on your résumés.

QUESTIONS FOR THOUGHT

1. In what other ways can science and technology help improve the lives of people with physical and mental challenges?

2. Are there times in which technology should not be used to aid people? Describe the situations and explain why.

3. In what ways has technology helped you achieve an important goal in life?

QUESTIONS OF STYLE

1. Throughout the essay, Mathewson uses "you," referring to the reader. What effect does this have on the overall tone of this piece?

2. The essay begins with a paragraph that reads as though it could have been written for a newspaper article. Why does Mathewson choose this approach? What does the story of the CEO with dyslexia add to the story of Mathewson's struggle with this challenge?

QUESTIONS OF STRATEGY

1. In paragraph 8, Mathewson offers a short process that explains how he worked with PC Write's basic spell-checking program. Trace the steps he takes as explained in this paragraph. Why does the author choose to explain the process he went through?

2. The discussion on dyslexia starts with Cisco CEO John Chambers but then moves to the personal narrative of the author. What does Mathewson achieve with this shift in focus?

QUESTIONS FOR WRITING

1. Matheson writes, "One thing I have learned in my climb is that you're judged more on how you deal with adversity than on your successes." Write an essay about a time when you had to overcome adversity. Begin by explaining what the situation was and then explain the steps you took to overcome the problem. Finally, reflect on the outcome of the situation.

*2. With a partner, write an essay on the uses of technology on campus and how it helps people with physical, mental, or learning challenges. Perhaps there are areas in which people with challenges could benefit from certain types of technology that hasn't been made available. Explore these possibilities.

3. Write a response to "The Dyslexic CEO" by James Mathewson. Jot down the main points in his essay and then give your opinion of each. Make sure your essay has an introduction, a thesis statement, strong explanation and support sentences, and a conclusion.

21

MOVIES

The mechanics of motion pictures are quite simple: A series of still photos, printed on a translucent strip and projected onto a large screen, move past our eyes at thirty-five frames per second (so fast the human eye cannot distinguish each frame), giving the illusion of movement. But what an illusion it is. For decades, from the earliest flickers of *The First Men On The Moon* to the blockbuster *Titanic* and beyond, movies have offered something completely unique to our society. Movies show us life in a way no other medium can.

For the general population, movies are entertainment. We shell out anywhere from six to ten dollars a ticket, load up on overpriced popcorn and soda, wander to a few empty seats, and wait for the magic. We see the exciting exploits of Indiana Jones and Luke Skywalker. We imagine ourselves saving the world alongside James Bond. We cry at the death scenes, scream at the scary parts, and then run back to the theater next week for the new show. We've been going to the movies since the beginning of the twentieth century and we have no signs of slowing down.

Seventy years ago, movies were not just entertainment; they were a way to get information and see the world. Before the advent of television, people flocked to movie theaters to see newsreels, mini-movies that told of important events in politics, sports, and the world. Because this was a way to get news, going to the "picture shows" was a necessity.

For people with the technical know-how and financial backing, movies can be a way to get a message to the public. Independent filmmakers like Spike Lee (*Do The Right Thing* and *Malcolm X*) and the Coen brothers (*O Brother, Where Art Thou?*) subvert the movie studios by raising money on their own, shooting their pictures, and then shopping the products to the studios for national distribution to theaters. Typically, most movies are generated by the studios themselves, and the studios control all elements of the movie, including cast choice, budget, and story. Taking the independent route means the filmmaker retains creative control but doesn't always have a large budget, access to top-name actors, or a way to get the films shown in theaters across the country. Some filmmakers have chosen to use the Internet to make and distribute their movies. With a digital video camera, certain software programs, and an Internet service provider, people have made short films for the entire world to see at a fraction of the cost of Hollywood films.

The readings in this section deal with the impact of motion pictures on our society. We are a society that says we are against violence of any kind, yet some of the most popular movies are filled with high body counts, blazing gun battles, and explosions. In the essay "One Poke Over the Line," John Leo examines violence in our entertainment. Over fifty years ago, Henry Myers, author of "Moving Pictures Evoke Concern," warned us of the dangers of motion pictures. The next time you decide to see a movie, consider the history, the culture, and the magic behind those flickering images.

Reading 27 | One Poke Over The Line
John Leo

BACKSTORY

A woman kills her stalker. A bounty hunter slays the demons guarding the treasure. The superhero and the villain throw punches, cars, and pieces of buildings at each other during their climatic battle. All of these movie scenarios have a common link: violence.

Violence in movies has always caused controversy. Many see it as entertainment and nothing more, while others argue that it is unnecessary and may, in some cases, catalyze violent tendencies in some viewers. John Leo, in a column written for *U.S. News and World Report*, says that although he enjoys these types of movies himself, perhaps the violence has gone too far.

LEXICON

bludgeons: hits repeatedly with great force

brutality: extremely harsh or mean behavior

cater: serve

cathartic: purifying; removing the bad

cynicism: assumption that people are insincere; sarcastic

decapitates: removes the head

decorously: in a calm, gracious manner

defy: resist

empathetic: able to identify with the emotions of others

endorsed: supported

gruesomeness: horribleness, usually bloody

impales: pierces with a sharp object

implicitly: not specifically stated but still understood

mandatory: required

meander: wander

mutilating: severely injuring by removing a necessary part

nihilism: philosophy that life and morals have little or no purpose

pastoral: from a clergy member in his or her official capacity

revel: take delight in; enjoy

sadism: delight in the pain of others

sympathetic: able to feel compassion for the pain of others

1   As a critic of violent entertainment, I have a flaw: I've always enjoyed it. When my wife heads for Cinema One to revel in some deeply empathetic movie about meaningful relationships, usually starring Meryl Streep or Shirley MacLaine, I meander off to Cinema Two for a film with more action, a higher body count and a few mandatory car crashes and explosions.

2   This is an absolutely conventional male attitude. If a meaningful relationship breaks out on screen, men usually go for popcorn. Most of us want action stories based on quest, challenge and danger (and therefore the likelihood of some violence). Like many males, I am especially partial to cartoon-like shoot'em-ups, such as the *RoboCop* and *Terminator* movies. If someone has to die, let it be a villainous stick figure rather than a recognizable human.

3   Now, however, I am bailing out. The dial has been turned up too far on gruesomeness and sadism, even in comic-book films. The most innocent-looking male action movie must be checked in advance for stomach-churning brutality. I knew I would not be going to see *Cape Fear* when a reviewer informed me that the DeNiro character "bites into the cheek of a handcuffed woman and spits out a Dinty Moore Chunky Stew-sized piece of flesh." Over-the-top hair-raising violence that would have been unthinkable in mainstream movies a decade or so ago now seems routine.

4   What's worse, the attitude toward the justification of violence has changed. At the beginning of *Terminator 2*, Arnold Schwarzenegger arrives from the future, naked and programmed for violence. He enters a bar and casually bludgeons a few pool players whose only offense is refusing to give him their clothes and a motorcycle. This is uncomfortably close to the common urban crime of attacking youngsters for their bikes or Starter jackets. Here that kind of violence is implicitly but rather clearly endorsed. After all, Arnold is bigger, stronger and has a nuclear war to stop. So beating up bystanders is OK.

5   *Codes of the West.* In the old Hollywood, the code was different. On the whole, violence among heroes was limited and a last resort. The deck was usually stacked to make nonviolence a nonoption at the end. But at least sympathetic characters were rarely shown enjoying violence or overdoing it. Now, as the social critic Mark Crispin Miller has written in *The Atlantic*, screen violence "is used primarily to invite the viewer to enjoy the feel of killing, beating, mutilating." The movie is set up for the viewer to identify with the hero and the fulfillment that violence brings him. Often, Miller says, the hero's murderous rage has no point "other than its open invitation to *become him* at that moment." This is not violence as last resort but as deeply satisfying lifestyle.

6   Michael Medved's book, *Hollywood vs. America,* is very sharp on another aspect of the new violence: It is often played for laughs. In the first *Predator* movie, the hero impales a man against a tree with his machete, then urges the victim to "stick around." In *Lethal Weapon 2,* Danny Glover jokes, "I nailed 'em both," after holding a nail gun to the heads of villains and puncturing their skulls. And in *Hudson Hawk,* Bruce Willis decapitates a bad guy and jokes, "I guess you won't be attending that hat convention in July." This is hardly hilarious humor, but it serves to suppress the moviegoer's normal emotional response to agony and mutilation. This flip attitude, very common in films now, is essentially sadistic.

7   In response to snowballing protests about screen violence, Hollywood has frequently tried to argue that fictional violence has a useful, cathartic effect: "I think it's a kind of purifying experience to see violence," says Paul Verhoeven, director of *Total Recall.* But a growing number of studies from the social sciences point away from this comforting thesis. The studies show that children exposed to violent entertainment tend to be more violent themselves and less sensitive to the pain of others. This makes screen violence a social problem and not, as Hollywood likes to argue, an individual problem for consumers. ("If you don't like the movie, don't go.")

8   Cardinal Roger Mahony, the Roman Catholic archbishop of Los Angeles, terrified the industry last winter by talking about a tough Hollywood film-rating code. But he dropped the idea and instead has issued a pastoral letter defending artistic freedom and asking Hollywood, ever so politely, to clean up its act. When violence is portrayed, he asks, "Do we feel the pain and dehumanization it causes to the person on the receiving end *and* to the person who engages in it? . . . Does the film cater to the aggressive and violent impulses that lie hidden in every human heart? Is there danger its viewers will be desensitized to the horror of violence by seeing it?" Good questions and no threat of censorship. Just an invitation to grow up.

9   Todd Gitlin, the Berkeley sociologist, put it less decorously, talking at a recent conference about "the rage and nihilism" that Hollywood is tossing on screen. He said: "The industry is in the grip of inner forces which amount to a cynicism so deep as to defy parody," reveling "in the means to inflict pain, to maim, disfigure, shatter the human image." Message to Hollywood from cardinal and sociologist: Try something else.

QUESTIONS FOR THOUGHT

1. Define *violence*. Then, watch a violent film. Record your reactions and discuss them with others who have seen the movie.

2. Movies are said to be mirrors of society. Is our society as violent as it is portrayed in some movies? Does seeing violence in entertainment encourage violent behavior? Should all forms of violence be removed from movies and other forms of entertainment?

*3. With a partner, make a case for the portrayal of violence in movies. What stories or historical events would lose their impact without the visuals of violence? Why is violence necessary to tell those stories?

QUESTIONS OF STYLE

1. "As a critic of violent entertainment, I have a flaw: I've always enjoyed it." This line opens Leo's essay. Why does he choose to open his essay this way?

2. In paragraph 3, Leo writes, "I knew I would not be going to see *Cape Fear* when a reviewer informed me that the DeNiro character "'bites into the cheek of a handcuffed woman and spits out a Dinty Moore Chunky Stew-sized piece of flesh.'" What is your reaction to this bit of description? Why does Leo use it?

3. Paragraph 5 starts with the subheading "Codes of the West." What does it refer to? What was the author's purpose in using that subheading?

QUESTIONS OF STRATEGY

1. The first three paragraphs of the essay are personal reflections on violence in film. Why does Leo include himself and his experiences in this essay? Why does he place them at the beginning?

2. Leo has researched violence in films and weaves insights from other sources throughout the essay. List the sources and note how they are used. What effect does this research have on Leo's argument? Is it effective?

3. When making comparisons between the types of movies women like and the types of movies men like, Leo is careful to select specific descriptions. For women's films, he writes "some deeply empathetic movie about meaningful relationships, usually starring Meryl Streep or Shirley MacLaine," while for men's movies, he says, "Like many males, I am especially partial to cartoon-like shoot 'em-ups, such as the *RoboCop* and *Terminator* movies." Why would Leo use these particular examples to make his point? How effective are these examples when making generalities about women and men?

QUESTIONS FOR WRITING

1. Write an essay describing the type or types of movies you enjoy watching. Brainstorm a list of these movies, then make a list of similarities between them. Choose three or four of those similarities and develop those ideas in your paper. Be sure to include explanations and examples in your essay, along with an introduction and a conclusion.

2. In paragraph 5, Leo writes,

   Screen violence "is used primarily to invite the viewer to enjoy the feel of killing, beating, mutilating." The movie is set up for the viewer to iden-tify with the hero and the fulfillment that violence brings him. Often, Miller says, the hero's murderous rage has no point "other than its open invitation to *become him* at that moment." This is not violence as last resort but as deeply satisfying lifestyle.

How does violence in movies reflect or affect violence we see in real life? Brainstorm violent scenes from movies you have seen or heard about. Compare the scenes to real-life violence you read about in newspapers and magazines. Jot down any connections you find and use them as the basis for an essay. If you find no connections, then write about what you think does cause real-life violence. Either way, be sure to develop your points with explanation, detail, and examples.

3. Return to Question 1 under "Questions for Thought" and jot down a definition of violence. Next, write a classification essay explaining the types of violence in movies and videos.

4. Write a response to John Leo's "One Poke Over the Line." Jot down the main points of his argument and then give your opinion. Make sure your essay has an introduction, a thesis statement, strong body paragraphs, and a conclusion. Add specific examples from movies to make your point, just as Leo does to make his.

*5. Find a student whose tastes in movies differ from your own. Together, rent or see two movies: one you enjoy watching and one the other person enjoys watching. As you watch, make note of the violent content of each film. After the screenings, discuss the violence in each movie and together write a comparison or contrast essay regarding that violence. Although the taste in films is different, was the tolerance for violence any different?

6. Rent or go to see a few foreign films with subtitles. (The Modern Languages Department at your school is a great resource for these films.) As you watch, make note of the violence in the films. How do other cultures use violence? Write an essay explaining your opinion.

Reading 28 Moving Pictures Evoke Concern
Henry Myers

BACKSTORY

When motion pictures became big social events and big box office, people swarmed to the theaters, much as they do today. Many movie critics say modern films are too violent, too rank, and too sexy. Interestingly enough, these concerns with movie content aren't recent. People have always wrestled with the purpose and content of movies, as can be seen in this essay, written over seventy-five years ago, by politician Henry Myers.

LEXICON

conspicuous: obvious

debauchery: indulgence in one's sexual desires; orgies

dissipation: giving oneself entirely to self-indulgence

dissoluteness: immorality

laudable: worthy of praise

pernicious: unwholesome; deadly

prurient: arousing sexual desire

ribaldry: vulgarity; coarse sexual comment

risqué: dirty; improper

sordid: dirty; mercenary

swamper: handyman or helper

unsavory: shady, shifty; morally suspect

1   Moving pictures, their educational influence for good or for bad, their growing importance as a factor in our civilization, the announced determination of those controlling the industry boldly to enter politics, and the desirability of regulation by law through censorship constitute a subject of acknowledged importance to the American people. . . .

2   The motion picture is a great invention, and it has become a powerful factor for good or bad in our civilization. It has great educational power for good or bad. It may educate young people in the ways of good citizenship or in ways of dissoluteness, extravagance, wickedness, and crime. It furnishes recreation, diversion, and amusement at a cheap price to many millions of our people—largely the young. It is the only form of amusement within the means of millions. It possesses great potential possibilities for good. It may furnish not only amusement but education of a high order.

3   Through motion pictures the young and the old may see depicted every good motive, laudable ambition, commendable characteristic, ennobling trait of humanity. They may be taught that honesty is the best policy; that virtue and worth are rewarded; that industry leads to success. Those who live in the country or in small interior towns, and who never visit large cities, may see pictured the skyscrapers, the crowded streets, the rush and jam of metropolitan cities. Those who live in the interior, and never see the seacoast, may see on the screen the great docks and wharves of seaports and see the loading and unloading of giant ocean steamers. Those who live in crowded cities, and never see the country or get a glimpse of country life, may have depicted to them all the beauties of rural life and scenery. All may see scenes of the luxuriant Tropics, the grandeur of Alpine Mountains, polar conditions, life in the Orient. The cities, palaces, cathedrals, ports, rural life, daily routine, scenic attractions, mode of living of every country on the globe, may be brought to our doors and eyes for a small price. The industry may be made an education to the young.

4   However, from all accounts, the business has been conducted, generally speaking, upon a low plane and in a decidedly sordid manner. Those who own and control the industry seem to have been of the opinion that the sensual, the sordid, the prurient, the phases of fast life, the ways of extravagance, the risqué, the paths of shady life, drew the greatest attendance and coined for them the most money, and apparently they have been out to get the coin, no matter what the effect upon the public, young or old; and when thoughtful people have suggested or advocated official censorship, in the interest of good citizenship and wholesome morals, the owners of the industry have resented it and, in effect,

declared that it was nobody's business other than theirs and concerned nobody other than them what kind of shows they produced; that if people did not like their shows they could stay away from them; that it was their business, and they would conduct it as they might please. At least they have vigorously fought all attempts at censorship and resented them. . . .

5   I have no doubt young criminals got their ideas of the romance of crime from moving pictures. I believe moving pictures are doing as much harm to-day as saloons did in the days of the open saloon—especially to the young. They are running day and night, Sunday and every other day, the year round, and in most jurisdictions without any regulation by censorship. I would not abolish them. They can be made a great force for good. I would close them on Sunday and regulate them week days by judicious censorship. Already some dozen or more States have censorship laws, with the right of appeal to the courts, and the movement is on in many other States.

6   When we look to the source of the moving pictures, the material for them, the personnel of those who pose for them, we need not wonder that many of the pictures are pernicious.

7   The pictures are largely furnished by such characters as Fatty Arbuckle, of unsavory fame, notorious for his scandalous debauchery and drunken orgies, one of which, attended by many "stars," resulted in the death of Virginia Rappe, a star artist; William Desmond Taylor, deceased, murdered for some mysterious cause; one Valentino, now figuring as the star character in rape and divorce sensations. Many others of like character might be mentioned.

8   At Hollywood, Calif., is a colony of these people, where debauchery, riotous living, drunkenness, ribaldry, dissipation, free love, seem to be conspicuous. Many of these "stars," it is reported, were formerly bartenders, butcher boys, sopers, swampers, variety actors and actresses, who may have earned $10 or $20 a week, and some of whom are now paid, it is said, salaries of something like $5,000 a month or more, and they do not know what to do with their wealth, extracted from poor people, in large part, in 25 or 50 cent admission fees, except to spend it in riotous living, dissipation, and "high rolling."

9   These are some of the characters from whom the young people of today are deriving a large part of their education, views of life, and character-forming habits. From these sources our young people gain much of their views of life, inspiration, and education. Rather a poor source, is it not? Looks like there is some need for censorship, does it not? There could be some improvement, could there not? . . .

QUESTIONS FOR THOUGHT

1. Write out Myers's basic concerns about the future of motion pictures. Now consider each concern as a prophecy, an event foretold. How accurate are the predictions Myers made?

2. In the second paragraph, Myers states, "It may educate young people in the ways of good citizenship or in ways of dissoluteness, extravagance, wickedness, and crime. It furnishes recreation, diversion, and amusement at a cheap price to many millions of our people—largely the young." Many modern critics share these concerns about modern movies. Other than their providing "recreation, diversion, and amusement at a cheap price," why are the young so drawn to movies? Why do they respond to their influence?

QUESTIONS OF STYLE

1. Myers's writing style is more formal than John Leo's ("One Poke Over the Line"). Note places where the style is particularly strong. How does this formal style affect Myers's argument?

2. In paragraph 3, Myers states, "through motion pictures the young and the old may see depicted every good motive, laudable ambition, commendable characteristic, ennobling trait of humanity. They may be taught that honesty is the best policy; that virtue and worth are rewarded; that industry leads to success." Why does Myers choose to include this idea in his argument?

3. Paragraph 9 ends this essay with a series of questions: "Rather a poor source, is it not? Looks like there is some need for censorship, does it not? There could be some improvement, could there not?" By asking these questions in this manner, what does Myers's presume about the reader's reaction to his argument? Are these answerable questions? What would answers reveal about the reader?

QUESTIONS OF STRATEGY

1. In paragraph 5, Myers writes, "I believe moving pictures are doing as much harm to-day as saloons did in the days of the open saloon—especially to the young." What is the basis of this comparison? Does Myers offer enough evidence to make a valid comparison?

2. Paragraphs 6 and 7 are set up as cause and effect. What is the basis of Myers's cause and effect argument here? Are evidence and support sufficient to make the argument convincing?

3. In explaining problem behavior within Hollywood, Myers provides specific star examples (Fatty Arbuckle, Virginia Rappe, and William Desmond Taylor). However, in the following paragraph, he lists general problems but not specific examples. Why does Myers choose to set up the details in this manner? How do they affect the overall impact of the essay?

QUESTIONS FOR WRITING

1. Watch a full-length movie produced before 1945 (the older the film, the better) and write a review. Note elements such as dialogue, storyline, acting, and so on. As you watch the film and prepare your review, keep in mind Myers's concerns about the medium.

2. Watch a series of the most popular films of the past five years. Note any trends in filmmaking and write an essay predicting the state of motion pictures in twenty or thirty years. How will the trends you see today affect the films of tomorrow?

3. Write an essay about films shown exclusively over the Internet. Be sure to discuss the types of films online, the attitudes of the filmmakers, and any trends that will affect Internet moviemaking. You may want to use one or two of these films as the basis for your essay.

*4. With a partner, argue the need for censorship. Each person should choose one side of the issue, research it, and then write a short essay supporting the position. Get together with your partner and join the two arguments into one essay on the concept of censorship.

5. Reread "Moving Pictures Evoke Concern" and then write a response to it, addressing each concern the author expresses in his essay. Be sure your essay follows standard reading response format.

22

CARTOONS

Drawings. Illustrations. Graphic literature. Sequential storytelling. The funnies. Comics. Toons. Whatever we call them, whatever form they are packaged in, almost everyone loves cartoons. We cut *Foxtrot* or *Garfield* out of our daily newspaper and share it with friends. As children (and adults), we watched *It's the Great Pumpkin, Charlie Brown,* and *How the Grinch Stole Christmas.* Almost everyone read Superman and Batman comic books as children, and many adults now read comic books such as *100 Bullets* and *From Hell* that are aimed at a more mature audience and published in hardcover. Every summer, millions of people stampede to movie houses to watch *The Lion King, Tarzan, Atlantis,* or any animated releases. In short, we love little paint and ink pictures.

Our fascination with cartoons, some say, is derived from every culture's love of visual art. Cartoons are just a mass-produced version of that type of art. While cartoons can be considered "art," original sketches of Snoopy hang in art galleries, and *Action Comics #1,* featuring the first appearance of Superman and published in 1938, is worth hundreds of thousands of dollars, cartoons can be a form of communication. Children are often taught lessons about life through picture books and comic books. Political ideas and commentary that would be deemed threatening in any other form can be expressed in caricature and the editorial cartoon. People who have reading challenges can often get the message by referring to illustrations. A new art form, computer-generated imagery (CGI), has developed from cartoons. With CGI, animators who once used pen, ink, and paper now use computers and software to design and animate characters. Some CGI is used to make special effects. In *Star Wars: Episode One,* for instance, Jar-Jar Binks is computer-generated. Even entire movies, such as *Toy Story, Shrek,* and *Final Fantasy: The Spirits Within,* have been generated by computer.

Whether line drawings, Saturday morning fare, or the new wave of computer generated imagery, cartoons can express what people see in ways other media may not. The "readings" in this chapter are cartoons that reflect the ideas and voices of their creators. With "A Very Special *Sesame Street,*" Ruben Bolling talks about the world-famous children's television program *Sesame Street* and what he feels is at the heart of the program. "Still Standing Tall," a selection from *Heroes,* follows. *Heroes* is an illustrated magazine dedicated to the firefighters, police officers, doctors, nurses, and others who risked their lives to help others on September 11, 2001, when two jet planes were hijacked and crashed into the World Trade Center in New York City. As you read each selection, reflect on the cartoons and how the illustrators challenge general perceptions of the art form.

Reading 29 | A Very Special *Sesame Street*
Ruben Bolling

BACKSTORY

Cartoons are often used to express opinions, as seen on the opinion pages of newspapers and magazines. Here, cartoonist Ruben Bolling, in his weekly comic strip *Tom the Dancing Bug*, expresses his view on the true nature of children's television programs. As you read the cartoon, think about the television programs you watched growing up. Is Bolling being unfair, or are children being socialized by television?

LEXICON

synchronizes: causes to move together

QUESTIONS FOR THOUGHT

1. Through this cartoon, Bolling suggests that *Sesame Street* and other children's television programs simply train children to watch television and become consumers. Do you agree with Bolling? Explain your answer.

2. Of all the popular children's programs currently on television, the author chose to use *Sesame Street* in his cartoon. Why? How does this reflect the overall message being expressed?

3. Was illustration the most effective way of delivering the author's point to the audience? If so, why was it effective? If not, what would have worked better, and why?

QUESTIONS OF STYLE

1. Although Bolling uses characters from *Sesame Street,* he doesn't have them speak in character. The characters use words and express an attitude they would never use or express on the show. Why does Bolling choose this technique? How does it work to make his point?

2. Irony is the expression of one idea when the opposite is expected. How is irony used in this piece? How does it affect the overall tone of the cartoon?

QUESTIONS OF STRATEGY

1. By using characters from *Sesame Street,* Bolling exploits a specific example to make his point. How effective is this single example? What other characters from children's television could have been used?

2. One of the characters says, "But more importantly, we're really teaching you how to become good little consumers of corporate culture." No examples or further explanations are provided. Why not? How do the pictures convey the meaning of the statement?

QUESTIONS FOR WRITING

1. Write an essay arguing the effectiveness in presenting opinion through a cartoon. Is the opinion clear in cartoon form? Does the cartoon form enhance the message or detract from it? Be sure to develop your thoughts with details and examples.

2. Watch a series of children's programs. Take notes on what you observe: lessons taught, images shown, length of segments inside the programs, nature of commercials during the program (if any), and popularity of the characters in the program. Write an essay stating whether you agree or disagree with Bolling's opinion of children's television. Present each of your points in a separate paragraph, and be sure that you develop each through explanation, details, and examples.

3. In this comic strip, Bolling implies that not watching television will help children develop their thinking abilities. Write an essay describing three activities that, once the television is off, children could do in order to develop these abilities. Be sure to include explanation, details, and example in your essay.

4. Find a cartoon in a newspaper or a comic book and write a reponse essay. Explain the cartoon and then write your reaction to it. Be sure to refer to the pictures as well as any words in the cartoon. Submit this essay to your instructor.

*5. With a partner, create your own political cartoon. (Visit your school's library for books containing a variety of political cartoons.) Write an essay about the process of creating the cartoon. Include your audience's reaction to the cartoon you created.

6. Find an assortment of political cartoons published in foreign newspapers and magazines. Write an essay comparing these cartoons to the ones you find in American publications. In your essay, compare and contrast these political cartoons.

Reading 30 Still Standing Tall
Walter Simonson

BACKSTORY

On September 11, 2001, two commercial jets were hijacked and forced into the two towers of the World Trade Center in New York City. Both buildings were leveled, and thousands of people died. Firefighters, police officers, rescue squads, and average men and women from across the country and the world offered whatever aid and assistance they could. Marvel Comics, publishers of such famous superhero comic books as *The Amazing Spiderman* and *Captain America,* published *Heroes,* an illustrated magazine in which artists and writers of comic books honored those who helped during the September 11 tragedy. In this piece, Walter Simonson drew a police officer and a firefighter standing where the fallen buildings once stood.

SEPTEMBER 11, 2001

QUESTIONS FOR DISCUSSION

1. What is your first reaction to this cartoon?
2. Could this image be effectively described in another creative medium? Which? Explain your answer.

3. Are there stories that should never be told in pictures? What stories? Why? Explain your answers.

QUESTIONS OF STYLE

1. The images in the drawing convey a simple idea: where the Twin Towers once stood, now stands a police officer and a firefighter. Why were these particular figures selected? How does the image affect your views of heroes?

2. Stories in comic books are often told with many pages and in many panels. What story is told in this single panel? Why does the artist choose to tell this story in only one panel?

QUESTION OF STRATEGY

1. The art in this panel, at first glance, may seem sketchy and unpolished. The characters have few distinguishing features other than their clothing. In what ways does this visual technique affect your interpretation of the term *hero*?

QUESTIONS FOR WRITING

1. Define *hero*. Read a comic book featuring a superhero such as Spiderman, Batman, Wonder Woman, or Superman. (For variety and a different perspective, read a superhero comic book from a country other than the United States.) Describe the way *hero* is defined in each of the comic books and the write a comparison/contrast essay about the two definitions.

2. The writers and artists responsible for creating *Heroes* donated their time to the project. When the magazine was published, Marvel Comics donated all proceeds to the Red Cross Disaster Relief Fund. Some people would consider these donations of talent and money "heroic." In what other ways can people be heroic? Write an essay explaining these ways.

3. Write and draw a comic strip about an act of heroism you witnessed or heard about. First, outline the event, telling who was involved, where the event took place, and what happened. If necessary, include dialogue. Next, sketch each scene. Pay close attention to the location of characters and other objects in the scene. Finally, write the dialogue and place it in the scene. (Don't be shy about your drawing abilities; the sketches don't have to be anything more than stick figures.) Reflect on the experience you illustrated and on the experience of illustrating it. What was different about this approach to storytelling than traditional written narrative storytelling?

4. Write a response to "Still Standing Tall." Jot down the ideas and feelings you get as you look at the picture and use those as the basis of your essay. Structure this response as you would a typical reading response essay.

*5. What types of heroes did you have when you were younger? With a partner, write a comparison and contrast essay about heroes from three or four cultures.

23

ADVERTISING

The primary goal of any business is to sell its products or services. The best way to sell a product or service is through advertising. Place an ad on a billboard downtown or take out a full-page ad in *USA Today,* and you guarantee yourself increased traffic and potential sales. Consumers need information about products before buying, and advertising can provide that information. Advertising, on the surface, works well for both business and consumer.

Look below the surface, however, and the concept of advertising can take on a darker meaning. Businesspeople spend millions of dollars each year to hire celebrities and professional athletes to push soda, deodorant, alcohol, even long-distance phone service on a viewing public. Ads, once seen only on billboards and between television shows, can now be found on websites, in classrooms, on t-shirts, in phone books, and even as part of local news programs. Some advertisers bypass traditional commercial venues and place their products within the shows and movies themselves. Just by watching a certain show, we are exposed to products that the stars wear, drive, or drink. Consumers rarely find content of value in commercials these days. Advertisers seem more interested in being clever and memorable. We can all sing jingles about a favorite snack food or remember a certain series of commercials for coffee, but what can we say about the products themselves?

The readings in this section focus on the nature of advertising and how it affects our lives. In "Ad to the Bone," Jeff MacGregor cautions that the use of ads in sporting events is getting dangerously out of control. Dirk Johnson, author of "When Money Is Everything, Except Hers," focuses on a young woman struggling to survive seventh grade, which has become almost unbearable due, in part, to the influence of advertising and consumerism.

The next time you go to a store, reflect on your purchases. Did you buy that soda because you like the brand or because you were influenced by an ad?

Reading 31 Ad to the Bone
Jeff MacGregor

BACKSTORY

Professional sporting events are sponsored by large corporations. Fans are not surprised when they see ads plastered around sporting arenas. In some sports, such as auto racing, many participants select sponsors in return for their public endorsement of a product or service. As we look at the relationship between sports and advertising, we might ask ourselves, "Where do we draw the line? When is enough enough?" Jeff MacGregor, in an essay originally published in *Sports Illustrated*, suggests that we should draw the line immediately because sports and advertising don't always mix.

LEXICON

Aegean: a section of the Mediterranean Sea near Greece

apt: appropriate

breezers: pants

cerebral: referring to the brain

cruller: small pastry

franchise: business granted the right to market a specific product or service

gouts: large splashes

imperialism: the drive to control resources by conquest

journeyman: worker of average ability

microcommercialism: idea of selling something on a small scale

mum: silent

neutrality: not taking a side in a conflict

phenomenon: an outstanding occurrence

proliferation: reproduction in mass quantity

retention: keeping; saving

saturation: thorough soaking

subconscious: the part of mental activity that is only slightly aware of what is happening

1   Watching a New York Rangers hockey game on television the other night, I saw, in a single rush up the ice, ads along the boards for GMC and Gulf, Dodge and Sharp and Snapple, IBM, Office Depot, Dunkin' Donuts, PaineWebber, Kodak, Amtrak, Bud Light, MetLife, American Express, Starter and Surge. I got my replays from the MCS Canon Cam and kept track of power plays with the AT&T scoreboard graphic. The Rangers sat on a bench underwritten by the History Channel. (How apt!) At the first intermission, they exited beneath a sign hawking Ranch 1 chicken. Then the commercials started.

2   Scientists say humans rarely use even 10% of their brain capacity. They keep mum on what we do with the other 90%. Longtime television sports viewers like me, though, know the truth. All additional cerebral storage space is devoted to commercial retention. I may not know my parent's phone number, but I can remember 30-year-old beer jingles as though I'd written them myself.

3   At a time when a journeyman point guard eats up the price of a private island in the Aegean, sports franchises and their television sponsors are desperately counting on fixed-position advertising to help pay their enormous freight. Commercials aren't enough anymore, not

since the remote control made them zappable. Broadcasters and franchises need to sell ad space you can't flip past or turn away from: Watch the game, see the spot. Whether it's the scrolling sign built into the scorer's table at a basketball game (Hardee's, Auto Zone, IBM) or the under-bumper NASCAR Cam (Valvoline, True Value, 1-800-How-'Bout-A-Kidney), certain forms of advertising are now inescapable. You take them in without really seeing them; they're in the very air—it's like we're inhaling them. A Mercedes logo hanging from the net at a tennis tournament you don't even remember watching is taking up space in your subconscious right now. (That's why you can't remember the Gettysburg Address.)

4   Any pretense to community or charity or even neutrality in the naming of golf tournaments, bowl games or stadiums was sold long ago. But there's still some available screen space, so that's being sold, too. Hence your Miller Genuine Draft sports ticker and CNN/SI's "The New Dodge Inside Sports" sports update.

5   I'm not even sure how effective this stuff is. Seeing Pavel Bure spit out a bloody tooth while he's sitting in front of a Dunkin' Donuts sign isn't likely to make me run out for a cruller. Nor is watching a stock car painted up like a box of Tide tumbling end over end at 180 miles per hour, gouts of flame billowing from its ruptured fuel tank while trailing a meteor shower of car and human body parts behind it, going to make me feel more confident about my next load of fine washables.

6   This phenomenon is even worse in Europe. Many of their leading social critics complain that popular American culture is a little *too* popular there, that McDonald's and Coca-Cola and Tom Hanks are just tools in the new age of Yankee commercial imperialism. What's really surprising is that there's any room left for them. Have you ever seen a Formula One race? Or a Swedish hockey game? Not a single square inch of salable ad space is wasted. From the toolboxes at Monaco to the butt of the goalie's breezers in Stockholm, there are endorsements for Elf or Adidas or Wheetabix plastered everywhere.

7   Which is probably the next move for North America's insupportable big-time sports economy. Auto racing is already there, a model of shameless commercial saturation, but in the decade ahead you'll begin to see the proliferation of pinched microcommercialism of on-uniform advertising in other sports as well. Can't we just skip a step and save everyone some trouble and confusion? Introducing your Ford Rangers! Your Mobil 1 Synthetic Oilers! Your Wishbone Salad Dressing Thousand Islanders!

8   I wasn't using my brain for anything important anyhow.

QUESTIONS FOR THOUGHT

1. How do advertisements affect your enjoyment of sporting events? Do you even notice them?

2. Consider advertisements in other media, such as product placement in television shows and movies. How do these forms of advertising affect your viewing experience?

3. Suppose you were chair of a committee designed to limit advertising. What types of advertisements would you limit? To what areas or places would you limit the display of advertisements?

QUESTIONS OF STYLE

1. In the opening paragraph of the essay, MacGregor gives a list of advertisements shown during the hockey game, then ends the paragraph with the sentence, "And then the commercials started." What does this paragraph prepare you for in the rest of the essay? What tone is conveyed?

2. In paragraph 7, MacGregor writes, "Can't we just skip a step and save everyone some trouble and confusion? Introducing your Ford Rangers! Your Mobil 1 Synthetic Oilers! Your Wishbone Salad Dressing Thousand Islanders!" Why does the author choose to use sentence fragments here? What effect do these fragments have on the overall tone of the essay?

QUESTIONS OF STRATEGY

1. In paragraph 5, the author says, "Nor is watching a stock car painted up like a box of Tide tumbling end over end at 180 miles an hour, gouts of flame billowing from its ruptured fuel tank while trailing a meteor shower of car and human body parts behind it, going to make me feel more confident about my next load of fine washables." Why does he choose this particular piece of detail to use as support? How well does the detail support the main idea of the paragraph?

2. Return to the list of ads mentioned in the first sentence of the essay. Why does MacGregor use detail in this way? How does the list set the tone for the essay?

3. At the end of paragraph 3, MacGregor writes, "A Mercedes logo hanging from the net at a tennis tournament you don't even remember watching is taking up space in your subconscious right now. (That's why you can't remember the Gettysburg Address.)" How do these two sentences show comparison and contrast? Which subject does MacGregor consider more valuable? Explain your answer.

QUESTIONS FOR WRITING

1. View a sporting event on television and make note of the types and amount of advertisement you see. Write an essay on the effects this advertisement had on your enjoyment of the event.

2. Write an essay discussing ways advertisements can enhance community events, health, education, and so on. Be sure to add an introduction and conclusion to your essay and to develop your points with details, explanations, and examples.

3. Reread "Ad to the Bone," watch a sporting event on television, and then write a response to MacGregor's essay. Be sure to quote your sources carefully and use your experience watching the sporting event to support your point of view.

*4. With a partner, create an ad campaign for your favorite beverage. Focus your ads on print media, radio, and television audiences. Target the ad to sports fans. Write the ad copy (the information about the product) and present your ad to your class. Write a process essay detailing how you plan to increase sales by showing this ad during the Super Bowl or another major sports event.

5. Write a response to "Ad to the Bone" from an athlete's point of view. In a persuasive essay, argue that advertising during sporting events should be encouraged. In your essay, explain who benefits from the ads (other than the advertisers) and how.

Reading 32   When Money Is Everything, Except Hers
Dirk Johnson

BACKSTORY

When most people think *advertisement,* they immediately think television commercials, billboards, or banner ads on websites. Product placement, however, is more subtle. People actually consume brand name products on screen. Sarah Michelle Gellar wears a certain brand of denim jeans on *Buffy the Vampire Slayer,* an teens rush to the nearest clothing store for that fashion. This creates an in-crowd who can afford to mimic people on the screen. But what about those who don't have the money, yet yearn to be part of that crowd? Dirk Johnson, in the following article published in the *New York Times,* wrestles with this question as he tells us about a young woman trying to fit into a society heavily influenced by advertisements.

LEXICON

affluence: riches, wealth

fret: worry

ostentatious: showy, pretentious

prestige: the ability to influence because of one's fame

savvy: shrewd

1   Dixon, Ill. Watching classmates strut past in designer clothes, Wendy Williams sat silently on the yellow school bus, wearing a cheap belt and rummage-sale slacks. One boy stopped and yanked his thumb, demanding her seat. "Move it, trailer girl," he sneered.

2   It has never been easy to live on the wrong side of the tracks. But in the economically robust 1990's, with sprawling new houses and three-car garages sprouting like cornstalks on the Midwestern prairie, the sting that comes with scarcity gets rubbed with an extra bit of salt. Seen through the eyes of a 13-year-old girl growing up at Chateau Estates, a fancy name for a tin-plain trailer park, the rosy talk about the nation's prosperity carries a certain mocking echo.

3   The everyday discussion in the halls of Reagan Middle School in this city about 100 miles west of Chicago touches on computer toys that can cost $1,000, family vacations to Six Flags or Disney World and stylish clothes that bear a Nike emblem or Tommy Hilfiger's coveted label. Unlike young people a generation ago, those today must typically pay fees to play for the school sports teams or band. It costs $45 to play in the youth summer soccer league. It takes money to go skating on weekends at the White Pines roller rink, to play laser tag or rock-climb at the Plum Hollow Recreation Center, to mount a steed at the Horseback Riding Club, to gaze at Leonardo DiCaprio and Kate Winslet at the Plaza Cinemas, to go shopping for clothes at the Cherryvale Mall.

4   To be without money, in so many ways, is to be left out. "I told this girl: 'That's a really awesome shirt. Where did you get it?'" said Wendy, explaining that she knew it was out of her price range, but that she wanted to join the small talk. "And she looked at me and laughed and said, 'Why would you want to know?'" A lanky, soft-spoken girl with large brown eyes, Wendy pursed her lips to hide a slight overbite that got her the nickname Rabbit, a humiliation she once begged her mother and father to avoid by sending her to an orthodontist.

5   For struggling parents, keenly aware that adolescents agonize over the social pecking order, the styles of the moment and the face in the mirror, there is no small sense of failure in telling a child that she cannot have what her classmates take for granted. "Do you know what it's like?" asked Wendy's mother, Veronica Williams, "to have your daughter come home and say, 'Mom, the kids say my clothes are tacky,' and then walk off with her head hanging low."

6   This is not the desperate poverty of Chicago housing projects, where the plight of empty pockets is worsened by the threat of gangs and gunfires. Wendy lives in relative safety in a home with both parents. Her father, Wendell Provow, earns $9 an hour as a welder. Her mother works part-time as a cook for Head Start, the Federal education program. Unlike students in some urban pockets, isolated from affluence, Wendy receives the same education as a girl from a $300,000 house in the Idle Oaks subdivision. The flip side of that coin is the public spectacle of economic struggle. This is a place small enough where people know the personal stories, or, at least, repeat them as if they did.

7   Even in this down-to-earth town, where a poor boy nicknamed Dutch grew up to become President, young people seem increasingly enchanted with buying, having, spending and status. R. Woodrow (Woody) Wasson, the principal at Reagan Middle School, makes it a point to sit down with every child and ask them about their hopes and dreams. "They want to be doctors, lawyers, veterinarians and, of course, professional athletes," said Mr. Wasson, whose family roots here go back to the 19th century. "I don't remember the last time I heard somebody say they wanted to be a police officer or a firefighter. They want to do something that will make a lot of money and have a lot of prestige."

8   He said a teacher in a nearby town has been trying to recruit high school students for vocational studies to become tool-and-die artisans, a trade that can pay $70,000 a year. "The teacher can't fill the slots," Mr. Wasson said. "Nobody's interested in that kind of work."

9   It is not surprising that children grow up believing that money is so important, given the relentless way they are targeted by marketers. "In the past, you just put an ad in the

magazine," said Michael Wood, the director of research for Teen-Age Research Unlimited, a marketing consultant in suburban Chicago. "Now savvy marketers know you must hit them at all angles—Web sites, cable TV shows, school functions, sporting events." He noted the growth of cross-promotions, like the deal in which actors on the television show *Dawson's Creek*, which is popular among adolescents, wear clothes by J. Crew and appear in its catalogue.

10   But young people get cues in their everyday lives. Some spending habits that would once have been seen as ostentatious—extravagant parties for small children, new cars for teenagers—have become familiar trappings for middle-class comfort. The stock market, although it is sputtering now, has made millionaires of many people in Main Street towns. Building developers hare recently won approval to build a gated community, which will be called Timber Edge.

11   "Wendy goes to school around these rich kids," her mother said, "and wonders why she can't have things like they do." A bright girl with a flair for art, writing and numbers, Wendy stays up late most nights, reading books. *The Miracle Worker* was a recent favorite. But when a teacher asked her to join an elevated class for algebra, she politely declined. "I get picked on for my clothes and living in the trailer park," said Wendy, who never brings anyone home from school. "I don't want to get picked on for being a nerd, too."

12   Her mother, who watched three other daughters drop out of school and have babies as teen-agers, has told Wendy time and again: "Don't lose your self-esteem."

13   One time a boy at school was teasing Wendy about her clothes—"they don't even match," he laughed—and her humble house in the trailer park. She listened for a while. He kept insulting her. So she lifted a leg—clothed as it was in discount jeans from the Farm & Fleet store—and kicked him in the shins. He told the authorities. She got the detention. It became clear to Wendy that the insults were not going to stop. It also became clear that shin-kicking, however deserved, was not going to be the solution.

14   She went to a guidance counselor, Cynthia Kowa Basler, a dynamic woman who keeps close tabs on the children, especially girls who fret about their weight and suddenly stop eating lunch. "I am large," she tells the girls, "and I have self-esteem."

15   Wendy, who knew that Mrs. Basler held sessions with students to increase their self-confidence, went to the counselor. "I feel a little down," Wendy told her. The counselor gathered eight students, including other girls like Wendy, who felt embarrassed about their economic station.

16   In this school named for Ronald Reagan, the students were told to study the words of Eleanor Roosevelt. One of her famous quotations was posted above the counselor's desk: "No one can make you feel inferior without your consent." As a group, the students looked up the definition of inferior and consent. And then they read the words out loud.

17   "Again," the counselor instructed.

18   "Louder," the counselor insisted. Again and again, they read the inspirational words.

19   In role-playing exercises, the children practiced responses to taunts, which sometimes called for nothing more than a shrug. "Mrs. Basler told us to live up to our goals—show those kids," Wendy said. "She told us that things can be a lot different when you're grown up. Maybe things will be the other way around then." Wendy smiled at the notion.

20   Life still has plenty of bumps. When Wendy gets off the school bus—the trailer park is the first stop, so everyone can see where she lives—she still looks at her shoes. She still pulls her shirt out to hide a belt that does not quite make the grade. And she still purses her lips to hide an overbite. But her mother has noticed her smiling more these days. And Wendy has even said she might consider taking an advanced course in math, her favorite subject. "I want to go to college," Wendy said the other day. "I want to become a teacher."

21   One recent day, she popped in to the counselor's office, just to say hello, then walked back down the halls, her arms folded around her schoolbooks. Mrs. Basler stood at the doorway and watched her skip away, a student with so much promise, and so many obstacles. For the girl from Chateau Estates, it is a long way from the seventh grade to college. "She's going to make it," the counselor said, with a clenched fist and a voice full of hope.

QUESTIONS FOR THOUGHT

1. "To be without money, in so many ways, is to be left out" writes Johnson in paragraph 4. Explain what this sentence means to you. In what ways can someone without money not be left out?

2. List a few of your immediate goals. Highlight the goals that focus on obtaining material things ("In five years, I would like to own a new BMW"). Beside each of these goals, write the reason that material object is important to you. Were any of these things influenced by ads or popular trends?

QUESTIONS OF STYLE

1. Reread paragraphs 16–19. Why does Johnson use this particular bit of dialogue here? How does it reflect the overall tone of the article?

2. When Wendy's story ends, we see her skipping away. She says she wants to go to college and become a teacher. Why does Johnson choose to end the article this way? Speculate on Wendy's future. Does she make it to college? Explain your answer.

QUESTIONS OF STRATEGY

1. This article has many passages of description. Jot down some descriptive sentences that stand out for you. Why do these particular passages impress you?

2. "When Money Is Everything, Except Hers," first published as a newspaper article, takes the form of a narrative. Why is this strategy effective? What other writing strategies could be used to convey the main ideas?

QUESTIONS FOR WRITING

1. In paragraph 12, Johnson writes, "Her mother, who watched three other daughters drop out of school and have babies as teen-agers, has told Wendy

time and again: 'Don't lose your self-esteem'." Write an essay in which you provide steps to help Wendy (or any young person in her situation) not lose her self-esteem. For ideas, visit your school's counselors or work with a partner.

2. Write a narrative about a time in which you had to overcome adversity as a young person. Describe the situation, the actions you took to deal with the problem, and the consequences of those actions. Reflect on the outcome. Would you have done anything differently? For inspiration, refer to the quote in paragraph 16: "No one can make you feel inferior without your consent."

3. Write an essay defining *counselor*. Who can or should be a counselor? What training or special skills should a counselor have? How involved should a counselor be with a student? Include the answers to these questions as you develop the thesis statement and main points to your essay.

4. Write a response to "When Money Is Everything, Except Hers." Perhaps you can compare and contrast your experiences in school with those of Wendy's in the essay, or perhaps you can write a narrative about your family life or school experiences when you were younger.

5. Examine ads found on television, in magazines, and in newspapers. What cultures are made popular through these ads? Write an essay comparing the cultures expressed in the ads with cultures you identify with, such as student culture or parent culture. As you develop your essay, be sure to add detail about both your culture and the ones found in the ads.

*6. With a partner, write an essay exploring ways young people get their selp-image and self-esteem other than mass media. (For ideas, survey members of your class or interview sociology or psychology instructors.) Be sure to explain each way and give specific examples.

PART V

Grammar and Mechanics Review

When I introduce grammar to my students, I often use the example of buying a car. Imagine I am a car salesman and you are looking for a car. I steer you to the finest car in the lot. It is fast, with a well-tuned engine. It is safe, with anti-lock brakes, air bags, and seat belts. The tires are brand-new. The warranty is top-notch. This car, you admit to yourself, is everything you ever wanted, but it has a small problem.

It looks like it was pulled out of a junkyard days ago.

The panels are mismatched. The roof is dented. The bumpers are scuffed. The outside of the car makes you skeptical of the claims I make about the insides of the car. In all likelihood, you would walk away from the lot and go buy a car elsewhere.

This is how readers respond to sloppy grammar and punctuation. You may have written the finest essay of your career. You may have uncovered secrets that will improve life for every person on Earth. But if words are misspelled and punctuation is out of place, if sentences are not complete, or if you have misused words, your readers won't take the content of your writing seriously. In fact, they may even stop reading altogether.

Grammar and mechanics are important to good writing. Understanding how they work will improve your composition. This grammar and mechanics handbook is designed to help you do that.

In chapter 24, you will be introduced to many parts of speech—nouns, pronouns, verbs, adverbs, prepositions, adjectives, conjunctions, and interjections—to provide you with the vocabulary and definition for the basics of grammar. Master parts of speech, and you can move to Chapter 25, which discusses how to build sound sentences. You will learn to identify and fix problems in agreement and with pronouns as well as sentence problems such as fragments, run-ons, and comma splices. Chapter 26 covers the effective use of punctuation—periods, question marks, exclamation points, commas, semicolons, colons, dashes and parentheses, quotation marks, apostrophes, and hyphens. The chapter also explores when to use capitalization in a sentence. The grammar and mechanics section is rounded out by Chapter 27, which offers information and advice on improving word choice, using a dictionary and thesaurus, avoiding wordiness, and improving your vocabulary.

Each chapter includes numerous exercises that will help you build your grammar skills. However, you need not worry about memorizing every rule. Feel free to use this handbook as a guide and look up a rule as you need to.

24

GRAMMAR "TOOLS"

To recognize how to correct errors in grammar and mechanics, you must start by understanding the eight **parts of speech** (nouns, pronouns, verbs, adjectives, adverbs, prepositions, conjunctions, and interjections). These parts, their functions, and the terms used to describe them are the "tools" that will help you build your grammar skills. This chapter will introduce you to the tools. If you are already familiar with them, it will refresh your memory.

NOUNS

Nouns are words that name a person, place, thing, idea, event, emotion, or quality. They commonly appear as the subject or the object of the action within a sentence.

Example: The <u>line</u> at the <u>box office</u> of the movie <u>theater</u> showing the new *Star Wars* <u>movie</u> wrapped around the <u>block</u>.

In this sentence, the action is centered on the nouns: the <u>line</u>, <u>office</u>, <u>theater</u>, <u>movie</u>, and <u>block</u>.

Categories of Nouns

Let's look at nouns in all the categories listed above.

Person A noun is a word or a name representing a human being or a group of people.

Example: <u>Cindy</u> went to meet her <u>boyfriend</u> at the nightclub, which was crowded with both <u>friends</u> and <u>strangers</u>.

Note that personal names are nouns.

Place A noun is a physical location, area, or environment, real or imagined.

Example: Some people believe that <u>studios</u> in <u>Hollywood</u> are the <u>birthplace</u> of all motion pictures, but many movies are made in <u>England</u> and <u>Australia</u> to cut costs.

Thing   A noun is something that can be experienced by one of the five senses. It can be seen, heard, smelled, tasted, or touched.

> *Example:* Sheila drank a <u>cup</u> of hot <u>tea</u> while she read the newest Harry Potter <u>book</u>, with some quiet <u>music</u> playing in the next <u>room</u>.

Idea   A noun is a concept, thought, plan, or impression.

> *Example:* Jerry had a sense of <u>freedom</u> when he graduated from high school.

Event   A noun is an occurrence or situation.

> *Example:* Gyasi wished that his <u>birthday</u> and <u>Christmas</u> came more than once a year.
>
> *Example:* The <u>concert</u> started two hours late.

Emotion   A noun is a feeling or a sensation.

> *Example:* We felt <u>happiness</u> and <u>relief</u> when our soccer team won the championship game by one goal.
>
> *Example:* <u>Sadness</u> fell over the family when Grandmother died.

Quality   A noun is a state of mind or physical being.

> *Example:* The lesson of *Beauty and the Beast* is that <u>beauty</u> is in the eye of the beholder.
>
> *Example:* The Disney movie of that fairy tale was the <u>favorite</u> of a generation of children.

Types of Nouns

Nouns can also be described as common or proper.

Common Nouns   **Common nouns** name one or more of a group or class of people, places, or things.

> *Examples:* woman, fan, dogs, park, mountain, ice cream, video game, dinner, baseball

Proper Nouns   **Proper nouns** identify specific people, places, or things. They begin with a capital letter.

> *Examples:* Steve, Paul McCartney, England, Louisiana, Coca-Cola, Columbus Day

Number of Nouns

Nouns can be singular or plural, showing number. They can also be described as countable and uncountable.

Singular Nouns   Singular nouns refer to one item or person.

> *Examples:* sister, hat, wizard

Plural Nouns   Plural nouns refer to two or more people or items. The plural is usually formed by adding an *s* to the singular noun:

Examples: sisters, hats, wizards

But there are exceptions. Nouns that end in *s*, *ss*, *sh*, *ch*, or *x* add *es* to form the plural. Some nouns ending in *o* add *es*.

Examples: porches, kisses, lashes, churches, foxes, tomatoes

Nouns ending in *f* or *fe* (but not *ff*) change the ending to *ve* and add *s*.

Examples: knives, selves

Nouns ending in *y* change the *y* to *i* and add *es* to form the plural.

Examples: parties, skies

But when the *y* is preceded by a vowel (*a*, *e*, *i*, *o*, *u*), then just add *s*.

Examples: highways, boys

Irregular nouns do not add an *s* at all but rather change internally to indicate the plural.

Examples: men, children, teeth

Collective Nouns   **Collective nouns** refer to a group but are singular in form.

Examples: team, choir, family

They can take a singular or a plural verb, depending on if they refer to the group as a unit or the group as a collection of individuals.

Example: The choir was surprised that the director was late.

Example: The choir were always jostling for position on the risers.

Countable Nouns   **Countable nouns** name items that can be expressed in terms of numbers.

Examples: one textbook, six tomatoes, several elephants

Uncountable Nouns   **Uncountable nouns** express things that can't be counted, so do not form a plural.

Examples: fear, confusion, joy, literature, flour, water, grass, army, trash, oxygen

Exercises

1. Underline the nouns in the following sentences, and then identify if they are common, proper, singular, plural, irregular, collective, or uncountable.

    a. The so-called British Invasion began with the Beatles.

    _____

    _____

b. This rock band from Liverpool began releasing records in 1963.

_____

_____

c. By the end of that year, their music had made them famous in England.

_____

_____

d. Their fifth single, "I Want to Hold Your Hand," skyrocketed to the top of the British charts.

_____

_____

e. One critic said they were the greatest composers since Beethoven.

_____

_____

2. Underline all the nouns in the following passage.

> But the excitement in England was tame compared to the welcome the Beatles received in the United States. The Beatles' manager, Brian Epstein, arranged for a performance on the popular Sunday evening television show, *The Ed Sullivan Show*. "I Want to Hold Your Hand" was now at the top of the charts in America, too. Ringo remembered that the four Beatles felt nervous and a bit sick during their flight to the United States. But when they landed at Kennedy Airport in New York, ten thousand screaming teenagers were on hand to greet them. More than seventy million Americans tuned into Ed Sullivan that Sunday. "Beatlemania," as the press called it, had taken hold of America.

PRONOUNS

Pronouns are substitutes for nouns, used instead of repeating the noun. They often indicate number and gender, and sometimes possession.

Personal Pronouns

Personal pronouns refer to people. They change form to show singular, plural, and whether they are used as the subject or an object of a sentence.

	singular	*plural*
subject	I	we
	you	you
	he, she, it	they

	singular	*plural*
object	me	us
	you	you
	him, her, it	them

Example: <u>I</u> am going to the theater tonight.

Example: Would <u>you</u> care to join me? If not, I will ask <u>him</u> to go.

Possessive Pronouns

Possessive pronouns show ownership.

singular	*plural*
my, mine	our, ours
your, yours	your, yours
his, her or hers, its	their, theirs

Example: The *Nutcracker* is <u>my</u> favorite ballet.

Example: Deanna said *Beauty and the Beast* was <u>hers</u>.

Indefinite Pronouns

Indefinite pronouns do not refer to a particular person, place, or thing. Examples are <u>anyone</u>, <u>someone</u>, <u>everyone</u>, <u>no one</u>, <u>each</u>. Indefinite pronouns are singular in number.

Example: I'll get tickets for <u>anything</u>, as long as it's a musical.

Example: <u>Someone</u> said most of the shows were standing room only.

Demonstrative Pronouns

Demonstrative pronouns refer to a specific thing or things. This type of pronoun points to one part of the whole and can be used with a noun or in place of a noun.

singular	*plural*
this	these
that	those

Example: <u>This</u> seat is good, but <u>that</u> seat in the front row is better.

Example: <u>These</u> tickets cost a lot.

Interrogative Pronouns

Interrogative pronouns are used when asking questions.

Example: <u>What</u> are the major differences between the movie version and the stage version of *The Lion King*?

Example: <u>Which</u> production is more colorful?

Example: <u>Whose</u> idea was this stage production anyway?

Example: <u>Who</u> designed the costumes for the stage production?

Relative Pronouns

Relative pronouns relate or correspond to another noun within the sentence. Relative pronouns are *who, which,* and *that.* These pronouns introduce **relative clauses,** which modify nouns.

Example: The Lion King, <u>which</u> started out as a Disney animated movie, is a wonderful stage production.

Example: Elton John, <u>who</u> has recorded hundreds of songs, did the music for *The Lion King.*

Example: The tickets <u>that</u> were sold for the first production of *The Lion King* are now collector's items.

Intensive Pronouns

Intensive pronouns end in *self* or *selves* and are added to a noun within the sentence to add emphasis or draw attention to it.

Example: The show <u>itself</u> had a simple plot, but the acting made it suspenseful.

Example: The actors <u>themselves</u> were surprised by the response to the production.

Reflexive Pronouns

Reflexive pronouns reflect the action back on the subject. Reflexive pronouns take the same form as intensive pronouns.

Example: The stage manager hurt <u>himself</u> when he fell into the scenery.

Example: I thought the actors lost <u>themselves</u> in their roles.

Exercises

1. Give an example of each of the following types of pronoun, and write a sentence using it.

    a. personal pronoun

b. possessive pronoun

_____

c. indefinite pronoun

_____

d. demonstrative pronoun

_____

e. interrogative pronoun

_____

f. relative pronoun

_____

g. intensive pronoun

_____

h. reflexive pronoun

_____

2. Return to the passage in Exercise 2 of the previous set (page 436) and underline every pronoun twice. Draw an arrow from each to the noun it refers to.

VERBS

Verbs are the action words in a sentence. They say what the noun is or does, or what is done to the noun.

Types of Verbs

Verbs indicate action by or the condition of a noun. Some are used with the main verb to indicate time or tense.

Action Verbs   **Action verbs** specify the action taken or received by a noun. They are usually the main verbs of a sentence.

Example: Susan <u>walked</u> to the art museum.

Example: The guard <u>said</u> the building was closed and <u>waved</u> her away.

Example: Susan <u>protested</u> and <u>stamped</u> her feet, for she <u>wanted</u> to do some research that afternoon.

Linking Verbs   **Linking verbs** connect the noun to a further description of its condition. Most often, linking verbs are a form of the verb <u>to be</u>. Linking verbs are also verbs that describe the five senses at work, such as <u>look</u>, <u>sound</u>, <u>smell</u>, <u>taste</u>, <u>feel</u>, <u>become</u>, <u>appear</u>, or <u>seem</u>.

Example: Susan <u>felt</u> tired after walking to the museum.

Example: She <u>was</u> sure she would never get her research done.

Example: Time <u>seemed</u> to be passing quickly.

Helping Verbs   **Helping verbs** are used in combination with other verb forms to express time or tense or obligation. Forms of the verbs *to be* and *have, do, should, could, would, shall, will,* and *may* are the most common helping verbs.

Example: Susan's research paper <u>is</u> focused on Van Gogh's paintings.

Example: If the museum <u>is</u> closed, she <u>could</u> go to the library.

Example: Susan <u>did</u> not think the assignment was an easy one.

Example: She <u>will</u> finish her research before she starts to write.

Tenses

The **tense** of a verb is its built-in indication of time—past, present, or future.

Present Tense   The **present tense** is a verb form indicating that the action is happening now. Often, these verbs have an *s* or *es* ending.

Example: Susan <u>thinks</u> the museum <u>is</u> the only place to find out more about Van Gogh's work.

Past Tense   The **past tense** is a verb form indicating that the action happened in the past. Often, a verb shows past tense by adding *ed* to the end of the verb.

Example: Susan <u>walked</u> back home after her disappointing trip.

Future Tense   The **future tense** is a verb form indicating that the action will happen in the future. The future tense is formed by the addition of the helping verbs *shall* or *will*.

Example: Next time, Susan <u>will</u> know to begin her research with the Internet.

Irregular Verbs

Some verbs do not follow the rules of endings when their tenses change. For example, the present tense *Susan thinks* does not become *Susan thinked* in the past tense but rather *Susan thought*. Verbs that do not follow the rules when changing tenses are called **irregular verbs**.

Irregular Verbs

Present Tense	Past Tense	Past Participle
begin	began	begun
bite	bit	bitten
blow	blew	blown
bring	brought	brought
buy	bought	bought

Present Tense	Past Tense	Past Participle
choose	chose	chosen
draw	drawn	drawn
drink	drank	drunk
eat	ate	eaten
fight	fought	fought
fly	flew	flown
give	gave	given
go	went	gone
hide	hid	hidden
know	knew	known
lay	laid	laid
lie	lay	lain
ride	rode	ridden
ring	rang	rung
rise	rose	risen
run	ran	run
see	saw	seen
shake	shook	shaken
sing	sang	sung
sink	sank	sunk
sit	sat	sat
speak	spoke	spoken
steal	stole	stolen
stick	stuck	stuck
swim	swam	swum
swing	swung	swung
take	took	taken
teach	taught	taught
tear	tore	torn
think	thought	thought
throw	threw	thrown
wake	woke	waked
wear	wore	worn
win	won	won
write	wrote	written

Number

Verbs take a singular or plural form, depending on the subject (noun) to which they are connected.

Example: My child <u>plays</u> in her sandbox all morning. (singular to agree with singular subject *child*)

Example: Children <u>play</u> on the beach all afternoon. (plural to agree with plural subject *children*)

Notice that in the singular for the third person, present tense, most verbs end in *s*.

Exercises

1. Give an example of each of the following verb types, and write a sentence using it.

   a. action verb

   _____

   b. linking verb

   _____

   c. helping verb

   _____

   d. present tense verb

   _____

   e. past tense verb

   _____

   f. future tense verb

   _____

2. Return to the passage in Exercise 2 of the first set of exercises (page 436) and circle every verb. In the margin, identify the kind and tense of each.

MODIFIERS

Sentences often contain words that identify and describe nouns and verbs. These words are called **modifiers**. There are two types of modifiers: adjectives and adverbs.

Adjectives

Adjectives describe or limit nouns and pronouns by adding detail.

Example: My <u>young</u> nephew is obsessed with the <u>bright yellow</u> Pokémon named Pikachu.

The nouns *nephew* and *Pokémon* are modified by placing descriptive words in front of them; these show that the nephew is young and that the Pokémon named Pikachu is bright and yellow.

Other examples: soft, beautiful, wobbly, tall, dented, creamy, rough

Pronouns as Adjectives   Possessive and demonstrative pronouns preceding nouns are also modifiers.

Examples: my hair, his guitar, their window, this shoe, these apples, those tunes

Adverbs

While adjectives modify nouns, **adverbs** modify verbs or the action in a sentence. They often end in *ly,* as with *quickly.* Adverbs can also modify adjectives and other adverbs.

Example: Steven's collection of trading cards has grown <u>quickly</u> within the past few months.

Example: He <u>eagerly</u> sells and trades with his friends.

Example: His brother Chris is the <u>only</u> other family member, though, who also collects trading cards.

Example: Chris takes his collection <u>very seriously</u>.

Exercises

1. Underline the adjectives in each of the following sentences. Underline articles twice.

   a. Santa's fluffy, thick beard tickled the young boy's round face.

   b. Seventeen strong people are needed to control the Thanksgiving Day parade float.

   c. A water hole during the dry season is the best place to find wild animals.

   d. Cool, clear water flowed over the rocks and under the covered bridge.

   e. Yesterday's newspapers are filed with old news, but old newspapers are filled with history.

  f. Journalism has been called the "rough cut" of history.

  g. These bananas were yellow yesterday, but this morning I noticed they were turning soft and black.

2. Write your own sentences using the adjectives below.

  a. red, spicy, dark

  _____

  _____

  b. cold, clicking, wet

  _____

  _____

  c. musty, orange, microscopic

  _____

  _____

  d. blue, red, yellow, strong, silky

  _____

  _____

  e. coarse, lanky, scrubbing, chartreuse

  _____

  _____

3. Underline the adverb in each sentence.

  a. A rescue mission began immediately after the plane went down.

  b. Silently, prayers were offered in support of the mission.

  c. After seven hours of searching, the divers moved farther and farther into the ocean.

  d. An hour later, someone spotted a figure barely moving on a piece of the plane.

  e. The pilot of the downed plane softly thanked the rescue crew.

4. Add an adverb to each of these sentences.

  a. The train moved along the track.

  b. The excess paint oozed down the wall.

  c. The marching band played the school's fight song.

  d. The crickets could be heard rubbing their legs together.

  e. In fact, all of the insect sounds drew our attention.

PREPOSITIONS

Words that demonstrate the relationship between two or more nouns are called **prepositions**. The thing, or noun, connected by the preposition to the subject is its **object**. Together, prepositions and their objects make **prepositional phrases**.

Example: Tammi finally had two front-row tickets <u>for</u> the Backstreet Boys concert <u>in</u> Philadelphia <u>after</u> waiting <u>about</u> two weeks.

Other examples: above, around, at, aside, beside, beyond, between, behind, in, inside, out, outside, through, throughout, under, up, with, within, without

Exercises

1. Underline the prepositional phrases in each sentence.
   a. There is at least one prepositional phrase within each sentence in this exercise.
   b. The briefcase with the leather straps is under the desk in Room 3B.
   c. Beyond the hill is the house that belonged to John's family.
   d. The actress with the bright red hair was in an episode of *The X-Files*.
   e. Every Friday night our family gathered in the living room to watch that show on television.

2. Connect the following nouns with prepositional phrases and then create sentences.

   Example: computer, file, history class

   The file <u>in the computer on the desk</u> disappeared <u>during history class</u>.

   a. CD player, toaster, television

   _____

   _____

   b. hat, wagon, horses, shotgun

   _____

   _____

   c. basketball, football, bat, shoes

   _____

   _____

d. textbook, beaker, lab table, chemical solution

_____

_____

e. school, gymnasium, bleachers, coach

_____

_____

CONJUNCTIONS

Conjunctions are words that connect parts of sentences or entire sentences. Three basic types of conjunctions are coordinating conjunctions, subordinating conjunctions, and adverbial conjunctions.

Coordinating Conjunctions

Coordinating conjunctions are words that connect words, phrases, or sentences that are grammatically equal. There are seven coordinating conjunctions.

Coordinating Conjunctions

Conjunction	Meaning	Example
and	connects two things that are equal or happen at the same time	Sally watched television, and I surfed the Internet.
but	shows a contradiction or unexpected turn of events	Sally watched Oprah, but she disliked the topic of discussion.
for	used when the second sentence explains the reason for the first sentence; has the same meaning as *because*	Sally didn't watch television, for she had homework to do.
nor	shows a negative choice or a choice where neither decision is viable	Sally didn't want to watch television, nor did she want to surf the Internet. (Note that Sally does not want to do either activity. Also note that the clause after the conjunction <u>nor</u> puts the helping verb in front of the subject.)

Conjunction	Meaning	Example
or	shows choice	Sally could watch television, or she could do her homework.
so	used for showing cause and effect when situations in the second clause occur due to situations in the first clause	Sally finished all of her homework, so she watched television to relax.
yet	similar in nature to <u>but</u>, but the contradiction is more extreme	Sally had homework to do, yet she watched television.

Subordinating Conjunctions

Subordinating conjunctions join clauses of sentences that are grammatically unequal. A **clause** is a sentence element that contains a noun and a verb. **Independent clauses** can stand alone and are complete in themselves. **Dependent clauses** are incomplete; they depend on an independent clause to make them complete. Here is where subordinating conjunctions come in. They join dependent clauses to independent clauses.

Example: I went to the Capitol <u>where</u> Congress was in session.

Note that "where Congress was in session" is a clause; it has both a noun *(Congress)* and a verb *(was)*. But it makes no sense by itself; it is a dependent clause. To complete its meaning, it needs the independent clause "I went to the Capitol."

There are many subordinating conjunctions. Most show time sequence. Others indicate cause, suggest where or when, show contrast, or set up conditions.

Subordinating Conjunctions

Conjunction	Indicates	Example
after	time sequence	After Sally watched television, she surfed the Internet.
although	contrast	Although Sally watched *Oprah*, she disliked the topic of discussion.
as	time sequence	As Sally watched television, she did her algebra homework.
as long as	time sequence	As long as Sally watched television, her brother stayed out of the room.
because	cause	Because Sally watched television, she did not finish her homework.

Continued

Conjunction	Indicates	Example
before	time sequence	Before Sally watched television, she called Tina to get the homework assignment.
even though	contrast	Even though Sally watched television, she got all the algebra problems right.
if	condition	If Sally watches television, she can't possibly do well on her homework assignments.
once	time sequence	Once *Oprah* is over, Sally will turn off the television.
since	cause	Since Sally watches so much television, her friends are less likely to call.
until	time sequence	Until Sally turns off the television, she won't read to Cora.
when	where or when	When Sally watches television, she can't hear anything you say to her.
where	where or when	Where there is a television, there you will find Sally.
while	time sequence	While Sally watched television, Tina finished her homework..

Adverbial Conjunctions

Adverbial conjunctions (also known as *conjunctive adverbs*) connect two independent clauses. Like coordinating and subordinating conjunctions, adverbial conjunctions show cause, addition, and contrast. Punctuation is important. A semicolon precedes the adverbial conjunction, and a comma generally follows.

Adverbial Conjunctions

Conjunction	Indicates	Example
consequently	cause	Sally watched television all night; consequently, she did not study for her history test.
furthermore	addition	Sally studied her history notes for two hours; furthermore, she decided not to watch television so she could read the textbook chapter again.

Conjunction	Indicates	Example
however	contrast	Sally thought she was prepared for the test; however, she did not pass it.
moreover	addition	Sally was discouraged about the failing grade; moreover, she wondered if she should drop the course.
nevertheless	contrast	Sally decided to stay in the course; nevertheless, she was uneasy in class and shy during discussions.
otherwise	contrast	Sally was determined to do better in history; otherwise, the tuition would be wasted.
therefore	cause	Sally reviewed her class notes daily; therefore, she did not have too much to memorize the night before the next test.

Exercises

1. List three of each of the following.

   a. coordinating conjunctions

   _____

   b. subordinating conjunctions

   _____

   c. adverbial conjunctions

   _____

2. Choose a coordinating conjunction, a subordinating conjunction, or an adverbial conjunction to complete each of the following sentences. Correct the punctuation if necessary.

   a. New York used to be the most populous state, _____ I think California is now.

   b. Cleveland _____ Buffalo are in what is called the Rust Belt.

   c. Industries in these cities have closed, _____ workers have lost their jobs.

   d. Some workers have moved away, looking for work; _____, others have stayed in their hometowns _____ tried to learn new skills.

   e. Industries have tended to gravitate toward the Sun Belt; _____, the populations of Sun Belt states have increased, too.

f. Either Rust Belt cities will have to attract new industry, _____ they will experience depopulation and a declining tax base.

g. Retirees also head toward Sun Belt states, _____ the cost of living is often less in this region, _____ the weather is often better.

INTERJECTIONS

We all use interjections when we talk with our friends. Wow! Pow! Holy Cow! These phrases aren't just in comic strips. **Interjections** are those short little words that attract attention. Most often, they're followed by exclamation points.

Example: <u>Wow</u>! I've just won the lottery!

Example: <u>Cool</u>! Let's go celebrate.

ARTICLES

There is one final part of speech—**articles.** These are the little words *a, an,* and *the* that appear before nouns.

Exercise

1. Add an appropriate interjection to the following sentences.

a. We have to cancel the game because of the rain.

b. I thought the test was tomorrow, not today.

c. Steven made the winning basket with only six seconds left in the final game of the championship.

d. Imagine winning 100 million dollars.

e. Did you see Franklin's new bike?

CHAPTER REVIEW

The basics or "tools" used to create sentences are nouns, pronouns, verbs, modifiers (adverbs and adjectives), prepositions, conjunctions, and interjections. These are the eight parts of speech.

Nouns name a person, place, thing, idea, event, emotion, or quality. Common nouns refer to groups or classes of things, while proper nouns identify specific people, places, or things. Proper nouns begin with a capital letter. Plural nouns are usually formed by the addition of *s,* but there are exceptions. Collective nouns refer to a group but are singular in form. Uncountable nouns express things that can't be counted, so do not form a plural.

Pronouns are substitutes for nouns, used instead of repeating the noun. They often indicate number and gender, and sometimes possession. Types of pronouns include personal pronouns, possessive pronouns, indefinite pronouns, demonstrative pronouns, interrogative pronouns, relative pronouns, intensive pronouns, and reflexive pronouns.

Verbs are the action words in a sentence. They say what the noun is or does, or what is done to the noun. They also indicate tense, or when that action is taking place. The three basic tenses are the past (verb adds *ed*), present (verb has an s ending in the singular), and future (needs a helping verb). Verbs that require more changes to show tense are called irregular verbs. Linking verbs, most often a form of *to be,* connect the noun to a further description of its condition. Helping verbs are used in combination with other verb forms to show tense or obligation.

Modifiers, words that identify and describe nouns and verbs, come in two basic types: adjectives, which modify nouns, and adverbs, which modify verbs and sometimes adjectives and other adverbs.

Prepositions demonstrate the relationship between two or more nouns. The thing, or noun, connected by the prepositions is its object. Together, prepositions and their objects make prepositional phrases.

Conjunctions connect parts of sentences or entire sentences. Three basic types of conjunctions are coordinating conjunctions, which connect words, phrases, or sentences that are grammatically equal; subordinating conjunctions, which join clauses of sentences that are grammatically unequal; and adverbial conjunctions, which connect two independent clauses.

Interjections are those short little words we use to get attention. Most often, they're followed by exclamation points.

Final Exercises

1. Read the following paragraph. Label each noun with *N,* each pronoun with *PN,* each verb with *V,* each adjective with *ADJ,* each adverb with *ADV,* each preposition with *P,* each conjunction with *C,* and each interjection with *I.* Draw an arrow between each pronoun and the noun it replaces.

Why has the world moved to e-mail? I know it is fast, and I know it can save paper, too. It just seems that we are missing out on something very important: spending time with people. When you write a letter, you are forced to sit down with your favorite pencil or shiny, new pen, and some very special, hand-picked stationery. A lot of thought went into making sure these materials were just right. A business letter doesn't belong on scented, flowery pink paper. On the other hand, a thank-you note doesn't belong on stiff, yellow legal pad paper, either. The idea here is that you spent time creating something unique before you sent it. Nothing like this happens with e-mail. Contacting friends by telephone is the best way to spend time with others. A friendly voice at the other end of the telephone can brighten a very dreary day at the office. If you are at home, that phone call can last for hours. A call can make business transactions run more smoothly. Everyone responds to human contact in a positive way. We should make contact and forget email.

2. Using a paragraph or essay you have written recently, label each noun with *N*, each pronoun with *PN*, each verb with *V*, each adjective with *ADJ*, each adverb with *ADV*, each preposition with *P*, each conjunction with *C*, and each interjection with *I*. Draw an arrow between each pronoun and the noun it replaces.

25

MAKING THE "TOOLS" WORK: Sentences

The parts of speech described in Chapter 24 are only "tools" of grammar. The place where we put these tools to work is in the **sentence**, the combination of words that is the basic unit of language. This chapter explains how sentences work and how fix those that don't. It also challenges you to recognize and correct common grammatical errors. Grammatical rules are signaled for you by a ▸.

SIMPLE SENTENCES

A **simple sentence** is composed of a single **independent clause**, which is a set of related words expressing a complete thought. It includes a subject and a verb as well as additional words such as an object (noun or pronoun), phrases, and adjectives. It can be short or long.

Example: Dogs bark.

Example: Small, high-strung dogs sometimes bark loudly in the middle of the night.

Subject

The **subject** of a sentence acts or is acted upon, or is described or identified. It is the doer of the action in the sentence. Subjects are usually nouns or pronouns. To identify the subject of the sentence, ask, "Who or what is doing the action?"

Example: <u>Franklin</u> is lost without his mobile phone.

Example: <u>He</u> has had one since he started working at night.

Example: The <u>phone</u> allows his sick grandmother to contact him.

Simple Subjects   **Simple subjects** are usually one word.

Example: <u>People</u> are starving in many parts of the world.

Compound Subjects   A **compound subject** is more than one linked noun or pronoun that relates to the same action (verb) within a sentence.

Example: <u>Franklin</u> and his <u>grandmother</u> live together.

Example: Either <u>Franklin</u> or his <u>brother</u> does the daily household chores.

Delayed Subjects   In some sentences, the subject is not at the beginning but in the middle or even at the end of the sentence. These are called **delayed subjects**; they often are found when the sentence begins with *here, there, where,* or *it*.

Example: After the newsreels and the coming attractions came the <u>feature presentation</u>.

Example: There are <u>several previews</u> before this movie.

Example: Here are your <u>popcorn and drink</u>.

***–ing* Subjects**   A verb ending in *–ing* and used as a noun, with or without additional words, can be the subject of a sentence. These *–ing* **words** are called **gerunds**.

Example: <u>Showing</u> the premiere of a new show after the Super Bowl usually boosts ratings.

Example: <u>Singing</u> is my favorite way to relax.

Infinitive Subjects   A verb preceded by the word *to* is an **infinitive**. Because an infinitive can function as a noun, it can be the subject of a sentence.

Example: <u>To sing</u> just sets my mind at ease.

Verbs

The **verb** is the action word in the sentence.

Simple Verb   A **simple verb** is a single verb.

Example: Jerold <u>ran</u>.

Compound Verb   A **compound verb** is more than one verb expressing actions relating to the subject.

Example: Jerold <u>ran</u> to the pizzeria, <u>picked up</u> his order, and <u>paid</u> for it with cash.

Agreement between Subjects and Verbs

In a sentence, the subject and verb must agree in number. When you revise something you've written, study each sentence to be sure that its subject and verb work together.

Here are some guidelines:

▸ Subjects and verbs must agree in number. If they don't, adjust the verb to fit the subject.

Example: <u>Wendy is</u> a victim of peer pressure.

▸ If the subject is singular and in the third person, the verb adds an *s* at the end. If the subject is plural, the plural verb does not end with an *s*.

Example: <u>Wendy wears</u> clothes from discount stores. (singular)

Example: The <u>actors</u> from her favorite television shows <u>wear</u> clothes from Abercrombie and Fitch. (plural)

Example: A <u>boy</u> at school <u>teases</u> Wendy about her clothes. (singular)

Example: <u>Boys</u> at school <u>tease</u> Wendy about her clothes. (plural)

▸ Even if words or phrases or clauses come between them, a subject and verb must agree.

Example: The <u>teasing</u>, which is really cruel, <u>makes</u> Wendy feel self-conscious.

▸ A compound subject connected by *and* takes a plural verb.

Example: Wendy's <u>counselor</u> and <u>history teacher have noticed</u> how uncomfortable she is.

▸ A compound subject connected by *or* or *nor* takes a singular verb.

Example: Neither the <u>counselor</u> nor the <u>teacher has reprimanded</u> the boys.

▸ If the subject closest to the verb is plural, then the verb is plural.

Example: <u>Wendy</u> or <u>her parents need</u> an appointment with the principal.

▸ Indefinite pronouns take a singular subject.

Example: <u>Everyone</u> in Wendy's history class <u>senses</u> her humiliation.

▸ Collective nouns designating a group as unit take a singular verb.

Example: The <u>class is</u> sympathetic to her.

▸ Collective nouns implying a collection of individuals take a plural verb.
Example: The <u>faculty are</u> divided on matters regarding student life.

Objects

The **object** receives the action of the verb in a sentence. It is always a noun or a pronoun. Prepositions also take objects.

Direct Objects   A **direct object** receives the action of an action verb. In the most common sentence structure, the direct object follows the verb.

Example: Troy picked up his <u>snowboard</u>.

Example: The skiers criss-crossed the <u>slope</u> behind him.

Indirect Objects   An **indirect object** designates to or for whom the verb's action is performed. Sometimes, but not always, the indirect object is preceded by *to* or *for*. A sentence can have both a direct and an indirect object.

Example: Troy gave his <u>ski instructor</u> a high-five after he negotiated the course without falling.

Example: The ski instructor waved <u>to Troy</u>, but Troy was already on the lift.

Objects of Prepositions   The noun or pronoun to which a preposition connects in a prepositional phrase is called the **object of a preposition**.

Example: Troy felt his legs give out <u>under him during the last run of the day</u>.

Exercises

1. For each sentence, put an *S* above the subject, a *V* above the verb, a *DO* above the direct object, (if any), and an *IO* above the indirect object (if any). Some sentences have more than one of these elements.

   a. It can be difficult to upgrade or repair your computer these days.

   b. The machines are designed to take a lot of use.

   c. My computer is three years old and is already obsolete.

   d. Will they make a computer that will never go out of style?

   e. Waiting for that day would be a waste of time.

   f. Calling a tech support center or buying a new computer may be the answer to my problems.

   g. I hate to be manipulated by companies that only have new sales in mind.

2. Check subject and verb agreement in each of the following sentences; correct any errors you find.

   a. *Thelma and Louise* appeal to women, but I'm not sure how many men liked the movie.

   b. To run away from responsibilities seem like a good idea, or at least a good fantasy.

   c. The ending of the movie is sad.

   d. When I saw it, everyone in the movie theater were upset.

e. As in all movies with a strong emotional impact, the audience walked out silently.

f. My friends and I have wanted to rent the movie and to see it again.

g. Neither they nor I has found a video rental store that carries it.

Active and Passive Voice

A verb's **voice** tells whether the subject is the actor of the sentence or is being acted upon. In **active voice**, the subject performs the action and is generally more important than the direct object of the sentence. In **passive voice,** the subject is acted upon.

Example: Marissa took back her overdue library books yesterday. (active)

Example: The five overdue library books were taken back by Marissa yesterday. (passive)

Notice how many more words the passive voice uses to make the same statement. Passive voice verbs always need helping verbs. Generally, the active voice is simpler and stronger.

› For stronger writing, use the active voice rather than the passive voice.

The passive voice is used when the person or thing performing the action is not named or does not need to be prominent.

Example: The potholes in the road were fixed yesterday.

Exercises

1. Read the following sentence. Put an *A* in front of active voice sentences and a *P* in front of passive voice sentences.

_____ a. One of the greatest film epics of all time is *Gone with the Wind*.

_____ b. The film was based on a book by Margaret Mitchell.

_____ c. Movie stars like Bette Davis, Tallulah Bankhead, Lana Turner, and Katherine Hepburn were considered for the role of Scarlett.

_____ d. But the role was eventually signed by Vivien Leigh, a British stage actress who had never been in an American film.

_____ e. Though she and the male star, Clark Gable, were reputed to have "no chemistry," Leigh was spectacular as Scarlett.

_____ f. Leigh got the Academy Award for Best Actress.

_____ g. *Gone with the Wind* was awarded Best Picture of 1939.

2. Recast the following passive voice sentences in the active voice. Some sentences you can just switch around, but others you will have to rewrite from scratch. One is probably best left in the passive voice.

a. The movie rights were sold to David O. Selznick by Margaret Mitchell for $50,000.

_____

b. The filming was begun with the scene of the burning of Atlanta.

_____

c. The sets had been used before, in the movie *King Kong*.

_____

d. At the premiere, stars in open cars riding down Macon Highway and Peachtree Street in Atlanta were cheered by 300,000 spectators.

_____

e. The movie was watched by President Franklin D. Roosevelt at the White House a week and a half later.

_____

COMPOUND SENTENCES

Two independent clauses can be combined to make one **compound sentence**. The clauses are joined by coordinating conjunctions, semicolons, or adverbial conjunctions.

Coordinating Conjunctions

Coordinating conjunctions connect two sentences into a single compound sentence. The coordinating conjunctions are *and, but, for, nor, or, so,* and *yet*. When combining two sentences with a coordinating conjunction, change the ending punctuation of the first sentence to a comma, then add the conjunction and the second sentence.

Example of two sentences: Survivor is a popular show. Giselle doesn't watch it.

Two sentences combined: Survivor is a popular show, but Giselle doesn't watch it.

Example of two sentences: He went to the mall last night. He came home with the latest video game system.

Two sentences combined: He went to the mall last night, and he came home with the latest video game system.

▸ Place a comma before the coordinating conjunction in a compound sentence.

Semicolons

Semicolons connect two complete sentences without any conjunction. When using semicolons, be sure that the two sentences you want to join are complete, of equal rank, and relate closely to each other.

Example: Enterprise is a popular show; it has been renewed for another season.

‣ Place a comma between independent clauses in a compound sentence that is not joined with a conjunction.

Adverbial Conjunctions

Adverbial conjunctions (also known as *conjunctive adverbs*) can be used at the connection of complete sentences. This conjunction shows how the two sentences relate to each other—through cause, addition, or contrast. The sentences are separated by a semicolon or a period, and a comma follows the adverbial conjunction.

Example: Frank spends all of his spare money on comic books; <u>therefore</u>, he has quite a large collection.

Example: Saturday is an exception, <u>however</u>; it isn't usually possible to go to three concerts on one night.

‣ When two sentences are joined with an adverbial conjunction, place a semicolon before or after the adverbial conjunction, (wherever the separation should be strongest), and a comma on the other side.

Exercises

1. Combine the following sentences into compound sentences, using coordinating conjunctions or adverbial conjunctions. Be sure to punctuate the sentences correctly.

   a. Basketball is a popular sport. It is the state of Indiana's favorite sport.

   b. In Indiana, every garage or country barn has a hoop. Every hoop sees action every day.

   c. College games attract huge audiences. High school games attract even larger audiences.

   d. Everyone in the state follows the high school playoffs. High school players become household names.

   e. In the old days, playoff games were broadcast by loudspeakers on the streets. People would stop to listen.

   f. Today the games are televised. People do not gather on the streets. They do not seem so excited.

   g. High school basketball in Indiana will always be known as "Hoosier Hysteria." Hoosiers are crazy about basketball.

2. The following paragraph is boring for its parade of simple sentences. Make some of the sentences compound by using coordinating conjunctions, semicolons, or adverbial conjunctions. You can also change some verbs if you want.

> Ronald Reagan was a movie star before he was president. He was a sports announcer and baseball writer in Des Moines. He left Des Moines for Hollywood. He arrived in Hollywood in 1937. He had major roles in the movies *Knute Rockne* and *Kings Row.* In *Bedtime for Bonzo*, his costar was a chimpanzee. He was president of the Screen Actors Guild. Later he was president of the United States.

COMPLEX SENTENCES

While compound sentences combine two independent clauses that are equal, **complex sentences** are composed of an independent clause and a dependent clause. Like an independent clause, a **dependent clause** has a subject and a verb, but it begins with a dependent word (subordinate conjunction or relative pronoun) and cannot stand alone. It gives additional information about the independent clause to which it is connected. A **relative clause** is a dependent clause introduced by a relative pronoun, such as *who* or *which*.

Example: We saw the new Broadway musical. (independent clause, full sentence)

Example: After we had dinner at the Savoy. (dependent clause, sentence fragment)

Example: We saw the new Broadway musical after we had dinner at the Savoy. (complex sentence)

Example: We saw the new Broadway musical, which was the most popular show on the circuit that spring. (complex sentence)

Dependent clauses can come either before or after the independent clause, depending on which idea you want to emphasize. However, keep in mind that the dependent clause generally conveys the less important content.

Example: After we saw the Broadway musical, we stopped for a bite to eat.

Example: We stopped for a bite to eat after we saw the Broadway musical.

‣ If the dependent clause comes before the independent clause, place a comma between the two clauses.

‣ Place a comma before relative clauses beginning with *who* or *which*, but not *that*.

Exercises

1. Connect the first sentence in each sentence pair with the last sentence using coordinating, subordinating, and adverbial conjunctions. Some of your sen-

tences will be compound, and some will be complex. Please note that, in some cases, a variety of conjunctions can be used.

  a. Soccer is a popular sport in Europe. It is becoming more popular in the United States.

  b. In soccer, there is no tackling. Nobody wears shoulder pads.

  c. In American football, all the players get tackled. Shoulder pads are a must.

  d. In American football, a player makes a touchdown. His team earns six points.

  e. In soccer, a player makes a goal. His team earns one point.

  f. Football is played a certain way in Europe. Football is played differently in the United States.

  g. Soccer has spread from Europe to the United States. American football is rarely played in Europe.

2. Rewrite the paragraph on Ronald Reagan in Exercise 2 on page 460, this time using compound and complex sentences.

3. Connect at least ten of the sentences within the paragraph below using coordinating, subordinating, and adverbial conjunctions to make compound or complex sentences. Feel free to reorganize sentences when necessary.

> Living without a car is easier than most people think. It may even lead to a better way of life. You own a car. You have to pay for the gas. Gas prices continue to soar. Keeping gas in your car can get expensive. You don't own a car. You don't have that expense. Another factor is public transportation. Cars are convenient. Buses and taxis can get you where you need to go. They are also less expensive than maintaining a car. Riding a bus gives you time to read or organize your day. Last, not having a car means you can be healthier. You can walk just about anywhere in town. You can ride your bike. This way, you can get exercise. You can also get where you need to be. Not owning a car can be a liberating experience.

4. Add the correct punctuation to the sentences in the following paragraph.

> Almost every movie carries a rating but most moviegoers don't know what the ratings mean or how they are assigned to a movie. The rating system can seem quite interesting yet it is very simple. A movie is made. Neither the filmmakers nor the studio can influence the rating for the movie is submitted to a ratings committee. This committee invites volunteers of different ages, genders, socioeconomic backgrounds, and races to watch the movie. The volunteers are given guidelines for each rating so they have something to follow in making their decision. The volunteers assign the movie a rating (G, PG, PG-13, R, or NC-17) and their work is done. The filmmakers are told of the decision of the committee. The majority of the movie people don't challenge the rating however those who are not happy have a choice. They can challenge the ratings board or edit the movie for a different rating. Many simply edit the offending parts and release the movie

with the altered rating. Directors have been known to challenge an NC-17 rating for it can limit the box-office potential of a movie. As a rule most movie distributors won't send movies rated NC-17 to theaters, however, sometimes even these movies get shown.

5. Take a paragraph you have written and find sentences that can be combined. Choose any combining style—compound or complex—and join the sentences. Make sure the sentences that are joined relate to each other and that appropriate punctuation is used.

SENTENCE STRUCTURE AND FUNCTION

Sentence structure is often determined by function. Sentences that ask questions, for example, are arranged in a different way from those that make statements.

Declarative Sentences

A **declarative sentence** makes a statement. Normally, the subject comes first, then the verb, and then the direct object.

Example: Cora took her niece to the waterfront to watch the boats.

Example: They did not notice the storm brewing in the west.

Interrogative Sentences

An **interrogative sentence** asks a question. Normally, the first word is an interrogative pronoun (*what, which, who, whose*) or another question word (*when, where, why,* or *how*), followed by the verb and then the subject.

Example: When did you get to school this morning?

Example: How long did it take you to log on?

Example: Was it below freezing on New Year's Eve?

▸ Place a question mark at the end of an interrogative sentence.

Imperative Sentences

An **imperative sentence** makes a command. Usually, the first word is a verb that specifies the action to be taken. The subject, however, often isn't stated but is understood to be *you*, the person addressed, who is to do the action specified.

Example: Go get help!

Example: Hand in your essay by the end of class today.

Example: Please go away.

When the emotion is strong, as in the first example above, imperative sentences end with an exclamation point.

Exclamatory Sentences

An **exclamatory sentence** is a declarative sentence that is so full of emotion it is followed by an exclamation point rather than a period. Sometimes it is not really a sentence but an interjection.

Example: I missed the opening episode of *West Wing* last night!

Example: Rats! I missed the opening episode of *West Wing* last night!

‣ Place an exclamation point at the end of an exclamatory sentence.

Exercises

1. Identify each of the following sentences as declarative (*D*), interrogative (*Int*), imperative (*Imp*), or exclamatory (*E*). Add the correct final punctuation.

_____ a. What do you think is the greatest movie of all time

_____ b. I vote for *Citizen Kane*

_____ c. No No *Gone with the Wind* is the greatest

_____ d. Tell me your opinion

_____ e. Which movie had the biggest box-office draw

_____ f. Who knows. They were both so long ago

2. Write one of each of the following types of sentences. Underline the subject, and circle the verb. Notice their relative positions.

a. declarative

_____

b. interrogative

_____

c. imperative

_____

d. exclamatory

_____

USING PRONOUNS CORRECTLY

Pronouns can make your sentences read smoothly or bring them to a screeching halt as the reader tries to find out what noun your pronoun is replacing. To work, each pronoun must agree in number, and sometimes in gender, with the noun it refers to. In the following sentence, underline the pronoun, and draw an arrow to the noun it replaces.

Example: John forgot his book.

In this example, there is no mistaking who is meant by *his*: it refers to *John*.

But pronouns are not always so easy to use. The following sections will help you make pronouns and **antecedents**—the nouns they refer to or replace—agree, and show you how to avoid embedding gender bias in your use of pronouns.

Pronouns and Antecedents

Usually, a pronoun refers to the nearest noun—but some sentences are complicated.

Example: My father told <u>his</u> brother that <u>he</u> had been a fool.

In this sentence, it is not clear if the father or the brother had been a fool. In such cases, it's best to rewrite the sentence.

Better: My father told his brother, "I've been a fool."

▸ The antecedent of a pronoun must be unmistakable; if it is uncertain, rewrite the sentence.

Agreement in Number

If a noun is singular, any pronoun that refers back to it has to be singular, too. If a noun is plural, the pronoun must be plural.

Example: The band conductor waved <u>his</u> arms in panic.

Example: The trombone players noticed that one of <u>their</u> number had fallen.

▸ Pronouns must agree in number with the noun they replace.

Collective Nouns   Remember that collective nouns refer to a group but are singular in form. If they designate a group as unit, any pronouns that refer to them must be singular.

Example: The <u>team</u> <u>was</u> depressed after losing <u>its</u> last game of the season.

However, if the collective noun designates a collection of individuals acting separately, any pronouns must be plural.

Example: The <u>team</u> <u>were</u> blaming each other for <u>their</u> loss.

▸ Pronouns referring to collective nouns can be singular or plural, depending on how the collective noun is used.

Indefinite Pronouns   Remember that indefinite pronouns are singular, so pronouns that refer to indefinite pronouns must be singular, too. Fill in the missing pronoun in the following sentence.

Example: Everyone was required to turn in ＿＿＿＿＿＿＿ textbook.

Did you select *his, her,* or *their*? *Their* is definitely incorrect, because *everyone* is singular. *His* would be correct if *everyone* in the group referred to is male. *Her* would be correct if *everyone* in the group referred to is female. Most likely the group is mixed, so you'll need to use this formulation: *his or her.*

‣ Pronouns referring to or replacing indefinite pronouns must be singular.

Agreement in Gender

‣ Pronouns must agree in gender with the nouns they replace.

Quite obviously, pronouns must be the same gender as their antecedents.

Avoiding Pronoun Bias

Because some personal pronouns have gender, you must be careful how you use them. Don't let your pronoun choice suggest that you think men, or women, are dominant. What pronoun would you use in this sentence?

Example: The brain surgeon was hoping _____ would not be called for another emergency that night.

Don't assume that all brain surgeons are men! If you don't know if the surgeon is male or female, how would you fill in the blank?
Here's another example.

Example: Everyone in the class hoped _____ would not be called on first.

You might have decided to use *he or she.* That would be correct.

Example: Everyone in the class hoped he or she would not be called on first.

Another solution that sometimes works is to change the noun to a plural, because plural personal pronouns do not signify gender.

Example: All <u>those</u> in the class hoped <u>they</u> would not be called on first.

Example: All class <u>members</u> hoped <u>they</u> would not be called on first.

‣ To avoid pronoun bias, use personal pronouns that agree in gender with the noun they replace or convert the noun and pronoun to plural forms.

Pronouns as Subjects and Objects

Personal pronouns have different forms as subjects and objects. Make sure you choose the correct form.

Pronouns as Subjects   For subjects of sentences, use the subject form of personal pronouns.

Example: When the telephone rang, <u>I</u> picked it up.

Example: <u>She</u> asked me to go to the movies with her.

Example: <u>We</u> decided to see the new Harry Potter movie.

Notice that pronouns that are the subjects of dependent clauses are in the subject form, too.

Example: You would think <u>I</u>'d recognize Lucinda's voice, but <u>I</u> didn't.

Example: We went a little early to the mall, for <u>we</u> knew the stores were having sales.

Example: Lucinda, <u>who</u> craves the latest fashions, found several two-for-one bargains.

▸ Use the subject form of personal pronouns for the subjects of independent and dependent clauses.

Pronouns as Objects   For objects in sentences, use the object form of personal pronouns.

Example: The big clock at the mall reminded <u>us</u> it was time for the show.

Example: The boys in the ticket line were noisy, and the manager scolded <u>them</u>.

Example: The woman in the ticket booth handed the tickets to Lucinda and <u>me</u>.

Example: Between you and <u>me</u>, I thought the scolding was not necessary.

Example: The manager told <u>us</u> to move along.

Sometimes, when there is more than one object, it helps to remove—temporarily—one of the objects so you can see more clearly which pronoun is right.

Example: Inside the theater, the boys were polite to Lucinda and _____

Example removing one object: Inside the theater, the boys were polite to <u>me</u>.

Correct pronoun: Inside the theater, the boys were polite to Lucinda and <u>me</u>.

▸ Use the object form of personal pronouns as direct objects, indirect objects, and objects of prepositions.

Who and *whom* deserve special explanation. Use *who* for the subjects of sentences and clauses, and *whom* when an object is needed.

Example: <u>Who</u> were those boys?

Example: I don't know <u>who</u> they were.

Example: To <u>whom</u> do you think their attentions were directed?

Dependent clauses starting with *who* or *whom* are particularly tricky. Start by finding the main verb of the dependent clause, and then look for its subject. That subject will be *who*, even if the dependent clause as a whole functions as an object to the main verb of the dependent clause.

Example: I thought they directed their attentions to <u>whoever</u> was sitting near them.

In this case, *whoever* is correct, because it is the subject of the dependent clause's verb, *was sitting.*
Sometimes it helps, again, to remove intervening words.

Example: Lucinda told me _____ she thought they liked.

Example removing intervening words: Lucinda told me <u>whom</u> they liked.

Correct pronoun: Lucinda told me <u>whom</u> she thought they liked.

In this case, *whom* is correct, because it is the object of *liked; they* is the subject of *liked.*

▸ For dependent clauses using *who* or *whom*, check the verb first. Its subject is *who*, and its object is *whom.*

Exercises

1. Circle the correct pronoun in the following sentences.
   a. The audience rose to (its, their) feet and screamed.
   b. Back in the men's locker room, everyone raised (his, their) arms and cheered.
   c. The coaches said the last season was (its, their) best.
   d. The team was united in (its, their) frenzy.
   e. Hank and I were glad (we, us) had decided to stick with sports (our, us) senior year.
   f. Coach Harvey congratulated Hank and shook (his, her, their) hand.
   g. He has been a mentor this year to (we, us).
2. Circle the correct pronoun in the following sentences.
   a. Sebastian and (I, me) are going biking after school.
   b. This is a favorite pastime for (we, us).
   c. The kids who play basketball at the park wave to (I, me) and Sebastian.
   d. Actually, they wave to (whoever, whomever) bikes on the path by the court.

e. We smile at (they, them) as we zoom by.

f. It gives (we, us) a thrill to go as fast as possible down the hill.

g. Sebastian slows down at the bottom, where there's a pothole that once made (he, him) fall.

3. Correct the pronouns in the following paragraph. You will need to rewrite some sentences to be sure pronoun antecedents are clear.

> My friend Karen and I spent last Saturday at the roller rink. The first pair of skates she rented were too small for her. The clerk at the rental desk said she could exchange it for another pair. This time, the clerk helped her try them on. She and her shoved the skate over her thick sock. The skate was still too small, so she got down a third pair, one size larger. This time the skates fit her perfectly. Then Karen and I went out onto the floor. They were playing a rock song with a powerful beat. We tried to keep in time to the music, but our concentration made us get in the way of whomever was close by. We decided to concentrate on us skating rather than on the music. Afterward a little kid who we almost tripped gave a weak smile to Karen and I. We thought we were doing a better job of staying out of the way of everyone, but they didn't always stay out of our way.

PROBLEM SENTENCES AND HOW TO FIX THEM

When revising your work, be aware of all the kinds of problems sentences can have. The most common ones to watch for are sentence fragments, run-ons, and comma splices.

Sentence Fragments

A complete sentence has a subject and a verb and expresses a complete thought. If any one of these is missing, what you have is not a sentence but a **fragment**. To discover fragments in your writing, ask yourself the following questions:

- Is there a verb? Is the verb complete?

If the answer is no, add a verb or complete the verb by adding a helping verb.

Example of a fragment: Sam Raimi <u>making</u> the new Spiderman movie.

Fragment fixed: Sam Raimi <u>is making</u> the next Spiderman movie.

- Is there a subject?

If the answer is no, add a subject or combine sentences.

Example of a fragment: Chang is happy. Finally saw the movie *Titanic.*

Fragment fixed: Chang is happy. He finally saw the movie *Titanic.*

Fragment fixed: Chang is happy because he finally saw the movie *Titanic.*

- Is a dependent clause standing alone, without an independent clause?

If the answer is yes, connect the dependent clause to an independent clause.

Example of a fragment: When he slid into home plate. Sean scored the winning run.

Fragment fixed: When he slid into home plate, Sean scored the winning run.

Example of a fragment: Because Delaney's team practiced every day for three weeks. The team got better.

Fragment fixed: Because Delaney's team practiced every day for three weeks, the team got better.

- Is a phrase or clause beginning with an *–ing* word (a gerund) or *to* followed by a verb (an infinitive) standing by itself?

If the answer is yes, connect the phrase or clause to an independent clause.

Example of a fragment: Hoping to end the rally. The manager replaced the pitcher.

Fragment fixed: Hoping to end the rally, the manager replaced the pitcher.

Example of a fragment: To win the championship game. Delaney's team needed a lot of practice.

Fragment fixed: To win the championship game, Delaney's team needed a lot of practice.

- Is an example standing by itself?

The phrase *for example* signals that more information is coming. Make sure that information is connected to a sentence. Write the sentence if you need to.

Example of a fragment: Delaney's team got better in many areas. For example, pitching, hitting, and fielding.

Fragment fixed: Delaney's team got better in many areas. For example, they improved their pitching, hitting, and fielding.

(Note that the collective noun *team* in these sentences is used as a plural noun, so the pronoun *their* is appropriate).

▸ Check every sentence to make sure it has a subject and a verb and expresses a complete thought.

Exercises

1. Place an *F* in the line beside the groups of words that are fragments. Place an *S* in the line beside the groups of words that are sentences.

    _____ a. Mark Price holds the NBA record for the best career in-season foul shot percentage.

_____ b. While the youngster's friends liked to try to shoot their foul shots.

_____ c. In the respectable overhand style.

_____ d. Judging by mechanics alone, this should be the case with just about every foul shot.

_____ e. Yet while Barry can easily sink nine out of ten shots, others fall short.

2. Rewrite the fragments in Exercise 1 as complete sentences.

3. Underline the fragments in the paragraph below. Then fix them.

> Using lots of trigonometry, Brancazio calculated the optimal angle of the arc from the free-throw line. If tossed at 32 degrees or less. The ball will likely hit the back of the rim. At angles greater than that, the ball has a chance. Of making a nice swish. The optimum angle, he calculated, is 45 degrees. Plus half the angle from the top of the player's hand to the rim. Of course. Lobbing a ball very high so that it comes down nearly straight into the basket. Would be the most efficient technique. But a shot like that is almost impossible to aim. His formula makes it possible for a player to shoot with the largest possible margin for error.

Run-ons

Run-ons occur when two or more sentences are placed together with no punctuation between them. To correct this problem, find the subject and verb for each sentence. Then focus on the point at which the first sentence ends and the second sentence begins. Add (1) a comma and a coordinating conjunction; or (2) an adverbial conjunction with a semicolon on one side and a comma on the other; or (3) a semicolon; or (4) a period, and capitalize the first word that follows. What you do depends on how, and how closely, the sentences are related.

Example of a run-on: The player made the free throw the team won the game.

Run-on fixed: The player made the free throw, and the team won the game.

Run-on fixed: The player made the free throw; consequently, the team won the game.

Run-on fixed: The player made the free throw; the team won the game.

Run-on fixed: The player made the free throw. The team won the game.

You can also make the first independent clause into a dependent clause by adding a subordinating conjunction.

Run-on fixed: When the player made the free throw, the team won the game.

▸ Two independent clauses cannot be in the same sentence together unless a coordinating conjunction, an adverbial conjunction, or a semicolon separate them. Alternatively, you can add a period and create two sentences.

Comma Splices

Comma splices mistakenly connect two independent clauses (sentences) with a comma. Remember, a comma is not strong enough to separate (or join) two independent clauses. To fix this problem, replace the comma with (1) a comma and a coordinating conjunction; or (2) an adverbial conjunction with a semicolon on one side and a comma on the other; or (3) a semicolon; or (4) a period, and capitalize the first word that follows. Note that these solutions are the same as for a run-on sentence.

Example of a comma splice: The player made the free throw, the team won the game.

Comma splice fixed: The player made the free throw, and the team won the game.

Comma splice fixed: The player made the free throw; consequently, the team won the game.

Comma splice fixed: The player made the free throw; the team won the game.

Comma splice fixed: The player made the free throw. The team won the game.

You can also make the first independent clause into a dependent clause by adding a subordinating conjunction.

Comma splice fixed: When the player made the free throw, the team won the game.

Exercises

1. Correct the run-ons and comma splices in the following sentences.

   a. Some people like baseball other people like basketball.

   b. I have always liked sports, I have never played them well.

   c. Watching baseball on television is fun, but I still like to go to the ballparks there is nothing like experiencing a live game.

   d. The crowd is constantly humming with excitement even if your team loses you are having a good time.

   e. Go to a ballpark on a summer afternoon you will fall in love with baseball.

2. Correct the run-ons and comma splices in the following paragraph.

   Professional basketball players are too good for the game. The shortest players are six feet tall and the rim is only ten or twelve feet high. Any good athlete that tall can jump that high. They have at least an hour or more to make hundreds of points, they make mistakes and millions of dollars. I think the officials should change the rules of basketball I think they should make the game a challenge for everyone. Put the hoops up higher, the players will have to jump further. Shorten the quarters to five minutes that will make players work harder to score so many points. Finally, instead of losing the ball, players could be fined for foul shots, double dribbling, and the like. When money is at stake, the players will change the way they play.

CHAPTER REVIEW

Sentences are the basic units of paragraphs and essays. When you're revising, you need to pay attention to each sentence to make sure it is correct and effective. At its most basic, each sentence must have a subject and a verb and express a complete thought. A simple sentence is composed of a single independent clause.

The subject of a sentence—a noun or pronoun—acts or is acted upon, or is described or identified. Simple subjects are usually one word. A compound subject is more than one linked noun or pronoun that relate to the same action (verb) within a sentence. In sentences with delayed subjects, the subject is in the middle or even at the end of the sentence. These delayed subjects are often found when the sentence begins with *here, there, where,* or *it*. A verb ending in *–ing* and used as a noun (called a *gerund*), with or without additional words, can be the subject of a sentence. A verb preceded by the word *to* is an infinitive. It functions as a noun and can be the subject of a sentence.

The verb is the action word in the sentence. A simple verb is a single verb. A compound verb is more than one verb expressing actions related to the subject. The subject and verb of a sentence must agree in number.

The object receives the action of the verb in a sentence. It is always a noun or a pronoun. A direct object receives the action of an action verb. Generally, the direct object follows the verb. An indirect object designates to or for whom the verb's action is performed. Prepositions also take objects. The noun or pronoun to which a preposition connects in a prepositional phrase is called the object of a preposition.

A verb's voice tells whether the subject is doing the action of the sentence or is being acted upon. In active voice, the subject performs the action. In passive voice, the subject is acted upon. The passive voice is used when the person or thing performing the action is not named or does not need to be prominent. For stronger writing, use the active voice rather than the passive voice.

Two independent clauses can be combined to make one compound sentence. The clauses are joined by coordinating conjunctions, semicolons, and adverbial conjunctions. The coordinating conjunctions are *and, but, for, nor, or, so,* and *yet.* When combining two sentences with a coordinating conjunction, change the ending punctuation of the first sentence to a comma, and then add the conjunction and the second sentence. Semicolons connect two complete sentences without any conjunction. Be sure that the two sentences you want to join are complete, of equal rank, and relate closely to each other before using a semicolon. Adverbial conjunctions show how the two sentences relate to each other—through cause, addition, or contrast. The sentences are separated by a semicolon or a period, and a comma follows the adverbial conjunction.

While compound sentences combine two independent clauses that are equal, complex sentences are composed of an independent clause and a dependent clause. Like an independent clause, a dependent clause has a subject and a verb, but it begins with dependent words (subordinate conjunctions or relative pronouns). They give additional information about independent clauses to which they are connected, but they are not complete sentences. A relative clause is a dependent clause introduced by a relative pronoun, such as *who* or *which*.

Sentence structure is often determined by function. A declarative sentence makes a statement. The subject comes first, followed by the verb, and then the direct object. An interrogative sentence asks a question. The first word is an interrogative pronoun or another question word, followed by the verb and then the subject. An imperative sentence makes a command. The first word is a verb that specifies the action to be taken. The subject is understood to be *you*, the person addressed, even if it is not stated. An exclamatory sentence is a very emotional declarative sentence. It is followed by an exclamation point rather than a period. Sometimes it is not really a sentence but an interjection.

Pronouns can make your sentences read smoothly or stop them altogether. To work, each pronoun must agree in number, and sometimes in gender, with the noun it refers to. If collective nouns designate a group as unit, any pronouns that refer to them must be singular. If the collective noun designates a collection of individuals acting separately, any pronouns must be plural. Indefinite pronouns are singular, and pronouns that refer to indefinite pronouns must be singular. Avoid gender bias in selecting pronouns. Personal pronouns have different forms as subjects and objects. Make sure you choose the correct form.

When revising your work, watch for and correct sentence fragments, run-ons, and comma splices. A fragment is an incomplete sentence, missing a subject or a verb or not expressing a complete thought. Run-ons occur when two or more sentences are placed together with no punctuation between them. Comma splices mistakenly connect two independent clauses (sentences) with a comma. To correct these two problems, find the subject and verb for each sentence. Then, focus on the point at which the first sentence ends and the second sentence begins. From there, you can add a comma and a coordinating conjunction; or an adverbial conjunction with a semicolon on one side and a comma on the other; or a semicolon; or a period, and then capitalize the first word that follows. What you do depends on how closely the sentences are related.

Final Exercises

1. Read the following paragraph, underlining the subject of each sentence and circling the verb. Make sure the subjects and verbs agree; correct any errors you find. Then, add the correct punctuation throughout.

Was life easier fifty years ago than it is today Many people want us to think so however I bet that is not the case There has always been problems Not everybody remember them accurately Racism and sexism were on television and in the movies then Schools were violent as they are now There was problems in government as well The difference is that we know about the trouble sooner Through cable television and the Internet we can find out about the world instantly. Was life easier in the past Ask yourself that question the next time you study history or read a newspaper

2. Connect the first sentence in each sentence pair with the last sentence using coordinating, subordinating, or adverbial conjunctions. Some of your sentences will be compound, and some will be complex. Please note that, in some cases, a variety of conjunctions can be used. Correct any pronoun errors you find.

   a. *Die Another Day* features the exploits of British superspy James Bond. It also focuses on vanity.

   b. The movie features a fantastic machine. It can change anyone's appearance.

   c. In the movie, a general's son wants to have his face changed by the machine. The machine gets ruined.

   d. The transformation is only half complete. The machine blows up.

   e. The general's son blames James Bond for his disfigurement. He wants to kill him.

   f. James Bond may have caused the machine to explode. The man's twisted thinking is also responsible for his plight.

   g. James Bond has a better way to change appearances. Different actors have played him throughout the years.

3. Combine each of the following sentence pairs to make compound or complex sentences. Check subject-verb agreement for each sentence and make changes, if necessary.

   a. Reality-based television shows are very popular. Game shows are not.

   b. One reality-based show were *The Osbournes*. It feature the family life of music star Ozzy Osbourne.

   c. Another reality-based show is *Big Brother*. Cameras spies on people twenty-four hours a day, seven days a week.

   d. *Who Wants to Be a Millionaire?* was extremely popular. The game show was shown many times every week.

   e. People lost interest in the show. The show was canceled.

4. Read through the following paragraph, correcting fragments, run-ons, and comma splices whenever necessary.

   Robots may seem like things from a science-fiction movie. But they are real. If you look closely at the toys on the market. Many are robots.

Take any radio-controlled car. For example. The cars are operated by some-one with a controller, that is a type of robot. There are more advanced toys like RoboPets, they can interact with each other. Also, robots can be found in kitchen appliances. Such as coffee makers and washing machines. Coffee makers can make a perfect cup of coffee whenever you want it. Washing machines can be programmed. To add bleach or fabric softener at certain times as well. When you get in a new car. You are also using a type of robot. Lights can signal that a door is ajar. Or that you are low on fuel. Guidance systems can direct you to nearby hotels or diners. None of these machines rival Data or R2-D2 those robots are years away. The robots we have today. Are the androids of tomorrow.

5. Correct all the mistakes you find in the following paragraph.

The Japanese art of paper-folding which is known as origami requires patience, practice, and paper. Patience is needed because it take a long time to master the folding techniques and many different kinds of folds need to be learned. For example the pocket fold, the valley fold, and the mountain fold. It is one of the most difficult. Even with instructions it still take patience. To make the proper folds. Practice is also required. Before you begin an origami project you should read about it. There are many books about origami and these books contain a lot of information about the history of origami, folding techniques, and the origami models but information does not guarantee results. I have two books on the subject, I still have a hard time making a dinosaur. Finally, you need a lot of paper and it have to be a certain type. They cannot be heavy since heavy paper tend to be too bulky to fold. If the paper is too thin it can tear too easily and they will not hold the creases very well. Save flyers and junk mail. Which is printed on appropriate paper and use them for practicing your origami models. Its colors can make interesting patterns that happen by chance. But everything else about origami deserve your close attention. If you have enough patience, practice, and paper, you will be soon decorating your living area with beautiful paper flowers, paper candy dishes, and paper animals.

26

PUNCTUATION AND CAPITALIZATION

On the surface, punctuation might seem to be just little marks inside and at the end of sentences that help separate—and sometimes join—ideas. But punctuation does more than that. It reflects the dramatic intent of the writer, as if the sentences were being spoken. It also reflects the writer's emphasis by drawing attention to certain words, phrases, or complete sentences.

To use punctuation effectively, you must be familiar with the following: sentence endings (period, question mark, and exclamation point), commas, semicolons, colons, dashes and parentheses, quotation marks, apostrophes, and hyphens.

Capitalization works somewhat like punctuation—a shape sending a signal to the reader. This chapter covers capitalization, too.

SENTENCE ENDINGS

The mark of punctuation at the end of a sentence tells you something about the nature of the sentence. Choose your mark wisely.

Period (.)

▸ Place a **period** at the end of a declarative sentence.

Example: ER is television's top-rated medical drama of the season.

▸ Note that periods are also placed at the end of abbreviations.

Examples: Tex., Dec., Mr.

Question Mark (?)

▸ Place a **question mark** at the end of an interrogative sentence.

Example: Is *ER* television's top-rated medical drama?

Example: What is television's top-rated situation comedy?

Example: Is *Friends* television's top-rated situation comedy?

Exclamation Point (!)

› Place an **exclamation point** at the end of an exclamatory sentence.

Example: I missed the season finale of *ER*!

› Exclamation points can also be after interjections.

Example: Rats! I missed the season finale of *ER* last night!

Exercises

1. Place end punctuation on the following sentences.
   a. Charlie signed up for the basketball team
   b. What did Charlie do
   c. He signed up for the basketball team
   d. Can he play
   e. Hey There's Charlie now
   f. Did you make the team
   g. Yes
   h. Congratulations That is wonderful news

2. Write the appropriate type of sentence for the sentence ending.
   a. a sentence ending in a period

   _____

   _____

   b. a sentence ending in an exclamation point

   _____

   _____

   c. a sentence ending in a question mark

   _____

   _____

COMMAS (,)

Commas separate items in a series or dependent and independent clauses. More specifically, commas separate:

• items in a series
• clauses in compound sentences

- clauses in complex sentences
- additional information
- interrupters
- piled-on adjectives
- items in addresses
- items in dates
- salutations in informal letters

Items in a Series

▸ Use commas to separate two or more nouns, adjectives, adverbs, and clauses in a series.

Example: I can't watch television without my remote, a soda, potato chips, and the channel guide.

Example: My mother has to clear the table, put away the leftovers, wash the dishes, and sweep the floors before she can watch the evening news.

▸ Be aware that some items are so naturally linked that no comma should separate them.

Example: Steven likes honey and peanut butter and jelly on his sandwiches.

Clauses in Compound Sentences

▸ Place a comma before the coordinating conjunction in a compound sentence.

Example: Actress Helen Hunt starred in *What Women Want,* and she had a major role in *As Good as It Gets.*

▸ Place a comma after an adverbial conjunction.

Example: Harry Potter is very popular in the United States; however, he was created by a British author.

Clauses in Complex Sentences

▸ If the dependent clause comes before the independent clause, place a comma between the two clauses. Otherwise, no comma is used.

Example: Because the new video games are so popular, many stores can't keep them in stock.

Example: Many stores can't keep the new video games in stock because they are so popular.

▸ Place a comma before relative clauses beginning with *who* or *which*, but not *that*.

Example: Even dentists' offices, which are not usually popular with children, are now stocked with video games. The games that involve spies and violence are often requested.

Additional Information

▸ Commas can set off additional information that begins with an *–ing* word from the rest of a sentence.

Example: Maleeka was excited about receiving the new Harry Potter book for her birthday, jumping up and hugging her mother.

▸ Commas can also set off additional information contained in a prepositional phrase at the beginning of the sentence.

Example: Within hours, all of the Harry Potter novels had been sold.

▸ Commas separate *for example,* in any position, from the rest of the sentence.

Example: For example, the new Harry Potter movie drew huge audiences during the holidays .

Example: One of the laws affected by the Internet is the right to privacy law, for example.

Interrupters

▸ Interrupters that break the flow of a sentence are set off by commas.

Example: Everyone in my family, my father and older sister most of all, loves Harry Potter.

Piled-on Adjectives

▸ Place commas between piled-on adjectives.

Example: The new, outrageous CD by Britney Spears is difficult to find.

▸ Be sure not to separate adverbs from the adjectives they modify.

Example: The incredibly popular CD by Mos Def is difficult to find.

Items in Addresses

> In formal addresses, commas separate titles from names and cities from states. A basic address looks like this:

> Sherlock Holmes, Private Investigator
> 555 Baskerville Lane
> Hounds City, NM 10000

> Note that no comma appears between the state and the ZIP code. Also, be sure to place commas around states following city names within sentences.

> *Example:* New York, New York, is home for many television networks.

Dates

> In dates, use a comma to separate day from month and month from year.

> *Example:* Pink Floyd's new CD will be released January 1, 2004.

> Also, be sure to use commas around dates and months within sentences.

> *Example:* The movie *JFK* deals with the events that led to November 23, 1963, the day Kennedy was assassinated.

> However, a comma is not needed between a month or season and year in a sentence.

> *Example:* Martin Luther King gave his "I Have a Dream" speech at the Lincoln Memorial in August 1963.

Salutations in Letters

> In a personal informal letter (one to a friend, relative, or acquaintance), a comma is used after the greeting.

> *Example:* <u>Dear Frank,</u>

> We are really enjoying the islands. It is just like living *Survivor.* Thanks for watching the dog.

> Remember to place a comma after the complimentary close of your letter as well.

> *Example:* <u>Yours,</u>

> Susie and Bill

Exercises

1. Place commas in the appropriate places within each sentence.
   a. Stephen King writer of horror novels like *Salem's Lot* has written a number of screenplays.

b. King's chilling spine-tingling stories are not for the faint of heart.

c. "Rita Hayworth and Shawshank Redemption" "Apt Pupil" and "The Body" are three of King's short stories that have been made into movies.

d. At times short writings with strong emotional impact are better than longer works and for King this format has been successful.

e. Men women and older children all seem to enjoy King's horror stories.

f. Because King's *The Shining* examines family relationships both parents and children can relate to it but it is also especially frightening to children.

2. Place commas in the appropriate places within this paragraph.

When I go see a movie I want to see something thought-provoking entertaining and positive. I think that the same criteria should be used for children's movies. In May 1977 *Star Wars* hit the big screen. I was thirteen at the time and I thought that was the best movie ever made. It is fun to watch even now because even after all these years I still feel like a kid cheering and clapping when Luke Skywalker destroys the Death Star. Now that I have my own children I am very careful about what I let them watch. Movies like *The Iron Giant* for example or *The Shining Toy Story Tarzan* and *Star Wars Episode One: The Phantom Menace* seem to appeal to them but I am not sure they are safe for my children. My kids may play with all the electronic action figures or buy glow-in-the-dark easy-to-spot light swords but they won't see the movies until we have discussed them.

3. Write a sentence with at least one comma for each situation below.

a. (items in a series)

_____

_____

b. (piled-on adjectives)

_____

_____

c. (additional information)

_____

_____

d. (an interrupter)

_____

_____

e. (dates)

_____

_____

SEMICOLONS (;)

Semicolons are stronger separators than commas. They are used much less frequently, primarily when commas will not do.

Items in a Series

▸ Commas are generally used to separate items in a series, but when one or more of the items has a comma within it, semicolons are needed.

Example: Those who spoke out at the meeting were Clara Whitherspoon, senior class <u>president; Andy</u> Hamner, a spokesperson for the residence hall <u>advisors; and</u> Thom Frablin, a freshman.

Clauses in Compound Sentences

▸ Use semicolons to separate two closely related independent clauses in a compound sentence that are not joined with a coordinating or subordinating conjunction.

Example: Superman is published by DC <u>Comics; Black</u> Panther is published by Marvel Comics.

Remember, a comma in this position, between clauses, would produce a sentence error called a *comma splice*.

▸ When two independent clauses are joined with an adverbial conjunction, place a semicolon before or after the adverbial conjunction (wherever the separation should be stronger) and a comma on the other side.

Example: The dean said she was willing to listen; however, when she heard the first students express strong opinions, she dismissed the meeting without letting everyone speak.

Exercises

1. Combine the following sentences using a semicolon or a semicolon and an adverbial conjunction.

   a. Swimming in the city pool is a great activity.

      Swimming in a muddy waterhole is not.

      _____

      _____

   b. We can stay until the end of the ballet.

      We can leave now.

      _____

      _____

    c. Susie did not have such a great time at the Jimmy Buffet concert. Her purse got stolen.

_____

_____

    d. Everyone should know how to balance a checkbook. Patience and some math skills are all that is required.

_____

_____

    e. I finally saved enough money to take a computer course. The class was filled.

_____

_____

2. Place semicolons in the correct spots in the following sentences.
    a. We wanted to get breakfast at the restaurant however, they were only serving lunch.
    b. My stomach growled I needed something to eat.
    c. We finally found a good restaurant moreover, they were serving breakfast all day.
    d. I ordered two bacon and egg sandwiches, my favorite Steve had cereal and a bagel, which looked really good and Jeri ate three pancakes with mounds of butter and gallons of syrup.
    e. That breakfast was filling we didn't eat again until 5 p.m. that evening.

COLONS (:)

Colons are used to introduce a word, phrase, or clause that in some way explains or parallels the first clause in a sentence. They are also used to introduce quotations, to separate main titles from subtitles, and they follow the greeting in a formal business letter.

Statement of Explanation

▸ Use a colon to separate a sentence and its explanation.

Example: Just one movie has broken every box-office record to date: Titanic.

Example: Titanic seems to have everything: history, high drama, incredible special effects, and a love story that will make you weep.

Quotations

▸ Colons also are used to introduce long quotations (two sentences or more) or block quotes (paragraph length).

Example: The article in *Rolling Stone* observed: "Hip-hop has taken the strategies of grass-roots organizing and used them to sell records and images. The result is a fad that spread like wildfire."

Example: The author then goes on to comment on hip-hop musician activists:

> There are some well-publicized, star-sponsored operations like Puff Daddy's House, which finances camps and other activities for inner-city youth, and Lauryn Hill's Refugee Project, which also works with at-risk urban youth. But even these operations have been criticized—perhaps unjustly—for being vanity charity activities, not really informed by an overall social or political strategy. It is sometimes hard to separate ego from good will, or good publicity from good works.

Titles and Subtitles

▸ Colons separate titles from subtitles.

Example: On January 1, 2001, I watched *2001: A Space Odyssey.*

Salutations in Business Letters

▸ In a business letter addressed to someone you do not know or know only in a professional or office setting, use a colon following the salutation.

Example: Dear President Bush:

Exercises

1. Place colons in the appropriate spots below.
   a. *Genius The Life of Albert Einstein* was an inspirational book for me.
   b. I learned about the single most important element for intelligence imagination.
   c. Another book that I enjoyed was *Riding the Waves The Beach Boys and Their Music.*
   d. The author believed that the Beach Boys were a very influential group in the 1960s. He claimed "The Beach Boys were not only the leaders in the surfin' sound. Their antics popularized the California life-style, and their colorful shirts were worn from White Plains to the White House."
   e. For me, though, there was only one influential band at the time the Rolling Stones.

DASHES AND PARENTHESES

Like commas, dashes and parentheses can be used to set off additional information or interrupters from the rest of a sentence. Dashes are less of a break than parentheses, which indicate that the information within them is nonessential.

Dashes (—)

Dashes are somewhat stronger than commas but not as strong as parentheses in setting information off from the rest of the sentence.

▸ Use dashes to set off interrupters.

Example: NYPD Blue—a show that pushed many boundaries when it debuted—seems tame when compared to other television dramas these days.

▸ A single dash at the end of a sentence works much like a colon.

Example: The Beatles' most successful movie was also a hit song—*A Hard Day's Night.*

Parentheses ( )

Information that is unnecessary to the rest of the sentence can be set off in **parentheses**.

Example: Many people don't know that Patrick Stewart (Captain Jean-Luc Picard from *Star Trek: The Next Generation*) made his name in theater before acting on television and in movies.

Exercises

1. Place dashes or parentheses in the appropriate areas in the following sentences.
   a. Sally's dream a pair of diamond-studded earrings costs more than $30,000.
   b. Jonah her husband fainted when he saw the price.
   c. Diamonds often called "a woman's best friend" are for men, too.
   d. In fact, much of the jewelry worn by women earrings and bracelets are now being worn by men.
   e. Amber a fossil resin rather than a precious stone has been very popular in jewelry recently.
2. Combine the additional information with each sentence using dashes or parentheses.
   a. Sentence: The Internet is a great place to find information.

Additional Information: The Internet is a network of computers.

_____

_____

b. Sentence: Ilene's father signed autographs at the car dealership Saturday.
Additional Information: Her father used to play professional football.

_____

_____

c. Sentence: The building's walls were made to withstand any pressure, including a dynamite blast.
Additional Information: The walls are three bricks thick.

_____

_____

d. Sentence: The winning lottery ticket was sold at McGuffey's Market on Hudson Street.
Additional Information: The ticket was worth $20 million.

_____

_____

e. Sentence: The student's essay was published in *Newsweek*.
Additional Information: The title of the essay was "Schools and Weapons: A Dangerous Mix."

_____

_____

QUOTATION MARKS (" ")

Quotation marks set off statements from sources and words or phrases used in unusual ways (slang and other irregular words), and titles of magazine articles and short works of literature.

Quotations and Dialogue

▸ Place quotation marks around words, phrases, and entire sentences that come from other writers or sources.

Example: Football coach Vince Lombardi once said, "Winning isn't everything; it's the only thing."

▸ Conversations within a piece of writing, called *dialogue,* are treated like quotations.

Example: "I was fifteen minutes late for class yesterday," Chazz told Larry.

Example: "Why? What happened?" asked Larry.

Example: "No big deal, really," Chazz said. "I just missed the bus."

Follow these rules for punctuating quotations and dialogue:

▸ Put only direct quotations in quotation marks. (In the example that follows, Chazz is quoted directly, Larry indirectly.)

Example: When Larry asked what had happened, Chazz replied, "I just missed the bus."

▸ Put commas, periods, and question marks inside the quotation marks.

Example: "Why? What happened?" asked Larry.

Example: "No big deal, really," Chazz said. "I just missed the bus."

▸ Close one set of quotation marks before opening another.

Example: "If you buy a car," Larry said, "then you would never be late for class."

▸ Use single quotation marks for a quotation within a quotation.

Example: "When Larry said 'If you buy a car, then you would never be late for class,' I almost laughed," said Chazz.

Slang and Unusual Words

▸ Quotation marks can also signal slang words, sarcasm, and words discussed as words.

Example: In the 1950s, high school students thought Elvis Presley was "cool."

Example: My grandmother, who was a teenager then, is really "cool" when she wiggles like Elvis.

Example: Words like "cool" never seem to die.

Titles of Short Works

▸ Put quotation marks around titles of magazine and journal articles and other short works of literature, like short stories and poems.

Example: My grandmother embarrasses me when she croons "Love Me Tender," but my grandfather loves it!

- Underline, or put in italics, the titles of magazine or journals and longer works of literature, published separately.

  Example: The article "Mr.right.com" was first published in *Essence* magazine.

  Example: <u>Suessical the Musical</u> was not a very popular Broadway show.

Exercises

1. Place quotation marks in the appropriate places in the sentences below. Some sentences may require the use of italics instead (you should underline).

   a. I think the assignment is due tomorrow, said Frank. We'd better get started.

   b. Are you nuts? Joannie asked. Even if we work all night, we still won't get this assignment done.

   c. We don't have a choice. If the instructor said, turn this assignment in tomorrow, we have to turn the assignment in tomorrow or fail, replied Frank.

   d. This assignment is the pits, added Courtney.

   e. Do you think the article, Remembering Elvis, published in last January's Rolling Stone, will give us some cool quotes? Maggie suggested..

2. Two friends are discussing plans for the weekend. One wants to go to shopping, while the other wants to go to the movies. Write their dialogue below, using single and double quotation marks as needed.

APOSTROPHES (')

Apostrophes, those single quotation marks that resemble floating commas, show ownership and contractions.

Ownership

▸ Use an apostrophe, followed by *s,* to show ownership or possession.

  Example: Challyne's skateboard was stolen last night.

  Example: Chris's skateboard needs new wheels.

▸ For plural owners, add an apostrophe only.

  Example: The Franks' home is for sale. (plural owner)

  Example: The Joneses' home is for sale. (plural owner)

▸ The apostrophe plus *s* can help your reader know if two people own separate items or have joint ownership of one item.

Example: Challyne's and Chris's skateboards need repair. (separate ownership)

Example: Challyne and Chris's new skateboard is the best on the market. (joint ownership)

An exception is the word *its,* which shows ownership (like *his* and *hers*) without an apostrophe.

Example: That motorcycle is hers.

Example: She needs to have its engine tuned soon.

Contractions

Apostrophes can also indicate the missing letters in **contractions** or missing numbers in dates.

Example: "The Summer of '69" was a great song.

Example: Isn't it amazing that some people thought rock 'n' roll would be just a fad?

Be aware that *it's,* which looks like a possessive, is a contraction for *it is* or *it has.*

Example: It's been a long time since I've heard a song by Elvis on the radio.

Exercises

1. Place the apostrophe in the appropriate place in the following sentences.
   a. The captains boat was christened *The Aquanaut.*
   b. *The ABCs of Painting* is a training video.
   c. "Thats exactly what the governments agents want you to think," said Fox Mulder.
   d. "Its not going to happen," the mother told her three girls. "I wont let it."
   e. "My watch must be broken," said Keith, "because its hands are not moving."

2. Rewrite the following phrases to show possession or ownership
   a. the mittens belonging to the kittens

   _____

   _____

   b. the hats belonging to the Gonzales girls

   _____

   _____

c. the labels belonging to the CDs

_____

_____

d. the airplane belonging to four pilots

_____

_____

e. the house belonging to the Thomases

_____

_____

HYPHENS (-)

Hyphens join words into compounds and, at the end of a line of type, divide words that run over onto the next line.

Compound Words

▸ Hyphens join words that work together, including numbers and colors, when each is equal, and words that function as a single adjective before a noun.

Examples: twenty-five, blue-green, tension-free semester, happy-go-lucky sophomore

Some words simply exist as compounds.

Examples: follow-through, ex-president, will-o'-the-wisp.

Runover Words

▸ If you or your computer runs out of space at the end of a line, place a hyphen at a natural breaking point in the word and continue the word on the next line. (Many computer programs do this for you automatically.)

A breaking point normally corresponds to a pronounced syllable, which is a single sound that always includes at least one vowel.

▸ Before you hyphenate a word, check a dictionary to be sure you've chosen the right place.

Examples: ti-ny, sta-ble, tap-estry or tapes-try, for-tunate or fortu-nate, co-ordination or coor-dination or coordi-nation or coordina-tion

▸ When a word is composed of separate elements, a safe breaking point is always between the elements.

Examples: care-less, clean-ing, pop-corn, ferry-boat, tumble-weed, multi-cultural

Exercises

1. Hyphenate the following words or phrases correctly. You can simply mark the hyphen above the line. Some words should not be hyphenated.

    a. seventy six

    b. seventy six year old grandmother

    c. red orange

    d. reddish orange

    e. the best ever summer vacation

    f. small minded roommate

    g. a last ditch effort

    h. runner up

    i. Major League baseball

    j. good for nothing loafer

2. Hyphenate the syllables in the following words. You can simply mark the hyphen above the line. Use a dictionary if you are uncertain and to check your work.

    a. baseball

    b. hesitate

    c. spotless

    d. colorful

    e. master

    f. educate

    g. nonsense

    h. categorize

    i. fuzzy

    j. hotdog

CAPITALIZATION

Capital letters are signals to the reader. Use them to indicate:

- the beginning of a sentence or quotation.
- proper nouns
- titles in front of names
- key words in titles
- religious terms
- titles of courses
- specific languages

Beginning a Sentence or a Direct Quotation

▸ Capitalize words that start sentences and direct quotations.

Example: A wise person once said, "You can catch more flies with honey than with vinegar."

▸ Do not capitalize the second part of a direct quote after the interrupter.

Example: "You can catch more flies with honey," a wise person once said, "than with vinegar."

Proper Nouns

▸ Capitalize personal names and the pronoun *I.*

Example: Sheila Evans, the travel agent, booked a round-trip flight to Paris, though I wanted to fly to Rome.

▸ Capitalize the names of groups, organizations, and ethnic group designations. References to racial and ethnic groups are not capitalized.

Example: The African-American organization NAACP, one of the oldest black civil right organizations in the country, investigated claims of racism against the Fraternal Order of Police.

▸ Capitalize days of the week and months but not seasons.

Example: Next Tuesday will be the first day of January, one of the coldest winter months.

▸ Capitalize street, city, state, and country names.

Example: My address in the United States is 550 Winterset Lane, Pittsburgh, Pennsylvania.

▸ Capitalize place names and regional designations like East, West, North and South when used as nouns but not as adjectives.

Example: According to the latest report, the Southern United States is the most rapidly growing region.

Example: Sunsets in the West, whether in the Rocky Mountains or over the Pacific Ocean, are often spectacular.

▸ Brand names, too, are proper nouns, and should be capitalized, but not the common name of the item.

Example: Toys 'R' Us usually has a wide selection of Barbie dolls, Hot Wheels cars, and Playstation video game cartridges.

Titles in Front of Names

▸ Capitalize titles, ranks, or offices when they appear before a personal name.

Example: Headquarters received a report from Captain Matthew Gideon about the heroic efforts of Kim Daniels, a private.

Key Words in Titles

▸ Capitalize every word in a title, except for prepositions, conjunctions, and articles.

Example: Arthur Miller's play *Death of a Salesman* was first produced more than fifty years ago.

Religious Terms

▸ Capitalize established religions, religious figures, and religious texts.

Example: Some of the teachings of Jesus found in the Gospels are similar to the teachings of the Buddha.

Titles of Courses

▸ Capitalize specific titles of courses or those with a numerical designation.

Example: My history exam was tough, but I passed my Sociology 201 midterm with flying colors.

Example: Now, all I have to study for is the midterm in Shakespeare's Tragedies.

Languages

▸ Capitalize names of languages.

Examples: Greta speaks German, Spanish, and French fluently.

CHAPTER REVIEW

Marks of punctuation are symbols that give signals to help with sentence clarity and flow. The most common form of punctuation is the period (.), used at the end of declarative sentences. Periods are also used at the end of abbreviations. Other sentence-ending punctuation includes the question mark (?), used for interrogative sentences, and the exclamation point (!), used for exclamatory sentences.

Commas (,) separate elements in sentences, including items in a series, clauses in complex sentences, clauses in compound sentences, additional information, interrupters, piled-on adjectives, items in addresses, items in dates, and salutations in informal letters.

Semicolons separate items in a series when commas have already been used, connect two closely related independent clauses in a compound sentence, and separate compound sentences joined with an adverbial conjunction.

Colons introduce a word, phrase, or clause that explains a sentence's first clause. They also introduce quotations, separate subtitles from main titles, and follow salutations in formal business letters.

Dashes and parentheses, like commas, may also be used to set off additional information in a sentence.

Quotation marks set off statements by others, words used in unusual ways, and titles of short works. Rules governing the punctuation of quotations include putting commas, periods, and question marks inside quotation marks, using single quotation marks for quotations inside quotations, and capitalizing the first word of a quotation.

Apostrophes are single quotation marks that show ownership and contractions.

Hyphens join words into compounds and divide them if a word has to be broken at the end of one line of type and continued on the next.

Capital letters are used for the first word at the beginning of a sentence or quotation, proper nouns, titles in front of names, key words in titles, religious terms, titles of courses, and languages.

Final Exercises

1. Punctuate the following sentences and capitalize where appropriate.
   a. susan mcknight's first edition copy of *the grapes of wrath* is priceless
   b. french is sinclair's first language but she can also speak swahili
   c. the new backstreet boys cd released on Monday sold out by Wednesday
   d. bob winstons birthday party will take place on thursday march 18 at the hyatt regency hotel, 1335 east westlake ave columbus ohio
   e. william shatner will forever be known as the first and first rate captain of the starship enterprise
   f. rabbi blum once told me belief in god is all you need
   g. the holiday season should be joyful however the expectations are so high that many people get depressed.
   h. in the summer of 99 the south experienced many strange weather patterns
   i. one farmer who had irrigated his crops during the drought that year lost most of his produce when too much rain fell at once causing his tomatoes cucumbers and cantaloupe to swell and burst
   j. You are at the mercy of the weather he said i knew that when i started
   k. one result of the drought was inevitable food prices increased
   l. Although tropical storms did bring more rain the drought carried on into the fall
   m. when the water table reaches normal is anyones guess
   n. what do forecasters predict for the growing season next year

2. Place the appropriate punctuation marks in the following paragraph, and capitalize where appropriate.

   a comedian once said 99% of success is showing up. This adage can be applied to getting a college education Attendance is a big part of success in college. it shows that you are serious about the class and as a result serious about your educational future. You wouldnt apply for a job and never go to work. Why would you pay for a class and never attend Going to class gives you an edge on the assignments In last semesters french class I had an instructor mr nowlen who never gave out a schedule. You had to be in class in order to know what was going to happen that week. Class is also great for one other important aspect of school socializing. People sometimes say class isnt a good place to meet people. I disagree I have met some great people during history class discussions which would have been boring otherwise Wow who would have thought that showing up for class could mean so much

3. Place the appropriate punctuation marks in the following business letter.

1335 westlake ave.
columbus oh
deerborne pumpkin farms inc
2323 cattlesberry ct
seattle Washington
June 18, 2000

dear ms deerborne

   The sodbuster 2010 shovel advertised in the October issue of *plants monthly* is a poor product and I am writing in response to your money back guarantee. On April 2 my husband emil received the shovel in the mail and the package was dented in three different places. When we got the box opened the shovel had come apart the head had separated from the body and everything had to be put back together again. Later that day, emil went to dig a hole and the shovels handle broke in two in fact, later we found it had broken in three places. We thought it was just a bad shovel until we started talking to some other people. This is what they had to say

   My sodbuster did nothing but break my wallet
   can you believe someone actually thinks that is a good shovel
   my replacement shovel never did get here

Given all of this evidence, we have decided to return the shovel's head the body and the handle to you for a full refund. We expect our money within two weeks after that we will get a lawyer.
Thank you for your time in dealing with this problem.
Yours
Emily atwood

4. Select a paragraph or essay you have recently written. Read each sentence carefully, making sure the sentence endings are appropriate and all other punctuation is right. Check capitalization as well. Correct mistakes.

27

WORD CHOICE

Writers are often said to have a way with words. In truth, the strength of your writing depends in part on your vocabulary. Not only is it important to have the words to express your thoughts, you must also be able to use these words appropriately. This chapter discusses tools that will help you select the perfect word for the perfect sentence.

IMPROVING WORD CHOICE

Often, when we hear children talking, we are amazed at the vocabulary they have acquired and use daily. But language acquisition can slow or even stop as we get older, limiting the number of words available for expressing ourselves. For writers, language is vital. You should always be on the lookout for ways to improve your vocabulary so you will have as wide a range of word choice as possible. The best tools for improving vocabulary are dictionaries and thesauri.

Using a Dictionary

Perhaps the most popular tool for improving your word choice is a **dictionary**. Dictionaries contain vital information about words, including their syllable breaks, pronunciation, formation of plurals or tenses, origin, parts of speech, and meanings. Synonyms (words with similar meanings) and antonyms (words with opposite meanings) may also be mentioned. See the example below for more detail.

> **team** (tēm) *n.* **1** Two or more beasts of burden harnessed together. **2** A group of peole working or playing together as a unit, esp. a group forming one side in a contest. — *v.t.* **1** To convey with a team. **2** To harness together in a team. — *v.i.* **3** To drive a team. **4** To form or work as a team: to *team* up. [<OE *tēam* offspring, team]

Syllables Almost every dictionary provides a syllable-by-syllable breakdown of each entry. This breakdown helps identify the structure or parts of the word and can tell you where hyphens belong if you have to break the word at the end of a line of type.

Pronunciation   Dictionaries include symbols and marks that indicate the standard way a word is pronounced. Accent marks tell you the syllable to emphasize when you say the word. The others letters and symbols explain the sound each letter or group of letters makes. For example, the word *team* is pronounced "tēm". The line over the *e* shows the long vowel sound (the sound of the vowel when it is said in the alphabet).

Formation of Plurals or Tenses   Dictionaries show you the forms of words, especially if plurals are irregular (that is, are not formed by simply adding –s, as in "man," "men") or tenses are irregular (that is, are shown by internal changes, as in "eat," "ate").

Origin   Dictionaries can also provide an extremely brief history of a word by noting where the word was first used. *Team* is Old English in origin but has connections to German and Dutch.

Part of Speech   Dictionaries give the part of speech (noun, pronoun, verb, adjective, adverb, preposition, conjunction, interjection) for each entry. Typically, *team* is used as a noun, but it can also be a verb.

Meanings   Finally, dictionaries reveal the meanings of words. Keep in mind that the more comprehensive the dictionary, the more extensive and detailed the list of meanings. *Team* has a number of meanings, such as:

Noun

- two or more beasts of burden
- a group of people working together in a coordinated effort

Verb

- to convey with a team
- to harness together
- to drive a team
- to join in a cooperative activity

Dictionaries and Word Choice

You know that dictionaries contain a lot of information. But how do you use that information when you're looking for the right word? You must look beyond the word's definition and consider its other aspects as well.

▸ Look up the meaning and make sure that it fits in the context of the sentence you are writing.

Example: That basketball collection went all the way to the championship undefeated.

Better: That basketball team went all the way to the championship undefeated.

‣ Look at the part of speech to make sure you are using the word correctly.

Example: The two sides team up during practice.

Better: The two sides play together during practice.

Exercise

Look at the underlined word in each sentence below. Find its dictionary definition. Should the word remain in the sentence, or should it be replaced? Explain your answer.

a. The waiter <u>sat</u> the tray on the counter.

b. <u>Respite</u> the demands of the child, the father did not buy the toy.

c. The scientist's <u>hypothesis</u> had been proven after the experiment.

d. The man decided to have <u>selective</u> surgery.

e. The mighty dinosaur moved slowly through the jungle, <u>razing</u> trees and smashing boulders.

Using a Thesaurus

Another good tool for improving word choice is the **thesaurus**. Like a dictionary, a thesaurus lists the meanings of words. Unlike a dictionary, it does so by providing synonyms and, sometimes, antonyms.

> **team,** *n.* **1.** [People working together, especially on the stage] — *Syn.* partners, combination troupe, company, duo, trio, foursome, sextette, scream-mates*, love team*, heart team*, dream team*; **see also organization** 3.
>
> **2.** [An organization, especially in sport] — *Syn.* contingent, aggregation, outfit, unit, crew, side, club; **see also organization** 3.
>
> **3.** [Draft animals] — *Syn.* rig, four-in-hand, pair, span, tandem, cart horses, string, matched team.
>
> **team,** *v.* — *Syn.* pull, couple, haul; **see draw.**

Synonyms   **Synonyms** (words with the same or a similar meaning) are listed after the entry. *Team* in the sense of a group of people working or playing together, has the following synonyms: partners, combination troupe, company, duo, trio, foursome, sextette, scream-mates, love team, heart team, dream team.

Antonyms   After synonyms are listed, **antonyms** (words with opposite meanings) are sometimes given. *Team* has no antonyms, but I bet you can think of an antonym for a word like *tall!*

Thesauri and Word Choice

You can use a thesaurus to find a better word—more precise, more vivid, more memorable—than the word you started with.

Example: The big, walking dinosaurs in the movie *Dinosaur* were very believable.

Big and *walking* are adjectives describing dinosaurs, but these words are not distinctive or powerful. You might want to replace them.

Example: The hulking, lumbering dinosaurs in the movie *Dinosaur* were very believable.

The choice of the words *hulking* and *lumbering* gives the reader a much more vivid picture of the dinosaurs. But beware: Not every word in a thesaurus entry works equally well.

Example: The pregnant, stepping dinosaurs in the movie *Dinosaur* were very believable.

Exercise

Write your assessment of the tone or feeling for each sentence. Then, using a thesaurus, find a replacement for the underlined word. Make sure the replacement word is accurate for the context and improves the flow and feeling of the sentence. Discuss your word choices with other members of the class.

a. Computers have helped people commit crimes in a <u>mixture</u> of ways.

   Tone: _____

   Replacement Word: _____

b. One type of computer crime is "hacking," or <u>entering</u> a secured computer's hard drive without permission.

   Tone: _____

   Replacement Word: _____

c. Criminals have also used the Internet to lure unsuspecting people into <u>discourse</u> rooms.

   Tone: _____

   Replacement Word: _____

d. Through online conversations, <u>villains</u> find out information such as your name, the type of computer you use, and websites you have previously visited.

   Tone: _____

   Replacement Word: _____

e. The <u>rhapsodical</u> writings of some members of chat rooms can be inviting, but beware of being tricked.

Tone: _____

Replacement Word: _____

Writing With Computers

DICTIONARIES AND THESAURI

Computer dictionaries and thesauri can be a great advantage. Many word processing programs signal your mistake if you misspell or misuse a certain word. Likewise, whenever you are looking for a different word, all you have to do is access your word processing program's thesaurus file and see what similar words are listed. These electronic tools are wonderful, but they have to be used carefully. No matter how powerful your word processing program is, the dictionary and thesaurus are limited. Words that are spelled correctly but used incorrectly or are unknown to the program's dictionary file will be flagged as incorrect. Your word processor's thesaurus program will reveal only a select number of synonyms. You may not find the word that you want or need for your writing task.

Spelling and Homonyms

Perhaps the most familiar use for a dictionary is to check and correct spelling. Dictionary definitions can tell you, for example, if you have used a word that is wrong even though it is pronounced just like the word you really want. Words that sound alike but are spelled differently are called **homonyms,** and they are a common source of confusion.

Common Homonyms

- To: toward something; a preposition
- Two: the number
- Too: an extreme

    Example: <u>Too</u> many people have <u>two</u> access keys <u>to</u> the safe.

- Their: shows possession
- They're: contraction for "they are"
- There: location

    Example: <u>They're</u> the first platoon to fly <u>their</u> flag on the island over <u>there</u>.

- Your: second-person possessive pronoun
- You're: contraction for "you are"

    Example: <u>You're</u> not where you are supposed to be in order to make <u>your</u> grand entrance.

- Hear: to listen
- Here: location

    Example: If you stand <u>here</u>, you can <u>hear</u> the concert better.

- Whether: shows a choice
- Weather: atmospheric conditions

    Example: <u>Whether</u> or not the forecast calls for rain, we will not take a chance on the <u>weather</u>.

- Who's: contraction for "who is" or "who has"
- Whose: shows ownership

    Example: <u>Who's</u> in charge here? I have to find out <u>whose</u> car was stolen.

- Straight: direct; without wavering
- Strait: a canal or a passage through water

    Example: Our tour took us <u>straight</u> through the Bering <u>Strait</u>.

- Peace: without aggression
- Piece: part of a whole

    Example: The soldiers took their weapons apart <u>piece</u> by <u>piece</u> to show that they wanted <u>peace</u>.

At times, commonly confused words do not sound exactly alike, but are close enough to be confusing.

- A: article used with consonant sounds
- An: article used with vowel sounds
- And: conjunction connecting two things

    Example: <u>An</u> egg for breakfast sounds good, <u>and</u> <u>a</u> steak for lunch sounds even better.

- Were: past-tense form of the verb *are*
- We're: contraction for "we are"

    Example: We <u>were</u> going to see a movie, but now <u>we're</u> going to the park instead.

- Then: shows sequence
- Than: shows comparison

    Example: I like anchovies more <u>than</u> pepperoni. I eat the pepperoni first. <u>Then</u> I can savor the anchovies.

- Clothes: garments
- Close: to shut; near
- Cloths: pieces of fabric

  Example: Please <u>close</u> the door so I can clean behind it with <u>cloths</u> made of old <u>clothes</u>.

- Fell: past tense of fall
- Feel: touch

  Example: I didn't <u>feel</u> well after I <u>fell</u> down the stairs.

- Accept: take
- Except: other than

  Example: The instructor said she would <u>accept</u> all of Steven's late assignments <u>except</u> for the last report.

- All ready: being fully prepared
- Already: happening before an implied time

  Example: By the time my computer was <u>all ready</u> to go, Jane was <u>already</u> online.

- Lose: opposite of win
- Loose: not restrained
- Loss: misplacement; removal

  Example: Due to the <u>loss</u> of their coach, the team had <u>loose</u> organization and went on to <u>lose</u> every game that season.

- Lay: place
- Lie: recline

  Example: I <u>lay</u> my glasses on the nightstand before I <u>lie</u> down .

- Good: describes things
- Well: describes actions, conditions, and the five senses at work

  Example: The nurse thought it was a <u>good</u> idea to see if the patient was feeling <u>well</u>.

Exercises

1. For each homonym pair, look up the definitions in a dictionary and write them next to the appropriate word.

   a. pair _____

   pear _____

b. its _____

  it's _____

c. way _____

  weigh _____

d. past _____

  passed _____

e. stationery _____

  stationary _____

f. role _____

  roll _____

g. principle _____

  principal _____

2. Read through the sentences below, locating any homonyms and correcting spelling, if necessary.

  a. Many people overlook the benefits that cloning can provide two humanity.

  b. Imagine loosing a kidney but having another one already to be implanted inside you.

  c. The new kidney would come from you're own sells.

  d. The same procedure could help create a strong hart to replace a week one.

  e. The problem of organ rejection would no longer exist since your body would automatically except your own well cells.

AVOIDING WORDINESS

Sometimes, if you are struggling to make a particular point, you write much more than necessary. Wordiness can actually work against your desire to be clear and precise. Here are some guidelines to help you avoid wordiness.

▸ Keep your focus on topic, audience, and purpose.
  To rein in your sentences, focus again on your topic (what you are writing about), audience (who is going to read it), and purpose (why you are writing in the first place). See how the TAP focus can help you eliminate words. Imagine encountering this sentence in a packet of material aimed at returning students:

  Example: English 101 is a three–credit hour course that meets three times a week for one hour each day or three hours one day a week and includes instruction about sentence writing, paragraph writing, and essay writing.

The topic is English 101. Because the audience are returning students, we can presume they understand how credit hours work. The purpose is to give an overview of the class. A rewrite may look like this:

Fixed: English 101, a three–credit hour course, includes strategies for writing sentences, paragraphs, and essays.

‣ Remove redundant words and phrases.
A clearly written sentence will carry more weight than a sentence loaded with repeated ideas. Carefully read every word and eliminate unnecessary repetition.

Example: At this present point in time, the president doesn't have enough knowledge to formulate a response to the question that has been asked, but he will review information and respond later.

"At this present point in time" is a way to say "now," or "presently." "Doesn't have enough knowledge to formulate a response" means "doesn't know." "The question that has been asked" can be condensed to "the question" (because all questions are asked). The new sentence would look like this:

Fixed: The president doesn't have an answer to your question now, but he will review information and respond later.

‣ Watch "there is" and "there are" constructions. When sentences begin with "There is" or "There are," the subject is delayed. Often, the subject can be brought to the beginning of the sentence, eliminating words and making the sentence stronger overall.

Example: There are six computer components needed for the upgrade.

Fixed: Six computer components are needed for the upgrade.

Exercises

1. Rewrite each sentence, cutting down on wordiness.

   a. The flaming orb in the sky gave us knowledge that the time of day was late evening.

   _____

   _____

   b. The group of very young human beings produced musical noise at the holiday concert.

   _____

   _____

c. Rupert's collection of spinning disks that produce musical sounds when played in a CD player exceeds in number more than five thousand and six.

_____

_____

d. The diminutive box that receives television transmissions is no longer in working order.

_____

_____

e. Watching too much television can give a human being an unpleasant feeling concentrated in the upper cranial area.

_____

_____

2. Edit the following paragraph for wordiness. Record your revised paragraph on the lines below.

A selective amount of the entirety of Mother's wisdom was accurate. She spoke to me often of tying the strings on my foot coverings before this writer would go outside the house to partake in pleasurable activities. At one point in time, I went from an upright position to a prone position because those strings got interwined in my feet. My female parental unit also articulated that I should refrain from consuming too many sweet foods before my scheduled eating times. This I did one time and experienced pains in my stomach for several sixty-minute time periods. Finally, I have a recollection of my mother stating that I should not intake food while I vocalized. She said this would cause me to lose the flow of air to my lungs and she was correct. I choked. Much of what my female parental unit said was factually based.

_____

_____

_____

_____

_____

_____

3. Read through a paragraph or essay you have written recently. Look for wordy areas, underline them, and then rewrite the problem areas.

AVOIDING CLICHÉS

Clichés are phrases that have been used so much that they are no longer effective or meaningful. For example, "as sharp as a tack" and "it was a dark and stormy night" are weary expressions. Here are some guidelines to help you avoid clichés.

- Examine the real meaning of the sentence. Clichés often hint at what you want to say, but they don't get it across with precision. Take a close look at each sentence to make sure you are getting your point across.

  Example: Taina is as smart as a whip.

  Better: Taina is very intelligent and does quite well in school.

- Rewrite the entire sentence or paragraph from a new perspective. Clichés reflect a tired approach to a topic. Consider viewing the topic from a different angle to get a new perspective.

  Example: It was a dark and stormy night.

  Better: Lightning flashed, thunder rolled, and rain splashed down as we drove through the darkness.

IMPROVING YOUR VOCABULARY

The best way to improve your word choice is to expand your vocabulary. Your everyday vocabulary can get you through the day, so you may need to make a special effort to learn new words. An increased vocabulary can help you:

- **Articulate your thoughts.** The English language has a huge number of words and can supply the perfect word for almost every situation. Improving your vocabulary allows you to work with precision.

- **Understand larger or deeper concepts.** Students can be quick to say that they "just don't get it" when they have to read and understand challenging material. At times, the difficulty stems from not understanding the words in the text. As you begin to understand the terms, you begin to understand the concepts.

- **Communicate with a larger audience.** An expanded vocabulary will allow you to reach all kinds of readers, or reach your regular readers in new and deeper ways.

New words don't just suddenly pop into your head. You must go out and find them, and then use them to make them your own.

Reading

Reading is, perhaps, the best way to improve your vocabulary. Not only will you be exposed to new words but also you will find new meanings and uses for words you already know. If you want, you can underline or highlight new words when you read. Although reading with a good dictionary at hand is a good idea, you may also use context clues to get an overall sense of a word or to help you figure out its meaning. At times, the definition of a word can be found within the words around it.

Example: The tornado ripped through the town, toppled trees, lifted cars off the ground, and dumped hail the size of golf balls.

The meaning of the word *tornado* is clear from this description of its power.

Index Card System

A more deliberate approach to vocabulary building involves creating a word list. Pay attention to words all around you and how they are being used. On a 3 × 5 index card, jot down one word you have heard, or learned, and its meaning. (You may need to consult a dictionary.) Arrange the index cards in a file box in whatever order you choose: alphabetically, by part of speech, or by meaning. Quiz yourself every so often on the spelling and meaning of each word in the file. Have the index cards handy for quick reference as you write.

Exercises

1. Try to grasp the meaning of each underlined word. Let the sentences around the words give you clues to their meaning. Write the meaning on the lines below.

   a. Television, like drugs, dominates the lives of its addicts. And though some lonely Americans leave their sets on without watching them, using them as electronic <u>companions</u>, television usually absorbs its viewers the way drugs absorb their users. Viewers can't work or play while watching television; they can't be out on the streets, falling in love with the wrong people, learning how to <u>quarrel</u> and compromise with other human beings. In short, they are <u>asocial</u>. So are <u>drug addicts</u>.

   (Hamill, "Crack and the Box")

   Companions: _____

   Quarrel: _____

   Asocial: _____

   Drug Addict: _____

   b. It has never been easy to live on the wrong side of the tracks. But in the economically <u>robust</u> 1990's, with sprawling houses and three-car garages sprouting like cornstalks on the Midwestern prairie, the sting that comes with <u>scarcity</u> gets rubbed with an extra bit of salt. Seen through the eyes of a 13-year-old girl growing up at Chateau Estates, a fancy name for a tin-plain trailer park, the rosy talk about the nation's <u>prosperity</u> carries a certain mocking echo.

(Johnson, "When Money Is Everything, Except Hers")

Robust: _____

Scarcity: _____

Prosperity: _____

2. Read a newspaper or magazine article. Underline five words that are unfamiliar to you. Try to grasp their meaning from the context. Then look them up in a dictionary to check their meaning.

CHAPTER REVIEW

Effective writing starts with the right words. Word choices can be improved by using a dictionary or a thesaurus, and these tools can help you build your vocabulary, too. Dictionaries give information on syllable breaks, pronunciation, formation of plurals or tenses, word origins, parts of speech, and, or course, meanings. Thesauri list synonyms and, sometimes, antonyms.

Use dictionaries and thesauri wisely to:

- **Select words with the right meaning.** A word may have many meanings and slight variations on meaning, so it is important to make your choice exactly.
- **Avoid commonly confused words.** Watch out for homonyms, words that sound alike but have different meanings and, usually, spellings.
- **Avoid clichés.** Well-worn phrases hurt the power of sentences. Rewrite clichés from a fresh perspective.
- **Avoid wordiness.** Using more words than is necessary gets in the way of your meaning. Keep your focus on your topic, audience, and purpose. Remove redundant words and phrases.

To build your vocabulary, read widely, and highlight and learn unfamiliar words. Use a dictionary to discover meanings that are not clear from the context. An index card system, in which you jot down unfamiliar words on 3 × 5 index cards, along with their meanings, and parts of speech, can help you keep track of new words and add them to your vocabulary.

Final Exercise

Rewrite the following paragraph. Be sure to pay attention to word choice, spelling and homonyms, clichés, and wordiness. Make the paragraph as trim and strong as you can.

Recently at this point in time, I have decided that two many things in the media are not accurate. Weather it is television talk shows, newspaper articles, or radio news, they're a lot of problems with the media's representation of the world in which we live in on a day-to-day basis. First, I want to converse about the television talk show. Talk shows started out as informational ways of getting information. Now, most talk shows just show augments, fisticuffs, and people stripping. It all seams very fake to me. I have even heard that the audience reactions are fixed or planned ahead of time. Too me, that isn't quality television in my opinion. Next, newspaper articles are sometimes biased or unclear. Just look at today's headlines in today's paper. I am sure that the headline leads you to think about won thing and the article says something else. Once I read a headline about a man who escaped from prison but the article said that he had not tried to escape from prison but he could have if he had wanted to. That information was not clear in the headline at all, not even a little bit. The third and last item I will discuss in this essay where information can be wrong is on the radio. I wake up every morning to melodious tones and some information about recent events that have taken place in the world. While radio news is shorter then television news, it still may not bee as accurate. Yesterday, I herd that there was a fight at city hall when in fact there wasn't. Information on television, in newspapers, and on the radio needs to be more correct.

GLOSSARY

Action verbs: Verbs that show action being done by or to the subject.

Active voice: Subject is taking action within the sentence; considered a strong sentence construction.

Adjectives: Words that describe or limit nouns or pronouns through added detail.

Adverbial conjunction: Words that connect phrases and sentences while showing cause, addition, and contrast. Also referred to as *conjunctive adverbs*.

Adverbs: Words that describe or identify verbs or actions within a sentence.

Antecedents: Nouns to which a pronoun refers.

Antonyms: Words with opposite meanings.

Apostrophes: Punctuation that shows ownership or expresses the idea that letters or numbers are missing in contractions (').

Appeal: A way of presenting information to an audience. Three types of appeals are an appeal to emotion, an appeal to reason, and an appeal to moral code.

Audience: The group of readers to which your writing is aimed. The different types of audiences include *friendly* (one that won't show much resistance to your point of view), *neutral* (ones who don't have a strong opinion favoring or opposing your point of view), and *unfriendly* (those who are opposed to your point of view).

Body paragraphs: Paragraphs that support the thesis statement of the essay. Each body paragraph is focused on one particular aspect of the topic.

Body sentences: Sentences that support the topic sentence in a paragraph. Usually provide explanation and examples.

Brainstorming: Writing down ideas in order to find what you want to explore in a piece of writing. Types of brainstorming include *freewriting, clustering,* and *jotting*.

Business writing: Writing centered on business or professional organizations, such as memos, resumes, cover letters, and thank-you letters.

Cause: The reason an event occurred.

Chronological order: Arrangement of events in a time sequence. Also called *time order*.

Classification: Defining a concept by identifying certain categories or characteristics.

Clause: A collection of words that contains a noun and a verb.

Clichés: Phrases that have been so overused that all meaning has been lost or weakened.

Climax order: An essay arrangement in which material is presented from least impressive to the most impressive.

Coherence: The clarity of a piece of writing to its audience.

Collective Nouns: Nouns that represent a group or unit.

Colon: Punctuation used to draw attention to a word or phrase mentioned in a preceding sentence (:).

Comma: Punctuation used to show separation of items in a series of clauses (,).

Comma splice: Two or more sentences connected with only a comma.

Common nouns: Nouns that represent everyday or generic items.

Comparison: Showing the similarities between two or more different concepts.

Complex sentence: The combination of an independent clause and a dependent clause into a single sentence.

Compound sentence: Two or more independent clauses connected into one sentence.

Compound subject: More than one noun or pronoun that acts as a subject within a single sentence.

Compound verb: Two or more verbs expressing action or state of being for the subject of a sentence.

Concluding paragraphs: The final paragraphs in an essay. Conclusions may reflect the main idea expressed in the thesis statement, or they may call the audience to take action.

Concluding sentence: The final sentence in a paragraph, often reflecting the *topic sentence.*

Conjunctions: Words that connect other words, phrases, and sentences.

Content: Information provided in a piece of writing.

Contrast: Showing the differences between two or more different concepts.

Coordinating conjunction: A word that connect phrases and sentences that are grammatically equal.

Countable nouns: Nouns that can be expressed in numbers.

Cover letter: A single page document expressing a person's interest in working for a particular person or company. Usually accompanied by a **résumé**.

Criterion: A characteristic of a topic used as a basis of classification.

Critical thinking: In-depth thinking in which a person analyzes information.

Dashes: Punctuation that sets off additional but non-essential information within a sentence (–).

Debatable thesis: A thesis statement that presents one side of an argument.

Declarative sentence: An independent clause that makes a statement. Usually followed by a period (.).

Definition: The meaning of a concept.

Delayed subject: A subject found in the middle or at the end.

Demonstrative pronoun: Pronoun that represents a specific thing or things.

Dependent clause: A collection of words that contains a subject and a verb and begins with a subordinating conjunction. These are not complete sentences.

Description: A piece of writing that appeals to the five senses: smell, touch, taste, sight, and hearing.

Details: The bits of information (colors, smells, sounds) that help develop a piece of writing.

Dialect: The way a person pronounces and enunciates words.

Dialogue: A written version of a conversation between two or more people.

Direct object: A noun that receives the action of a verb.

Documentation: A record of research and information.

Dominant impression: The overall feeling or attitude expressed by the author in an essay.

Editing: Making final mechanical, word choice, spelling, punctuation, and capitalization changes in a draft.

Effect: The impact or influence that an event can have on other events.

Essay: A carefully arranged group of paragraphs, all focused on a central topic. Essays generally include an *introduction*, a *thesis statement*, *body paragraphs*, and a *conclusion*.

Evidence: Factual information that verifies claims. Evidence could consist of research, history, statistics, expert testimony, and personal experience.

Exclamation point: Puntuation placed at the end of an exclamatory sentence (!).

External documentation: Documentation of research materials listed on a Works Cited or Bibliography page.

Findings: Conclusions drawn from research.

Fragment: A sentence that is missing a subject, a verb, or a complete thought.

Future tense: The condition of a verb that shows the action of a sentence has yet to happen.

Gerunds: Verbs ending in –*ing* used as nouns. A gerund can be the subject of a sentence.

Helping verbs: Verbs that show time, tense, or obligation when used with other verbs.

Homonyms: Words that sound the same but have different spellings and meanings.

Imperative sentence: An independent clause that makes a commend. The first word of an imperative sentence is usually a verb or a direct address (*you*).

Indefinite pronouns: Pronouns that do not represent a certain person, place, or thing.

Independent clause: A collection of words that contains a subject, a verb, and a complete thought.

Indirect object: The noun or pronoun to whom or for whom the verb's action is directed.

Infinitive subject: A verb preceded by the word *to* and used as a subject.

Informed opinion essay: An essay in which the writer is giving a point of view about a single aspect of a topic, using personal perspective and very limited research as support.

Intensive pronouns: Pronouns added to nouns for effect. These pronouns usually end in *–self* or *–selves*.

Interjections: Short words or phrases that reflect strong emotion, usually followed by exclamation points (!).

Internal documentation: A style of referring to outside sources within the body of a research paper.

Interrogative pronouns: Pronouns used when asking questions.

Interrogative sentence: An independent clause that asks a question. Usually followed by a question mark (?).

Introduction: Opening paragraphs of an essay.

Irregular nouns: Nouns that do not take the *–s* ending to be plural.

Irregular verbs: Verbs that do not follow the *–ed* rule when changing to the past tense.

Jargon: Technical or specific language created and used by a particular group.

Linking verbs: Verbs that connect a noun to other description within a sentence.

MLA: Modern Language Association; also a style for presenting documentation.

Materials: Items needed to successfully create or build something.

Mechanics: Sentence structure, parts of speech, and other elements dealing with grammar.

Memo: A short note or letter that provides information to those within an organization or company. Also called *memorandum*.

Method: An explanation within a research paper of how the research was conducted.

Modifiers: Words that describe or identify nouns and pronouns.

Narrative: A type of essay in which the author recounts a series of events that focus on a central point.

Nouns: Words that represent a person, place, thing, idea, event, emotion, or quality.

Object: Nouns or pronouns connected through prepositions; the receiver of the action from a verb

Order of importance: A descriptive organizational pattern in which the author describes the most important element first, the next important element second, and so on.

Outline: The "skeleton" or basic arrangement of a piece of writing.

Outside sources: Information that comes from sources other than personal experience, including magazines, newspapers, scholarly books and journals, television, radio, Internet, and general reference materials.

Paragraph: A short way to express information, most paragraphs are at least three sentences long and includes a topic sentence, body sentences, and a concluding sentence.

Parentheses: Punctuation that sets off additional but non-essential information within a sentence ( ).

Parts of speech: The eight basic sections of the English language (nouns, pronouns, verbs, adjectives, adverbs, prepositions, conjunctions, and interjections) that are used to create sentences.

Passive voice: A sentence structure by which the ubject is being acted upon; considered a weak sentence construction.

Past tense: The condition of a verb that shows the action of a sentence has already happened.

Peer review: Having another writer critique a piece of writing before submitting it to the intended audience.

Period: A dot placed at the end of a declarative sentence (.).

Personal pronouns: Pronouns that substitute for nouns that relate to people.

Plagiarism: The act of using someone else's words, thoughts, ideas, or research without giving appropriate credit.

Possessive pronouns: Pronouns that show ownership.

Prepositions: Words that show relationships between two or more nouns or pronouns.

Prepositional phrase: A group of words that begins with a preposition and end with an object.

Present tense: The condition of a verb that shows the action of a sentence is taking place now.

Prewriting: Planning a piece of writing.

Problem Statement: The main idea of a narrative essay, written as a thesis statement.

Process: The step-by-step explanation of how to complete a task. The traditional approach focuses on the sequential order of the steps in the process, while the formula approach puts more emphasis on the steps themselves.

Pronouns: Words that substitute for nouns.

Proofreading: Checking the final draft of an essay for errors of any type.

Proper nouns: Nouns that represent specific items. Proper names begin with a capital letter.

Purpose: Reasons the writer created a piece of writing.

Question mark: Punctuation placed at the end of an interrogative sentence (?).

Quotation: A reference taken from another piece of writing. A direct quote is a word for word reference. An indirect quote is one restated in your own words. A line quote is a single sentence or two taken from a source, while a block quote is a paragraph or two taken from a source.

Quotation marks: Punctuation used to express dialogue or to draw attention to unusual words or phrases (" ").

Reading response: An essay in which the author is discussing points made in another essay by another author.

Relative clause: A dependent clause that begins with a relative pronoun (who, that, which).

Reflexive pronouns: Pronouns that place the action back onto the subject.

Relative pronouns: Pronouns that relate to or correspond to other nouns within a sentence.

Research papers: Essays in which the author gathers information from a number of outside sources and shares that information with the audience.

Résumé: A one or two page document explaining job qualifications. Most resumes include contact information, work objectives, work history, job-related skills, education, interests, and references. Usually submitted with a *cover letter*.

Revision: Adding to, deleting from, reorganizing, or otherwise changing a rough draft to improve it.

Rough draft: An unpolished piece of writing in paragraph or essay form.

Run-ons: Two or more sentences that are connected without the appropriate punctuation or conjunction.

Selecting: The process of choosing what information to include in a piece of writing.

Semicolon: Punctuation that, by itself, connects two independent clauses; looks like a comma with a period above it. (;).

Sentence: A group of words containing a subject, a verb, and a complete thought. Also called an *independent clause*.

Simple subject: One word that acts as the subject of a sentence.

Simple verb: A single word that expresses action or state of being in a sentence.

Six Journalists' Questions: The six basic questions that must be answered when writing a narrative: *who* are the characters, *what* is the situation, *when* did the events occur, *where* did the events occur, *why* did the events occur, and *how* were the characters affected by the events.

Spatial order: A descriptive organizational pattern that focuses on the arrangement of items.

Structure: The layout of a piece of writing.

Style: Words and attitudes used to express a piece of writing. Also called *tone*.

Subject: A noun or pronoun that does the action within a sentence or is being acted upon, described, or identified.

Subordinating conjunction: Words that connect phrases and sentences that are grammatically unequal.

Synonyms: Words with similar meanings.

Tense: The condition of a verb that shows time (past, present, future).

Thank-you letter: A polite letter sent after an interview that expresses thanks for the opportunity to discuss employment.

Thesis statement: the controlling idea of an essay, usually found at the end of the introduction.

Topic: who or what the paragraph or essay is about. Topics include *academic topics* (ones usually assigned in college courses) and *self-reflective topics* (ones generated through diaries and journals).

Topic sentence: The controlling idea of a paragraph.

Transitions: Words or phrases that move the reader from one thought to another smoothly.

Uncountable Nouns: Nouns that can't be expressed in numbers. These nouns do not form plurals.

Unity: Connection of all the parts of an essay.

Verbs: Words that show action in a sentence or the state of being of the subject within a sentence.

Voice: With verbs, explains whether the subject is taking action or is being acted upon.

Works Cited: A listing of research materials referenced in a research paper. See also *External documentation*.

Writing strategy: A way a topic can be presented to an audience, including *narrative, process, description, definition and classification, cause and effect, comparison and contrast,* and *persuasion.*

CREDITS

Text Credits

"Selections from the Allen Notebooks" by Woody Allen from *The Norton Anthology of Expository Prose,* 4th ed. Ed. Arthur M. Eastman. W. W. Norton, New York. 1975. 113.

"Send Your Children to the Libraries" by Arthur Ashe from *The New York Times,* February 6, 1977. Copyright © 1977 by the New York Times Co. Reprinted by permission.

Excerpt from "Music" by Allan Bloom. Reprinted with the permission of Simon & Schuster from *The Closing of the American Mind* by Allan Bloom. Copyright © 1987 by Allan Bloom.

TOM THE DANCING BUG © Ruben Bolling. Reprinted with permission of Universal Press Syndicate. All rights reserved.

"Confrontations, Common Bonds" by Michael J. Bugeja from *Writer's Digest,* March 1997. Reprinted by permission of Michael J. Bugeja, author of *Guide to Writing Magazine Nonfiction.*

"Television Changed My Family Forever" from *Move On: Adventures in the Real World* by Linda Ellerbee. Reprinted by permission of Linda Ellerbee, journalist, author, and award winning producer.

Research Project "The Best 4-Year College for Me" by Erica Gates. Originally published on the Internet website of Germanna Community College, December 10, 1996. Reprinted by permission of Erica Gates-Cline.

"Goldson's Good Life on a Shoestring" by Yonason Goldson. Originally published online. Reprinted by permission of Troikamagazine.com.

"Crack and the Box" by Pete Hamill from *Esquire,* May 5, 1990. Reprinted by permission of International Creative Management, Inc. Copyright © 1990 by Pete Hamill.

"When Money Is Everything, Except Hers" by Dirk Johnson from *The New York Times,* October 14, 1998. Copyright © 1998 by the New York Times Co. Reprinted by permission.

"The Day That I Sensed a New Kind of Intelligence" by Garry Kasparov from *Newsweek,* March 25, 1996. Reprinted by permission of Garry Kasparov.

From "Preliminaries," which appears in *Koppett's Concise History of Major League Baseball*, by Leonard Koppett. Reprinted by permission of Temple University Press. Copyright © 1998 by Temple University. All rights reserved.

"How Scott Weiland Got Sober" by Greg Kot from *Rolling Stone,* July 5, 2001. Copyright © 2001 Rolling Stone LLC. All rights reserved. Reprinted by permission.

Excerpt from "Polaroids" by Anne Lamott. From *Bird by Bird* by Anne Lamott, copyright © 1994 by Anne Lamott. Used by permission of Pantheon Books, a division of Random House, Inc.

"I'd Like to Use Essay Tests, But…" by Marilla Svinicki. This essay is a publication of The POD Network, *Essays on Teaching Excellence*. Reprinted by permission of The POD Network.

"Hello, Darkness, My Old Friend" by Richard Talcott from *Astronomy*, May 2001. Reproduced by permission. Copyright © 2001 *Astronomy* Magazine, Kalmbach Publishing Co.

"Gravity's Rainbow" by Guy Trebay from *The Village Voice*, October 8, 1996. Reprinted by permission of *The Village Voice* and Guy Trebay.

Memo "To The Davidson College Community" from President Robert F. Vagt, January 12, 1998. Reprinted by permission of Robert F. Vagt.

"The Good E-Book" by Jacob Weisberg from *The New York Times Magazine*, June 4, 2000. Copyright © 2000 by Jacob Weisberg. Reprinted with permission of The Wylie Agency, Inc.

"Estella's Choice" by Dana White from *Women's Sports and Fitness*. September 2000, 54–57.

Image credits

Page 2, Drawing by author's son, Kai Hall; page 2, © Photo by Anne Katrine Senstad; page 116, © Remy Courseaux; page 117, Reproduced by permission, *Astronomy*, Elisabeth Rowan, © 2001 Kalmbach Publishing Co.; page 174, © Hulton Archive/Getty Images; page 174, © Art Directors/Helene Rogers; page 382, © AP/Wide World Photos; page 381, © Photo by Cam Garrett; page 384, © Gail Albert Halaban/Corbis Outline; page 400, Diagram by Nigel Holmes.

INDEX